CORRECTIONAL MENTAL HEALTH HANDBOOK

This book is dedicated to the memories of our fathers:
Thomas J. Fagan (1926-1989)
and
Robert H. Ax (1908-1993)

CORRECTIONAL MENTAL HEALTH HANDBOOK

THOMAS J. FAGAN
ROBERT K. AX
Editors

SAGE Publications
International Educational and Professional Publisher
Thousand Oaks ▪ London ▪ New Delhi

For information:

 Sage Publications, Inc.
2455 Teller Road
Thousand Oaks, California 91320
E-mail: order@sagepub.com

Sage Publications Ltd.
6 Bonhill Street
London EC2A 4PU
United Kingdom

Sage Publications India Pvt. Ltd.
B-42 Panchsheel Enclave
New Delhi 110 017 India

Printed in the United States of America

Library of Congress Cataloging-in-Publication Data

Correctional mental health handbook / edited by Thomas J. Fagan and Robert K. Ax.
      p. cm.
Includes bibliographical references and index.
ISBN 0-7619-2753-0 (cloth)
     1. Prisoners-Mental health services—Handbooks, manuals, etc.
I. Fagan, Thomas J., 1949- II. Ax, Robert K., 1952-
RC451.4.P68 C6685 2003
365′.66—dc21

                                        2002015734

This book is printed on acid-free paper.

02   03   04   05   10   9   8   7   6   5   4   3   2   1

Acquisitions Editor:	Jerry Westby
Editorial Assistant:	Vonessa Vondera
Production Editor:	Sanford Robinson
Copy Editor:	D. J. Peck
Typesetter:	C&M Digitals (P) Ltd
Indexer:	Karen McKenzie
Cover Designer:	Michelle Lee

Contents

Introduction

Thomas J. Fagan and Robert K. Ax

We have been providers of mental health services within correctional settings for most of our professional careers, and between us we have more than 40 years of correctional mental health experience. Over the years, we have repeatedly made the same three observations. First, the number of criminal offenders with mental health problems has been increasing steadily. In fact, correctional settings appear to be taking the place of state mental hospitals as primary sites for the treatment of mentally ill individuals in some states.

Second, the academic community has historically placed very little emphasis on correctional facilities as places of employment when they prepare their students for mental health practice, and as a result, they have provided their students with very little training specific to this setting. Indeed, some faculty have even discouraged their students from seeking employment as correctional mental health providers. Although some graduate programs now offer training in forensic mental health, these programs typically deal more with pre-confinement issues such as the assessment of mental health concerns as they relate to determinations of competency to stand trial, criminal responsibility at the time of the offense, and mitigating factors that might influence sentencing of criminal offenders. Few graduate programs offer courses that deal specifically with the many assessment, treatment, and management issues faced by correctional mental health workers who are tasked with providing mental health services and programs to mentally ill criminal offenders during their incarceration and with preparing them for their eventual return to the community.

EDITORS' NOTE: The editors extend a special thanks to David W. Roush, in the School of Criminal Justice at Michigan State University, for his support of this project, his assistance in identifying potential chapter authors, and his willingness to review material and provide meaningful feedback.

Third, mental health professionals who do choose to work in a correctional setting often face difficulties in adjusting to a work environment where their services are considered subordinate to the primary missions of this work setting. Unlike other mental health settings where rehabilitation and alleviation of suffering are the primary foci for all staff, such as psychiatric hospitals and community mental health facilities, correctional settings are tasked first with protecting society from criminal elements and second with punishing felons by separating them from society for specified periods of time. Neophyte correctional mental health professionals therefore have the dual challenges of adjusting to their supporting role within the correctional environment and developing services and programs that are effective without interfering with the primary missions of the correctional setting or with the staff who are tasked with accomplishing these missions. Obviously, some mental health professionals are better suited to these challenges than are others, but without guidance and mentoring, few are able to navigate these difficult waters successfully.

It is with these observations in mind that we began this handbook. Certainly, with the dramatic increase in the number of individuals with mental disorders in corrections, the need for well-trained mental health professionals within this setting has expanded. As mental health professionals have entered this field, they have begun to define roles beyond those traditionally assumed by mental health providers in other settings. Our goal in preparing this book was to provide a general overview of correctional mental health roles, issues, services, and programs to as broad an audience as possible.

More specifically, we hope that this handbook will serve as a resource to academic programs considering the development of courses in correctional mental health or as an adjunct to existing forensic courses. We believe that the material in this book does a good job of introducing the diverse field of correctional mental health to students preparing to enter the mental health profession by exposing them to the various populations found in correctional practice as well as to the many roles, issues, services, and programs provided by correctional mental health professionals.

We also expect this handbook to help clarify for mental health professionals entering the field of corrections their roles within the larger correctional community. It is too easy for neophyte correctional mental health professionals to make faulty assumptions about the importance of their role within the larger correctional organization and, as a result, to end up in conflict with the very organization they wish to serve.

Finally, we wanted this handbook to serve as a guide for correctional administrators tasked with developing or supervising mental health programs and professionals. Very often, the training and focus of correctional administrators has not been on mental health services or programs. In some cases, correctional administrators might even view mental health professionals and programs as "necessary evils" dictated by the courts. Over the years, we have seen how mental health programs that are well integrated with the more custodial aspects of correctional work can enhance the smooth and orderly running of a facility. We have also seen how mental health programs that do not attempt to coordinate their activities with those of other institutional departments can easily fail. It is our hope that this book will provide correctional administrators with an overview of mental health issues and aid them in deciding which services and programs can benefit their facilities and offer them ideas on how best to integrate them into their overall institutional operations.

Organizationally, this handbook is divided into three broad sections. In the first section, administrative, organizational, and ethical issues are presented. Chapter 1 presents a three-level model for developing and implementing mental health services and programs within a correctional setting. Using this service delivery model, Level 1 services would be defined as those basic mental health services provided to all offenders, Level 2 services would be those offered to special offender groups or populations, and Level 3 services would be those offered on a consultative basis to the institution. Chapter 2 discusses who the mental health professionals are that enter correctional work. This chapter discusses the academic preparation, training, and experience of mental health professions in general as well as what roles these professionals have played and what problems they have typically faced when they enter the correctional arena. Chapter 3 discusses the ethics of correctional mental health practice. Perhaps no single area is more misunderstood and confusing to the correctional administrator than this area. Unfortunately, neophyte mental health professionals entering correctional work also sometimes misunderstand this area and find themselves in what they believe to be serious ethical dilemmas. This chapter helps to define some of the ethical standards and guidelines that govern the practice of mental health in general and provides a thought-provoking framework for understanding how to implement these standards within a correctional setting.

The second and largest section of this handbook focuses on the many services and programs offered to detainee and inmate populations. Loosely following the three-level service delivery model presented in Chapter 1, this section describes in more depth mental health services and programs offered to individual offenders (Level 1) and to groups of offenders who share similar qualities or special needs (Level 2). Chapter 4 presents basic mental health services that should serve as a necessary core within any correctional setting. Certainly, other services or programs can be added to this core as resources allow, but no correctional setting is successfully meeting the mental health needs of its population without the provision of these basic services. Chapters 5 through 10 discuss the general characteristics, treatment needs, and management concerns of specific groups or populations of inmates. Chapter 5 highlights what is perhaps the largest special needs population in corrections today—the substance-abusing or dependent offender. Chapter 6 discusses individuals with significant mental impairment and the special challenges that these individuals present to correctional mental health professionals and administrators. Chapter 7 discusses female offenders, a group that has been growing faster than other segments of the correctional population. Chapter 8 deals with sexual offenders and predators. Chapter 9 discusses juvenile offenders. Chapter 10 covers other special offender populations such as military prisoners, geriatric offenders, and inmates with terminal medical problems that affect their mental health.

The third and final section of this handbook presents various clinical and consultative activities offered by mental health professionals within correctional settings. Chapter 11 discusses routine mental health services offered to institution staff through employee assistance programs and also describes special services offered to staff who have responded to or witnessed highly stressful critical incidents during the performance of their correctional duties. Chapter 12 presents the multiple roles for mental health professionals in training correctional staff. This chapter also discusses the importance of training mental health staff as they enter the correctional arena. Chapter 13 highlights a variety of consultative roles offered by mental health professionals to other institution departments or to the institution as a whole. Some of these roles are fairly traditional, such as consulting with case management staff on program planning or release preparation for inmates, but other roles are less traditional, such as training hostage or crisis negotiators. Chapter 14 stresses the importance of and need for good evaluative research as we attempt to expand the programs and services we provide during an era of cost containment and conservative fiscal management. It has become increasingly clear over the years that the "one program fits all" model has not been very successful. What the authors of this chapter propose is a research-based correctional practice that seeks to determine which programs work best with which offenders in which types of settings. The book concludes with Chapter 15, which highlights several future directions or trends in correctional mental health.

In selecting authors for the various chapters, we sought people with solid corrections or academic credentials. Our authors represent a good cross section of federal, state, and local correctional mental health practitioners with many years of hands-on experience in dealing with correctional mental health issues. Many of them are leaders in their fields. We also sought to include several authors from the academic community who have special interest and expertise in correctional mental health. We are very appreciative of the time and effort all of the authors put into their respective chapters, are pleased with the finished product, and hope that the reader finds each chapter to be informative and helpful in understanding the complexities and rewards of correctional mental health work.

PART I

ADMINISTRATION, ORGANIZATION, AND ETHICS

CHAPTER 1

Mental Health in Corrections: A Model for Service Delivery

Thomas J. Fagan

The housing and treatment of both criminal offenders and individuals with mental disorders in prisons and jails has been a recurring theme in corrections since confinement became a socially accepted means of punishment (Roberts, 1997). As early as the 1600s, when workhouses were the punishment of the day in Europe, there are documented cases in which relatives confined unruly family members rather than having these individuals tarnish the families' reputations (Spierenburg, 1995). To accomplish this, family members were required to petition a magistrate for permission to confine these individuals. Although many of these noncriminal individuals worked, a minority—usually from wealthy or distinguished families—were able to avoid labor by being isolated in small homes where the homeowners cared for them.

During the early 1800s, Americans were confining various groups—including criminals, the mentally ill, orphans, delinquents, and the chronically unemployed—in their prisons and jails, often in the same facility (McShane & Williams, 1996). This practice resulted in deplorable living conditions and prompted reformers such as Dorothea Dix to lobby state legislatures for the creation of separate facilities to house the mentally ill. With her success came the advent of mental asylums, the removal of many noncriminal individuals with mental disorders from prisons and jails, and the hope of treatment rather than punishment for these individuals. However, with overcrowding and a lack of adequate treatment staff, the hope of treatment quickly vanished and the warehousing of the mentally disordered in these asylums became the norm.

In addition, with the spread of mental asylums came a new class of mentally ill individuals. These individuals were both mentally ill and criminally dangerous. For these individuals, a number of hybrid arrangements in both prisons and asylums were developed (Morris, 1995). Prisons managed these cases either by housing them with regular criminals or by placing them in separate housing units within the prisons. Some correctional systems even developed separate prison psychiatric hospitals to manage these individuals. Asylums or state hospitals developed secured wards for these types of mentally disordered criminal offenders. These wards provided minimal treatment coupled with the added security found in prisons and jails. This bifurcated system continues even today in many states.

By the early 1900s, medical and behavioral scientists began to play a more prominent role in the thinking and policymaking of corrections. From their point of view, crime could be diagnosed and treated like any other medical condition or illness. As behavioral scientists began to work with prison and jail populations and apply the language and methodologies of medicine to these populations, it became clear to them that these populations were not homogeneous. Rather, offenders needed to be classified based on their security requirements as well as on their mental status (Rotman, 1995). Once again, the idea of segregating individuals with mental disorders from other criminal offenders was reinforced. In addition, the need for mental health treatment staff within the correctional environment became evident. According to Rotman (1995), by 1926, there were more than 100 psychiatrists and psychologists employed in correctional settings.

The medical model, with its emphasis on diagnosis and treatment, prevailed through much of the 20th century. It was applied to both mentally disordered and criminal offenders. Programs and other rehabilitative efforts became the buzzwords within the correctional community. However, by the mid-1970s, there was a growing feeling that few, if any, of these efforts were having any significant impact on the recidivism rate of treated offenders. Much of this pessimism was fueled by reviews of available research at the time, which failed to produce any conclusive links between rehabilitative efforts and declines in correctional recidivism rates (DiIulio, 1991; Martinson, 1974). These findings were sufficient to shift correctional policy away from the medical model.

By the late 1980s, a more balanced view about rehabilitation and correctional programs began to emerge, thanks in part to the extensive research efforts of Canadian social scientists such as Gendreau, Cullen, Ross, and Goggins (Cullen & Gendreau, 1989, 2000; Gendreau, 1996; Gendreau & Goggins, 1997; Gendreau, Goggins, & Smith, 1999; Gendreau & Ross, 1979, 1987), who were able to demonstrate that some correctional treatment programs were effective at reducing recidivism rates. This more balanced view, which is the prevailing approach used in most correctional facilities today, offers a variety of correctional programs (e.g., educational, vocational, religious, mental health, work) to offenders with the hope that offenders will participate in programs that will provide them with the role models and skills they will need to be more productive members of society on their release from prison.

Mental Illness in Prisons and Jails: Current Status

Three factors appear to be contributing to the current rapid rise in the number of individuals with mental disorders found in today's correctional environment. First, today's "law and order" sentiments regarding crime, which began during the 1980s, have resulted in a variety of "get tough" legislative actions, including the abolishment of parole, the introduction of determinant sentencing, changes in competency/criminal responsibility standards, and "three strikes" legislation. The cumulative effect of these actions has been to place more individuals in prison for longer periods of time. The number of individuals confined in America's prisons and jails today is fast approaching 2 million. Because some percentage of this population is likely to possess mental illness, the number of individuals with mental disorders will likely increase proportionately to increases in the number of confined individuals.

Second, with the development of psychotropic medications during the 1950s, there has been a national movement toward downsizing the locked wards of psychiatric hospitals in favor of mainstreaming mental health patients and providing them with community-based services. Although this notion was commendable, most state and federal budgets did not provide adequate funding to support these community-based programs. The result has been a dramatic increase in the number of persons with mental illness found among the ranks of the homeless and the incarcerated (Torrey, 1988; Torrey, Stieber, & Ezekiel, 1992). In a de facto sense, today's prisons and jails have assumed many of the functions formerly the responsibility of state psychiatric hospitals (McConville, 1995).

Estimates regarding the number of individuals with mental illness in today's prisons and jails have varied somewhat. In one study cited by McConville (1995), 37% of men and 56% of women serving sentences of more than 6 months in England were suffering from diagnosable mental disorders. In two studies conducted by the Bureau of Justice Statistics (Beck & Maruschak, 2001; Ditton, 1999), there were approximately 284,000 to 291,000 offenders with mental illness incarcerated in the nation's prisons and jails in 1998. Using self-report data indicating either a mental condition or an overnight stay in a mental hospital as a definition of mental illness, Ditton (1999) found that approximately 16% of all state prisoners, 7% of all federal prisoners, 16% of all local jail offenders, and 16% of all probationers were mentally impaired. Ditton also noted that state prisoners with mental conditions were more likely that other inmates to be incarcerated for violent offenses (53% vs. 46%), more likely than other inmates to be under the influence of drugs or alcohol at the times of their current offenses (59% vs. 51%), and more than twice as likely as other inmates to have been homeless during the 12 months prior to their arrests (20% vs. 9%). In their annual survey of state and federal correctional systems, Camp and Camp (1998) asked participants to provide the percentage of their offenders who were involved in mental health programs. Reports ranged from a low of less than 1% in several smaller states to a high of 18% in the state of Ohio. Finally, Fazel and Danesh (2002) studied the prevalence rates of mental illness in the prisons and jails of 12 Western countries. They found that approximately 4% of their surveyed sample were diagnosed with psychotic disorders, 10% with major depression, and 47% with antisocial personality disorder.

Third, America's war on drugs has resulted in a dramatic increase in the number of incarcerated individuals confined for drug-related offenses, including use, possession, and/or distribution of narcotics. Begun, Jacobs, and Quiram (1999) reported that the actual number of state prison inmates confined for drug offenses increased from 19,000 (6% of the total inmate population) in 1980 to approximately 234,000 (23% of the inmate population) in 1996. Mumola (1999) noted that the number of federal inmates held for drug-related offenses was much higher and accounted for about 63% of the current federally sentenced inmate population. Interestingly, Camp and Camp (1998) reported that only about 14% of all incarcerated individuals were involved in some form of drug treatment on January 1, 1998.

Using the figures just cited as a rough guide, several observations might be made. First, if approximately 16% of all incarcerated individuals at the state prison and local jail levels and approximately 7% of all incarcerated federal offenders have a primary diagnosis of significant mental impairment, then it is safe to assume that as these prison and jail populations continue to grow, so too will the number of incarcerated individuals with significant mental impairments. Second, if substance abusers who participate in treatment are added to this figure, then an additional 14% of the inmate population may be considered mentally disordered. This figure includes only those offenders seeking treatment for substance abuse. There are many other offenders who decline treatment, some of whom may have a diagnosable substance abuse problem. Last, if better functioning inmates with some mental disturbances (e.g., anxiety and mood disorders, adjustment disorders to incarceration or to medical illnesses such as HIV/AIDS) and personality disorders (e.g., borderline personality disorder, antisocial personality disorder) are added to this equation, then the percentage of mentally diagnosable offenders becomes even higher.

In short, there is a large and growing population of mentally disordered individuals currently confined in our nation's correctional facilities. Although the placement of mentally disordered individuals in prisons and jails is not a new phenomenon, certainly the number of confined individuals with mental disorders is far greater today than at other times in our history. How correctional settings identify, manage, and treat these individuals has an impact not only on the long-term mental health of this disordered population but also on the work and living conditions found within prisons and jails.

While mental health practitioners work diligently to address the diverse needs of this population within prison and jail settings, correctional policymakers, with growing support from the general public, have begun to examine alternatives to incarceration for nonviolent offenders both with and without diagnosable mental disorders (Schiraldi & Greene, 2002). This movement to seek alternatives to confinement has been aided by a need to contain costs as state and federal revenues shrink during tighter economic times. Certainly, drug and mental health courts, home confinement, reforms in mandatory sentencing laws, and increases in compassionate releases for terminally ill and elderly offenders all are examples of this shift in public sentiment and correctional policy. If these reforms take hold, then they may signal a stabilization, or perhaps even a decline, in the number of future offenders placed in prisons and jails. However, for the current time, correctional mental health practitioners are left with the problem of how best to manage and treat mentally disordered offenders in a setting that does not also embrace rehabilitation as its primary goal and that has limited funds and an expanding population.

Mental Health Services in Prisons and Jails: A Conceptual Model

Providing mental health services in prisons and jails has always been a somewhat contentious subject. When too few services are offered, the psychotic and/or suicidal behaviors of offenders with mental disorders can easily disrupt the smooth and orderly running of a correctional facility. Untreated offenders with mental illness frighten some criminal offenders but may also be victimized by other offenders. Their idiosyncratic behavior often alienates them from other offenders (thereby leaving them isolated), creates housing dilemmas and management difficulties for correctional staff, and may lead to liability issues for correctional administrators. When a broad range of services is provided to offenders with mental illness, cries of coddling criminals are sounded in some public arenas. Others wonder why criminals can have access to services that are sometimes difficult for the average law-abiding citizen to receive.

Assessing which mental health services to offer within a correctional facility can also be difficult to determine and may be influenced by several factors. Certainly, the size and clinical needs of the population being served represent one key factor. The overall mission of the facility in which the services are being offered (e.g., jail, prison, prison hospital, high-security facility, boot camp, private prison) may also be a defining factor. The funding level for mental health services will also be critical. Limited funding obviously results in a limited number of staff available to provide services. When staff resources are restricted, mental health staff are forced to either prioritize their time and offer services only to those whose needs are most immediate and critical or extend the reach of their services by training paraprofessionals to carry out some basic service delivery functions.

Even when adequate funding is available for mental health staff, sometimes it is difficult to find mental health professionals who are willing to work within a correctional environment. Many view this environment as unwelcoming and antithetical to the objectives of treatment. This problem is further compounded by the fact that many correctional facilities are located in rural or remote areas where community-based treatment providers are limited and, therefore, in greater demand. Finally, service delivery may be influenced by the skills, experiences, and treatment biases of the service provider; by the willingness of the service provider to train and use paraprofessionals and correctional staff as treatment extenders; and by the support and respect of correctional administrators for program and service initiatives and staff.

Given all of the preceding conditions and caveats, there are any number of ways of organizing and conceptualizing the delivery of mental health services in a correctional environment. The conceptual model that follows is one way of accomplishing this task. It is meant to provide correctional workers and other readers who may be unfamiliar with mental health services—and, more particularly, mental health services within a correctional environment—with a conceptual framework through which to view, organize, and evaluate mental health services within prisons and jails.

The conceptual model presented in what follows outlines three levels of service. Level 1 services are basic, are provided to individual offenders, and are often mandated by correctional accrediting bodies such as the National Commission on Correctional Health Care and the American Correctional Association. Level 2 services are offered to specific target groups or populations within prisons and jails and may or may not be mandated by correctional accrediting bodies. Level 3 services involve systemic interventions and/or consultations, often at the institution or agency level. This conceptual model is additive in nature. In other words, Level 2 services should generally not be added until most Level 1 services are implemented, and Level 3 services should not be added until most Level 2 services are being addressed. Presented another way, if the number of service providers is limited, then Level 1 services should be their primary target. If additional staff resources are added, then Level 2 followed by Level 3 services should gain more attention. This model represents one way of prioritizing service delivery when resources are limited.

Level 1 Services

Level 1 services are basic mental health services available to all offenders. Although use of these services may be affected by the demographics of the population being served (e.g., males, females, juveniles, detainees, high- vs. low-security offenders), they represent what should be considered a minimal level of mental health service. Their primary purpose is to provide for the detection, diagnosis, short- and long-term treatment, and referral of offenders with significant mental health problems—problems that may be potentially life threatening or that may seriously disrupt the smooth running of an institution. The availability of Level 1 services also serves the secondary purpose of providing offenders with a support system throughout their incarceration. Level 1 services include initial intake assessments, acute crisis intervention, brief counseling, individual psychotherapy/ case management targeting primarily the seriously disturbed offender, detention/ segregation reviews, special mental health evaluations, and maintenance of mental health records.

Initial intake assessments are typically conducted with one or more of the following purposes in mind:

1. To identify emotional, intellectual, and behavioral deficits and/or significant mental impairment

2. To identify specialized treatment needs (e.g., psychotropic medication, suicide monitoring, alcohol/drug detoxification or treatment)

3. To provide baseline data for mental health staff to use during future contacts with offenders

4. To provide useful information to other institution staff (e.g., assault potential, escape risk, potential adjustment problems, special housing/program needs)

5. To inform offenders about the availability of mental health services and how to access them

At a minimum, initial intake assessments involve a clinical interview with the offender. As time and resources permit, these assessments may also involve a review of relevant historical data, a period of behavioral observation, and psychological testing. Intake assessments may be conducted at institutions specifically designed for this purpose (i.e., diagnostic and assessment centers), or they may be conducted at regular correctional institutions. The most important issue is that they be conducted prior to the inmate's placement in the general inmate population. These assessments are usually completed by mental health professionals, medical staff, or specially trained correctional workers. Ordinarily, these assessments are begun soon after the offender's arrival at the facility and are completed within 14 days. In a study conducted by the Bureau of Justice Statistics (Beck & Maruschak, 2001), it was reported that nearly 70% of all state correctional facilities screen all inmates for mental illness during the intake process.

Crisis intervention services are used by mental health professionals whenever offenders present themselves with significant mental health problems that may endanger either their lives or the lives of other offenders. Two obvious examples are offenders who are either suicidal or blatantly psychotic. Suicidal inmates may require special housing, continuous monitoring, and follow-up treatment to prevent them from harming themselves and to assist them through a short crisis period to a more rational mental state. Psychotic offenders may pose a danger to those around them or may become victimized by other offenders as their behavior becomes more bizarre. These individuals may require housing changes (to protect them from more predatory offenders), increased monitoring, and medication to stabilize their mental states. If they cannot be stabilized in a reasonable period of time, then they may need to be referred to a facility better able to meet their specific treatment needs (e.g., prison psychiatric hospital, psychiatric ward in a state hospital).

Brief counseling services are offered to offenders who have specific problems that are causing them some degree of mental distress. These problems vary across inmates and depend in part on offenders' ability to cope with unexpected or challenging events and on their individual support network. Brief counseling is typically short term in nature (i.e., one to four sessions) and focused on solving a specific problem. For example, some offenders seek brief counseling early in their incarceration to help them adjust to the structure of a correctional environment or to the separation from loved ones. Other offenders seek brief counseling during their incarceration as problems surface between themselves and other inmates, staff, or family members. Still others manage their confinement without distress but require brief counseling as they begin to face the idea of returning to the community. Because of its short-term, problem-specific nature, brief counseling is the most frequently provided service to offenders.

Individual psychotherapy is ordinarily conceptualized as a service sought by individuals who are interested in making significant behavioral, emotional, and/or attitudinal changes. It tends to be long term in nature and is broader in scope than brief counseling. It may focus on the development of greater personal insight or on the development of specific skills. Because it is more time-consuming and involved than brief counseling, it requires a significant commitment on the part of both the offender and the mental health professional. In many correctional facilities, the number of offenders in individual psychotherapy is limited by staff shortages and by a lack of will on the part of offenders to make the time and energy commitments needed to successfully complete this type of therapy. Many criminal offenders lack insight into the harmful, self-destructive nature of their behavior and often do not see the need for individual psychotherapy. Beck and Maruschak (2001) reported that approximately 71% of all state correctional facilities provide counseling/ therapy by trained mental health professionals to their inmate populations.

Within the context of this discussion of Level 1 services, individual psychotherapy is defined more narrowly to focus only on those long-term monitoring, case management, and therapeutic services provided by mental health professionals to individuals who are suffering from serious mental disorders. Put another way, individual psychotherapy may be defined here as the long-term follow-up of services begun during a period of acute crisis. Once stabilized, individuals with serious mental disorders often require regular monitoring to ensure that they comply with their medication regimens and do not disrupt the orderly running of the institution. They may also need various adjustments in their institutional circumstances (e.g., housing and job changes) to accommodate the lingering symptoms of their disorders. Last, these individuals may need assistance in developing more useful coping skills to avoid future occurrences of their disorders. To accomplish these objectives often requires a long-term commitment on the part of mental health professionals to work with seriously disordered offenders.

Detention/segregation reviews are mental health assessments completed on individuals who are housed in an administrative detention or disciplinary segregation unit for periods of 30 days or more. Offenders who violate institution rules, need to be separated from other offenders, or are pending transfer to another facility are typically found in this type of housing unit. Because these units restrict an offender's access to treatment staff as well as program, work, and recreational activities, there is a concern among correctional professionals that this level of isolation may have a negative effect on the offender's mental state over an extended period of time. Detention/segregation reviews are designed to assess the offender's adjustment to his or her surroundings, to determine whether continued isolation will have a negative effect on the offender's mental status, and to gauge whether the offender poses a threat to self, staff, or other inmates.

Special mental health evaluations are completed on offenders for many reasons. For example, when mental health concerns are identified during the initial intake screening process, a more detailed evaluation may be required to arrive at a definitive diagnosis, to assess what treatment options are needed, and to determine where best to provide them (i.e., locally or in a hospital setting). As offenders reach parole eligibility dates, parole boards will sometimes request assessments to determine how great a potential risk the offenders would pose to the community if parole were granted. Courts refer individuals for special assessments before their trials begin whenever those individuals' mental competence to participate in their trials or their mental responsibility at the times of the offenses is questioned. Courts also refer convicted individuals for special assessment, on occasion, to gain a better understanding of the offenders' mental status and programming needs prior to imposing final sentences. Institution disciplinary committees, much like courts, may refer inmates who have violated institution rules for special assessment to determine mental competence and responsibility prior to their participation in disciplinary hearings. Mental health assessments may also be completed on offenders who are referred by correctional staff when bizarre behavior is noted or other mental health concerns are raised.

Maintenance of mental health records is an essential component of the delivery of correctional mental health services. It is not uncommon in correctional settings for several staff members working various shifts to provide treatment services to offenders. It is also routine in larger correctional systems for inmates to move from one facility to another. Last, it is not unusual for offenders to "doctor shop" until they find someone willing to provide them with a particular service (e.g., tranquilizing medication). The only way for care to be continuous is to routinely document when services are given or denied. Documentation of mental health services is sometimes part of a larger medical record, but it may also be maintained as a stand-alone file. Keeping accurate mental health records can also be very helpful when offenders or their families raise issues of correctional malfeasance.

Collectively, the Level 1 services just described define the minimum standard for the delivery of mental health services within a prison or jail setting. Although these services may be provided by qualified full-time, part-time, or contract mental health staff, they all are considered essential services. Accrediting organizations, such as the National Commission on Correctional Health Care and the American Correctional Association, have numerous standards that define each of these activities and propose minimal guidelines for how they should be performed in prisons and jails. Practically speaking, Level 1 services might be considered the "no frills" package of correctional mental health services. They are sufficient to address the serious individual mental health needs of a correctional population so long as an adequate number of trained staff members is available to provide these services. Although setting reasonable staffing guidelines is fraught with problems too numerous to list here, a very general guideline of one mental health provider for every 500 offenders is a standard that a number of systems, including the Federal Bureau of Prisons, have found satisfactory.

In some correctional agencies, in-house mental health professionals also offer Level 1 services to employees through employee assistance programs (EAPs). Most EAPs focus on staff who are experiencing emotional, behavioral, mental health, or substance abuse problems that are having a negative impact on their job performance. They assist staff in identifying the nature and extent of their problems, provide short-term interventions, and refer staff with long-term treatment needs to available community resources. EAP counselors sometimes serve as an agency contact point for community treatment providers when employees are preparing to return to work after extended absences for treatment. Some correctional agencies choose not to use in-house treatment staff and instead offer EAP services through contracts with community-based mental health professionals or agencies.

Level 2 Services

Level 2 services consist of programs and services offered to specific groups of offenders who possess similar problems or characteristics or who share specific mental health treatment needs. Common problems or characteristics might be found among offenders who share specific demographic features such as age (young vs. old) and gender (male vs. female). They might also be found among offenders who fall within a specific diagnostic category such as substance abuse, stress-related disorders, sex offenses, psychosis, or HIV status. Finally, offenders who share a specific status, such as military prisoner, penitentiary inmate, or illegal alien, might experience similar problems or concerns. In each of these cases, offenders can best be treated in a group format where both similarities in pathology and support from peers can be used to promote positive therapeutic change.

Although there has been considerable debate over the years regarding the value of group programs in the correctional environment (Cullen & Gendreau, 2000; DiIulio, 1991; Martinson, 1974), there is strong empirical evidence that some correctional group treatment programs are effective at reducing recidivism rates. Gendreau (1996) and Gendreau, Goggins, and Smith (1999) provided excellent summaries of the literature in this area. This literature defines a number of key elements that are necessary for effective correctional treatment programming. Among these elements are the following:

1. Programs are presented in a correctional environment that is both supportive of programming initiatives and stable in terms of social climate and staff resources.

2. Stakeholders in the program (e.g., community sources, correctional administrators, program providers, correctional staff) agree that the program has value and is consistent with the institution's mission and values.

3. Treatment providers are appropriately trained and have professional credibility with offenders, staff, and correctional administrators.

4. Role models are provided to offenders that are within their reach (e.g., corrections employees or community figures as opposed to sports celebrities).

5. Programmatic goals are clearly stated and target specific criminogenic factors such as pro-criminal attitudes and associations, impulsivity, and risk-taking behaviors.

6. Programmatic emphasis is on basic cognitive-behavioral, problem-solving skills that clearly relate actions to consequences and demonstrate respect for authority.

7. Relevant post-program support systems are developed that use whatever human and financial resources are available within both the correctional and community settings to aid and support program goals.

Even if group treatment programs were not successful at reducing prison recidivism rates, DiIulio (1991) proposed that group treatment programs serve more than rehabilitative functions within a correctional environment. He noted that treatment programs have a humanizing effect on the correctional environment and can serve as valuable incentives for offenders to engage in good behavior. His research, as well as the work of Lissner, Cornell, Pompi, and Gable (1998), has suggested that effective programs equate with safer, less costly prison operations, as measured by factors such as reduced inmate idleness, lower offender assault and rule infraction rates, better inmate-staff relationships, and higher staff morale and retention.

Although this book contains many examples of effective correctional treatment programs, two examples of special populations requiring special programs will suffice in this section to illustrate types of Level 2 services/programs.

Drug Abuse Treatment Programs. With so many individuals being confined today for substance-related offenses, it is no surprise that one of the most common types of correctional programs currently is in the area of drug abuse treatment. Drug abuse treatment programs in prisons and jails use many of the same treatment models that are found in community treatment settings. It is not uncommon to find 12-step programs, such as Alcoholics Anonymous and Narcotics Anonymous, in today's prisons and jails. These programs define alcohol or drug abuse as a medical disease that can be treated and stress the value of peer support in overcoming the disease.

Lipton (1995), in a review of several independent and geographically diverse substance abuse programs for offenders, found positive findings for offenders who participated in substance abuse intervention programs in prisons and community-based follow-up settings. He noted a sizable contrast between the post-release outcomes of treatment participants compared with those of inmates who did not participate in treatment.

One of the newer approaches to drug abuse treatment describes itself as biopsychosocial in nature. This type of program stresses the importance of biological, psychological, and social factors as contributing factors in substance abuse. Treatment using this model stresses personal responsibility in overcoming substance abuse and is typically cognitive-behavioral in its approach. It educates clients about the effects of substance abuse on all aspects of their lives, teaches skills to improve interpersonal communication, targets criminal and faulty thought patterns that contribute to substance use, assists participants in identifying situations that historically have triggered substance use, helps individuals to develop healthier lifestyle choices, and supports people when they transition back into their communities following program completion. Preliminary data from the Triad Drug Evaluation Project (Pelissier et al., 2000), a National Institute on Drug Abuse-sponsored program currently evaluating selected biopsychosocial residential drug abuse treatment programs in the Federal Bureau of Prisons, have yielded some promising results. This study reported a 25% reduction in recidivism rates and a comparable reduction in behavioral problems from program participants. (See Chapter 5 for a more detailed discussion of substance abuse issues in corrections.)

Female Offender Treatment Programs. Female offenders have emerged over the past several years as a special correctional population in need of additional attention. Historically, this has been a relatively small population. However, over the past decade, the rate of females being admitted to correctional facilities has risen steadily. Greenfield and Snell (1999) reported that between 1990 and 1998, the number of women confined in prisons grew by an annual average of 8.5%. Over that same period, prison populations nationwide increased an average of 6.7% annually. The authors also found a 42% increase in the number of felony convictions for women in state courts between 1990 and 1996. Their study indicated that in 1998, there were approximately 84,000 female offenders confined in prisons, with an additional 866,000 females under the supervision of parole and probation authorities. Camp and Camp (1998) reported that female offenders represented approximately 6.4% of the total prison population on January 1, 1998.

Anyone who has worked with both male and female offenders is quick to point out that the emotions, attitudes, and behaviors of these populations are very different (Morash, Bynum, & Koons, 1998). For example, female offenders struggle significantly more with family separation and child care issues than do male offenders (Gabel & Johnston, 1995). Female offenders are frequently more avid and demanding consumers of medical care, Level 1 mental health services, and other correctional programs and services (Ditton, 1999). When female offenders group together, it is often around issues involving support and nurturance. Male offenders tend to group together around power and control issues. Although both populations can be manipulative, their techniques differ. Female offenders tend to use flirtation, seduction, and sexuality to achieve their objectives. Male offenders are more likely to use threats and other coercive techniques.

One theme that has emerged as significant among female offenders is the large number of these offenders who come to prisons and jails with significant trauma from physical abuse, sexual abuse, and/or domestic violence histories. Various studies have suggested that anywhere from 50% to 80% of female offenders have abuse and/or domestic violence histories when they arrive at prisons (Belknap, 1996; Herman, 1992; Marcus-Mendoza, Sargent, & Chong Ho, 1994; Pollack-Byrne, 1990; Walker, 1994). Within this population of abused female offenders, Marcus-Mendoza et al. (1994) also found high rates of drug abuse (39%) and alcohol abuse (19%). Based on these data, there is a clear need for correctional programs that address the trauma associated with this abuse and that provide female offenders with the skills and confidence needed to avoid returning to these types of relationships post-release.

Similar to prisons housing male offenders, female institutions have historically offered an array of educational, vocational, medical/mental health, religious, and recreational programs for their residents. However, until recently, few institutions have offered programs that meet the specific treatment needs of incarcerated women with significant abuse histories. Group programs are now emerging in several federal facilities that specifically address the trauma histories of abused female offenders. These programs have several components, including information about trauma to educate about the symptoms and effects of trauma, skills building to enhance general coping abilities, wellness and health awareness to promote healthier lifestyle choices, and more traditional psychotherapy to deal with the long-term effects of trauma. (See Chapter 7 for a more detailed discussion of female offender management and treatment issues.)

Staff Services. Level 2 services may also be provided to correctional staff who share similar problems or characteristics. For example, correctional work, like law enforcement work in general, can be extremely stressful. To address this issue, correctional mental health professionals might offer staff special group training in stress management that provides them with a variety of stress reduction techniques. In addition, correctional workers are sometimes exposed to situations that are extremely traumatic (e.g., staff/inmate murder, staff/inmate suicide, riot or hostage incident, natural disaster, physical or sexual assault). It is not unusual for these individuals to experience a variety of post-trauma symptoms. Through the use of critical incident stress debriefing techniques, which are typically done in small groups of six to eight individuals, correctional mental health professionals have been able to assist employees in working through the effects of traumatic incidents so that they may return to work.

Level 3 Services

Level 3 services involve the application of behavioral science principles at an institution or agency level through consultation and other systemic interventions. The training that mental health professionals receive in the behavioral sciences can be very helpful to correctional administrators tasked with managing the overall correctional environment. Mental health professionals have tapped into their social science backgrounds to successfully develop classification systems used to manage diverse offender populations more efficiently (Alexander & Austin, 1992; Kane & Saylor, 1982; Solomon & Baird, 1982). These classification systems have typically attempted to separate predatory offenders from weaker offenders in an effort to provide safer living conditions for all offenders. Mental health professionals have also been asked to use their conflict resolution skills to mediate disputes between or among dysfunctional departments within correctional institutions and between labor and management.

Correctional administrators interested in objectively measuring the social climate of an institution have used the psychometric talents of behavioral scientists. These talents have also been tapped to identify the characteristics of successful employees. As these characteristics have been identified, psychometricians have then been able to develop empirically derived selection criteria that can be used to screen for these characteristics among current employees and prospective new employees. Knowledge of what qualities a successful correctional employee must possess also has implications for leadership development and succession planning strategies within an agency. These also are areas where mental health professionals can offer assistance.

Many of the skills currently taught to all correctional workers for use in managing criminal offenders have their roots in the behavioral sciences. Examples of these skills include effective interpersonal communication skills, active listening skills, confrontation avoidance procedures, conflict resolution methods, and crisis negotiation techniques. Mental health professionals employed by correctional agencies are in an excellent position to provide training in these skill areas to all or specially selected correctional workers as one way of significantly improving the overall climate within their system.

Mental health professionals are also in a position to train specific correctional staff to serve as mental health paraprofessionals so that program opportunities can be increased and staff-inmate contacts can be maximized. Correctional counselors are frequently the beneficiaries of this type of training. Mental health staff may also train correctional officers, work detail supervisors, and other staff who come into daily contact with offenders regarding signs and symptoms of mental illness and suicide. This type of training increases the sensitivity of all staff to inmates with these types of problems, helps to reduce staff fear and misunderstanding about these issues, and provides staff with useful techniques for managing these offenders when their behavior becomes troublesome. In essence, this type of training for staff aids them in becoming treatment extenders and allows the reach of mental health professions to extend beyond their offices and clinics.

Finally, correctional mental health staff are in a unique position, based on their regular contacts with both offenders and other staff, to observe negative or destructive patterns or trends within the correctional environment. This information, along with recommendations for corrective action, can be extremely valuable to correctional administrators.

Conclusions

Obviously, mental health professionals bring different personalities, talents, and interests to their work in corrections. More traditional mental health professions view their role within the correctional environment as that of direct service providers. These individuals tend to stay in their offices and provide Level 1, as well as some Level 2, services to offenders and staff who are willing to come to their offices for assistance. In many ways, these treatment providers have set up "private practices" within correctional settings. Although this model may be valuable to individual recipients, its merit, from a correctional administrator's or worker's perspective, is often difficult to assess. From such a perspective, it may be viewed positively but more likely will be seen as an example of coddling inmates or advocating for the rights of inmates.

Some correctional mental health providers approach their correctional work using more of a community mental health model. They see themselves as more then just basic service providers and believe that they can, through early screening, education, and effective intervention, either prevent or at least minimize problems that affect individuals as well as the systems in which they operate. These treatment providers see clearly the value of reaching out into the offender population, assessing group needs, and providing effective intervention strategies that are both economical and efficient. These mental health professionals often view themselves as part of a larger correctional team or system and, as a result, are more likely to approach problems from this perspective. Level 3 services, such as training staff to serve as treatment extenders and to be more knowledgeable and sensitive about particular offender mental health needs, are appropriate ways of addressing offender needs while at the same time tackling some of the systemic factors that may be exacerbating these problems. When mental health providers use a community mental health model, they are consulting routinely with staff at all levels of the institution, are getting staff more involved in treatment interventions as treatment extenders, and (as a result) are often viewed more favorably by both offenders and correctional staff, who see them more as team players who are sensitive to both inmate and staff issues.

Although correctional systems benefit from mental health providers who use both the "private practice" and "community mental health" models, the most effective mental health delivery systems within correctional settings are hybrids of both models. They provide an array of services and programs from all three levels and blend them into one seamless, comprehensive mental health delivery system that addresses both offender and staff needs at the individual, group, and systemic levels.

Although correctional mental health professionals are in a position to see first-hand the value of their services and programs to participating offenders, correctional administrators might not yet share the same positive views regarding the overall value of mental health services and programs to the correctional environment. Mental health professionals can easily provide numerous testimonials from offenders who have benefited from mental health services and programs, but these findings are obviously not very empirical. During this era of cost containment, mental health professionals need to develop more empirical methods of demonstrating the value of their services and programs not only from a "positive change" perspective but also from a cost containment and "value-added" basis. Lissner et al. (1998) proposed one model for accomplishing this task and, using this model, have been able to illustrate the clear social and financial benefits of at least one mental health program in the correctional environment. Obviously, additional research is needed in this important area to prove what correctional mental health professionals have known for many years—that correctional mental health services and programs are cost-effective, can produce positive prosocial change in offenders, and can help to humanize the correctional environment for both staff and offenders.

References

Alexander, T., & Austin, J. (1992). *Handbook for evaluating objective prison classification systems.* Washington, DC: National Institute of Corrections.

Beck, A. J., & Maruschak, L. M. (2001). *Mental health treatment in state prisons, 2000* (Bureau of Justice Statistics Special Report, NCJ 188215). Washington, DC: U.S. Department of Justice, Office of Justice Programs.

Begun, A. M., Jacobs, N. R., & Quiram, J. F. (Eds.). (1999). *Prisons and jails: A deterrent to crime?* Wylie, TX: Information Plus.

Belknap, J. (1996). *The invisible woman: Gender, crime, and justice.* Belmont, CA: Wadsworth.

Camp, G. M., & Camp, C. (1998). *The corrections yearbook, 1998.* Middletown, CT: Criminal Justice Institute.

Cullen, F. T., & Gendreau, P. (1989). The effectiveness of correctional rehabilitation: Reconsidering the nothing works debate. In L. Goodstein & D. MacKenzie (Eds.), *American prisons: Issues in research and policy* (pp. 23-44). New York: Plenum.

Cullen, F. T., & Gendreau, P. (2000). Assessing correctional rehabilitation: Policy, practice, and prospects. In J. Horney (Ed.), *NIJ criminal justice 2000: Vol. 3. Policies, processes, and decisions of the criminal justice system* (pp. 109-176). Washington, DC: U.S. Department of Justice, National Institute of Justice.

DiIulio, J. J. (1991). *No escape: The future of American corrections.* New York: Basic Books.

Ditton, P. M. (1999). *Mental health and treatment of inmates and probationers* (Bureau of Justice Statistics Special Report, NCJ 174463). Washington, DC: National Criminal Justice Reference Service.

Fazel, S., & Danesh, J. (2002). Serious mental disorder in 23,000 prisoners: A systematic review of 62 surveys. *The Lancet, 359,* 545-550.

Gabel, K., & Johnston, D. (1995). *Children of incarcerated parents.* New York: Lexington Books.

Gendreau, P. (1996). The principles of effective intervention with offenders. In A. Hartland (Ed.), *Choosing correctional options that work* (pp. 117-130). Thousand Oaks, CA: Sage.

Gendreau, P., & Goggins, C. (1997). Correctional treatment: Accomplishments and realities. In P. Van Voorhis, M. Braswell, & D. L. Lester (Eds.), *Correctional counseling and rehabilitation* (pp. 271-279). Cincinnati, OH: Anderson.

Gendreau, P., Goggins, C., & Smith, P. (1999). The forgotten issue in effective correctional treatment: Program implementation. *International Journal of Offender Therapy and Comparative Criminology, 43*(2), 180-187.

Gendreau, P., & Ross, R. R. (1979). Effectiveness of correctional treatment: Bibliography for cynics. *Crime & Delinquency, 25,* 463-489.

Gendreau, P., & Ross, R. R. (1987). Revivification of rehabilitation: Evidence from the 1980's. *Justice Quarterly, 4,* 349-408.

Greenfield, L. A., & Snell, T. L. (1999). *Women offenders* (Bureau of Justice Statistics Special Report, NCJ 175688). Washington, DC: National Criminal Justice Reference Service.

Herman, J. L. (1992). *Trauma and recovery.* New York: Basic Books.

Kane, T., & Saylor, W. (1982). *Security designation/Custody classification of inmates.* Washington, DC: U.S. Bureau of Prisons.

Lipton, D. S. (1995). *The effectiveness of treatment for drug abusers under criminal justice supervision.* Washington, DC: U.S. Department of Justice, National Institute of Justice.

Lissner, A. R., Cornell, D. M., Pompi, K. F., & Gable, R. J. (1998). The value of treatment in prison. *Cornell Papers, 2,* 1-15.

Marcus-Mendoza, S. T., Sargent, E., & Chong Ho, Y. (1994). Changing perceptions of the etiology of crime: The relationship between abuse and female criminology. *Journal of the Oklahoma Justice Research Consortium, 1,* 13-23.

Martinson, R. (1974, Spring). What works? Questions and answers about prison reform. *The Public Interest,* pp. 22-54.

McConville, S. (1995). Local justice: The jail. In N. Morris & D. J. Rothman (Eds.), *The Oxford history of prisons: The practice of punishment in Western society* (pp. 297-327). New York: Oxford University Press.

McShane, M. D., & Williams, F. P. (Eds.). (1996). *Encyclopedia of American prisons.* New York: Garland.

Morash, M., Bynum, T. S., & Koons, B. A. (1998). *Women offenders: Programming needs and promising approaches* (NIJ Research in Brief). Washington, DC: National Institute of Justice.

Morris, N. (1995). The contemporary prison. In N. Morris & D. J. Rothman (Eds.), *The Oxford history of prisons: The practice of punishment in Western society* (pp. 227-259). New York: Oxford University Press.

Mumola, C. J. (1999). *Substance abuse and treatment of state and federal prisoners* (Bureau of Justice Statistics Special Report, NCJ 172871). Washington, DC: National Criminal Justice Reference Service.

Pelissier, B., Rhodes, W., Saylor, W., Gaes, G., Camp, S. D., Vanyur, S. D., & Wallace, S. (2000). *TRIAD drug treatment evaluation project: Final report of three-year outcomes—Part 1.* Washington, DC: Federal Bureau of Prisons, Office of Research and Evaluation.

Pollack-Byrne, J. M. (1990). *Women, prison, and crime.* Pacific Grove, CA: Brooks/Cole.

Roberts, J. W. (1997). *Reform and retribution: An illustrated history of American prisons.* Lanham, MD: American Correctional Association.

Rotman, E. (1995). The failure of reform. In N. Morris & D. J. Rothman (Eds.), *The Oxford history of prisons: The practice of punishment in Western society* (pp. 169-197). New York: Oxford University Press.

Schiraldi, V., & Greene, J. (2002, May). Public opinion shifts as states re-examine prison policies in face of tightening budgets. *On the Line, 25*(3), 1-2, 7.

Solomon, L., & Baird, C. (1982). Past failures and future potentials. In L. Fowler (Ed.), *Classification as a management tool: Theories and models for decision makers* (pp. 5-9). College Park, MD: American Correctional Association.

Spierenburg, P. (1995). The body and the state: Early modern Europe. In N. Morris & D. J. Rothman (Eds.), *The Oxford history of prisons: The practice of punishment in Western society* (pp. 49-77). New York: Oxford University Press.

Torrey, E. F. (1988). *Nowhere to go: The tragic odyssey of the homeless mentally ill.* New York: Harper & Row.

Torrey, E. F., Stieber, J., & Ezekiel, J. (1992). *Criminalizing the seriously mentally ill.* Washington, DC: Public Citizens Health Research Group and National Alliance for the Mentally Ill.

Walker, L. E. A. (1994). *Abused women and survivor therapy.* Washington, DC: American Psychological Association.

CHAPTER 2

Correctional Mental Health Professionals

Phil Magaletta and Jennifer Boothby

Since the dawn of corrections, there have been incarcerated men and women who have suffered from mental illnesses. Given the manifestation of such illnesses, be it the expression of odd thoughts, the acting out of behaviors disruptive to institutional life, or a general inability to cope with the stressors of the prison environment, administrators have had to ask the question: What exactly can be done for and with such individuals, and who is to perform such work? This question remains as relevant today as it was in the past, perhaps even more so. Multiple streams have converged to maintain the need for mental health services in corrections as well as to create the means by which these professional services can be provided.

The need for mental health services can be seen as a continuing outgrowth of the volume of those being incarcerated, concomitant with less viable alternatives for community-based residential treatment of those with mental disorders. (See Chapter 1 for a discussion of deinstitutionalization of the mentally ill.) In addition, the existing literature suggests that incarcerated individuals have a high prevalence rate of both current and previous mental illness. Compared with community samples, prevalence rates are elevated for a range of disorders, including the severe mental illnesses, substance abuse, and learning disorders (Guy, Platt, Zwerling, & Bullock, 1985;

AUTHORS' NOTE: Opinions expressed in this chapter are those of the authors and do not necessarily represent the opinions of the Federal Bureau of Prisons or the U.S. Department of Justice.

Palermo, Gumz, & Liska, 1992; for reviews of this literature, see also Diamond, Wang, Holzer, Thomas, & Cruser, 2001; Sigurdson, 2000).

Beyond the intrinsic offender needs, social changes over the past several decades have expanded the opportunity for mental health professionals to offer services in the correctional environment. One major change has been the significant growth in the cadre of professional mental health providers. Penal institutions have remained a social structure in America for more than 200 years, and the unmet mental health needs of the incarcerated has been mentioned in the literature since at least 1850 (Barnes, 1968). However, it was not until after World War II that the majority of the mental health professions, which could potentially meet these needs, began to blossom. Since that time, the mental health field has witnessed the emergence of new specializations within core professions (e.g., psychiatric nursing), the expansion of degree programs within existing mental health professions (e.g., the M.A., M.S., Ph.D., and Psy.D. are now offered in clinical psychology), and the birth of new fields of professional mental health practice (e.g., the addictions counselor).

A second trend that has broadened the opportunity for mental health professionals to practice in corrections has been the steady emergence of legal opinions mandating that mental health services be provided to incarcerated individuals. For example, in *Estelle v. Gamble* (1976), it was ruled that withholding medical care from inmates constituted a violation of the Eighth Amendment. These findings were expanded to include mental health treatment in *Inmates v. Pierce* (1980). *Ruiz v. Estelle* (1980) established that, in addition to other services, inmates should have access to a range of mental health services and that these services should be provided by sufficient numbers of trained mental health providers.

Congressional mandates have also influenced mental health care in corrections. This has been most evident in the area of substance abuse treatment. The Anti-Drug Abuse Act of 1986 defined drug abuse as a priority and focal point of treatment in prisons. The Anti-Drug Abuse Act of 1988 actually provided the means for funding such treatment programs.

Buttressing these mandates, various professional groups—including the American Correctional Association, the National Commission for Correctional Health Care, the American Medical Association, the American Psychological Association, the American Psychiatric Association, and the American Association for Correctional Psychologists—have issued standards for the delivery of mental health and substance abuse services in jails and prisons. The importance of these standards cannot be overstated, as federal and state courts continually reference them as a measure of culpability during inmate suits alleging inadequate mental health treatment (Steadman, McCarty, & Morrissey, 1989). Providing the parameters for programs and practices, these standards typically focus on issues concerning the administration of mental health programs, staffing, continuing professional development, and the identification and management of offenders with mental illness, substance abuse problems, and those at risk for suicidal thinking and/or behavior.

At the organizational level, opportunities for service provision have also grown as correctional administrators have become better educated about, and more confident in, the contributions that mental health professionals can make to the joint "custody and care" missions of their respective institutions. Related to this, the growth in newly constructed correctional institutions in concert with the retirement of many correctional administrators has resulted in the advancement of correctional administrators who are generationally distinct from their predecessors. Many in this new group have worked side by side "in the field" with correctional mental health professionals. This has enabled administrators to develop a knowledge base concerning when and how to use their professional mental health staff.

Finally, advancing technologies have also expanded the role and ability of mental health professionals to access the correctional environment and provide services to its inhabitants. Mental health providers no longer need to walk through the gates of the prison. The use of low-cost televideo technology has emerged as an effective means for delivering a range of mental health services to incarcerated individuals (DeLeon, 2000; Magaletta, Ax, Bartizal, & Pratsinak, 1999; Magaletta, Fagan, & Ax, 1998; Magaletta, Fagan, & Peyrot, 2000; Magaletta & Herbst, 2001). In this scenario, the professional logs on to the technology from his or her office and meets over real-time audiovisual equipment with the inmate, who remains in the institution.

The Correctional Mental Health Professions

General Professional Considerations

In general, a profession is defined as having a unique body of knowledge, with members who possess specific skills or techniques developed on the basis of this knowledge (Keith-Spiegel & Koocher, 1985). A professional's relationship to society and the public implies trustworthiness and competence. To ensure this, professions develop mechanisms to ensure consistency, regulate practice, and balance the self-interests of the profession with the interests of the public. Mechanisms may be legal, such as licensing requirements, which legally certify professional competencies before permitting professionals to practice. Other mechanisms, such as codes of ethics, are designed to be self-regulatory and provide moral and behavioral guides for professionals. (See Chapter 3 for a discussion of ethical issues.) Very often, professions mandate that their members continue to develop their competencies and skills throughout their careers through the use of continuing education. Although there are many unique skills and competencies across the various correctional mental health professionals, all are dedicated to applying their unique talents to their correctional work.

A recent estimate regarding the number of mental health and paraprofessional counseling staff (excluding those practicing in juvenile facilities and private correctional institutions and those employed on a part-time contractual basis) working in U.S. federal and state jails and prisons is 10,341. This accounts for an average of 3.6% of the correctional employees in any given facility (Camp & Camp, 1999). Understanding the similarities and differences among the mental health professions is essential for planning and developing a solid mental health delivery system. A brief examination and explanation of the types of mental health professions that exist in today's prisons and jails is presented in what follows.

Psychiatrists

The profession of psychiatry is rooted in medical practice and is the oldest of the mental health professions. Psychiatrists begin their postbaccalaureate education by attending 4 years of medical school, where they are broadly trained as physicians and earn a medical doctor (M.D.) degree. This is followed by a 1-year internship in which physicians rotate through clinical subspecialties, including internal medicine and neurology. Following the internship, a 3-year residency in psychiatry begins. The residency usually involves training in hospitals, emergency rooms, and outpatient clinical settings, and particular subspecialties (e.g., child and adolescent psychiatry) may be developed and pursued. It is during the residency that these physicians acquire their core knowledge regarding the etiology and biology of mental illness and the special skills needed to treat individuals with mental illness, particularly in a medical setting. Aspiring psychiatrists typically develop their diagnostic and treatment skills under the supervision of more experienced psychiatrists using a mentorship training model.

Because psychiatrists are first trained as physicians, they are most likely to use extensive medical record reviews and patient interviews as their primary diagnostic tools and to use biological modalities, such as psychotropic medications, in the treatment of individuals with mental disorders. Psychiatrists (and other medical doctors) are currently the only mental health treatment providers authorized to independently prescribe such medication. Administering psychotropic medications represents one of the mainstays of psychiatric work in corrections. In addition, psychiatrists may be active in assessing the mental competence and/or criminal responsibility of individuals pending trial on criminal charges. They may also be asked for mental health information by the courts to assist in sentencing decisions following convictions.

Most nonmedical correctional facilities employ psychiatrists on a part-time contractual basis primarily to medically manage their inmates with the most severe forms of mental illness. However, psychiatrists may be employed full-time in correctional reception and diagnostic centers or in correctional medical and psychiatric hospitals. Of the 10,341 full-time mental health professionals and paraprofessionals mentioned previously, 431 were psychiatrists.

Current psychiatric training is heavily steeped in the biological bases of behavior and often does not emphasize training to conduct individual or group psychotherapies. For these therapeutic interventions, other mental health professionals with more specific psychotherapy training may be better qualified.

Psychologists

The profession of psychology is rooted in the study of human behavior. Psychologists apply behavioral science principles and methods to the identification, assessment, prevention, and/or treatment of individual, group, and/or family problems. Psychologists have an advanced degree in either clinical or counseling psychology. Clinical psychologists undertake education and training focused largely on the assessment and treatment of individuals with mental disorders, while the training of counseling psychologists is more focused on the treatment of "normal" individuals with more transient nonpathological difficulties in adjustment.

The educational requirements for both clinical and counseling psychologists traditionally include the completion of a doctoral degree (either the doctor of philosophy [Ph.D.] degree in clinical or counseling psychology or the doctor of psychology [Psy.D.] degree). This degree typically requires 5 years of postbaccalaureate graduate work—4 years in an academic psychology department or professional school setting and 1 year in a supervised internship focused specifically on the provision of mental health services to a clinical population. The internship is usually completed at another institution independent of the university or professional school granting the doctoral degree.

It is notable that psychologists, unlike other mental health professionals, receive a comprehensive mental health education in that it integrates psychological theory, science, and practice. Students are exposed to a range of theory and knowledge that includes course work on the biological, psychological, and social bases of human behavior. During their training, they are also taught research design and methodology. Prior to receiving their doctorate degree, many psychologists have already completed two original research projects: the *thesis* and the *dissertation*. Finally, concurrent with this academic work, students are also developing core skills and competencies in performing clinical tasks (e.g., psychological interviews; psychological assessments; individual, marital, family, and/or group psychotherapies) under the supervision of other doctoral-level licensed psychologists (Goldenberg, 1983).

Although the doctoral degree is the required degree in most states for a person to be licensed as a psychologist, individuals may also receive a master's degree (typically 2 years of postbaccalaureate training) in psychology. In most states, these individuals are required to work under the supervision of a licensed doctoral psychologist, and in some states, they may be licensed as professional counselors. Although little survey data exist, one recent study (Boothby & Clements, 2000) suggested that many state correctional systems employ doctoral psychologists and individuals with a master's degree in psychology at approximately the same rates. However, some prison systems, including two of the largest (the California Department of Corrections and the Federal Bureau of Prisons), have adopted the standard for community practice and hire only doctoral-level psychologists.

Psychologists are, by virtue of their education and training, perhaps the most versatile in the range and type of services they offer the correctional environment. It is likely that this versatility factors into psychologists being the most frequently employed mental health professionals in today's correctional environment (Camp & Camp, 1999). Correctional psychology's ranks have grown from a mere 78 during the 1940s (Burton, 1948) to more than 2,000 in 1998 (Camp & Camp, 1999).

It is interesting to note, however, that the functions and roles of the psychologist in corrections have remained somewhat consistent throughout the past 50 years. Corsini and Miller (1954) described the job functions of 43 correctional psychologists as performing various assessments, conducting individual and group psychotherapy, conducting research, engaging in administrative duties, and consulting and training institution staff. Nearly 50 years later, Bartol (1998) categorized their roles into diagnosis and assessment, treatment/intervention, and research planning and evaluation. Between the 1950s and the 1990s, several studies have reported similar findings regarding the roles and functions of psychologists in corrections (Bindman, Neiberg, Gilbert, & Haughey, 1961; Boothby & Clements, 2000; Clements, 1987; Otero, McNally, & Powitzky, 1981; Smith & Sabatino, 1990).

Psychologists practicing in today's correctional facility are active participants in many aspects of the correctional environment. Correctional psychologists conduct crisis, individual, and group psychotherapy with general population inmates as well as those offenders with mental disorders or substance abuse problems. They also perform psychological evaluations of offenders either at the request of the courts or for classification, diagnosis, treatment planning, intake screening, and crisis intervention purposes. Psychologists regularly consult with prison administrators about issues related to the mental health needs of both staff and inmates, perform various administrative duties, and train correctional staff to manage high-risk inmates, such as those with mental illness and those at risk for suicide, more effectively. Psychologists also use their extensive knowledge about specific psychotropic medications to screen candidates for referrals to consulting psychiatrists and to monitor the progress of offenders who are placed on psychotropic medications.

As the aforementioned functions assert, the role of the psychologist leaves little time for conducting research, and psychologists in today's correctional facilities rarely exercise this skill. It is interesting to note, however, that although these psychologists do not capitalize on this skill, many do express an interest in staying active and using this skill in their employment (Boothby & Clements, 2000; Federal Prison System, 1983; Otero et al., 1981).

Social Workers

The field of social work has much to offer correctional systems. The educational underpinning of social work focuses on the interplay between the person and the social context in which the person operates. Social workers typically earn a master of social work (M.S.W.) degree, which entails 2 years of postbaccalaureate education. Throughout their education, social workers accumulate a variety of supervised field experiences at hospitals, social services agencies, and clinics. Traditionally, social workers have studied the operations of social service agencies and programs (e.g., social security, Medicare, welfare programs) and case management and have applied this study when making home visits and coordinating after-care services for hospital-discharged patients within the community. However, during recent years, the role of social workers has expanded to include training in individual, family, marital, and group psychotherapies. Within corrections, social workers provide both traditional case management services, such as release planning for inmates requiring special assistance prior to community release, and newer treatment functions, such as individual and group therapy, often for inmates with chronic mental illness or substance abuse problems. With their therapeutic training and background in case management, it is not unusual to find correctional social workers assuming duties in, or being supervised or administered by, one of several correctional departments. Medical services, psychology services, and unit management all may employ social workers.

Other Mental Health Professionals

Although the professions just discussed are the mainstay of prison mental health treatment, other mental health professions are represented as well. Most often, these additional service providers are found on inpatient mental health units, where prisoners with chronic mental illness and those in acute distress reside.

Psychiatric nurses are nurses who are specifically trained to deal with the unique nursing and medication issues of patients with mental illness such as comorbid physical and emotional problems (Peternelj-Taylor & Johnson, 1995). Most nurses have completed 2 years of course work, had additional supervised field experience, and taken a qualifying exam that leads to becoming a registered nurse (R.N.). Alternatively, some nurses have also earned a bachelor's degree in nursing, and others go on to receive a specialized master's degree that is necessary to acquire limited prescribing authority. Those psychiatric nurses with limited prescribing authority are certified registered nurse practitioners.

Recreation therapists are involved in planning and implementing recreational and leisure time activities and education for patients. These activities might include organized sports, such as basketball and softball, or independent projects, such as hobbies and crafts. These activities are designed to develop, restore, or maintain the emotional, cognitive, and physical behaviors that are necessary for leisure and social involvement. They also facilitate adjustment to the hospital environment, and it is in such a medical or hospital correctional setting that recreation therapists are employed. Recreation therapists are distinct from other recreation specialists in that they work with a particular, and not the general, population of inmates. They are also distinct in that they are certified by a professional body of recreational therapists and have earned a bachelor of arts degree from a college or university with a recreation therapy program.

Music therapists and art therapists are also sometimes employed to work with the prison mental health population, although the number of such institutions is small and the budgeting for such positions is rare. Music therapy can be defined as the prescribed use of music by a qualified person to effect change in the psychological, physical, cognitive, or social functioning of persons affected by physical and/or emotional illness. Music therapists have earned a bachelor's degree in music therapy and may also have a master's degree. Art therapy provides a vehicle for social interaction and self-expression for those suffering from physical and/or emotional illnesses. Some art therapists have earned a bachelor's degree with specialized course work in art therapy. Others have received specialty training in some other area of art and apply this knowledge to work with patients.

Treatment Teams

Many correctional systems employ a team approach to mental health treatment, with several treatment providers—such as a psychiatrist, a psychologist, and a social worker—consulting together about treatment for a specific inmate. In this model, each provider brings a unique perspective and a specific set of skills to the treatment process, resulting in a comprehensive and informed treatment approach. In this model, the psychiatrist manages the medication needs of the offender, the psychologist provides psychotherapy as needed, and the social worker finds suitable placements for inmates with mental illness either when they are returned back into the general population of a regular correctional institution following treatment at a correctional medical facility or when they are released into the community following completion of their sentences.

Paraprofessionals

As the name implies, mental health paraprofessionals perform functions similar in process to other mental health professionals, but they have not experienced the formal schooling or training of professionals. As a result, they typically work under the direction and supervision of a professional mental health worker. They are most likely to be found in correctional settings either assisting inmates in their day-to-day adjustment to prison life or conducting fairly didactic, psychoeducational groups (e.g., anger management, social skills training) that have a highly structured, predetermined format. *Correctional counselors* in the unit management philosophy are prime examples of this type of paraprofessional.

A common question in corrections is whether or not inmates themselves can be used as paraprofessionals to deliver services to other inmates. A simple and resounding "no" is the best course of action. Inmates should rarely, if ever, be used to conduct or offer mental health services (Metzner, 1997). Their lack of professional training and supervision, and the potentially volatile situations that could emerge with the misuse of information gleaned in the context of "therapy," are just a couple of the reasons for the aforementioned declaration. For inmate therapeutic programs with identified inmate "leaders," constant supervision from correctional personnel is always recommended.

Mental Health Professionals: Common Correctional Challenges

The correctional work environment is relatively complex, and the delivery of mental health services is not its primary mission. There is also a dearth of available training experiences and literature on what exactly constitutes effective practice for mental health professionals who choose to work in corrections. For these reasons, it is not surprising to find several challenges that consistently emerge for correctional mental health professionals.

The Challenge of Limited Knowledge

Due to the unique nature of the prison environment, neither staff nor inmates who enter the prison for the first time feel prepared for the experience (Brodsky, 1982). Mental health professionals in corrections are no exception. Although they possess a unique body of knowledge and have received some degree of training in its application, few have a sufficient understanding of the correctional environment or have received any didactic instruction on this setting and how it interacts with that body of knowledge (Farrington, 1980; Levinson, 1985; Smith, Paskewicz, Evans, & Milan, 1986). Classes that could provide even brief information on contextual variables in corrections, such as criminology, law, sociology, and even the workings of the criminal justice system itself, are rarely offered in any of the academic degree programs noted earlier.

Despite the dearth of available academic training, there are several notable exceptions. The University of Alabama has offered a Ph.D. program in clinical psychology with a specialty in correctional psychology for nearly 20 years. Also, there are several academic programs offered at the doctoral level that focus on "forensics" (Bersoff et al., 1997; Melton, Huss, & Tomkins, 1999; Pietz, DeMier, Dienst, Green, & Scully, 1998). These programs typically offer a joint Ph.D./J.D. degree, although it should be noted that beyond medical centers, most correctional employers would not regularly use the skills of a forensic mental health professional. In terms of supervised experience in a correctional mental health setting, there are numerous correctional facilities that receive students for training, although there continues to be wide variance in the type and quality of training offered. At the doctoral level for clinical and counseling psychologists, the Federal Bureau of Prisons continues to offer one of the most comprehensive and best-organized correctional predoctoral psychology internship programs. Positions are currently available in 10 institutions, and the American Psychological Association has accredited all of these programs except the newest one, which is seeking accreditation. A leader in this type of correctional training experience, the bureau has placed more than 500 psychologists in internship positions, thus helping them to complete their requirements for the doctoral degree.

Given the overall difficulty in finding balanced preparation for correctional work, it is not surprising to find its more subtle manifestations—the dearth of professional organizations for correctional mental health professionals, low membership in such organizations where they do exist (Boothby & Clements, 2000), and a virtually nonexistent literature base on the clinical supervision of the correctional mental health professional (Norton, 1990). It is interesting to observe that in the studies that have examined the mental health professional's role and functions, inquiry about or mention of any clinical supervisory function, in either giving or receiving supervision, is consistently absent. The one study that does raise the supervision function (Ferrell, Morgan, & Winterowd, 2000) reported that mental health professionals who practiced group therapy in corrections were less satisfied with the individual supervision they had received, as compared with their other job duties.

Despite the lack of formal training opportunities, the absence of an actual training curriculum, and the paucity of a correctional mental health literature base designed to orient a mental health practitioner to the correctional environment, there do appear to be certain core areas that would benefit all correctional mental health professionals. Crisis intervention techniques, substance abuse treatment models, group therapy methods, and empirically documented treatment interventions with offenders would begin a list of core subjects. A brief survey of the current criminal justice system, its various manifestations, and its history would also be helpful in providing clinicians with a contextual base in which to understand their practice environment.

Mental health professionals entering the correctional environment would also benefit from an exploration of the literature on therapeutic approaches with racially and culturally diverse populations. There really is no more diverse place in the world than a prison. In an interesting summary, Corsini (1945) wrote that the prison psychologist must have the skill and ability to "enter into good rapport with the widest variety of individuals, in the age group from 16 to 80, negros and whites, mental ages 6 to 20, former annual incomes nothing to a million dollars" (p. 103). The only thing that has happened in prisons since that time is the expansion of nearly all of the aforementioned parameters (Milan, Chin, & Nguyen, 1999; Pietz et al., 1998). One method of gaining a greater appreciation for cultural diversity issues would be for correctional mental health workers to link up with other social institutions that intrinsically serve a more reflective teaching mission and that might support the correctional mission. Hospitals and universities would be obvious choices (Gormally & Brodsky, 1973; Lovell & Jemelka, 1998; Megargee, 1995).

To be certain, there is some degree of learning that can only be gleaned from experience. The following may be heard by more seasoned correctional personnel: *The prison itself will teach you your trade. The question is, are you willing to be taught, and who will you allow to be your teacher—other professionals, the inmates, the line staff, the administration, or all of them?* It is imperative, however, for those mental health professionals who are working in the correctional environment and who possess research expertise to begin studying their clinical prison experiences in an effort to expand the formal knowledge base regarding correctional mental health issues. Given the diagnostic complexities of offenders, the paucity of empirically documented treatment approaches with such offenders, and the fact that such work will occur within a setting whose primary mission is not treatment, it behooves correctional mental health professionals to continue exploring new ways of and content for training future correctional mental health professionals.

The Challenge of Limited Resources

The challenge of limited resources has affected every aspect of corrections as state and federal legislatures, along with correctional administrators, attempt to keep pace with the burgeoning jail and prison populations. Although the number of mental health professionals in corrections has grown, it has not kept pace with the increasing inmate population (Boothby & Clements, 2000), and it certainly has not risen proportionately with the increasing number of inmates with mental illness. Further compounding this problem is the reality that, in any given set of mental health positions, there is likely to be one or more vacancies waiting to be filled, such that the group of mental health providers in a given institution is always "one short" (Lovell & Jemelka, 1998).

The clear implication here is that, in addition to clinical skill, the more effective mental health professionals in today's correctional environment will be those who can set and manage multiple priorities effectively. Chapter 1 provided one method for establishing and setting such priorities. Beyond priority setting, mental health professionals can expand the scope of their services by placing greater emphasis on the use of paraprofessionals and community volunteers. For example, Alcoholics Anonymous (AA) districts maintain lists of members who have identified themselves as willing to discuss the principles of AA with professional groups or staff. In addition, these members, in most cases, are able to provide community AA contacts who may be interested in volunteering to conduct AA meetings inside prisons. There are currently approximately 2,500 active AA groups in American prisons (Alcoholics Anonymous World Services, personal communication, March 10, 2001). Similar groups, such as Narcotics Anonymous, also exist. Local churches may also provide fertile ground for soliciting volunteers with an interest in aiding inmates with mental health needs. The growth of such church-based prison programs (e.g., Prison Ministries, KAIROS, Alternatives to Violence), as well as the reemergence of "faith-based" programs in prisons, attests to the effective use of these resources.

The Challenge of Patience in an Action-Oriented Environment

A chaplain once remarked that what he missed least about working in prison was the "tyranny of the urgent." Those who have worked in corrections immediately recognize the meaning and feel of this phrase. Sandwiched between inmates who demand phone calls and throw feces and administrators who ask the professional to "do something with" or "fix" inmates, the push for the mental health professional to take immediate action is almost palpable.

This is a predictable challenge because prisons are male-dominated cultures with much anxiety. These factors create and favor an active problem-solving approach (Levant & Pollack, 1995; Magaletta & Herbst, 2001). Mental health professionals are encouraged to pause and remember that their most effective skill may lie in their ability to listen effectively. The effective use of this skill often seems at odds with the correctional environment, which commands a sense of urgency for the multitude of interventions that are required on a daily basis. However, it is only by listening carefully that more active problem-solving techniques can be pursued effectively. The challenge for correctional mental health professionals is to balance this reality within themselves and their clinical practice, despite the press of the correctional environment for immediate action.

The Challenge of the Joint Mission

Despite the fact that all correctional employees receive their paychecks from the same source, the question of who exactly the mental health professional works for may still be a challenge with which some mental health professionals struggle. This polarizing trend between the "custody" and "care" missions of the penal institution can be traced back to the early 1800s (Barnes, 1968). Any type of social containment is likely to yield a series of dichotomous outcomes, and the aforementioned polarization has also been documented between correctional officers and administrative staff (Cheek & Miller, 1983; Pogrebin, 1980).

Today's mental health professional must be flexible enough to recognize the reality that although there are two missions in a prison, the balance of these missions will be in constant fluctuation and dependent on several factors, most of which will not be under the professional's control. The particular personalities and previous experiences of the administrative staff, the current inmate population and its degree of volatility, and the current political and social climate regarding the application of justice in the state or country all are critical in determining the balance of the joint missions.

What is likely to be under the control of mental health professionals is the relationships they have with their institution and the staff therein. Given their expertise in communication skills, mental health professionals may use these skills to improve or facilitate their relationships with the current administration (Morgan, Winterowd, & Ferrell, 1999). This skill may also be used both formally and informally to educate staff on how mental health interventions with inmates serve the greater needs of the institution and the employees' work environment. Understanding the importance of different responsibilities, as well as the "language" of each layer in the correctional system, is crucial in this scenario. For example, a housing unit officer is likely to be receptive to feedback about how exactly to refer an inmate for mental health evaluation when the officer believes the inmate is exhibiting signs and symptoms of mental illness or suicide, whereas an administrator is likely to be interested in hearing about the potential benefit of decreased disciplinary rates as the result of a residential treatment program.

On the other side of the house, administrators benefit from seeing their employees as having unique strengths or a professional body of knowledge that can be used in a specific manner to aid in the mission of the institution. The "one size fits all" mentality, particularly as it applies to the day-to-day operation of an institution, seems to be a poor use of existing resources. Except in cases of emergency (and there are certainly plenty of these), it is difficult to explain why an administrator might employ a highly trained mental health professional to make bologna sandwiches. Likewise, administrators who are aware of the professionals' range of skills are in a better position to ask why only individual interventions are being made when group interventions may reach more inmates.

Despite the historical prevalence of the joint "care versus custody" mission battle in many correctional institutions, the salience of the problem appears to be waning. Brodsky (1996), a psychologist who has studied mental health professionals in corrections for more than 30 years, noted that the treatment-custody debate has all but disappeared from the correctional-clinical literature. Perhaps leading this trend, Levinson (1985) reported that, as compared with seasoned correctional psychologists, new psychologists were less concerned with how they would be perceived by their correctional colleagues and more concerned with how the system actually worked. He wrote,

It came as a considerable surprise that psychology services in the Federal Prison System had over the years gained a sizable degree of credibility. Many of the battles that the author thought were still ongoing, apparently, have been won. Being accepted by fellow correctional workers is no longer the major issue it was back in the days of the dinosaurs. (p. 43)

More recently, Steadman et al. (1989) surveyed jail mental health professionals and their administrative and line staff compatriots. They reported that "the overall level of conflict in mental health service programs for this type of correctional facility was less than would be suggested by the sociological literature" (p. 100). In their survey of mental health professionals, Ferrell et al. (2000) reported that respondents were satisfied with the degree of support they received from their administrative personnel. One would hope that this trend will continue as the field of correctional mental health further develops. This will save correctional mental health professionals from having to choose between the two missions and will lead them to learn and develop in ways that will effectively and efficiently assist in the achievement of both missions.

Self-Care for Mental Health Professionals

In a recent study examining correctional mental health professionals practicing group therapy (Ferrell et al., 2000), the majority of respondents reported being satisfied with their work. However, most anyone working in corrections will eventually encounter the despair, hopelessness, and web of self-pity that flavor most prisons. Correctional mental health professionals are particularly likely to experience this as they immerse themselves day in and day out with the exact struggles yielding this flavor. Writing about self-care for mental health professionals, Norcross (2000) quoted Sigmund Freud: "No one who, like me, conjures up the most evil of those half-tamed demons that inhabit the human beast, and seeks to wrestle with them, can expect to come through the struggle unscathed" (Freud, 1905/1933, p. 184). The relevance of this statement for those who work in corrections is immediately obvious. How mental health professionals care for themselves given this reality is an essential determinant for their overall quality of life and their careers.

Freud's ability to see and name his "scathing" is an effective self-care strategy and highlights the following point. To be able to name what is happening (or at least reflect on what might be happening) and to maintain a sense of balance when one has no idea what is happening are essential self-care skills. To truly recognize the complexity of correctional mental health work is an effective start. Although a solid base of literature exists concerning the "side effects" (e.g., mild anxiety, moderate depression, emotional exhaustion, disrupted relationships) of traditional mental health practice (Norcross & Guy, in press), it is wise to consider additional factors that are likely to produce such effects in correctional mental health providers.

Prisons themselves, and particularly higher security prisons, are dangerous places. Correctional mental health workers must be aware of the constant potential for danger that lurks beneath the precarious "control" of institution life and the reality of the crimes that were committed by those incarcerated. At the same time, one cannot allow such awareness to result in paralyzing fear. Each correctional mental health worker also has to adjust to the various security measures (e.g., waiting for other staff to open a secure door) over which they have no control.

There are what Tewksbury (1993) called "interactional" (environment interacting with professional duty) stresses. Mental health providers must cope with the reality of not being in control of the daily operations of the facility. They may be called out of a treatment session on a moment's notice to respond to an emergency. They may have scheduled 10 inmates to be seen on a particular day but then need to reschedule these appointments due to an institutional lockdown. Overt confrontations between or directly with inmates, although infrequent, always loom on the horizon. Being the recipient of threats, as well as the lightning rod for the projection of blame, is common.

In addition to learning about and adjusting to the prison environment, mental health professionals must adapt their theoretical perspectives to the unique challenges of working with offenders themselves. Prisoners can be diagnostically complex (Silber, 1974), and the entirety of their presenting pathologies are rarely experienced in most training clinics. Lovell and Jemelka (1998) summarized this best:

> These are hard cases. In the case of prisoners, mental illness is not just an unfortunate overlay on an otherwise stable life. The participants have survived, often just barely, perinatal complications, developmental disabilities, childhood abuse and neglect, brain damage, social ostracism, failures in school and work, drug and alcohol abuse, or multiple suicide attempts. Usually not just one but many of these factors interact in complex ways. (p. 63)

Given these realities, the correctional mental health professional's basic assumptions concerning mental health theory may need to be challenged. For example, most training programs implicitly teach professionals to believe what clients tell them (Meloy, 1996). The core conditions of therapeutic change in insight-oriented therapy—namely mutual trust, confidentiality, and voluntary enrollment—may need reworking in the correctional environment (Schlesinger, 1979).

Correctional mental health clinicians who want to take better care of themselves may also wish to reflect on where and how they experience the potential stresses in their work. Different people respond in different ways to different responsibilities and layers of the correctional environment. For example, some may have an extremely difficult time performing rounds in segregation but feel perfectly at home doing group therapy with general population inmates. Others may enjoy individual therapy but experience stress when conducting administrative matters. It is a helpful practice to understand how stress manifests itself in one's life. Are personal stressors present in one's work, in relationships with others, in one's mind, or viscerally in one's body? With an understanding of such matters, the correctional mental health professional is in a better position to make the necessary adjustments to accommodate high-stress days or duties with effective self-care strategies.

One final area worth monitoring by correctional mental health professionals is how much personal responsibility they assume for the results of their therapeutic efforts with inmates. In therapy with inmates, mental health workers need to be able to clearly distinguish between the therapeutic work and the outcome of that work. There are times when focusing solely on results is troubling (Schlesinger, 1979). Merton (1985) provided interesting food for correctional thought:

> Do not depend on the hope of results. When you are doing the sort of work you have taken on, . . . you may have to face the fact that your work will be apparently worthless. . . . As you get used to this idea, you start more and more to concentrate not on the results but on the value, the rightness, the truth of the work itself. And there too a great deal has to be gone through. (p. 294)

When clinicians do decide to place value on the results of their work, they should consider whose criteria to use (Strupp & Hadley, 1977). What society, the inmate, the clinician, and the correctional administrator would consider to be "effective results" are likely to be very different from one another.

References

Barnes, H. E. (1968). *The evolution of penology in Pennsylvania.* Montclair, NJ: Patterson Smith.

Bartol, C. R. (1998). *Criminal behavior: A psychosocial approach.* Upper Saddle River, NJ: Prentice Hall.

Bersoff, D. N., Goodman-Delahunty, J., Grisso, J. T., Hans, V. P., Poythress, N. G., & Roesch, R. G. (1997). Training in law and psychology. *American Psychologist, 52,* 1301-1310.

Bindman, A. J., Neiberg, N. A., Gilbert, R. R., & Haughey, D. W. (1961, June). The psychologist's function on a state level. *Mental Hospitals,* pp. 6-9.

Boothby, J. L., & Clements, C. B. (2000). A national survey of correctional psychologists. *Criminal Justice and Behavior, 27,* 716-732.

Brodsky, C. M. (1982). Work stress in correctional institutions. *Journal of Prison and Jail Health, 2,* 74-102.

Brodsky, S. L. (1996). Twenty years of criminal justice and behavior. *Criminal Justice and Behavior, 23,* 5-11.

Burton, A. (1948). The status of correctional psychology. *Journal of Psychology, 28,* 215-222.

Camp, C. G., & Camp, G. M. (1999). *The corrections yearbook 1999: Adult corrections.* Middletown, CT: Criminal Justice Institute.

Cheek, F. E., & Miller, M. D. S. (1983). The experience of stress for corrections officers: A double-blind theory of correctional stress. *Journal of Criminal Justice, 11,* 105-120.

Clements, C. B. (1987). Psychologists in correctional institutions: Getting off the treadmill. In E. K. Morris & C. J. Braukmann (Eds.), *Behavioral approaches to crime and delinquency* (pp. 521-541). New York: Plenum.

Corsini, R. J. (1945). Functions of a prison psychologist. *Journal of Consulting Psychology, 9,* 101-104.

Corsini, R. J., & Miller, G. A. (1954). Psychology in prisons, 1952. *American Psychologist, 9,* 184-185.

DeLeon, P. (2000). The importance of seeing the "bigger picture." *Psychotherapy Bulletin, 35,* 6-12.

Diamond, P. M., Wang, E. W., Holzer, C. E., Thomas, C. R., & Cruser, D. A. (2001). The prevalence of mental illness in prison: Review and policy implications. *Administration and Policy in Mental Health, 29,* 21-40.

Estelle v. Gamble, 429 U.S. 97 (1976).

Farrington, D. P. (1980). The professionalization of English prison psychologists. *Professional Psychology, 11,* 855-862.

Federal Prison System. (1983). *Psychology services manual* (Program Statement 5310.6 Archived Document). Washington, DC: Author.

Ferrell, S. W., Morgan, R. D., & Winterowd, C. L. (2000). Job satisfaction on mental health professionals providing group therapy in state correctional facilities. *International Journal of Offender Therapy and Comparative Criminology, 44,* 232-241.

Freud, S. (1933). Fragment of an analysis of a case of hysteria. In *Collected papers of Sigmund Freud* (Vol. 3). London: Hogarth. (Original work published 1905).

Goldenberg, H. (1983). *Contemporary clinical psychology.* Belmont, CA: Wadsworth.

Gormally, J., & Brodsky, S. L. (1973). Utilization and training of psychologists for the criminal justice system. *American Psychologist, 28,* 926-928.

Guy, E., Platt, J. J., Zwerling, I., & Bullock, S. (1985). Mental health status of prisoners in an urban jail. *Criminal Justice and Behavior, 12,* 29-53.

Inmates v. Pierce, 489 F. Supp. 638 (1980).

Keith-Spiegel, P., & Koocher, G. P. (1985). *Ethics in psychology.* New York: McGraw-Hill.

Levant, R. F., & Pollack, W. S. (Eds.). (1995). *A new psychology of men.* New York: Basic Books.

Levinson, R. B. (1985). The psychologist in the correctional system. *American Journal of Forensic Psychology, 3,* 41-43.

Lovell, D., & Jemelka, R. (1998). Coping with mental illness in prisons. *Family and Community Health, 21,* 54-66.

Magaletta, P. R., Ax, R. K., Bartizal, D. E., & Pratsinak, G. J. (1999). Correctional telehealth. *Journal of the Mental Health in Corrections Consortium, 44,* 4-5.

Magaletta, P. R., Fagan, T. J., & Ax, R. A. (1998). Advancing psychology services through telehealth in the Federal Bureau of Prisons. *Professional Psychology: Research and Practice, 29,* 543-548.

Magaletta, P. R., Fagan, T. J., & Peyrot, M. F. (2000). Telehealth in the Federal Bureau of Prisons: Inmates' perceptions. *Professional Psychology: Research and Practice, 5,* 497-502.

Magaletta, P. R., & Herbst, D. (2001). Fathering from prison: Common problems and successful solutions. *Psychotherapy, 38,* 88-96.

Megargee, E. I. (1995). Assessment research in correctional settings: Methodological issues and practical problems. *Psychological Assessment, 7,* 359-366.

Meloy, J. R. (1996). *The psychopathic mind.* Northvale, NJ: Jason Aronson.

Melton, G. B., Huss, M. T., & Tomkins, A. J. (1999). Training in forensic psychology and the law. In A. K. Hess & I. B. Weiner (Eds.), *The handbook of forensic psychology* (pp. 700-720). New York: John Wiley.

Merton, T. (1985). *The hidden ground of love.* New York: Farrar, Strauss, & Giroux.

Metzner, J. L. (1997). An introduction to correctional psychiatry: Part II. *Journal of the American Academy of Psychiatry and the Law, 25,* 571-579.

Milan, M. A., Chin, C. E., & Nguyen, Q. X. (1999). Practicing psychology in correctional settings: Assessment, treatment, and substance abuse programs. In A. K. Hess & I. B. Weiner (Eds.), *The handbook of forensic psychology* (pp. 580-602). New York: John Wiley.

Morgan, R. D., Winterowd, C. L., & Ferrell, S. W. (1999). A national survey of group psychotherapy services in correctional facilities. *Professional Psychology: Research and Practice, 30,* 600-606.

Norcross, J. C. (2000). Psychotherapist self-care: Practitioner-tested, Research-informed strategies. *Professional Psychology: Research and Practice, 31,* 710-713.

Norcross, J. C., & Guy, J. D. (in press). *Leaving it at the office: Psychotherapist self-care.* New York: Guilford.

Norton, S. (1990). Supervision needs of correctional mental health counselors. *Journal of Addictions and Offender Counseling, 11,* 13-19.

Otero, R. F., McNally, D., & Powitzky, R. (1981). Mental health services in adult correctional systems. *Corrections Today, 43*(1), 8-18.

Palermo, G. B., Gumz, E. J., & Liska, F. J. (1992). Mental illness and criminal behavior revisited. *International Journal of Offender Therapy and Comparative Criminology, 36,* 53-61.

Peternelj-Taylor, C. A., & Johnson, R. (1995). Serving time: Psychiatric mental health nursing in corrections. *Journal of Psychosocial Nursing and Mental Health Services, 33,* 12-19.

Pietz, C. A., DeMier, R. L., Dienst, R. D., Green, J. B., & Scully, B. (1998). Psychology internship training in a correctional facility. *Criminal Justice and Behavior, 25,* 99-108.

Pogrebin, M. (1980). Challenge to authority for correctional officers. *Journal of Offender Counseling, Services, and Rehabilitation, 4,* 337-342.

Ruiz v. Estelle, 503 F. Supp. 1256, 1323 (1980).

Schlesinger, S. E. (1979). Therapy on a treadmill: The role of the prison psychotherapist. *Professional Psychology, 10,* 307-317.

Sigurdson, C. (2000). The mad, the bad, the abandoned: The mentally ill in prisons and jails. *Corrections Today, 62*(7), 70-78.

Silber, D. E. (1974). Controversy concerning the criminal justice system and its implications for the role of mental health workers. *American Psychologist, 29,* 239-244.

Smith, R., Paskewicz, C., Evans, J., & Milan, M. (1986). Development, implementation, and results of a correctional mental health professional training needs assessment. *Journal of Offender Counseling, Services, and Rehabilitation, 11,* 95-106.

Smith, R. R., & Sabatino, D. A. (1990). Roles and functions of psychologists in American correctional institutions. *Journal of Offender Rehabilitation, 16,* 163-174.

Steadman, H. J., McCarty, D. W., & Morrissey, P. (1989). *The mentally ill in jail.* New York: Guilford.

Strupp, H., & Hadley, S. W. (1977). The tripartite model. *American Psychologist, 32,* 187-196.

Tewksbury, R. (1993). On the margins of two professions: Job satisfaction and stress among post-secondary correctional educators. *American Journal of Criminal Justice, 18,* 61-77.

CHAPTER 3

Correctional Mental Health Ethics Revisited

John T. Dignam

My first full-time position as a therapist was in a spouse abuse treatment program. Treating court-ordered, mostly resistant clients was a challenge for a neophyte clinician such as myself. In an effort to enhance my skills, I attended a seminar on brief therapy offered by the Palo Alto Mental Research Institute group, whose model is well known for its emphasis on strategic or tactical interventions to facilitate change (cf. Fisch, Weakland, & Segal, 1982). The audience was an eclectic group of professionals, one of whom had identified herself during introductions as a psychotherapist with a Rogerian, person-centered orientation. After days of listening to the presenter suggest the use of paradoxical statements or even intentional misdirection as perfectly acceptable and effective therapeutic tools, she could no longer contain her distress over the promotion of such "ingenuine" behavior on the part of a helping professional. She interrupted his case presentation by standing up and asking in an exasperated voice, "Don't you think it's highly unethical to lie to your patients?" Without hesitation, the presenter replied, "No. I rather believe it is highly unethical to offer patients therapy that doesn't work."

The point in this author recalling this charged and memorable exchange is not to advance or refute the debatable proposition that honesty and efficacy are

AUTHOR'S NOTE: Opinions expressed in this chapter are those of the author and do not necessarily represent the opinions of the Federal Bureau of Prisons or the U.S. Department of Justice.

inherently incompatible when doing therapy. Rather, it is offered to exemplify a larger issue relevant to the ethical practice of psychotherapy and mental health treatment provision in general. Competent and well-intentioned clinicians sometimes struggle, both with each other and within themselves, over what appear to be conflicting ethical imperatives that arise when abstract ethical absolutes seemingly collide with the practical realities of serving one's client(s) meaningfully and effectively. Ethical conflicts of this kind may be more prevalent, or at least are more conspicuous, in the field of correctional psychology or in any correctional mental health discipline.

More than two decades ago, Monahan (1980) recognized the unique ethical questions inherent in practicing forensic psychology in general, and his seminal book contained chapters that introduced the more circumscribed nexus of ethics and correctional psychology in compelling and thought-provoking ways (Brodsky, 1980; Clingempeel, Mulvey, & Repucci, 1980). Since then, there have been very few professional publications devoted exclusively to this topic. Ivanoff and Smyth (1997) discussed ethical issues and concerns in their chapter on social workers practicing in corrections, but the most recently published work on ethical issues in correctional psychology in particular was written by Weinberger and Sreenivasan (1994). Their reexamination of this subject included a presentation of hypothetical vignettes designed to highlight the range of potential ethical dilemmas faced by correctional mental health practitioners, most of which are rarely encountered in other settings. These authors' position was that such dilemmas naturally arise in correctional environments due to a basic and unavoidable conflict between two opposing philosophical models: treatment versus security. (Clingempeel et al. [1980] referred similarly to a "custody versus treatment" conflict.) Because the primary mission of the institutions in which they work is security and control, correctional mental health staff are often required to assume roles and responsibilities in addition to, and presumably inconsistent with, that of therapists or helpers. Thus, they inevitably find themselves in ethical binds from which the only ultimate escape, according to Weinberger and Sreenivasan (1994), is a bifurcated system, like those found in some state correctional agencies, in which decision-making power for mental health treatment and corrections stems from separate and independent authorities.

It is most certainly true that correctional psychologists and other correctional mental health practitioners struggle with their share of ethical challenges and that careful consideration and debate of relevant ethical issues must occur to resolve them satisfactorily. But it can also be argued—and is in this chapter—that many such conflicts are often more apparent than real and that their presumed inevitability seems to be based largely on an incomplete or biased understanding of correctional environments and their missions. Indeed, this seems particularly true of Weinberger and Sreenivasan (1994), whose broad-brush analysis of the topic relied on oversimplified "straw man" arguments and betrayed a naive, nearly hostile perspective on corrections in general.

The first step in any critical discussion of correctional mental health ethics, then, should be a plenary examination of the unique and complex context in which correctional mental health professionals practice. And for those professionals who wish to maintain the highest standards of ethical conduct and prevent ethical dilemmas from occurring in the first place, a full appreciation, understanding, and acknowledgment of the context in which they practice, as well as their important role in it, is essential. So, before discussing confidentiality, dual relationships, or any other particular ethical issue, what follows is an informed but admittedly different perspective on the correctional environment from that found in other works on professional ethics in correctional mental health practice. There are two objectives in doing so. First, it is hoped that this explication will demonstrate that corrections, although certainly unique in many ways as a behavior setting for practitioners, has much more in common with other clinical work environments than has been recognized previously. Second, this framework, if accepted as a valid representation of the correctional context, should help to crystallize correctional mental health practitioners' thinking about specific ethical issues and should serve as a blueprint for guiding ethical conduct and decision making.

The Correctional Context

Prisons are neither the hellish dungeons nor the lavish country clubs about which liberal and conservative critics alike sometimes hyperbolize. Nor do they resemble the classic Hollywood depictions of anarchical asylums run by evil and corrupt staff, who take pleasure in thwarting the virtuous tendencies of the most innocent of inmates while colluding with the few truly sociopathic criminal inhabitants to do so. The reality of correctional institutions is far less sensational and far more complicated. The actual conditions under which incarcerated offenders exist vary widely and depend on institution security levels, jurisdiction (federal, state, or local), training requirements and opportunities for staff, size of facility, available funding and other resources, executive leadership, and many other factors. Of course, however different they may be, all correctional settings must meet strict governmental and other minimum standards (e.g., safety, health, environmental), and regular monitoring occurs accordingly.

The caliber of staff who work in correctional facilities, as in nearly any workplace, runs the gamut from highly dedicated professionals who take their work seriously, to those who benignly put in the hours to get their paychecks, to the relative few whose corruption, exploitative behavior, or general misconduct are usually detected sooner or later. The population of inmates in their charge is similarly diverse in terms of backgrounds and motivations, although they do share one common characteristic: They all broke the law or at least were convicted of doing so. (In the case of pretrial and presentence inmates, they are in custody based on evidence of having done so.) The implications of this fact, as well as other inmate-related issues that should inform and guide correctional mental health practitioners' ethical behavior, are discussed at greater length later.

Treatment Versus Security: A False Dichotomy

As mentioned previously, those who have written about ethical issues for correctional mental health workers usually point to a fundamental conflict between treatment and security concerns as the source of many ethical dilemmas. But the premise that those two interests are naturally in conflict is debatable and seems to be based on a one-dimensional definition of "security." The purpose of maintaining effective security and control within the confines of a correctional institution is much more than keeping those incarcerated inside. Another primary goal is to protect inmates from each other and from themselves, thus promoting the safety and general welfare of offenders. This is hardly inconsistent with a psychological treatment philosophy. Indeed, effective treatment is less likely to occur in environments where patients or clients feel unsafe or threatened constantly.

Moreover, the presupposition that treatment goals are ipso facto diametrically opposed to the necessary objectives of security and control in a correctional institution is only remotely valid if one presumes a severely limited range of treatment goals or if one believes that treatment issues are relevant only in the vacuum of the dyadic or group session. Consider as an example the treatment of pedophilia in a prison setting. A reasonable treatment goal undoubtedly would be avoidance of child pornography or related items. Another part of maintaining "security" in a prison entails periodically searching offenders' cells to find and confiscate contraband, of which child pornographic material would be an example. Treatment staff should promote or even participate in those security activities, which are perfectly consistent with treatment goals, and the best in-prison sex offender treatment programs do just that. To do otherwise artificially compartmentalizes treatment issues and communicates to the patient that the clinician is less than wholly committed to therapeutic objectives.

To argue, in effect, for an arbitrary division of labor, such that custodial staff enforce treatment goals but treatment staff just talk about them in the name of maintaining the necessary "trust" between therapist and patient, risks sacrificing a truly meaningful therapeutic alliance in which the most difficult and real problems can be uncovered and conquered "head-on." In fact, those lines are already blurred—and appropriately so—in other institutional treatment settings. Patient rules and regulations are not ignored, or at least should not be, by treatment staff in places such as inpatient psychiatric units, group treatment homes, and residential drug treatment centers. Indeed, adherence to such rules and regulations, along with other signs of responsible behavior on the part of the patient, are usually monitored and assessed as indicators of treatment progress or failure. For example, if a psychologist on a psychiatric inpatient unit were asked to sit on a panel to help determine what privilege reductions or sanctions should occur in the case of a patient who struck another patient during a group, most informed observers would not think that the psychologist was in the throes of an ethical dilemma. Yet similar circumstances have been viewed elsewhere (Weinberger & Sreenivasan, 1994) as tantamount to an ethical crisis for the correctional mental health professional.

Of course, one could counter the preceding argument by pointing out that the critical difference between an institutional treatment setting and a prison is that the mission of the former is precisely therapeutic, while the mission of the latter is not. But that argument relies, again, on a limited view of the nature of corrections. Correctional facilities can and should be places that shape and reinforce responsible prosocial behavior on the part of offenders, not only through treatment and established programs but also through role modeling, education, structure, and consistent application of rewards and punishments. Indeed, the very term *correctional* intentionally connotes that positive change is an expected outcome of incarceration. Ideally, then, correctional settings should be therapeutic in the broadest sense, and they often are despite preconceived notions to the contrary. Although it would be naive to think that all such facilities are always operated with that lofty goal exclusively in mind, it is nonetheless true that individual offender behavior change in a positive direction is one goal of corrections.

Thus, rather than being in constant conflict, most practical elements of both "treatment" and "security" models are highly complementary if they are applied consistently and intelligently. Indeed, they should be applied in concert if the ultimate goal is holistic and lasting change. An alternative model to the false dichotomy of treatment versus security is what this author calls the "management-treatment continuum," along which all custodial and traditional treatment activities fall. At the lower end of that spectrum, for example, are activities such as counting inmates, imposing a disciplinary sanction for fighting, and other correctional staff functions designed primarily to manage offender behavior. At the upper end lie more conventional therapeutic activities such as psychotherapy and Alcoholics Anonymous meetings. And in the middle are common occurrences in correctional (and other) treatment settings such as restraining a decompensating psychotic inmate, imposing a treatment-relevant disciplinary sanction for brewing alcohol on a drug treatment unit, and placing a depressed offender on a suicide watch. But all of the tasks on that continuum have a common purpose: to effect and promote positive change across a wide range of behavioral, cognitive, and emotional domains. Therefore, all correctional staff—not just mental health professionals—work together toward what could be called a "collaborative rehabilitation" of offenders, not unlike partnerships between professionals and paraprofessionals in institution treatment settings. The implications of this perspective for correctional mental health workers' ethical conduct are significant and are explored in subsequent sections of this chapter.

Who Is the Client?

That question, which was the title of Monahan's (1980) groundbreaking book referred to earlier, is a fundamental one for correctional mental health workers to answer in charting a course of ethical conduct on the job. In the first organized survey on ethical issues faced by psychologists working in criminal justice systems (Clingempeel et al., 1980), the majority of whom were in correctional settings, variations on that very question underlay many of the ethical dilemmas reported by respondents to an even greater extent than the so-called custody versus treatment conflict. The nature of correctional mental health work, given the many and varied tasks clinicians are asked to perform, ensures any number of client candidates at varying times. The crux of the ethical issue here is usually couched in terms of the clinician's perceived divided loyalties between the competing interests of the offender versus the institution or, more broadly, the criminal justice system or "society." From a conventional perspective, *who* the client *is* depends largely on *what* the clinician *does*. If one is engaged in individual psychotherapy with an inmate, then the offender is the client or, more accurately, the "primary" client. If one is conducting an evaluation for a parole board to proffer an opinion on recidivism risk, then the system is the primary client and the clinician presumably risks taking action contrary to the "best interests" of the offender.

A more perspicacious look at a correctional mental health worker's list of actual and potential clients reveals that it is arguably quite long: the offender, the institution, "society," the courts, the warden, the government, taxpayers, fellow correctional staff, the offender's family, defense attorneys, probation and parole officers, the agency for which one works, the offender's victims, researchers, prosecutors, the offender's cell mate, and so on. Of course, those are not mutually exclusive categories of clients, nor are their interests necessarily mutually exclusive. But it is important for correctional mental health staff to fully grasp who all of their proximal and distal constituents are in answering the topic question, "Who is the client?" And clinicians should not have to put even the broader categories of offender versus the correctional system versus "society" in separate boxes when it comes to determining the focus of their therapeutic loyalty. Or, as Monahan (1980) himself so aptly put it, "'Who is the client?' is not a multiple-choice question." The objectives and interests of each obviously can overlap. Monahan was certain, however, that there are always instances in which the correctional psychologist must struggle with agonistic allegiances between the offender and the criminal justice system. Thus, his qualified conclusion was that the inmate and the system both are clients of the clinician "*in different roles and with varying priorities*" (p. 5, italics in original).

But is this necessarily true? The answer depends entirely on one's analysis of the alleged disparate interests of the two or more clients. Take, for example, the situation of conducting a parole board evaluation alluded to earlier. If a clinician were to render an opinion about an offender that there was moderate to high risk of recidivism, this would surely influence the board, and a likely outcome would be denial of parole. Presumably, any internal ethical struggle would hinge on the clinician's knowledge that the outcome would not be in the offender's interests and that the clinician in effect would be taking action contrary to the inmate's general welfare. But that analysis relies on a fairly narrow view of what constitutes the offender's interests or welfare. It seems a perfectly defensible position to expand one's view of a client's welfare beyond that which affords him or her the most immediate personal relief or comfort (and, perhaps, more immediate relief or comfort to the clinician as well). Or, in other words, it is certainly not unreasonable for a clinician to genuinely believe that an offender's true best interests are served by his or her remaining in prison. A correctional mental health professional should accept responsibility for making judgments, imperfect as they may be, that the offender's long-term therapeutic interests and welfare may be quite different from how they appear on the surface, that those longer term interests are more relevant to the actual goals of engaging in that particular clinical activity in the first place, and that they are probably going to be much more compatible with the interests of the other clients (e.g., "society") in most cases.

So, who is the client? At the risk of seeming overly simplistic, the answer may just be that simple: everyone, perhaps with no or very few qualifiers or caveats. And just as was argued previously with regard to the false dichotomy of treatment versus security, the presumed relative incompatibility of interests among the correctional mental health worker's various clients may be overstated and far less axiomatic than is commonly believed by practitioners and others. Certainly, there are unavoidable value judgments that are inherent in any position on this issue. But despite that potential for bias, a fresh and critical look at our time-honored assumptions about the natural divisions between offenders' and institutions' stakes in the process and about the outcomes of mental health treatment in corrections is overdue.

There is another dimension to the question "Who is the client?" that is highly relevant to correctional mental health ethics but is generally not addressed in that context: What is the nature of the client population? Notwithstanding the fact just discussed that correctional mental health practitioners have multiple clients, the focal point of their efforts obviously is the offender. And although it would be unfair and inaccurate to categorize inmates, particularly mentally ill inmates, as demonstrably different from patients one might encounter outside prison walls in terms of their symptoms and general motivations for treatment, there are important differences that mental health staff need to be cognizant of so as to function competently and effectively in the correctional environment. First and foremost, from a diagnostic perspective, it is a fact that offenders will meet criteria for antisocial personality disorder, and certainly adult antisocial behavior, in disproportionately higher numbers than in an otherwise similar nonoffender population (cf. American Psychiatric Association, 1994). (For practitioners in the juvenile justice system, the same obviously would be true for the disruptive behavior disorders.) Individuals who fit descriptions of the psychopath (Hare, 1996) will also be overrepresented in offender groups. Given this clinical reality, practitioners in corrections often need to (or should) fortify traditional treatment modalities with other interventions or assessments as necessary.

Even those offenders who are not constitutionally or otherwise diagnosable with antisocial or psychopathic labels are likely to exhibit behavior that presents additional clinical challenges for the correctional mental health professional. Whether influenced by the environmental press and demand characteristics of the unique behavior settings of correctional institutions, by inmate peers, by justified or unjustified anger and bitterness, or by desperation, offenders are arguably more likely to display behaviors such as resistance, reactance, "staff splitting," hostility, attempts to achieve secondary gain, and a host of other clinical distractions for clinicians than would be the case in another venue. "Distractions" is hardly the right term, however, because the point is this: These behaviors do not constitute mere obstacles to effective treatment but rather are legitimate targets of treatment that correctional mental health professionals must be prepared to tackle given the nature of the clinical population.

Finally, it should be reemphasized that offenders generally have something in common: a history (or at least a significant episode) of behaving in illegal irresponsible fashion and often failing to take responsibility or be otherwise accountable for that and other antisocial behaviors. This pervasive characteristic of the population in question not only is a legitimate target for treatment; it is arguably one of the most important issues to address therapeutically. And for any treatment along those lines to be effective and sustainable, alternatives such as the management-treatment continuum and collaborative rehabilitation approaches described earlier are bound to have greater impact than more traditional approaches to treatment. This is true because these alternative approaches afford more opportunities for holding offenders accountable for their behavior across different situations and over longer periods of time than do traditional approaches. Once again, if the ultimate goal is meaningful lasting change in offender behavior, then this seems to be a more than reasonable argument.

Who Is the Provider?

That corollary question should also be asked and explicated for the full correctional context to be understood and appreciated. The term *collaborative rehabilitation* was coined earlier to describe how all correctional staff—not just mental health providers—have a potential role to play in promoting positive change consistent with therapeutic goals and can work together to achieve those goals. It is naive to think that correctional mental health staff, who see and interact with their patients for a relatively small percentage of the time as compared with other staff, generally have as good an understanding of, or exert as significant an influence over, inmates as they may believe. (This could also be said of mental health providers in general, who may see their clients as infrequently as 50 minutes per week or less, but that loaded topic is beyond the scope of this chapter.) This is not to say that the efforts of skilled and dedicated clinicians have not had a tremendously positive impact on the mental health and general well-being of many offenders. Indeed, it is undoubtedly true that some inmates' very lives have been saved by capable mental health staff who intervened during times of crisis, and it is probable that many more have found psychologists, social workers, psychiatric nurses, counselors, and other helping professionals to be among the few or only sources of empathy and emotional solace while they were incarcerated. Rather, in the broader context and across all offenders, it is impossible for correctional mental health clinicians to detect those who are in crisis or otherwise in need of service, to fully and accurately assess their clients' true conditions and progress, or to effect positive change in general without the help of other correctional staff.

It is not enough, nor is it fair, to regard the input or assistance of nonclinical staff as necessary only when convenient or unavoidable or for information flow to be unidirectional (i.e., from correctional staff to clinician). To conduct truly comprehensive assessments or realize meaningful treatment or programmatic success, there should be a genuine collaboration between mental health and other staff in correctional settings. Take, for example, the success of formal suicide prevention programs, which are fairly commonplace at this juncture in the course of correctional mental health program development. Their success is due in no small measure to one of these programs' primary components: nonclinical staff training on identifying and managing potentially suicidal inmates. More than providing skills, such training communicates the expectation that all are responsible for detecting inmates in crisis and forces collaboration between clinical and nonclinical staff (cf. Couturier, 2001). It seems to be not much of a leap to believe that similar success can be achieved in other mental health treatment and assessment programs by tapping underused human resources and expanding one's conception of who comprises the "treatment team."

Some may regard the prospect of partnering with nonclinical staff in treating offenders as fraught with insurmountable obstacles (not to mention ethical concerns) given providers' perceptions, often well founded, that correctional staff generally have little interest in or motivation for doing so. But perhaps this is because that role has not been adequately defined for them and/or because mental health staff have not reached out sufficiently to begin bridging the perceived "civilian versus custody" chasm. Mental health providers in corrections, in this author's view, have an ethical obligation to do whatever is in their power to preserve and improve the quality of patient care. And if including and regarding other correctional staff as essential members of the treatment team can reasonably be shown to be one step in achieving that goal, then ethical "sacred cows" may need to be questioned and possibly eschewed to promote that arguably higher ethical imperative. This is not to say that correctional staff can or should be trained as therapists or that correctional mental health professionals can or should delegate that and other technical tasks to others. What is called for here is an expanded definition of "treatment." The actions and interventions of correctional staff should be viewed as more than merely behavioral correlates that happen to be compatible with treatment goals; rather, they should be viewed as part-and-parcel of an offender's treatment plan. So, who is the provider? If the argument just made is valid and workable, then the answer is, to varying extents, everyone who works in a correctional facility.

Ethical Issues

Now that the correctional context and this author's perspective have been elucidated for the reader, a discussion of specific ethical issues can commence with that context and perspective in mind. Although this chapter is intended to be relevant for all correctional mental health providers, selected standards from the American Psychological Association's (1992) ethical principles are used merely as a way of anchoring and guiding the discussion. Be advised that the topics that follow in no way constitute an exhaustive list of ethical standards or issues of which correctional mental health practitioners should be aware. Rather, they were selected for review based on this author's experience of which issues are typically the most contentious and debated among correctional mental health providers in addition to their particular relevance to corrections as a unique clinical setting.

Privacy and Confidentiality

All mental health providers are generally bound by their respective ethical codes to maintain the privacy and confidentiality of patient information to the greatest possible extent. The qualifier that ends the preceding sentence is appropriate because it is also generally recognized that there are not only necessary and reasonable limits to such confidentiality rights, such as those defined by statute or regulation, but also limitations as to what the clinician can do to protect those rights absolutely. For example, in correctional settings, patient records do not belong to the clinician, as would be the case in private practice; rather, they are the property of the government agency that employs the clinician. (Increasingly, courts are also acknowledging that patient records are rightly the property of the patients themselves, with minimal exceptions.) This is the case not only in corrections, of course; this potentially significant limit to confidentiality also exists in many other institutional settings as well. But there are additional limits to client privacy and confidentiality unique to corrections that correctional clinicians must confront. Reports of some clinical activities (e.g., intake evaluations), for example, are typically forwarded to inmate files other than the patient records and are readily accessible to nonclinical staff. Mental health providers—indeed all staff—who work at correctional facilities are also expected to report any security violations or concerns, regardless of the circumstances under which such information was learned. And there may be other legitimate obstacles to preserving patient confidentiality depending on institution rules or unforeseen situations that can arise in the course of an individual inmate's journey through the criminal justice system.

Given this reality, it can be argued that the more important ethical consideration for correctional mental health staff with regard to confidentiality is not to preserve privacy per se but rather to ensure that all recipients of service are fully aware of the relatively severe limits to their right to privacy and confidentiality. And of course, informing potential clients of all limits and restrictions on privacy should occur prior to engaging in therapy or assessment activities, and if other limits arise during the course of treatment or evaluation, clients must be apprised accordingly as soon as is reasonably possible. A frequent complaint from clinicians is that this practice most assuredly has a considerable "chilling effect" on any therapeutic relationship and that the inevitable lack of trust must certainly prevent clients from disclosing their true inner selves, thereby dooming any therapeutic endeavor to failure from the start. This is a debatable point about which all correctional clinicians must be sensitive and vigilant. But the only logical alternative is to not provide services, which is ethically indefensible, or to engage in the similarly unethical practice of assuring inmate clients that their privacy and confidentiality will be protected to a greater extent than is possible or likely.

The latter practice undoubtedly occurs often for any number of reasons. Some correctional mental health staff might not be sufficiently aware of all the limitations to privacy and confidentiality in their facilities and agencies. Or they might assure their clients that information will be kept confidential out of a reflex of previous experience and training without completely thinking through either the environment in which they have chosen to work, with its unique demands and rules that pose unusual restrictions on privacy, or the ethical implications of promising something they cannot possibly deliver with confidence. Still others probably follow a middle-of-the-road strategy, asserting to their patients that confidentiality will be maintained with only a few remote exceptions and then adopting a minimalist documentation style that results in little, if any, clinically relevant information making it to the patients' records but affording the clinician a sense of having lived up to his or her pledge.

There is a corollary standard to the superordinate privacy and confidentiality standard in the American Psychological Association's (1992) code of ethics labeled "minimizing intrusions on privacy," which refers to psychologists' obligation to include in reports only information that is "germane to the purpose for which the communication is made." Some might argue that the middle-of-the-road strategy is consistent with, or even mandated by, this standard. But that misses the spirit of the standard, which is not to advocate sparse or minimal documentation but rather to caution psychologists about disclosing immaterial data to others (e.g., a client's sexual orientation in a substance abuse treatment progress report). In point of fact, intentionally omitting clinically relevant data from patients' records is most certainly unethical in itself insofar as it jeopardizes continuity of care for patients who will be seen in the future by other professionals who will likely rely on previous records for history and treatment planning purposes. This is particularly true in corrections, where inmates frequently are transferred to other facilities and also ordinarily pass through the different phases of custody—pretrial, prison, "halfway house," and probation—during which any number of mental health, medical, or other correctional professionals may need access to relevant clinical information to assist the offenders effectively.

This raises an important related question for correctional mental health providers: Who should have access to information in patient records? Certain mental health reports, as noted previously, are usually required by institutional or agency rules to be part of other inmate records and are accessible by other staff, and this limit to confidentiality obviously should be communicated to patients. But beyond that, most correctional clinicians would maintain that nonclinical staff should have no further access to clinical information about patients or to patient records without consent or unless statutory or other recognized limits exist. This conventional wisdom and practice is, in this author's opinion, worthy of more careful thought and possible reevaluation. If one agrees with the propositions put forth in previous sections of this chapter, such as that all staff who work in correctional facilities are "providers" in varying degrees and that a more panoptic view of what constitutes "treatment" of offenders may be in order, then a logical subsequent question might be the following: Why *shouldn't* nonclinical staff have access to patient information? With the obvious exceptions of disclosures that would raise truly serious ethical concerns, such as providing access to raw test data or to other materials that require professional interpretation, it seems perfectly reasonable—indeed advisable—for other members of the "treatment team" to be well informed about their clients.

Recognizing that this idealized view of how correctional facilities should operate does not always exactly match reality at this point in time, this author is certainly not advocating giving all staff complete and unfettered access to all patient information. But again, correctional mental health staff should seriously consider the potential benefits to their clients of expanding the treatment team, as it were. And if clinicians do include and involve other staff in treating inmates and/or facilitating their prosocial behavior, then clinicians need to act less like bodyguards of patient information and more like responsible gatekeepers of relevant clinical data that, if shared for the purpose of improving the quality of patient management and care, would be difficult to question on ethical grounds so long as potential and actual clients are made aware of this possibility. No one questions, for example, the need for patient records on inpatient psychiatric units to be readily accessible to licensed practical nurses or paraprofessionals involved in the patients' care. Why should a different standard exist in correctional settings? An important caveat is the ethical necessity of training all treatment team members to maintain appropriate privacy of clinical information such that it is used solely for treatment or behavior management purposes and is shared only with those who have a legitimate "need to know" related to those treatment or behavior management goals.

Dual or Multiple Relationships

Over more than a decade as an administrator of correctional mental health programs, this author has not heard clinicians from the field voice concerns more often or more loudly about any other ethical issue than the problem of dual or multiple relationships. Specifically, when asked or required to perform "correctional" tasks, such as relieving an officer on a housing unit (which entails holding his or her keys and maintaining security on the unit) and participating in a "shakedown" (i.e., a search for contraband) in an institution, many clinicians push the ethical "panic button" and alert the world that a multiple relationship problem is in danger of occurring. This author himself, early in his correctional career, reacted similarly under such circumstances, but that was before more thoroughly researching the American Psychological Association's (1992) ethical standard on multiple relationships. The intent of that standard is to prohibit psychologists from entering into personal, financial, or other extra-therapeutic relationships with clients that would taint their professional judgments, impair their objectivity and performance, or otherwise cause harm to or exploit the clients. After a thoughtful and comprehensive review, it would be difficult to find a "correctional" task that truly rises to any of those thresholds. A correctional mental health provider may be uncomfortable when performing tasks other than those that are strictly therapeutic or forensic in nature, but performing a task that is merely *different from* a clinician's typical regimen certainly is not tantamount to behaving unethically, at least not in the context of dual or multiple relationships.

An ethical concern would definitely exist, in this author's view, if the performance of correctional duties by a mental health provider had a measurable negative impact on his or her ability to serve clients. For example, if a psychologist agreed or was compelled to work a correctional post for an extended period of days or weeks, and this resulted, or could reasonably be shown to result, in a significant reduction in the quantity and/or quality of services he or she was able to provide to inmate clients in need, then that psychologist and others responsible for managing clinical services at that facility would be faced with an ethical issue (not to mention a problem of inefficient human resource use) that would require confrontation and swift resolution. But the point is that the ethical issue to be confronted under that circumstance has nothing to do with a dual or multiple relationship problem. Rather, it has much more to do with the general ethical principle of keeping patients' general welfare as one's paramount concern and actively avoiding behavior or circumstances that would cause them undue harm.

Thus, unless it can be demonstrated that clients' welfare will be jeopardized or that they will be exploited or harmed in the process, the performance of security-related tasks by clinicians who work in corrections does not appear to pose significant ethical problems, let alone a multiple relationship issue. Indeed, if one accepts the premise that "treatment" and "security" have been arbitrarily compartmentalized by those who have written about correctional mental health ethics, and that meaningful therapeutic relationships and lasting change are more likely to occur if correctional clinicians venture away from their "comfort zones" and become more involved in the totality of the inmate management-treatment continuum, then the prospect of clinicians engaging in correctional work poses not so much an ethical "red flag" as it does a "yellow light" through which mental health providers can proceed but with caution.

Clarification of Role

A related but qualitatively different ethical issue is role conflicts and clarification. A new set of ethical standards specifically for psychologists who engage in forensic activities was added in the most recent iteration of the American Psychological Association's (1992) code. Although written primarily for the practitioner who performs forensic work in the strictest sense of that term (i.e., expert testimony and other consultation related to civil and criminal court proceedings), one of the standards of that new set, "clarification of role," has relevance here. The essence of the standard is that clinicians have an obligation to avoid taking on potentially conflicting roles in the course of their work and should communicate and clarify for clients what they can and should anticipate in terms of clinician behavior and other conditions in light of those potentially conflicting roles. So, for example, if a psychologist in private practice were asked to conduct a competency evaluation for a criminal court proceeding on the same individual with whom he or she has been engaged in psychotherapy over the past year, then the psychologist would be ethically obligated to explain to the client that there would be additional limits to confidentiality during the course of conducting the competency evaluation. As a practical matter, of course, this is purely hypothetical because the psychologist would have a more compelling ethical obligation to refuse to do the competency evaluation in the first place and would most likely recuse himself or herself from the forensic case.

Unfortunately, not only are role conflicts more likely to occur in correctional mental health than in most other settings, but staff also have much less flexibility in satisfactorily resolving them than the psychologist would in the preceding example. Forgetting for the moment that there may be times when clinicians engage in non-clinical correctional tasks, there is great potential for role conflicts even within the boundaries of the strictly clinical work of correctional mental health providers. It would not be unusual for a clinician to be providing intensive psychotherapy to the same inmate on whom the clinician now must conduct a suicide risk assessment, the results of which will be shared with many others and used in behavioral management decisions, and at a later time be asked to conduct an evaluation of the same inmate for the parole board. So, the question is not whether role conflicts, as conceptualized within the field of mental health ethics, exist for correctional mental health professionals. Rather, there are two other questions more relevant to this discussion. First, what should clinicians do about the potential for role conflicts so as to maintain their ethical integrity? Second, are role conflicts, as defined earlier, necessarily problematic for correctional mental health providers interested in treating offenders and changing offender behavior?

The second question is addressed first. Surely the reader has deduced by now that this author's answer is a qualified *no*. Concerns over keeping conflicts of interest or objectivity out of therapeutic and evaluative relationships are understandable and commendable from a strict ethical perspective and should be heeded whenever possible given the potential for client confusion, mistrust, or harm. But in the case of offenders and the total environments (both physical and psychological) in which they must be met, it is impractical to believe, and perhaps unethical to demand, that the conditions under which clinicians attempt to effect any lasting or significant behavior change in a positive direction can or should be antiseptically free of all such perceived conflicts. A rethinking of the traditional rules and concepts that govern the ethical practice of mental health services provision seems to be in order in the face of the many complexities inherent in treating and managing inmates in a meaningful holistic manner. Although it may be viewed in the larger professional community as the "right" thing to do, it is not sufficient, nor is it ethical in the broadest sense, to rely exclusively on conventional methods that thus far have been less than wholly successful in solving what often appear to be the intractable problems of offenders. Otherwise, correctional mental health workers and others in that larger professional community may only be able to figuratively say, as a wit once put it, "The operation was a success, but the patient died."

Regardless, whether the clinician becomes more comfortable with the prospect of role conflicts or not, he or she has at least one unambiguous ethical responsibility in this regard. In answer to the first question as to what correctional mental health providers should do to maintain their ethical integrity in the face of potential role conflicts, it is clear that an effort must be made to communicate to all offenders with whom such providers are engaged clinically what this potential really means for them. Just as clinicians should clarify all of the restrictions on privacy and confidentiality, they should also review with offender clients what the latter could expect to happen in the event that the clinicians are required to take on a different clinical role with the offenders in the future. It is also advisable to use this opportunity to make sure that offender clients fully understand the reality of the correctional environment, that is, that clinicians may be called on and will function in a nonclinical correctional capacity at times when necessary. Although most inmates understand this reality intuitively, clarifying it in advance of embarking on a therapeutic or evaluative relationship prevents confusion and also provides a chance to discuss the correctional context and explain the clinician's multifaceted role in it as more than "cop" one day and "therapist" the next day. It may also be advisable, here or at other more appropriate times, to help offender clients understand that the clinician is not necessarily an advocate of the inmates per se so much as he or she is an advocate of the rehabilitative process and concomitant treatment goals. Frank discussions in this regard may also reduce the likelihood of staff splitting or other such resistances in the future. And skilled helpers can certainly communicate such ideas in ways that also communicate the more salient issue of overall concern for offenders' mental health and welfare. Regardless, the most important point here is that setting expectations and clarifying roles in this manner satisfy an ethical imperative and should be done as much in advance as possible.

Boundaries of Competence and Maintaining Expertise

Given the nature of the primary clinical population in question, it is also ethically imperative for correctional mental health providers to be sufficiently knowledgeable and competent to treat offenders. Correctional mental health is most accurately regarded as a specialty area, not merely a setting where generalists can ply their trade with patients who happen to be inmates. As discussed previously, there are certain clinical differences between inmates and other populations that correctional mental health staff should be prepared to confront as well as other unique challenges that stem from offenders' circumstances and both their natural and less comprehensible reactions to being incarcerated. So, for example, rather than ignoring or dismissing an offender's criminal lifestyle as not pertinent to treating his or her drug addiction, the correctional clinician should understand how the two are inexorably linked and should recognize that the former is just as valid and necessary a target of treatment as the latter.

Mental health providers in corrections can begin or continue to meet this ethical obligation by augmenting their training and experience with continuing education in areas pertinent to working with offenders in addition to that necessary to maintain their basic skills. Independent study options include reading on topics such as criminal personality—both seminal works (e.g., Yochelson & Samenow, 1976, 1977, 1985) and more recent expositions in this field (e.g., Walters, 1990, 1999)—as well as the closely related topic of psychopathy (Cleckley, 1976; Hare, 1981, 1996). Because it is well established that suicide is more likely to occur among incarcerated offenders than among the general population (Hayes, 1995), correctional clinicians also would be well advised to become much more familiar with the art and science of suicide risk assessment (Shea, 1999; White, 1999), especially given the relative lack of attention paid to this subject in graduate schools and other basic training forums (Bongar & Harmatz, 1989). Finally, it is equally important for correctional mental health providers to recognize that they cannot be all things to all patients. The full range of mental and behavioral disorders can be found in prisons, and clinicians need to be careful that they act within the boundaries of their expertise. The relative lack of options that correctional mental health staff may have in terms of referral sources as compared with professionals in the community, as well as the typically high inmate-to-mental health staff ratios in correctional facilities, may present significant difficulties in this regard. But when severe or complex cases present challenges beyond those that correctional clinicians can handle, they are ethically bound to seek peer consultation, contractual or other assessment and treatment alternatives, and any creative means necessary to ensure that the mental health and welfare of their patients is preserved to the greatest extent possible.

Finally, there is another ethical issue relevant to competence and integrity that can arise for mental health professionals who practice in correctional settings. There are occasions when correctional administrators may exert pressure, either unwittingly or not, on mental health professionals' clinical decision-making processes to achieve outcomes consistent with other management decisions. For example, a particular administrator may always wish to transfer mentally ill inmates, regardless of their current level of functioning, to a hospital or another setting whenever possible to avoid the potential for disruption or other costs (e.g., suicide watches) and obviously must rely in part on his or her local mental health clinicians to justify such actions. Although it should be clear to the reader by now that this author believes strongly that correctional mental health workers are members of a larger team and can be effective only if they work in concert with administrators and other staff, this position should not be construed as an admonition to "go along to get along." On the contrary, correctional clinicians should fully embrace their role as the local mental health experts by considering only the relevant facts as well as the broadest definitions of client welfare and interest in rendering judgments and recommendations about each individual offender's treatment and/or management needs. To do otherwise is tantamount to behaving unethically and sacrificing professional integrity. In this author's experience, the clinicians who ultimately gain the respect of correctional managers and other staff are those who strive to work effectively as part of the larger correctional team but who voice their professional opinions confidently and without apology during those rare times when they happen to conflict with other agendas.

Summary and Conclusions

The preceding discussion has focused on only some of the many ethical issues of which correctional mental health providers should be aware. The primary purpose of this chapter was to challenge the conventional and often imprecise views that some in the professional community maintain with regard to corrections and, within that context, to offer measured guidance on some of the more basic but often debated ethical issues as well as to propose alternative conceptions of what constitutes ethical behavior for mental health clinicians in a correctional environment. The frustrations often felt by those who do such work should be met with more than head shaking and hand wringing over the status quo. They should instead incite one to action and more creative thought as to how we might view and structure our systems of service delivery and patient care differently and to maximum effect. It is this author's view that mental health professionals in corrections, given their stake in the process and the stakes of their long list of constituents cited earlier, should continuously question the value of traditional models that are not producing results and strive to think "outside the couch," so to speak.

Ethical standards can and should evolve accordingly as philosophies and structures of mental health service delivery models change. After all, they are not merely derived from careful considerations as to what conditions and professional behavior would most likely promote and enhance patient/client welfare; mental health ethical codes are also shaped in part by the prevailing social mores at the time of their inception. Consider, for example, the ethical standards on privacy and confidentiality. In a larger historical context, it is likely that the acute emphasis on individual rights to privacy that underlie the essence and timbre of those ethical standards was at least partly influenced by the value society places on individualistic self-interest. Contrast this with a burgeoning alternative social philosophy, responsive communitarianism (Etzioni, 1999), which seeks to balance individual rights with social responsibility and the "common good." The communitarian view of privacy is that it is indeed an important right, but one that can be relinquished if public health or public safety is threatened in any way. So, with regard to offender treatment and rehabilitation, if one could argue successfully that further limiting inmates' rights to patient/client confidentiality increased the chances for treatment success and ultimately resulted in offenders becoming productive members of society, or otherwise led to less harm overall to the community, then from a communitarian perspective, this infringement on privacy rights would be acceptable and tolerated. Indeed, communitarian proponents argue for far fewer privacy rights being afforded to sex offenders, presumably including therapist-patient confidentiality rights, so as to protect the public.

The point, of course, is not to advance this particular alternative view as necessarily desirable or workable; rather, it is to illustrate that current ethical standards, as vitally important as they are in guiding responsible clinician behavior and protecting the welfare of clients, were not created in a social vacuum and should not be considered to exist in a vacuum. Nor should they be thought of as clinical ends in and of themselves. Existing ethical standards should be constantly evaluated in terms of whether they continue to facilitate humane, high-quality, and effective patient care. If, over time, they were found in any way to significantly limit or hinder positive treatment outcomes, whether in correctional or other settings, then a careful and methodical process of reevaluation in collaboration with the larger community of mental health professionals would be in order. During the interim, in providing correctional mental health services, the clinician must adhere to established ethical standards to the best of his or her ability, and when ethical dilemmas arise, the clinician is responsible for seeking assistance to resolve them satisfactorily and in accord with those established standards and applicable laws, statutes, and regulations. But correctional mental health practitioners also have a responsibility to use their own judgments and experience as additional guides in charting an ethical course of conduct as they face the many challenges and complexities of treating and assessing offenders.

References

American Psychiatric Association. (1994). *Diagnostic and statistical manual of mental disorders* (4th ed.). Washington, DC: Author.

American Psychological Association. (1992). *Ethical principles of psychologists and code of conduct.* Washington, DC: Author.

Bongar, B., & Harmatz, M. (1989). Graduate training in clinical psychology and the study of suicide. *Professional Psychology: Research and Practice, 20,* 209-213.

Brodsky, S. L. (1980). Ethical issues for psychologists in corrections. In J. Monahan (Ed.), *Who is the client?* (pp. 63-92). Washington, DC: American Psychological Association.

Cleckley, H. (1976). *The mask of sanity* (5th ed.). St. Louis, MO: C. V. Mosby.

Clingempeel, W. G., Mulvey, E., & Repucci, N. D. (1980). A national study of ethical dilemmas of psychologists in the criminal justice system. In J. Monahan (Ed.), *Who is the client?* (pp. 126-153). Washington, DC: American Psychological Association.

Couturier, L. (2001). Suicide prevention in a large state department of corrections. *Corrections Today, 63*(5), 90-97.

Etzioni, A. (1999). *The limits of privacy.* New York: Basic Books.

Fisch, R., Weakland, J. H., & Segal, L. (1982). *The tactics of change: Doing therapy briefly.* San Francisco: Jossey-Bass.

Hare, R. D. (1981). Psychopathy and violence. In J. R. Hays, T. K. Roberts, & K. S. Soloway (Eds.), *Violence and the violent individual* (pp. 53-74). Jamaica, NY: Spectrum.

Hare, R. D. (1996). Psychopathy: A clinical construct whose time has come. *Criminal Justice and Behavior, 23,* 25-54.

Hayes, L. M. (1995). *Prison suicide: An overview and guide to prevention.* Mansfield, MA: U.S. Department of Justice, National Institute of Corrections, National Center on Institutions and Alternatives.

Ivanoff, A., & Smyth, N. J. (1997). Preparing social workers for practice in correctional institutions. In A. R. Roberts (Ed.), *Social work in juvenile and criminal justice settings* (pp. 309-324). Springfield, IL: Charles C Thomas.

Monahan, J. (Ed.). (1980). *Who is the client?* Washington, DC: American Psychological Association.

Shea, S. C. (1999). *The practical art of suicide assessment: A guide for mental health professionals and substance abuse counselors.* New York: John Wiley.

Walters, G. D. (1990). *The criminal lifestyle: Patterns of serious criminal conduct.* Newbury Park, CA: Sage.

Walters, G. D. (1999). *Changing lives of crime and drugs: Intervening with the substance abusing offender.* New York: John Wiley.

Weinberger, L. E., & Sreenivasan, S. (1994). Ethical and professional conflicts in correctional psychology. *Professional Psychology: Research and Practice, 25,* 161-167.

White, T. W. (1999). *How to identify suicidal people: A systematic approach to risk assessment.* Philadelphia: Charles Press.

Yochelson, S., & Samenow, S. (1976). *The criminal personality: Vol. 1. A profile for change.* New York: Jason Aronson.

Yochelson, S., & Samenow, S. (1977). *The criminal personality: Vol. 2. The change process.* New York: Jason Aronson.

Yochelson, S., & Samenow, S. (1985). *The criminal personality: Vol. 2. The change process* (Rev. ed.). New York: Jason Aronson.

PART II

SERVICES
AND PROGRAMS

CHAPTER 4

Basic Mental Health Services: Services and Issues

Robert Morgan

A s discussed in Chapter 1, Level 1 or basic mental health services include mental health services that are available to all inmates confined in a prison or jail setting and include both assessment and treatment services. Basic mental health services are distinguished from rehabilitation services in that the former focus on symptom reduction and coping within the prison, whereas the latter focus on reducing criminal behavior and attitudes and reducing recidivism (Adams, 1985; Morgan, Winterowd, & Ferrell, 1999). Not only do basic mental health services contribute to the operation and security of a correctional environment, but offenders in need of mental health services have a right to receive the appropriate treatment (Metzner, Cohen, Grossman, & Wettstein, 1998). In fact, policies and procedures for correctional mental health services insist on the availability of basic mental health services (e.g., Cohen & Dvoskin, 1992; Metzner, 1993, 1998). As noted, the goal of basic mental health services is not to rehabilitate or prepare offenders for release but rather to identify offenders with psychological or psychiatric problems and initiate treatment services for these offenders. This chapter focuses on both clinical and administrative issues faced by mental health practitioners as they attempt to deliver Level 1 services to offenders within the correctional setting.

Typical Mental Health
Problems Exhibited by Offenders

The increased incarceration of the severely and persistently mentally ill is well documented (e.g., Condelli, Bradigan, & Holanchock, 1997; Hodgins, 1995; Steadman, Morris, & Dennis, 1995; Torrey, 1995). Mentally ill offenders who enter correctional facilities may require continuous mental health services to maintain emotional and behavioral stability throughout the period of incarceration. (See Chapter 6 for a thorough review of managing and treating mentally disordered offenders.) However, the mentally ill are not the only offenders who may be in need of mental health services.

Correctional institutions are stressful environments (Hassine, 1996; Santos, 1995; Toch, 1992), and the mere act of being incarcerated presents many existential concerns (Morgan, Ferrell, & Winterowd, 1999). Offenders must deal with existential issues, including loss of freedom and finding meaning in one's life (particularly for offenders facing long prison sentences), as well as with other issues resulting from incarceration such as family separation/disruption, unresolved financial difficulties, imposition of structure in one's life, loss of previous coping strategies, and fear of the prison environment itself (e.g., physical or sexual violence) (Santos, 1995). Certainly, some offenders will thrive under the environmental structure and unwritten inmate rules of conduct, many will adapt and blend into the prison environment, but others will experience adjustment difficulties and emotional distress. Thus, it is not surprising that newly incarcerated offenders may experience anxiety, depression, and/or other psychological disturbances. Basic mental health services are necessary to assist these offenders in their adjustment to their newfound lives as inmates.

Mental health professionals intervene to assist offenders in their transition to, or their return to, a correctional environment. It is noted that assisting inmate adjustment to the correctional environment may have unintended consequences in that behaviors that are functional in a correctional environment are not necessarily functional in the free world (Homant, 1986). Nevertheless, offenders experiencing severe adjustment difficulties become a concern for the safety and operation of a correctional institution and must be addressed.

Psychological symptoms are not limited to newly incarcerated offenders; rather, chronic anxiety and stress are inevitable by-products of being incarcerated. Offenders with both short- and long-term prison sentences will encounter numerous stressors and life issues with which they must deal. Previously mentioned issues, such as family separation and fear of violence, as well as numerous existential issues, such as feelings of loss of control, making sense of one's life, and the loss of freedom, are reoccurring sources of stress throughout one's incarceration. However, it should be noted that even offenders nearing their release dates experience feelings of anxiety and apprehension regarding their impending release (a process that offenders refer to as "getting short"). The closer offenders get to their release dates, the more they begin to contemplate their lives outside of prison. Issues such as reintegrating into the free world, being reacquainted with family members, finding a job, and avoiding criminal behavior become areas of concern.

Certainly, these are important issues for offenders to contemplate prior to release; however, such issues, by their nature, result in worry, concern, and anxiety, and they frequently necessitate referrals to mental health professionals. Thus, offenders in any stage of incarceration may be in need of mental health services.

Basic Mental Health Services

Basic mental health services consist of four broad areas: assessment, acute crisis intervention, brief therapeutic intervention, and special mental health evaluations. Each service area has a specific goal or function within the correctional institution. Each also involves specific clinical and administrative issues that the clinician must be aware of and address. These service areas, as well as the accompanying clinical and administrative issues, are briefly discussed next.

Assessment

Assessments are conducted to identify offenders at risk for psychological or behavioral problems and are typically conducted during the orientation phase of one's incarceration (i.e., initial intake assessments) or when requested by other correctional personnel. Many correctional treatment programs are available for inmates in need of services (e.g., substance abuse programs, HIV treatment programs, programs for violent and/or mentally ill offenders); however, inmates might not always self-refer for such programs (e.g., Morgan, Winterowd, & Ferrell, 1999). Thus, initial intake assessments or requested assessments are useful for identifying offenders at risk or in need of services.

As described in Chapter 1, initial intake assessments are conducted to identify "emotional, intellectual, and behavioral deficits" as well as "specialized treatment needs" of newly incarcerated offenders. Those offenders in need of services are then referred to the appropriate treatment services. Initial intake assessments work well for those offenders seeking help; however, of concern is the number of inmates who are in need of services but who are unwilling or unlikely to ask for help. The task of mental health professionals, then, is to identify those offenders who are in need of assistance but who are unwilling to acknowledge this need. Without the assistance of a "crystal ball," this task becomes arduous, and unfortunately, some at-risk offenders may slip through the cracks, at least temporarily.

Fortunately, offenders with emotional, intellectual, or behavioral problems who avoid detection at the time of intake will invariably be referred back to the mental health department for further assessment. The very nature of a secure correctional setting is conducive to the monitoring and maintenance of offenders. Although security constraints may be a hindrance to offenders (e.g., Kummerlowe, 1995), security staff serve the dual purposes of protecting the public and protecting incarcerated offenders from one another. Thus, security personnel help to identify offenders having trouble integrating into the mainstream prison population and frequently refer these individuals for mental health services. Such mental health referrals are critical in the maintenance of a secure correctional environment and afford those offenders in need of services ample opportunity to obtain treatment.

Acute Crisis Intervention

Unfortunately, an emotionally or behaviorally disturbed offender may remain undetected until such time as a crisis occurs. Acute crisis intervention is a necessary component of the basic mental health services and includes services for suicidal offenders, mentally disordered offenders, dangerous offenders, victims of sexual assault/abuse, and the developmentally disabled/retarded.

Suicide is a serious issue for mental health professionals working in secure correctional settings because it is the leading cause of death in lockups and jails and is the second leading cause of death in prisons and correctional institutions (Reynolds, 2000). Mental health professionals play a critical role by providing suicide prevention services and therefore must be cognizant of factors that increase the probability of suicidal behavior. These factors include demographic variables (e.g., young adults and older white males are at greater risk), presence of mental illness, recently incarcerated, placement in segregation, previous suicide attempts, suicidal threats, and lack of a social support system (Ax, 1999; Sherman & Morschauser, 1989). Fortunately, mental health professionals in correctional settings have structural opportunities (e.g., on-site observation) that private practitioner colleagues do not have. Once an offender has been identified as at risk for suicide (or for self-mutilation), he or she can be placed in an observation room with minimal possessions and provided frequent contact with a mental health professional. This contact allows for the establishment of a therapeutic alliance, and counseling is initiated to assist the offender in dealing with his or her problems and concerns. Psychopharmacological medications may be instituted as an adjunct therapy to alleviate the symptoms of mental illness (e.g., depression, anxiety) that contribute to hopelessness and suicidal ideation.

Acute crisis intervention services are also necessary for offenders with mental illness. The goal of acute crisis intervention for the mentally ill is emotional and behavioral stability. Treatment of mentally disordered offenders (see Chapter 6) is a constitutional right (Cohen, 1988, 1996; Cohen & Dvoskin, 1992) and typically includes long-term follow-up and the use of psychopharmacological treatment. Crisis intervention for offenders with mental illness, however, refers to inmates who are actively psychotic and/or who present a danger to themselves or others. Such services are not designed for long-term therapeutic purposes; rather, the goal is to stabilize the offenders and help them to remain in the general prison population. At times, it may be necessary to remove an offender from the general prison population for his or her safety as well as that of others; however, this is a short-term strategy, and the goal is to return the offender to the general prison population as soon as is safely possible. In addition to environmental controls, acute services will likely include the use of psychotropic medications, intensive counseling, and (in some systems) assistance in establishing a social support network. As offenders begin to stabilize, they will typically be transitioned into long-term treatment programs, where the goal is mental illness awareness and long-term emotional and behavioral stability.

Other prominent issues in correctional settings include issues of dangerousness and sexual assault. Although instances of assault (physical or sexual) have been exaggerated by the popular media (e.g., *American Me, Shawshank Redemption, American History X*), assaults do occur (e.g., Edens, Poythress, & Lilienfeld, 1999; Hemmens & Marquart, 1999). Mental health professionals will be called on not only to identify those offenders at risk for perpetrating such offenses but also to identify potential victims of such offenses. In addition, crisis intervention services will be necessary for those who already have been victimized. Mental health professionals encounter problems with confidentiality when potential perpetrators or victims of physical or sexual assaults are identified. Mental health professionals are trained to protect the confidentiality of their clients; however, in correctional settings, the institutions are also the clients and must be notified when potential perpetrators or victims are identified (Monahan, 1980). This often results in conflicting feelings of mental health professionals who are unaccustomed to such practices. (See Chapter 3 for a more detailed discussion of this issue.) Nevertheless, institutional staff must be informed of potential problems (both perpetrators and victims) for the safety of all.

What about after an assault has occurred? Certainly, an abused offender will experience problems (e.g., anxiety, depression, guilt, shame, fear) resulting from the assault (much like other offender victims), and mental health professionals need to be prepared to assist with such issues. This may be particularly problematic for mental health professionals working with offender victims who have previously been perpetrators of abuse themselves. Mental health professionals may suddenly find themselves unempathetic to such individuals, and almost certainly, correctional staff will have little empathy for such persons. Thus, a therapeutic and supportive environment may be surprisingly difficult to establish. Nevertheless, mental health professionals must develop a helping attitude and offer supportive services regardless of the environmental pressures against such services or these professionals' own biases and prejudices. Last, it should be noted that issues of post-traumatic stress disorder are not uncommon in correctional environments (e.g., Teplin, Abram, & McClelland, 1996) and may warrant particular attention for victims of physical and/or sexual attacks.

Another special needs group that may require the use of crisis intervention services is developmentally disabled or mentally retarded offenders. These offenders are more likely to experience adjustment difficulties (particularly in response to the structured environment), are less likely to participate in rehabilitative services, and are more likely to have lengthened prison stays (Gardner, Graeber, & Machkovitz, 1998). Developmentally delayed or mentally retarded offenders are also more likely to experience rules infractions (Santamour & West, 1977) than are their non-disabled counterparts. It is also possible that developmentally disabled or mentally retarded offenders are more likely to be victimized by other offenders because they might not recognize or comprehend situations in which they are being taken advantage of. Thus, crisis intervention services might be necessary to assist these offenders in their adjustment to both the correctional environment and their offender peers. Of concern is the tendency of developmentally delayed or mentally retarded offenders to resist efforts of assistance and their unwillingness (or inability) to acknowledge their need for help. Seeking mental health services in a correctional environment may be perceived as a sign of weakness, and mentally retarded offenders may be particularly sensitive to such perceptions. Thus, mental health professionals must be cognizant of this issue and be prepared to find paradoxical methods of helping this special needs group in spite of these offenders' resistance to help.

Therapeutic Services

As indicated previously, the goal of basic mental health services is not to rehabilitate offenders but rather to stabilize offenders with emotional or behavioral problems so that they can maintain functioning within the current correctional environment. This is accomplished via brief individual or group psychotherapy services. Analogous to a managed care model of maintaining functioning, brief individual or group psychotherapy services aim to help offenders adapt to their environment and cope with their incarceration.

Brief therapeutic services may be as succinct as 1 to 4 sessions or have an upper limit of 25 sessions (Koss & Butcher, 1986). Although individual psychotherapy may be offered for those offenders who desire rehabilitation (i.e., those who desire significant behavioral, emotional, and/or attitudinal change as described in Chapter 1), this service tends to occur less frequently due to issues of staff availability and infrequent requests by offenders for such services. Thus, consistent with nonincarcerated psychotherapeutic services, particularly services governed by managed care, individual and group counseling services tend to be brief in nature and focus on symptom reduction and increased adaptation.

Brief individual psychotherapy services tend to serve different functions from group psychotherapy services within the correctional environment. Individual psychotherapy services tend to be implemented with more disturbed or mentally disordered offenders, whereas group psychotherapy services tend to be more problem focused on issues such as anger management, stress management, and problem solving (Morgan, Winterowd, & Ferrell, 1999). Given the effectiveness of group psychotherapy services (Morgan & Flora, in press) and limited resources of mental health departments in correctional facilities (Wilson, 1990), group psychotherapy services may be the treatment of choice. Given current concerns regarding overcrowding, a treatment option that allows mental health providers to reach a large number of offenders in a time-efficient manner will certainly be viewed as favorable by correctional administrators, particularly when this treatment approach results in positive outcomes on a variety of outcome measures (Morgan & Flora, in press).

Not surprisingly, offenders may be resistant to seek out mental health services. It has been speculated that inmates' attitudes toward rehabilitation programs tend to be negative (Rappaport, 1982), with feelings of suspiciousness being prominent (e.g., Mathias & Sindberg, 1985) in a "we against them" atmosphere (Demuth, 1995) in which inmates may view therapists as "cops" and treatment sessions as "snitch sessions" (Mobley, 1999). Thus, mental health providers in correctional settings will need to be adept at dealing with resistance and using paradoxical methods for engaging some offenders in the treatment process. Given manipulative tendencies by even the most motivated offender clients, psychotherapists in corrections, even more than in most other settings, must be self-aware and knowledgeable of their personal limitations. Then, to be truly effective with incarcerated offenders, mental health therapy providers must develop the ability to

> empathize without sympathy, confront without demeaning, care without carrying, direct without controlling, see manipulation as a poor coping strategy rather than a personal assault, find satisfaction in erratic progress toward limited and clearly defined goals, tolerate the ambiguities and conflicts of the setting, and accept their own limitations. (Mobley, 1999, p. 627)

Special Mental Health Evaluations

Still another service provided by mental health professionals in correctional settings is special mental health evaluations. These evaluations tend to be a service for the criminal justice system rather than for offenders and consist of parole board and disciplinary hearing assessments, segregation reviews, hospital referrals, and court-ordered pretrial and/or presentence evaluations.

Risk assessments, a common practice in forensic psychiatry and psychology, attempt to predict the likelihood that individuals will engage in future violence (Arrigo, 2000; Melton, Petrila, Poythress, & Slobogin, 1997). Similarly, correctional mental health professionals will be asked to conduct mental health evaluations for parole boards, disciplinary hearing officers, or correctional staff responsible for institutional transfers and classification reductions. Such evaluations are requested by those who are involved in determining offenders' outcomes. Parole boards need to evaluate risks of future violence, disciplinary hearing officers need to evaluate risks of continued rules violations, and correctional staff need to evaluate risks of escapes or other potential problems if offenders are transferred to less secure institutions. Mental health professionals assist in these decisions by evaluating offenders' mental states and their potential for impulsive behavior. Of concern, however, is the relatively poor accuracy of mental health professionals' predictions regarding future behavior of offenders (Arrigo, 2000; Melton et al., 1997; Monahan, 1981). Actuarial methods have been developed for identifying repeat criminal offenders (e.g., Statistical Information on Recidivism, Violence Risk Appraisal Guide), particularly sex offenders (e.g., Minnesota Sex Offender Screening Tool, Rapid Risk Assessment of Sexual Offense Recidivism, Sex Offender Risk Appraisal Guide); however, these methods have not been modified for correctional environments or for predicting the behavior of incarcerated offenders.

Mental health professionals are also asked to participate in segregation reviews to offer professional opinions regarding the mental health functioning of segregated offenders. Offenders are placed in segregation due to institutional rules violations. Mentally disordered offenders are more likely to be placed in segregation (DiCataldo, Greer, & Profit, 1995; Hodgins & Cote, 1991) because of more adjustment difficulties resulting in rules infractions and disciplinary write-ups. Segregation is an isolated experience, and many offenders, especially mentally disordered offenders, may experience extreme psychological reactions to this isolation (Miller & Young, 1997). Thus, mental health professionals participate in segregation reviews to monitor the mental health functioning of all segregated offenders. If an offender begins to decompensate, then mental health professionals will provide crisis intervention services in an attempt to stabilize them. Unfortunately, many offenders, particularly offenders with mental illness, will continue to decompensate if maintained in segregation and may require transfer to treatment-oriented correctional settings for emotional or behavioral stabilization.

One difficulty frequently encountered by mental health professionals responsible for segregation reviews is nontreatment correctional staff's perceptions of offenders in segregation as manipulators and as the "worst of the worst." Thus, there is little compassion, even for the severely mentally ill, and as a result, mental health professionals will often make decisions that are viewed as unfavorable by correctional staff. Staff resistance often results, and mental health professionals may be "educated" as to the manipulative behavior of offenders. Peer pressure to leave such offenders in segregation is often present. Nevertheless, mental health professionals have a responsibility to offenders and must respond in any fashion necessary to facilitate psychological stability.

Court-ordered pretrial and/or presentence evaluations are a more formal type of special mental health evaluation. At the local and state levels, mental health professionals from the community typically conduct these types of evaluations in jails, lockups, or assessment and diagnostic centers. Mental health professionals in state-operated correctional facilities typically do not offer pretrial evaluations because state offenders have typically been convicted and sentenced prior to being housed in a prison setting. However, in the federal criminal justice system, both correctional medical centers and regular correctional facilities are sometimes used as evaluation centers for offenders awaiting (a) pretrial evaluations to assess their competency to stand trial and/or their mental states and levels of criminal culpability at the times of the alleged offenses or (b) presentence evaluations to provide sentencing judges with information regarding offenders' mental status and treatment needs. Therefore, mental health professionals in the Bureau of Prisons may be asked to conduct both pretrial and presentence evaluations. In these cases, the mental health professional will conduct an evaluation, write a formal report for the court, and (if requested to do so) testify at the hearing. One benefit of this type of process is that mental health professionals will have increased contact with and observation of offenders, possibly allowing for more accurate conclusions and opinions. Of concern, however, is the possibility of dual roles. Frequently, a pretrial or presentence offender will be in need of treatment and will likely reach out to the mental health professional with whom he or she has had the most contact, typically the evaluator. Care must be taken to avoid dual roles in that a mental health professional who is conducting an evaluation via court order should not be dually involved in the offender's treatment. In these cases, it is more appropriate for the evaluator to refer the offender to another mental health professional for treatment.

Mental Health Records

Maintenance of mental health records serves several functions in a correctional setting. First and foremost, proper documentation is a professional responsibility of all mental health professionals (e.g., American Psychological Association, 1992), but this issue may be even more prominent in a correctional setting. Incarcerated offenders tend to be litigiously minded because that is the strongest avenue of revenge they have in dealing with perceived slights by the criminal justice system. In fact, many offenders appear to anxiously await potential maltreatment by correctional staff, health staff, and/or mental health professionals so that they can file lawsuits against anyone remotely involved in the perceived maltreatment. Offenders may claim that these lawsuits are attempts to correct a flawed system. However, often the true motivation lies in seeking recognition among one's peers or in seeking revenge against any or all persons contributing to one's continued incarceration. Regardless of the motivation, accurate record keeping is critical for protecting mental health professionals and combating frivolous lawsuits.

Accurate record keeping is also essential for continuity of care. It is of no surprise that offenders are prone to malinger for the benefits of mental health services. Benefits such as the acquisition of psychotropic medications, facility transfers, and even the temporary relief from one's work while attending a treatment session all are potential secondary gains. Given the number of treatment staff (e.g., health professionals, mental health professionals, substance abuse counselors, unit team staff), particularly in large correctional systems, offenders will frequently attempt to maneuver around professionals as needed until they receive the desired benefits. Thus, accurate and detailed record keeping is necessary for proper continuity of care and to prevent "doctor shopping" from occurring.

Fortunately, not all offenders try to manipulate the system, and for those offenders truly in need of services, accurate record keeping may be the only mechanism in place to ensure appropriate delivery of services. This is particularly important for offenders requiring crisis intervention services outside of normal work hours. Mental health professionals typically are not familiar with all offenders incarcerated at a particular institution, and when they are called in for emergency services (e.g., late at night, on weekends), the only information they might have access to is the mental health records. Only accurate and appropriately detailed records will allow the responding mental health professionals to facilitate treatment that is consistent with previous treatment protocol and that is best able to meet the needs of the offenders in crisis.

Accurate and detailed record keeping may also serve another function that is important to the institution at large. Frequently, mental health professionals and correctional administrators find themselves at odds with different goals, that is, treatment versus confinement (Morgan, Winterowd, & Ferrell, 1999); however, these conflicts are likely to be less problematic when mental health departments can "prove" their worth to the functional operation of the facility. On more than one occasion, this author has been involved in national audits of a correctional facility where one of the highlighted results was on the quality of mental health record keeping. In fact, in one such audit, the mental health records clarified other custody issues and clearly documented a continuity of care that was otherwise not documented. Thus, the mental health records protected the institution at large from further scrutiny. Such instances further highlight the contribution of mental health services, broadly speaking, to institutions at large and will endear mental health services to the administration or at least enhance administrative tolerance for what may otherwise be viewed as an unnecessary program (i.e., institutional cost).

Liability Issues and
Basic Mental Health Services

As indicated previously, incarcerated offenders have a right to basic mental health services. One question is who is liable for such services. Certainly, during the delivery of such services, mental health professionals are responsible for the quality and appropriateness of services delivered. Of greater concern to correctional administrators, however, is who is responsible for ensuring the delivery of such services.

Offenders have successfully sued jails, prisons, and prison systems under federal statutes regarding the right to mental health services (Cohen, 1988). Thus, although mental health professionals are responsible for the services they provide, ultimately, correctional systems are responsible for ensuring that appropriate services are being delivered, that is, that the mental health departments are meeting the standards documented as necessary in the policy and procedure manuals of the correctional systems.

One concern with regard to liability is staffing issues. Correctional systems are responsible for employing sufficient numbers of staff to provide the basic mental health services mandated by policy (e.g., Cohen, 1996). Of interest, and yet to be challenged, is the issue of non-doctoral-level mental health professionals providing mental health services in correctional facilities. Particularly, questions regarding quality assurance issues remain paramount (Morgan, Winterowd, & Ferrell, 1999) and must be addressed. This appears to be more of an issue for state correctional systems, which tend to use the services of non-doctoral-level professionals; in the Federal Bureau of Prisons and in the California Department of Corrections, mental health services are generally provided by doctoral-level psychologists. Correctional administrators in systems employing non-doctoral-level professionals may be at risk for legal action brought by offenders who claim that adequate mental health services are not being provided. At the very least, such correctional systems should participate in or encourage research to investigate such possibilities and to ensure that they are complying with mandated policy regarding the delivery of mental health services.

With regard to liability issues, an opportunity may exist for mental health professionals to further endear themselves to correctional administrators. As indicated previously, mental health treatment goals and correctional goals of security may at times be incompatible (e.g., McDougall, 1996; Morgan, Winterowd, & Ferrell, 1999); however, the two factions must meet on common ground. Who better to facilitate this than mental health professionals? With open lines of communication (a mental health specialty) and research skills, mental health professionals have many ways in which to endear themselves to correctional administrators. By maintaining basic mental health services that are state-of-the-art as well as consistent with determined policy, mental health professionals relieve administrators of such liability concerns. This favor may be returned in the form of leniency when mental health professionals are attempting to develop innovative treatment programs.

Conclusions

Basic mental health services are available to all incarcerated offenders in jails, lock-ups, prisons, and other correctional environments. The goals of basic mental health services are not to rehabilitate offenders but rather to facilitate or maintain offenders' emotional or behavioral states to allow them to remain in the general prison population. Certainly, mental health professionals have an interest in more innovative treatment strategies, and such opportunities abound in correctional settings (see Chapters 5 to 10). However, the basic mental health services as described in this chapter include those services that must be offered to meet offender psychological/psychiatric needs. These services are designed to meet minimal standards of care and to help maintain a secure and functional correctional environment.

References

Adams, K. (1985). Addressing inmate mental health problems: A new direction for prison therapeutic services. *Federal Probation, 49,* 27-33.

American Psychological Association. (1992). Ethical principles of psychologists and code of conduct. *American Psychologist, 47,* 1597-1611.

Arrigo, B. A. (2000). *Introduction to forensic psychology: Issues and controversies in crime and justice.* San Diego: Academic Press.

Ax, R. K. (1999). *Suicide prevention.* Unpublished manuscript, Federal Correctional Institution, Petersburg, VA.

Cohen, F. (1988). *Legal issues and the mentally disturbed prisoner.* Washington, DC: National Institute of Corrections.

Cohen, F. (1996). Offenders with mental disorders in the criminal justice-correctional process. In B. D. Sales & D. W. Shuman (Eds.), *Law, mental health, and mental disorder* (pp. 397-413). Pacific Grove, CA: Brooks/Cole.

Cohen, F., & Dvoskin, J. (1992). Inmates with mental disorders: A guide to law and practice. *Mental and Physical Disability Law Reporter, 16,* 339-346.

Condelli, W. S., Bradigan, B., & Holanchock, H. (1997). Intermediate care programs to reduce risk and better manage inmates with psychiatric disorders. *Behavioral Sciences and the Law, 15,* 459-467.

Demuth, P. W. (1995). The relationship between maintenance of the criminal code and group denial in a substance abuse population: Its effect on treatment. *International Journal of Offender Therapy and Comparative Criminology, 39,* 77-81.

DiCataldo, F., Greer, A., & Profit, W. E. (1995). Screening prison inmates for mental disorder: An examination of the relationship between mental disorder and prison adjustment. *Bulletin of the American Academy of Psychiatry and the Law, 23,* 573-585.

Edens, J. F., Poythress, N. G., & Lilienfeld, S. O. (1999). Identifying inmates at risk for disciplinary infractions: A comparison of two measures of psychopathy. *Behavioral Sciences and the Law, 17,* 435-443.

Gardner, W. I., Graeber, J. L., & Machkovitz, S. J. (1998). Treatment of offenders with mental retardation. In R. M. Wettstein (Ed.), *Treatment of offenders with mental disorders* (pp. 329-364). New York: Guilford.

Hassine, V. (1996). *Life without parole.* Los Angeles: Roxbury.

Hemmens, C., & Marquart, J. W. (1999). Straight time: Inmates' perceptions of violence and victimization in the prison environment. *Journal of Offender Rehabilitation, 28,* 1-21.

Hodgins, S. (1995). Assessing mental disorder in the criminal justice system: Feasibility versus clinical accuracy. *International Journal of Law and Psychiatry, 18,* 15-28.

Hodgins, S., & Cote, G. (1991). The mental health of penitentiary inmates in isolation. *Canadian Journal of Criminology, 33,* 175-182.

Homant, R. J. (1986). Ten years after: A follow-up of therapy effectiveness. *Journal of Offender Counseling and Rehabilitation, 10,* 51-57.

Koss, M. P., & Butcher, J. N. (1986). Research on brief psychotherapy. In S. L. Garfield & A. E. Bergin (Eds.), *Handbook of psychotherapy and behavior change* (3rd ed., pp. 627-670). New York: John Wiley.

Kummerlowe, C. (1995). Coping with imprisonment: A long-timer's view. In T. J. Flanagan (Ed.), *Long-term imprisonment: Policy, science, and correctional practice* (pp. 41-50). Thousand Oaks, CA: Sage.

Mathias, R. E., & Sindberg, R. M. (1985). Psychotherapy in correctional settings. *International Journal of Offender Therapy and Comparative Criminology, 29,* 265-275.

McDougall, C. (1996). Working in secure institutions. In C. R. Hollin (Ed.), *Working with offenders: Psychological practice in offender rehabilitation* (pp. 94-115). Chichester, UK: Wiley.

Melton, G. B., Petrila, J., Poythress, N. G., & Slobogin, C. (1997). *Psychological evaluations for the courts: A handbook for mental health professionals and lawyers* (2nd ed.). New York: Guilford.

Metzner, J. L. (1993). Guidelines for psychiatric services in prisons. *Criminal Behaviour and Mental Health, 3,* 252-267.

Metzner, J. L. (1998). An introduction to correctional psychiatry: Part III. *Journal of the American Academy of Psychiatry and the Law, 26,* 107-115.

Metzner, J. L., Cohen, F., Grossman, L. S., & Wettstein, R. M. (1998). Treatment in jails and prisons. In R. M. Wettstein (Ed.), *Treatment of offenders with mental disorders* (pp. 211-264). New York: Guilford.

Miller, H. A., & Young, G. R. (1997). Prison segregation: Administrative detention remedy or mental health problem? *Criminal Behavior and Mental Health, 7,* 85-94.

Mobley, M. J. (1999). Psychotherapy with criminal offenders. In A. K. Hess & I. B. Weiner (Eds.), *The handbook of forensic psychology* (2nd ed., pp. 603-639). New York: John Wiley.

Monahan, J. (1980). *Who is the client? The ethics of psychological intervention in the criminal justice system.* Washington, DC: American Psychological Association.

Monahan, J. (1981). *The clinical prediction of violent behavior.* Rockville, MD: National Institute of Mental Health.

Morgan, R. D., Ferrell, S. W., & Winterowd, C. L. (1999). Therapist perceptions of important therapeutic factors in psychotherapy groups for male inmates in state correctional facilities. *Small Group Research, 30,* 712-729.

Morgan, R. D., & Flora, D. B. (in press). Group psychotherapy with incarcerated offenders: A research synthesis. *Group Dynamics: Theory, Research, and Practice.*

Morgan, R. D., Winterowd, C. L., & Ferrell, S. W. (1999). A national survey of group psychotherapy services in correctional facilities. *Professional Psychology: Research and Practice, 30,* 600-606.

Rappaport, R. G. (1982). Group therapy in prison. In M. Seligman (Ed.), *Group psychotherapy and counseling with special populations* (pp. 215-227). Baltimore: University Park Press.

Reynolds, J. B. (2000). *Correctional psychiatry.* Unpublished manuscript, Northwest Missouri Psychiatric Rehabilitation Center.

Santamour, M., & West, B. (1977). *The mentally retarded offender and corrections.* Washington, DC: U.S. Department of Justice, Law Enforcement Assistance Administration.

Santos, M. G. (1995). Facing long-term imprisonment. In T. J. Flanagan (Ed.), *Long-term imprisonment: Policy, science, and correctional practice* (pp. 36-40). Thousand Oaks, CA: Sage.

Sherman, L. G., & Morschauser, P. C. (1989). Screening for suicide risk in inmates. *Psychiatric Quarterly, 60,* 119-138.

Steadman, H. J., Morris, S. M., & Dennis, D. L. (1995). The diversion of mentally ill persons from community-based services: A profile of programs. *American Journal of Public Health, 85,* 1630-1635.

Teplin, L. A., Abram, K. M., & McClelland, G. M. (1996). Prevalence of psychiatric disorders among incarcerated women: I. Pretrial jail detainees. *Archives of General Psychiatry, 53,* 505-512.

Toch, H. (1992). *Mosaic of despair: Human breakdowns in prison* (Rev. ed.). Washington, DC: American Psychological Association.

Torrey, E. F. (1995). Jails and prisons: America's new mental hospital [editorial]. *American Journal of Public Health, 85,* 1611-1613.

Wilson, G. L. (1990). Psychotherapy with depressed incarcerated felons: A comparative evaluation of treatments. *Psychological Reports, 67,* 1027-1041.

CHAPTER 5

Substance Abuse Treatment Programs in Prisons and Jails

Roger H. Peters and Charles O. Matthews

Approximately 3% of the U.S. population was incarcerated or under other types of correctional supervision in 1999 (Office of National Drug Control Policy [ONDCP], 2001), among the highest rates of the developed countries in the world. The number of prisoners incarcerated in state and federal prisons nearly doubled during the 1990s, continuing a trend begun during the previous decade. During that time, the jail capacity in the United States rose from 389,000 to 652,000, and jails operated at more than 93% capacity (Bureau of Justice Statistics, 2000a). The cost of this rapid growth is overwhelming, amounting to nearly $40 billion spent on prisons and jails in 2000 (Justice Policy Institute, 2001). This includes approximately $24 billion to incarcerate nonviolent offenders—many of them drug offenders. Of the 1.3 million prisoners currently under state, federal, and local jurisdictions, 21% of state prisoners, 59% of federal prisoners, and 26% of jail inmates were incarcerated for drug offenses (Bureau of Justice Statistics, 2000b; ONDCP, 2001). The United States incarcerates significantly more individuals for drug offenses than the combined European Union incarcerates for all offenses, despite the fact that the European Union has a much larger population than the United States (Justice Policy Institute, 2001).

Current Issues Related to Drug Offenders in Prisons and Jails

Policy Trends Affecting the Incarceration of Substance-Involved Offenders

Among the factors serving to increase U.S. jail and prison populations are changes in law enforcement practices, new sentencing laws and policies adopted during the 1980s and 1990s, and new policies adopted regarding release from incarceration. Law enforcement practices that have influenced the rates of arrest and incarceration include drug operations targeting street-level users and sellers. These operations have led to a significant rise in the level of arrests and convictions for drug possession and sales. The Sentencing Reform Act of 1984 abolished parole for federal offenders and limited time off for good behavior. Other legislative changes affecting rates of incarceration include mandatory minimum sentencing provisions for a range of state and federal prisoners that resulted from enactment of legislation such as the Anti-Drug Abuse Act of 1986. The Anti-Drug Abuse Act of 1994, in conjunction with other state legislation, established mandatory minimum sentences for various drug offenses (U.S. Department of Justice, 1997c). Mandatory minimum sentences have led to significant increases in time served for drug offenses, that is, from an average of 22 months to 33 months (Bureau of Justice Statistics, 1995).

Approximately $30 billion was spent in the United States on adult corrections in 1998 (National Center on Addiction and Substance Abuse [CASA], 2001), including $24 billion (81%) on substance-involved offenders. In many states and localities, the costs for jail and prison construction have adversely affected the ability to fund education, social services, and other public services. In light of the burdensome costs of incarcerating nonviolent offenders, states have begun to reexamine minimum mandatory sentencing laws. Several state initiatives have focused on the need to focus more on treatment and rehabilitation rather than on incarceration for drug-involved offenders. In New York, the state court system has developed plans for offering substance abuse treatment to virtually all nonviolent offenders (Finkelstein, 2000). Recent ballot initiatives in Arizona and California have required that treatment be provided in lieu of incarceration for nonviolent drug offenders. For example, California's Proposition 36, enacted in 2001, excludes further incarceration as a condition of probation for nonviolent drug offenders and requires the court to order participation and completion of a substance abuse treatment program. Other similar state ballot initiatives are likely to be introduced in other states within the next several years.

The Need for Correctional Treatment

There have been many links drawn between substance abuse and criminal behavior (ONDCP, 2000). More than half of all jail inmates reported being under the influence of alcohol or drugs at the times of their offenses (Ditton, 1999). Substance abusers report significantly greater criminal activity and have more extensive criminal records than do nonusers (Ball, 1986; Collins, Hubbard, & Rachal, 1985), while those with greater histories of criminal activity are more likely to report prior substance abuse (Belenko & Peugh, 1998). In many cases, criminal activity (e.g., property crime, prostitution, drug trafficking) results from attempts to support a drug habit.

Results from the Arrestee Drug Abuse Monitoring program (National Institute of Justice, 2000) indicate that approximately two thirds of recent adult arrestees in metropolitan jails test positive for drugs, and 70% of all jail inmates were arrested for drug offenses or reported using drugs on a regular basis (Bureau of Justice Statistics, 2000c). Polydrug use remains a significant problem, with as many as 45% of female inmates and 40% of male inmates testing positive for more than one drug in certain areas. In prisons, lifetime prevalence of drug abuse or dependence disorder was reported to be 58%, including 46% for drug dependence (Peters, Greenbaum, Edens, Carter, & Ortiz, 1998). The prevalence rates of substance abuse and dependence for inmates in jails and prisons are significantly greater than those for the general population (Robins & Regier, 1991).

In recognition of the scope of substance abuse problems among jail and prison inmates, as well as the amount of time available to provide services for sentenced inmates in these settings, substance abuse treatment programs appear to provide a viable strategy for reducing drug use and criminal recidivism. Incarceration is also seen as a good opportunity to capitalize on periods of crisis and self-reflection among inmates as well as an optimal time to provide treatment to promote major lifestyle changes (Lipton, 1995).

History and Scope of Correctional Treatment Services

Although the U.S. Congress first established correctional substance abuse treatment programs during the 1920s, there was not widespread development of prison-based programs until the 1980s. Earlier efforts lost momentum due to a report indicating that correctional treatment was ineffective (Martinson, 1974) and to elimination or reduction of Law Enforcement Assistance Administration (LEAA) block grants. Federal initiatives, such as Project Reform and Project Recovery, helped to establish therapeutic communities (TCs) in a number of state prison systems during the 1980s and 1990s and promoted sharing of information regarding program interventions and implementation strategies.

During the past several years, there has been renewed interest in correctional treatment due to prison overcrowding, coupled with rapid cycling of drug offenders through the criminal justice system (Lipton, 1995). Although the Center for Substance Abuse Treatment (CSAT) funded the Model Programs for Correctional Populations initiative from 1990 to 1997, the majority of new funding for correctional treatment programs has been provided through the U.S. Department of Justice's Residential Substance Abuse Treatment (RSAT) Formula Grant Program. This program provided $270 million from 1996 to 2000 for the development of treatment programs within state and local correctional and detention facilities (U.S. Department of Justice, 1997b). An additional $550 million was authorized for the 1996-2000 period through the Byrne Formula Grant Program, which provides ongoing block grants to states through the U.S. Department of Justice's Bureau of Justice Assistance to support drug prevention, treatment, and other crime prevention programs.

Substance abuse treatment services for offenders have not kept pace with the growing need for these services in jails and prisons (Belenko & Peugh, 1998; Lurigio, 2000; Peters & Matthews, 2002; Simpson, Knight, & Pevoto, 1996). In the most recent national survey of correctional and detention facilities, only 56% of state prisons and 33% of jails provided substance abuse treatment services (Substance Abuse and Mental Health Services Administration [SAMHSA], 2000). Private contractors provide approximately one third of these treatment services. Only 21% of treatment services in jails and 31% of those in state prisons are provided in specialized treatment units apart from the general inmate population. Many existing correctional treatment programs are not comprehensive in scope and rely on peer counseling approaches such as Alcoholics Anonymous (AA) and Narcotics Anonymous (NA). Similarly, the staff:inmate ratio is quite low for many correctional treatment programs, for example, averaging 1:25 in state prisons (SAMHSA, 2000).

There is also an emerging gap between the number of jail and prison inmates who need substance abuse treatment services and the scope of services available in prisons (CASA, 1998). Only 1% to 5% of state and federal prison budgets are currently spent on substance abuse treatment (CASA, 1998). As a result, only 10% to 12% of prison inmates receive any form of substance abuse treatment (Bureau of Justice Statistics, 1999; Simpson et al., 1996). The estimated number of inmates identified as needing but not receiving prison treatment grew from 477,000 in 1990 to 691,000 in 1996 (CASA, 1998). This finding is supported by federal survey results indicating that self-reported inmate involvement in treatment declined from 25% to 10% between 1991 and 1997 (Bureau of Justice Statistics, 1999).

Several surveys have examined the scope of substance abuse treatment programs in jails. These include the American Jail Association survey (Peters, May, & Kearns, 1992), which identified 28% of jails reporting substance abuse treatment services. Of jails reporting these services, only 18% involved paid staff and only 7% had a comprehensive level of services that included group therapy, drug education, transition planning, and referral to community treatment. Few jails provided transition services for inmates with substance abuse treatment needs. The size of treatment programs, the size of program budgets, and the hours of weekly treatment increased with the size of the jail.

A 1998 survey conducted by the Bureau of Justice Statistics (2000c) found that 43% of jails reported substance abuse treatment programs. There were again rather wide disparities between large and small jails in the proportions providing treatment services. Among the jails surveyed, 64% reported self-help programs (e.g., AA/NA), 30% provided drug education services, and only 12% provided a combination of treatment, self-help groups, and drug education programs. A striking finding of the survey was that only 4% of jail inmates received any type of treatment services during their current incarcerations and that less than 2% received counseling services.

Standards for Substance Abuse Treatment Services in Prisons and Jails

Legal Standards

Legal standards indicate that inmates have limited rights to substance abuse treatment in prisons and jails (Cohen, 1998). The courts have consistently rejected a general constitutional right to substance abuse rehabilitation or treatment in correctional facilities (*Marshall v. United States,* 1974). The main exception to this rule is if conditions in a correctional facility demonstrate "deliberate indifference" to inmates' serious medical needs. Serious medical needs are defined as those diagnosed by a physician as requiring treatment or those that are so obvious that a layperson would easily recognize the necessity for medical attention (*Pace v. Fauver,* 1979). For instance, in *Palmigiano v. Garrahy* (1977), the court found that conditions in a Rhode Island prison were below constitutional standards. In its findings, the court linked the prison's failure to identify inmates with substance dependence problems as a contributing factor to increased drug trafficking within the institution, increased suicide risk, and overall deterioration of the prison. As a result, the court ordered the prison to implement substance abuse treatment services that addressed the withdrawal needs of inmates and that met minimal professional organization and federal agency standards.

In contrast to the limited legal mandate for substance abuse treatment in jails and prisons, case law consistently recognizes inmates' rights to medical treatment for withdrawal and other serious medical problems associated with substance abuse (Cohen, 1998; *Pedraza v. Meyer,* 1990; *United States ex rel. Walker v. Fayette County, Pennsylvania,* 1979). For example, when a detainee or an inmate has been placed on methadone maintenance, the courts have required medical care for the associated withdrawal symptoms but have not required continuance on methadone maintenance (Cohen, 1998). Substance abuse screening in prisons and jails also appears to have a stronger legal basis than does substance abuse treatment (e.g., *Alberti v. Sheriff of Harris County, Texas,* 1975; *Palmigiano v. Garrahy,* 1977; Peters, 1993b; *Ruiz v. Estelle,* 1980), due partly to the need to identify and treat potentially life-threatening sequelae of addiction such as withdrawal.

During the past few years, new case law has emerged that defines AA and NA as religious-based treatment programs (*Griffin v. Coughlin,* 1996; *Kerr v. Farrey,* 1996). As a result, jails and prisons that require inmate participation in AA or NA groups as a condition of maintaining desirable security classification or institutional privileges have been found to violate the First Amendment, which prohibits coerced involvement in religious activities. Prison or jail authorities can address this issue by removing coercive requirements or by incorporating nonreligious treatment alternatives (Cohen, 1998).

Professional Standards

A range of professional standards have also been developed that have helped to shape the evolution of correctional substance abuse treatment services

(Cohen, 1998; Peters, 1993b; Peters & Steinberg, 2000). Among the most influential of these standards are those developed by the National Commission on Correctional Health Care (NCCHC) and by the American Correctional Association (ACA), which are similar to the previously discussed legal requirements but are generally more explicit and demanding.

The following substance abuse services are listed as "essential" by the NCCHC (1996, 1997) for both jails and prisons:

- Management of intoxication and withdrawal, including medical supervision, use of written policies and procedures, and provisions for transferring inmates experiencing severe overdose or withdrawal to a licensed acute care facility
- A comprehensive health assessment (including substance abuse history) conducted within 7 days after arrival in prison or within 14 days after arrival in jail
- A mental health evaluation conducted within 14 days of arrival in jail or prison, including an evaluation of substance abuse history (these services are listed as "essential" for prisons and as "important" for jails)

Standards for "Inmates With Alcohol or Other Drug Problems" have been developed by the NCCHC for both jails and prisons. The NCCHC lists the following correctional services as "important":

- Written policies and actual practice to identify, assess, and manage inmates with substance abuse problems
- Opportunities for counseling provided to all inmates with histories of substance abuse problems
- Accreditation of counselors who provide substance abuse treatment services
- Use of existing community resources, including referral to specified community resources on release

The ACA's (1990, 1991, 2000) standards for jail and prison substance abuse treatment are similar to those developed by the NCCHC but are more detailed and explicit regarding appropriate programmatic elements. Like the standards of the NCCHC, the ACA's standards call for mandatory screening of inmate substance abuse during the initial health examination. The ACA also recommends that substance abuse assessment be conducted through the use of a standardized battery that includes screening and sorting procedures, clinical assessment and reassessment, assessment for substance abuse program assignment that is appropriate to the needs of individual inmates, referral, and drug testing and monitoring. ACA standards indicate the use of routine diagnostic assessment, identification of problem areas, development of individualized treatment objectives and goals, and efforts to address counseling and drug education needs.

Other services recommended by the ACA include the use of a standardized "needs assessment" administered to investigate the inmate's substance abuse history, medical exams to determine medical needs and/or observational requirements, development of individualized treatment plans by a multidisciplinary treatment team, pre-release relapse prevention education including risk management, and development of an aftercare discharge plan with the inmate's involvement. The ACA also calls for use of staff who are trained in substance abuse treatment to design and supervise the program, a written treatment philosophy with goals and measurable objectives, selection and training of recovered alcoholics/addicts as employees or volunteers, inclusion of self-help groups as adjuncts to treatment, relapse prevention and management, and efforts to motivate addicts to receive treatment through incentives such as housing and clothing preference. ACA standards also endorse the use of a range of treatment services, culturally sensitive treatment approaches, and pre-release and transitional services, including coordination with community programs to ensure continuity of supervision and treatment.

Correctional Substance Abuse Treatment Programs

A wide range of correctional substance abuse treatment programs have been developed during the past 20 years. The most comprehensive of these are located in prisons, which typically offer greater resources, include a wider range of institutional settings, and involve longer periods of confinement than do jails. There are numerous treatment program descriptions available in the literature for both prisons (Early, 1996; Inciardi, 1993; Leukefeld & Tims, 1992; Peters & Steinberg, 2000; Wellisch, Prendergast, & Anglin, 1994; Wexler & Lipton, 1993) and jails (Peters, 1993a; Peters & Matthews, 2002; Tunis, Austin, Morris, Hardyman, & Bolyard, 1996). The following section highlights a few of the more comprehensive prison substance abuse treatment systems and is offered to provide examples of the scope and intensity of services that can be provided in these settings. The following descriptions are based on written program descriptions and reports, published articles, and phone interviews conducted with correctional treatment system administrators.

Federal Bureau of Prisons

The Federal Bureau of Prisons (BOP) has a long history of providing substance abuse treatment and has redesigned its programs during the past 15 years, following passage of the Anti-Drug Abuse Acts of 1986 and 1988. The Violent Crime Control and Law Enforcement Act of 1994 required BOP to provide treatment to all eligible inmates, including those with substance use disorders, who are willing to participate in treatment (BOP, 2001). The BOP drug treatment approach employs an evidence-based biopsychosocial treatment model to modify attitudes, values, and thinking patterns associated with substance abuse and criminal behavior. As described in the following section, substance abuse treatment services are provided at differing levels of intensity, with community transitional treatment services provided following release from custody.

Residential Drug Abuse Treatment. The most intensive level of substance abuse treatment offered by BOP is the Residential Drug Abuse Treatment Program. Currently, 47 BOP institutions operate Residential Drug Abuse Treatment Programs and provide services to more than 12,500 inmates per year (BOP, 2001). All inmates applying to the residential drug abuse program must have a *DSM-IV* (*Diagnostic and Statistical Manual of Mental Disorders,* fourth edition) diagnosis of substance dependence or abuse and must volunteer for treatment. These programs are termed *residential* because inmate participants are housed separately from the general prison population. Residential programs are 9 to 10 months in duration, and all provide a minimum of 500 hours of substance abuse treatment. Typically, Residential Drug Abuse Programs provide 3 to 4 daily hours of substance abuse treatment 5 days per week. Additional time in residential treatment programs is spent on skills training, education, prison industries, and/or other inmate programs. Staff in Residential Drug Abuse Treatment Programs consists of a doctoral-level psychologist who supervises the drug abuse treatment staff members, each of whom carries a caseload of no more than 24 inmates.

Residential treatment programs use a standard cognitive–behavioral treatment curriculum that targets substance abuse and criminal thoughts and behavior, with the goal of increasing personal responsibility for abstinence and recovery. Services include traditional individual and group therapy as well as teaching positive skill-building techniques such as rational emotive therapy (RET), rational behavior therapy (RBT), and interpersonal skills. The three phases of treatment are (a) *orientation,* which serves to engage inmates into treatment and where inmates learn the rules of the program and understand their commitment to treatment; (b) *intensive treatment,* where inmates are introduced to RET/RBT and develop interpersonal skills to get along with others and target criminal thinking errors; and (c) *relapse prevention,* where inmates develop a relapse prevention plan and a reminder of the skills they will require when they leave the unit. Two wraparound modules provide inmates with a wellness plan that focuses on their emotional, physical, and spiritual wellness as well as a personal change plan that identifies for the inmates their levels of motivation and readiness for change (Prochaska, DiClemente, & Norcross, 1992). In most cases, on completion of the program, inmates either are transferred back to the general prison population or are released to a BOP Community Corrections Center, where they continue to participate in drug abuse treatment.

Nonresidential Drug Abuse Treatment. Nonresidential treatment programs are available in every BOP institution and serve inmates who are unable to participate in residential programs due to minimal time remaining on their sentences or to other reasons. Inmates in nonresidential programs are housed in general population units. Treatment includes development of individualized assessment and treatment plans, individual counseling, and group therapy. Group activities include relapse prevention planning and examination of thinking errors associated with substance abuse and criminal behavior. Treatment intensity varies by institution, from a minimum of 1 hour per month to approximately 2 hours per week of services. Nonresidential substance abuse treatment programs are provided to more than 8,000 inmates per year (BOP, 2001). These programs also provide at least 1 year of mandatory aftercare for inmates who have completed Residential Drug Abuse Treatment Programs and who have returned to the general population. In addition, 12-step groups are available to support the treatment process.

Drug Abuse Education. The least intensive treatment service offered by BOP is a 30- to 40-hour drug abuse education course. Drug abuse education is available at every BOP institution and is provided to more than 15,000 inmates per year (BOP, 2001). Drug abuse education is required for inmates identified as needing treatment through an initial psychological assessment and a review of records. Inmates are also required to attend this course if substance use contributed to the commissions of their crimes, if the sentencing courts recommended treatment, or if community supervision was violated as a result of substance use. Drug abuse education provides inmates with the facts of their drug use or trafficking behaviors, including the biological costs to their selves as well as the costs to their families and communities. Drug abuse education also includes a self-assessment to help inmates determine how substance abuse has affected different areas of their lives. Inmates are also provided with an orientation to the range of substance abuse treatment programs offered by BOP, and those with substance use disorders are encouraged to volunteer for the Residential Drug Abuse Treatment Program.

Transitional Services. Any inmate in need of drug abuse treatment who is transferred to the community through BOP Community Corrections Centers or is selected for home confinement is eligible to participate in Transitional Drug Abuse Treatment. In addition, inmates who complete the institutional residential drug abuse program are required to participate in this program, where drug treatment is provided through community-based treatment providers that, whenever possible, follow the same treatment philosophy as does BOP. Transitional Drug Abuse Treatment coordinators and their staff monitor inmate treatment compliance and progress. Community-based Transitional Drug Abuse Treatment services are provided to more than 8,500 inmates per year (BOP, 2001).

Future Directions. A multisite National Institute on Drug Abuse (NIDA)-funded outcome study of BOP's Residential Drug Abuse Treatment Programs demonstrated significantly lower rates of relapse and recidivism for male treatment completers than for an untreated matched group at 3 years post-release (Pelissier et al., 2000), indicating that BOP's current treatment model is effective for that population. To further improve outcomes, the National Institute of Corrections and the Institute of Behavioral Research at Texas Christian University recently implemented a process evaluation of BOP Residential Drug Abuse Treatment Programs to identify treatment components that are effective and those that should be altered. Specific objectives of the project include assessment of inmate engagement and change during treatment, monitoring of inmate reactions to treatment that represent barriers to recovery, identification of program attributes and intervention strategies associated with treatment effectiveness, and dissemination of effective assessment systems and treatment models for correctional populations (Leukefeld, Tims, & Farabee, in press).

An emerging realization for BOP is that, to adequately maintain substance abuse treatment gains, more attention must be paid to associated inmate problems such as mental health and medical concerns, anger and violence problems, and learning disabilities. Program staff have begun to develop ancillary treatment strategies to address these problems within BOP institutions. For example, specialized services are being explored for those inmates with neurologically based cognitive deficits. Such services could include special interview scales to determine whether additional cognitive rehabilitation and/or pharmacological interventions may be needed to assist inmates in comprehending and mastering the goals of drug treatment. Ancillary services must also be considered when planning community reentry. In addition to drug abuse aftercare, many inmates require access to mental health, educational, vocational, employment, financial, medical, and religious services, as well as housing assistance and gang intervention programs, to ensure treatment success and enhance community safety (Leukefeld et al., in press).

Florida Department of Corrections

The Florida Department of Corrections (FDC) has a long history of supporting innovative prison-based substance abuse program services. During the early 1970s, with funding through the LEAA, FDC developed several of the first correctional TCs in the country in addition to specialized substance abuse programming for female inmates and youthful offenders (Chaiken, 1989; FDC, 1995). Financial shortfalls experienced by the state and elimination of LEAA funding eventually led to significant reductions in these services. Following the drug epidemic of the 1980s, the state renewed its commitment to prison-based substance abuse program services and established Comprehensive Substance Abuse Program Services. FDC redesigned its system in 2000 to provide substance abuse services for inmates assigned to major institutions, work camps, forestry camps, road prisons, and work release centers (FDC, 2000). All inmates are screened for substance abuse problems at reception centers. Inmates identified as needing substance abuse program services are placed on an electronic roster and prioritized for placement in appropriate substance abuse programs. FDC offers a range of substance abuse program services of varying levels of intensity in both institutional and community corrections settings.

An administrative rule change enacted in July 2000 made participation in substance abuse program services mandatory for selected FDC inmates. As of July 2001, Chapter 944 of the Florida statutes incorporated mandatory substance abuse program participation for inmates who meet selected criteria. These criteria include inmates who (a) are considered a "public safety risk" due to substance abuse such as those convicted of DWI manslaughter, (b) are identified as substance abusers through standardized self-report instruments, (c) have histories of unsuccessful completion of an FDC residential substance abuse program, (d) are recommended for substance abuse programming by sentencing authorities, (e) have multiple substance-related convictions, or (f) have participated in drug court. Budget shortfalls in 2001 resulted in elimination of all non-federally funded FDC substance abuse program staff positions, although plans have been made to replace these staff positions through contracts with private agencies.

Residential Therapeutic Communities. Long-term residential TC programs are currently located in 13 major FDC institutions. Inmates are housed in an existing institution dormitory that is separated from the general inmate population. Duration of the TC program ranges from 9 to 12 months, according to completion of individual program goals. This TC model uses a hierarchy in which residents strive to gain upward mobility within the TC (e.g., better jobs, greater privileges, higher status) through complying with rules, participating in all activities, and displaying motivation. This TC model is highly structured and emphasizes responsibility, accountability, discipline, consistency, and learning through consequences and also targets both substance abuse and criminal behavior.

Clinical staff provide or supervise TC activities 7 days per week for a minimum of 60 structured program hours per week. Activities include TC meetings, structured leisure and wellness activities, process and psychoeducational groups, individual counseling, support group activities, educational and vocational activities, and reentry planning. These services are designed to teach skills necessary for successful transition back to the community.

Co-occurring Disorders Residential Therapeutic Communities. FDC has developed two treatment programs for inmates who have co-occurring mental health and substance use disorders. These include an 80-bed unit for male inmates at the Zephyrhills Correctional Institution and a 40-bed unit for female inmates at the Broward Correctional Institution. The Residential Substance Abuse Treatment for State Prisoners Formula Grant Program, operated by the U.S. Department of Justice, funds both programs. These programs are long-term (8- to 12-month) residential TCs designed to address the specific needs of inmates with co-occurring substance abuse and mental health disorders and were among the first of their type developed in the country. Services include specialized psychoeducational skills development groups, medication groups, psychiatric consultation, group and individual counseling, and other services provided within a TC modified for this population.

Intensive Outpatient. Intensive outpatient programs are located at approximately 31 FDC correctional institutions and provide services to inmates housed with the general prison population. The length of stay is from 4 to 6 months, with flexibility provided to accommodate individualized service plan goals. Each inmate receives at least 12 hours of program activities per week for a minimum of 4 days per week.

Outpatient and Reentry/Transitional Services. Three service tracks are provided at 31 FDC facilities and are intended primarily for inmates who are not released from incarceration after completion of the intensive outpatient or residential programs.

The first track is a 4-month relapse prevention program, designed for inmates who have at least 2 months remaining on their sentences and who have completed an intensive outpatient or residential program. The second track is a nonintensive outpatient program of up to 4 months in duration for inmates who have at least 2 months remaining on their sentences and who have no opportunity to participate in intensive outpatient or residential programming before their release. The third track is a weekly transitional program, typically during the last 30 to 60 days of incarceration, for inmates who have completed either of the other two tracks. Inmates in this third track are scheduled for release or transfer to a work release center, work camp, road prison, or forestry camp.

Other Substance Abuse Program Services. Other services offered by FDC include weekly motivational and readiness classes for inmates who are awaiting admission to intensive outpatient or residential substance abuse programs. Weekly alumni groups are also provided for inmates who have completed an intensive outpatient or residential substance abuse program. Recovery and support groups, including AA/NA, are coordinated by substance abuse staff and are available for program participants as well as inmates residing in the general prison population. In addition to the institutionally based services already outlined, FDC offers a range of noncustody substance abuse services through its Community Corrections programs. These include drug testing and assessment, case management and monitoring provided by Treatment Alternative to Street Crime services, detoxification, and varying intensities and lengths of outpatient treatment as well as secure and nonsecure residential treatment. Residential programs include Probation and Restitution Centers and diversion programs.

Future Directions. FDC is planning to enhance reentry programs for inmates returning to the community. FDC is also enhancing coordination with drug courts and existing reentry programs to provide a continuum of correctional substance abuse program services. Plans are in place to expand the scope of youthful offender (ages 14 to 18 years) substance abuse programs and to increase cognitive-behavioral components of these programs. Due to recent state and federal legislation, correctional faith-based substance abuse programs are also expected to expand in the near future.

Oregon Department of Corrections

The Oregon Department of Corrections (ODC) has a long history of innovative substance abuse programming, including the Cornerstone Therapeutic Community that opened in 1976 and operated for 20 years. ODC's substance abuse service system focuses on four key principles of evidence-based practice: (a) assessment of inmates' needs at intake, (b) matching treatment to inmates' needs, (c) integrating mental health and substance abuse treatment when appropriate, and (d) providing well-developed transitional treatment and reentry services (G. Field, personal communication, July 12, 2001). A treatment matching system has been implemented in which inmates are assessed and receive services appropriate to their individual needs, replacing an older "menu" style approach in which inmates selected services. Along with this reorganization, ODC has developed a linked, computerized treatment system to track inmates and ensure that they receive the appropriate services despite transfers between institutions. Currently, about three quarters of inmates assessed as needing services receive them before leaving prison. ODC offers six levels of alcohol and drug services to inmates in state correctional institutions, as described in the following sections.

Residential Therapeutic Communities. ODC operates three residential TCs for inmates with well-established criminal behavior and severe substance abuse disorders. Inmates remain in these programs for the last 9 to 12 months of their incarceration. The Powder River Alcohol and Drug Program is a 50-bed program for male inmates and also provides specialized treatment for sex offenders with substance abuse disorders. The Turning Point program has a 50-bed unit for women and a 50-bed unit for men and is intended for inmates with severe substance use disorders and high levels of criminality combined with moderately severe co-occurring mental disorders. Each of these programs is isolated from the general inmate population. These intensive TC programs provide approximately 30 hours of services per week and features a 1:5 staff ratio. The programs focus on developing a positive treatment culture among the inmates and provide an emphasis on the following: (a) substance abuse education and treatment, (b) family-related problems, (c) independent living skills, (d) linkage to community aftercare services, and (e) modifying criminal thinking, behavior, and lifestyle.

Dual Diagnosis Programs. Although the Turning Point program includes dual diagnosis treatment for inmates with moderately severe co-occurring mental disorders, ODC also provides specialized dual diagnosis treatment for inmates who have more severe co-occurring mental disorders. The Bridgepoint program for men (60 beds) and the In Focus program for women (60 beds) are TCs modified for the unique needs of inmates with more severe co-occurring mental disorders (e.g., lower intensity and slower pace of treatment). These programs have a high staff ratio of 1:7.5, ensuring more individual attention to each inmate, but provide fewer hours of services per week (12 to 15 hours) than the previously described residential TCs. Similar to the more intensive TCs, inmates are admitted to these programs for approximately the last 9 to 12 months of their sentences. Dual diagnosis programs also include a major focus on aftercare placement in the community.

Pre-Release Day Treatment. ODC operates three Pre-Release Day Treatment Programs for male inmates with moderately severe substance disorders who are enrolled in services during the last 6 to 7 months of their sentences. These programs provide 12 to 15 hours per week of classes and counseling groups to prepare inmates for sober living after release to the community. Success Through Education and Planning (50 beds) admits inmates with minimum-security classification, while Steps to Freedom (70 beds) admits those with medium-security classification. Freedom and Recovery (50 beds) is a bilingual, bicultural Spanish/English program and admits primarily Spanish-speaking inmates. One of the most important parts of these programs is developing close working relationships with community corrections agencies. Community corrections and substance abuse treatment staff provide "in-reach" services to inmates in these ODC programs, either in person or by telephone. This allows aftercare services to begin prior to release so as to increase the likelihood of ongoing involvement in post-release services.

Other Substance Abuse Treatment Services. The Summit program is an intensive 6-month coed TC-oriented boot camp that focuses on development of self-discipline in a military setting. In addition to drill practice, physical work and exercise, education, skills training, and cognitive change classes, 6 hours per week of alcohol and drug services are provided.

Substance abuse counseling groups are also provided in most ODC institutions by contract counselors and consist of 2 hours per week of structured group counseling over a 6-month period. These services are designed for inmates who have moderate substance abuse problems, live in the general prison population, and have no more than 3 years remaining on their sentences. Culture- and gender-specific treatment groups are readily available, including groups in Spanish and intensive case management for pregnant or postpartum female inmates. Participation in 10-hour Alcohol and Drug Education Workshops is a prerequisite to involvement in group treatment. These workshops provide basic substance abuse education and address motivation issues through use of an inmate self-assessment workbook. ODC also maintains a large 12-step meeting program. Individuals from local self-help communities have small contracts to recruit, select, and train approximately 200 community volunteers to facilitate in-prison AA/NA meetings. Currently, 800 inmates participate in these groups each week, and the groups are held in all ODC institutions.

Future Directions. Plans are under way within the ODC substance abuse treatment system to expand reentry and transitional services as well as dual diagnosis services. In addition, the entire ODC system is implementing a sequencing model of services in which inmates will work on their education needs during the first few months of incarceration, on their employment skill needs during the middle phase of incarceration, and on substance abuse and other transition needs during the last year of incarceration. Among other advantages, this model is intended to increase the efficiency of providing pre-release treatment and transitional services. The approach is expected to assist in ODC's ongoing efforts to prioritize group treatment services for inmates who are serving the last 6 months of their sentences, reduce inmate movement between institutions during this time, and focus on addressing key transitional service needs.

Correctional Treatment Outcome Research

A recent meta-analysis (Pearson & Lipton, 1999) of the prison and jail substance abuse treatment outcome literature demonstrated support for the efficacy of treatment in prison-based TCs in reducing criminal recidivism but did not support the effectiveness of boot camps and "drug-focused group counseling" programs, which were often poorly defined and less structured in comparison with TCs. Compared with the relatively large body of literature describing outcomes in prison substance abuse treatment programs, far fewer research studies have focused on jail-based treatment programs. Jail studies generally are less methodologically rigorous than those conducted in prisons and are characterized by the use of limited outcome measures. One inherent difficulty in conducting treatment outcome research in jails is that these settings typically provide a shorter duration of incarceration than do prisons, limiting the types of residential treatment approaches that can be provided.

An increasing number of prison and jail treatment outcome studies have been conducted over the past 10 years, as summarized in two recent reviews (Pearson & Lipton, 1999; Peters & Matthews, 2002). These studies provide strong evidence for the effectiveness of prison TCs (Inciardi, Martin, Butzin, Hooper, & Harrison, 1997; Knight, Simpson, Chatham, & Camacho, 1997; Knight, Simpson, & Hiller, 1999; Martin, Butzin, Saum, & Inciardi, 1999; Pelissier et al., 2000; Wexler, DeLeon, Thomas, Kressel, & Peters, 1999; Wexler, Melnick, Lowe, & Peters, 1999) and consistent evidence for the effectiveness of jail substance abuse treatment in reducing recidivism and relapse and in extending the length of time that participants remain in the community without arrest (Hughey & Klemke, 1996; Peters, Kearns, Murrin, Dolente, & May, 1993; Santiago, Beauford, Campt, & Kim, 1996; Taxman & Spinner, 1996; Tucker, 1998; Tunis et al., 1996). Promising approaches such as cognitive-behavioral therapies, methadone maintenance, and 12-step programs will require additional research to establish their effectiveness in correctional settings (Pearson & Lipton, 1999).

Existing research indicates that involvement in post-release community services is likely to improve outcomes for both prison and jail treatment programs (Hiller, Knight, & Simpson, 1999; Inciardi et al., 1997; Knight et al., 1997; Martin et al., 1999; Wexler, Melnick, et al., 1999). In addition, treatment of relatively longer length seems to be more effective within both prisons (Siegal et al., 1999; Wexler, Falkin, & Lipton, 1990) and jails (Santiago et al., 1996; Swartz & Lurigio, 1999; Swartz, Lurigio, & Slomka, 1996; Tunis et al., 1996). The optimal duration of treatment appears to be somewhat shorter in jails (1.5 to 5 months [Santiago et al., 1996; Swartz et al., 1996]) than in prisons (9 to 12 months [Wexler et al., 1990]), although additional research is clearly needed in this area.

Economic benefits from reductions in criminal recidivism related to involvement in jail treatment have been estimated at $156,000 to $1.4 million per year per program (Center for Substance Abuse Research, 1992; Hughey & Klemke, 1996). Similarly, the cost-effectiveness of intensive prison TC services was demonstrated in a recent study (Griffith, Hiller, Knight, & Simpson, 1999). Based on this analysis, TC services were found to be cost-effective only when an aftercare component was included. These services were the most cost-effective with offenders at higher risk of criminal recidivism.

Additional research is needed to identify the characteristics of inmates who respond most favorably to various types of treatment approaches and interventions as well as to identify strategies for matching inmates to jail and prison treatment programs and to follow-up programs in the community. Few studies have examined the effectiveness of non-TC treatment programs in correctional settings. As mentioned previously, the optimal lengths and types of prison treatment and aftercare linkages need to be explored in greater detail. The effects on treatment outcomes of program components, such as educational/vocational services and parenting responsibility and skills classes, are not well known and should be examined. It would also be useful to understand the benefit of adding specialized interventions, such as dual diagnosis, domestic violence, and cognitive-behavioral strategies for modifying criminal behavior, to traditional correctional substance abuse treatments. Both prison and jail substance abuse treatment outcomes research would benefit from the use of random assignment and examination of varied types of treatment modalities and interventions.

Treatment Approaches for Special Populations

Co-occurring Mental Health and Substance Abuse Disorders

An estimated 3% to 11% of jail and prison inmates have co-occurring substance use and mental health disorders (Abram & Teplin, 1991; National GAINS Center, 1997; Peters & Hills, 1993; Teplin, 1990; Teplin, Abram, & McClelland, 1996). Individuals with co-occurring disorders in correctional settings have more pronounced problems related to employment, social relationships, and mental health functioning and also have poorer institutional adjustment and more difficulty with cognitive tasks associated with treatment than do inmates who do not have mental health disorders (Edens, Peters, & Hills, 1997). Many inmates with co-occurring disorders are nonviolent offenders who repeatedly cycle through the criminal justice system, due partly to difficulties in treating this population in existing community mental health and substance abuse treatment systems (National GAINS Center, 1998).

Inmates with co-occurring disorders are often undetected in jails and prisons, and as a result, they might not receive treatment services for either disorder. Nondetection of co-occurring disorders often leads to misdiagnosis, neglect of appropriate treatment interventions, and poor treatment outcomes (Drake, Alterman, & Rosenberg, 1993; Teague, Schwab, & Drake, 1990). In many cases, poor treatment outcomes are misattributed to staff or programmatic issues rather than to untreated mental health or substance use disorders.

Several recent treatment programs for co-occurring disorders have been developed in state prisons and in BOP (Edens et al., 1997). These programs provide an intensive and structured set of treatment activities that are sequenced in several phases, arranged with progressively less intensive services provided over time. These specialized prison dual diagnosis treatment programs often include an orientation phase that is focused on motivation and engagement in treatment. Additional phases include intensive treatment and a final phase focused on relapse prevention and transition services. In-prison programs typically use modified TC approaches and provide extended involvement in treatment, an emphasis on psychoeducational approaches, shorter duration of treatment sessions, smaller client caseloads, and abbreviated group treatment sessions with a greater focus on experiential exercises (Edens et al., 1997). These programs tend to be less confrontational and provide more individual support and counseling activities in comparison with most traditional substance abuse treatment programs (McLaughlin & Pepper, 1991; Sacks & Sacks, 1995).

A number of programs were recently funded by SAMHSA to provide a diversion from jail for inmates who have co-occurring disorders (National GAINS Center, 1998). Pre-booking diversion programs focus on training and coordination between law enforcement and community mental health and substance abuse treatment agencies to promote placement of individuals in treatment facilities instead of jail. Several of these programs include crisis response teams that respond to incidents reported by law enforcement. Post-booking diversion programs involve cooperative arrangements with courts, prosecutors, the defense bar, community supervision agencies, and community treatment agencies to identify and divert offenders who are eligible for community treatment facilities in lieu of prosecution or as a condition of receiving reduced sentences. These programs feature staff that are able to identify eligible cases and to negotiate with prosecutors and the defense bar to provide community disposition and involvement in treatment services as a condition of release from jail. Post-booking diversion programs contain several common elements, including (a) early identification of new arrestees who have co-occurring disorders, (b) completion of screening and needs assessment for both disorders, (c) counseling and discharge planning, (d) use of criminal justice liaisons who can work effectively with both treatment systems and the criminal justice system, and (e) referral and monitoring in the community (Conly, 1999).

Treatment of Female Inmates

The population of female inmates in jails and prisons has risen dramatically during the past decade, with drug offenders representing more than a third of the women incarcerated during this period (Bureau of Justice Statistics, 2000b). Substance-abusing females differ significantly from substance-abusing males with regard to their demographic and substance use backgrounds and treatment needs. In comparison with their male counterparts in community samples, female substance abusers have been found to be less educated, to be more frequently unemployed, to have more prior substance abuse treatment episodes, to report higher levels of daily cocaine use, to have higher rates of Axis I affective disorders such as anxiety and depression, and to report higher rates of sexual and physical abuse (Brady, Grice, Dustan, & Randall, 1993; Regier et al., 1990; Wechsberg, Craddock, & Hubbard, 1998). These same gender differences have been described among offender populations (Acoca, 1998; Henderson, 1998; Lockwood, McCorkel, & Inciardi, 1998; Messina & Prendergast, 2001; Peters, Strozier, Murrin, & Kearns, 1997; Peugh & Belenko, 1999). Significant differences have also been observed in the development and progression of alcohol and drug problems among male and female offenders, with women beginning substance abuse at an older age than men but exhibiting an accelerated progression from use to abuse (Haas & Peters, 2001). The pattern of substance abuse among female offenders is also more likely to be determined by their significant opposite-sex relationships (Henderson, 1998).

Despite the growing need for substance abuse services among female offenders in jails and prisons, there is a significant shortage of treatment capacity for this population (Henderson, 1998; Peugh & Belenko, 1999; Wellisch, Anglin, & Prendergast, 1993a). Fewer than 11% of female offenders are involved in substance abuse treatment (Wellisch, Anglin, & Prendergast, 1993b), although the need for treatment is significantly higher. Many of the treatment programs available to women are coed, where staff and male participants significantly outnumber female participants (Lockwood et al., 1998). Comprehensive services for female offenders are less likely to be offered in programs serving both men and women than in those serving female offenders exclusively (Wellisch et al., 1994). Programs designed for female offenders are relatively scarce, typically offer limited intensity and duration of services, do not assess the full range of psychosocial problems among substance-abusing female inmates, and do not have sufficient resources to treat the majority of allied problems such as sexual abuse and domestic violence (Wellisch et al., 1994).

A number of specialized correctional substance abuse treatment programs have recently been developed for female offenders (Peugh & Belenko, 1999; Wellisch et al., 1993b). Several of these successful programs feature common elements, including (a) support for specialized programming within the corrections system and in the community, (b) treatment options of differing intensity, (c) transition planning prior to release from prison, and (d) ongoing supervision following release to the community (Wellisch et al., 1993a). Because of the interrelated psychosocial problems reflected within this population, Peters et al. (1997) recommended adoption of a co-occurring disorders treatment model in developing substance abuse treatment services that adheres to the following principles:

- Assessment and treatment approaches should address the interactive nature of different psychosocial problems.
- An extended period of assessment should be provided reflecting the complexity of psychosocial problems among female offenders.
- When multiple psychosocial problems are present, each problem should be treated as equally important as the foci of clinical interventions.
- In general, co-occurring problems should be treated simultaneously rather than sequentially.
- The areas of more severe functional disturbance should determine the sequence of treatment services for female inmates. These areas should be addressed earlier in the course of treatment.
- Mental health services should be a core element of treatment, not isolated from other substance abuse services for women.
- All treatment and correctional staff should receive training regarding the nature of co-occurring problems and disorders.

Specialized correctional treatment programming for female inmates is generally provided apart from males and is geographically isolated from the general prison population (Peters & Steinberg, 2000). Females with professional training who can also serve as role models should staff correctional treatment programs. Programs often feature females as program directors and include staff who have knowledge and experience in working with persons with problems related to physical/sexual abuse, parenting issues, and sexually transmitted diseases. Roles of correctional officers and treatment staff should be easily distinguishable to reduce conflicts regarding security and treatment issues and to enhance confidentiality of clinical information shared with staff during treatment (Wellisch et al., 1993b).

Within residential treatment settings such as TCs, a number of treatment modifications for women have been developed (Lockwood et al., 1998; Stevens, Arbiter, & Glider, 1989). These include promotion of a supportive and safe therapeutic environment, with the use of coercion and punishment moderated by concerns about duplicating past "abuse" experiences. (See Chapter 7 for a more detailed discussion of trauma and abuse among female offenders.) Gender-specific groups, individual counseling, and other activities are used to enhance trust and bonding with treatment staff and other participants. Specialized gender-specific programs also focus on developing relationship skills and on coordinating with social welfare agencies. Several treatment programs for female offenders provide opportunities for participants to maintain contact with their children given that separation from children may greatly influence recovery goals and engagement in treatment (Wellisch et al., 1993b). Vocational training and job readiness services are also critically important given that female offenders are often released to the community as the primary financial providers for their children but frequently do not have adequate job skills or training.

Only a few studies have examined treatment effectiveness among female offenders and have focused primarily on TC programs. Findings from these studies have been inconclusive. Several studies (Messina & Prendergast, 2001; Wexler et al., 1990) have found reductions in recidivism and higher rates of employment and positive parole discharge associated with in-custody treatment involvement. However, a recent study within the BOP treatment programs (Rhodes et al., 2001) did not provide evidence for the long-term effectiveness of substance abuse treatment for female prisoners. Additional research is clearly needed in this area to determine specific treatment outcomes related to varying levels of treatment intensity within different modalities (e.g., TCs, day treatment programs).

Future Directions and Trends in Correctional Substance Abuse Treatment

Linking Correctional and Community Treatment

Transition services need to be developed to provide linkages between correctional treatment and the community (CSAT, 1998). Many offenders who are treated in jails and prisons tend to relapse and may return to crime if they do not receive ongoing post-release services. Research studies indicate that the positive effects of in-prison treatment may be undermined if offenders are not involved in follow-up treatment services (Inciardi et al., 1997). Transition services and post-release treatment services typically are not funded by jail or prison authorities, and this often leads to the discontinuation of offenders' treatment participation after they are released from custody.

Several jurisdictions have developed effective strategies for bridging the gap between institutional services and community treatment. One example of innovative post-release transition services is the Opportunity to Succeed (OPTS) program developed by CASA. OPTS program sites provide an intensive blend of supervision, substance abuse treatment, case management, and social services that begin on release from institutional treatment programs and continue for up to 2 years (CSAT, 1998; CASA, 1998). Other key ancillary services needed by substance-involved offenders in both institutional and community settings include mental health counseling and psychiatric consultation, literacy skills, and educational and vocational programs.

Treatment-based drug court programs offer an alternative model for linking jail treatment programs and community treatment services. Drug courts have been established throughout the country and represent a dramatic change in how the courts respond to drug-involved offenders (Cooper, 1997; CSAT, 1996; U.S. Department of Justice, 1997a, 1998). Drug courts provide extended involvement in treatment coupled with judicial and community supervision and offer an important opportunity to divert nonviolent property and minor drug offenders from jails and prisons. Although typically operated by the criminal courts, drug courts have formed productive partnerships with jails and prisons to develop coordinated reentry approaches (Huddleston, 1998; Tauber & Huddleston, 1999).

The first phase of treatment in some drug court programs is completed in jail, with the provision of intensive services that focus on a comprehensive psychosocial assessment, substance abuse education, and engagement in and orientation to treatment. In other drug court programs, an initial in-jail treatment component is optional, depending on the severity of drug treatment needs and the importance of a secure treatment setting. Jail treatment may also be used to house inmates who are awaiting placement in drug court treatment programs in the community. Another major function of jail treatment programs is to provide more intensive services on a short-term basis for drug court participants who relapse or commit other major infractions. Partnerships between jails and drug courts are characterized by flexibility in addressing the individual needs of drug court participants and continued monitoring of participants who are placed in custody and noncustody settings.

Several states have also implemented reentry drug courts for inmates who have received treatment in prisons (Tauber & Huddleston, 1999). Inmates who receive "split sentences" to prison and follow-up involvement in drug courts are placed under the supervision of sentencing judges when they are released from prison. Community drug court programs may conduct initial assessments of offenders' service needs, community safety, and institutional risk prior to sentencing. Key issues in developing reentry court arrangements with prisons include the need to establish statewide jurisdictional authority for the courts so that the courts are able to regain jurisdiction once offenders are released from prison. Post-release community supervision must also be fully supportive of the reentry drug court model and must be involved in drug court team meetings and decision making. Other key issues facing prison reentry drug court programs are resources to support ongoing treatment following release from prison and the need for specialized "tracks" (e.g., mental health, youthful offenders, female offenders) to supplement post-release drug court activities.

Effective transition and reentry services may include "inreach" and "outreach" models, in which community program staff and services are brought to the institution and in which institutional staff initiate contact with community services. Contractual arrangements have also been made in some areas to provide specialized transition services. Case managers, often assigned to provide transition services, are familiar with a wide range of community services and are in regular contact with treatment programs, residential placements, offenders' family or social supports in the community, and other social services. Effective transition models from correctional treatment settings typically include the following components (CSAT, 1998):

- Early pre-release planning
- Development of a community reentry and/or relapse prevention plan
- Linkages between treatment, health care, and other service systems identified in the plan
- Coordination of transition plans with community supervision (e.g., including treatment provisions of plans as conditions of supervision)
- Monitoring the offender's transition to ensure that linkages have been made to transition services and that the offender has successfully adapted to new housing, employment, and treatment services

Expanding Treatment Alternatives to Incarceration

In addition to expanding the scope of correctional treatment services, there is a pressing need to develop alternatives to incarceration within the community (American Bar Association, 1994). Within a particular jurisdiction, different programmatic elements of these services might include (a) screening and assessment of drug offenders in community supervision, pretrial services, and other court settings related to eligibility for and placement in treatment services; (b) court liaison; (c) case management services for "high-risk" cases (e.g., offenders with co-occurring mental health disorders); (d) a continuum of substance abuse treatment programs of graduated intensity (e.g., outpatient, halfway house, residential) that provide priority placement for offenders; (e) coordinated planning efforts among courts, community supervision, and treatment agencies; and (f) specialized training for law enforcement, courts, detention, community supervision, and treatment as well as cross-training involving multiple professional disciplines that are involved in management, supervision, and treatment of drug offenders.

The Crime Bill recently passed by Congress provides momentum to expand alternatives to incarceration programs through funding for the development and evaluation of drug courts. Drug courts provide a promising diversionary approach that has now been implemented in approximately 500 jurisdictions throughout the country (Cooper, 1997; U.S. Department of Justice, 1998) and have been found to provide a cost-effective means of managing nonviolent offenders. In many jurisdictions, day reporting centers, halfway houses, and/or intensive outpatient programs have also been used effectively with drug offenders who would otherwise be committed to prison (CSAT, 1995).

New Directions in Correctional Treatment Research

There has been a significant growth during the past 15 years in the number of controlled experimental studies examining substance abuse treatment outcomes in correctional populations. This is due largely to funding support provided by NIDA and sustained efforts by a small but dedicated group of researchers in the field. Additional funding for drug court and other diversion programs has been provided by the National Institute of Justice and by the Office of Justice Programs' Drug Courts Program Office. The growing body of correctional research points consistently to the general effectiveness of comprehensive substance abuse treatment services in jails and prisons, as measured by reductions in criminal recidivism, substance abuse, and overall costs to the taxpayer. Research also demonstrates the positive effects of treatment duration on outcomes, particularly when post-release services, such as community-based residential programs for offenders who have received in-prison treatment, are provided.

Research is now under way to examine the effectiveness of specialized correctional treatment interventions for offenders with co-occurring mental health disorders, for female offenders, and for youthful offenders. A cohort of NIDA-funded drug court studies examining the long-term outcomes and cost-effectiveness of these programs are near completion. Other current research projects funded by the federal government examine outcomes associated with offender reentry programs that involve employment/vocational training, substance abuse services, case management, and community supervision. Additional research is clearly needed to examine alternatives to traditional TC treatment models employed in jails and prisons. For example, intensive outpatient approaches, day treatment, and other types of structured alternatives to TCs have proved to be effective within community settings and should be examined more closely in jails and prisons. The duration of treatment needed in residential and other alternative programs has not been well defined and is worthy of additional research. Given the high dropout rates among intensive correctional treatment programs, research should also identify and test promising strategies for engaging and retaining offenders in these programs.

References

Abram, K. M., & Teplin, L. A. (1991). Co-occurring disorders among mentally ill jail detainees: Implications for public policy. *American Psychologist, 46,* 1036-1045.

Acoca, L. (1998). Defusing the time bomb: Understanding and meeting the growing health care needs of incarcerated women in America. *Crime & Delinquency, 44,* 49-69.

Alberti v. Sheriff of Harris County, Texas, 406 F. Supp. 649 (S.D. Tex. 1975).

American Bar Association. (1994). *New directions for national substance abuse policy* (Special Committee on the Drug Crisis). Washington, DC: Author.

American Correctional Association. (1990). *Standards for adult correctional institutions* (3rd ed.). Lanham, MD: Author.

American Correctional Association. (1991). *Standards for adult local detention facilities* (3rd ed.). Lanham, MD: Author.

American Correctional Association. (2000). *Standards supplement.* Lanham, MD: Author.

Ball, J. C. (1986). The hyper-criminal opiate addict. In B. D. Johnson & E. Wish (Eds.), *Crime rates among drug abusing offenders* (final report to the National Institute of Justice, pp. 81-104). New York: Narcotic and Drug Research Inc.

Belenko, S., & Peugh, J. (1998, Fall). Fighting crime by treating substance abuse. *Issues in Science and Technology,* pp. 53-60.

Brady, K., Grice, D. E., Dustan, L., & Randall, C. L. (1993). Gender differences in substance use disorders. *American Journal of Psychiatry, 150,* 1707-1711.

Bureau of Justice Statistics. (1995). *Prisoners in 1994* (NCJ-151654). Washington, DC: U.S. Department of Justice.

Bureau of Justice Statistics. (1999). *Substance abuse and treatment: State and federal prisoners, 1997.* Washington, DC: U.S. Department of Justice.

Bureau of Justice Statistics. (2000a). *Prison and jail inmates at midyear 1999.* Washington, DC: U.S. Department of Justice.

Bureau of Justice Statistics. (2000b). *Prisoners in 1999.* Washington, DC: U.S. Department of Justice.

Bureau of Justice Statistics. (2000c). *Special report: Drug use, testing, and treatment in jails.* Washington, DC: U.S. Department of Justice.

Center for Substance Abuse Research. (1992, Spring). Washington County explores a structure for success. *CESAR Reports,* pp. 1, 5.

Center for Substance Abuse Treatment. (1995). *Planning for alcohol and other drug abuse treatment for adults in the criminal justice system* (Treatment Improvement Protocol, Series 17). Rockville, MD: Author.

Center for Substance Abuse Treatment. (1996). *Treatment drug courts: Integrating substance abuse with legal case processing* (Treatment Improvement Protocol, Series 23). Rockville, MD: Author.

Center for Substance Abuse Treatment. (1998). *Continuity of offender treatment for substance use disorders from institution to community* (Treatment Improvement Protocol, Series 30). Rockville, MD: Author.

Chaiken, M. (1989). *In-prison programs for drug-involved offenders* (National Institute of Justice, Issues and Practices series). Washington, DC: U.S. Department of Justice.

Cohen, F. (1998). *The mentally disordered inmate and the law.* Kingston, NJ: Civic Research Institute.

Collins, J. J., Hubbard, R. L., & Rachal, J. V. (1985). Expensive drug use in illegal income: A test of explanatory hypotheses. *Criminology, 23,* 743-764.

Conly, C. (1999, March-April). Coordinating community services for mentally ill offenders: Maryland's Community Criminal Justice Treatment Program. *American Jails,* pp. 9-16, 99-114.

Cooper, C. S. (1997). *1997 drug court survey report: Executive summary.* Washington, DC: American University, School of Public Affairs, Justice Programs Office.

Ditton, P. M. (1999). *Mental health and treatment of inmates and probationers* (Bureau of Justice Statistics special report). Washington, DC: U.S. Department of Justice.

Drake, R. E., Alterman, A. I., & Rosenberg, S. R. (1993). Detection of substance use disorders in severely mentally ill patients. *Community Mental Health, 29,* 175-192.

Early, K. E. (1996). *Drug treatment behind bars: Prison-based strategies for change.* Westport, CT: Praeger.

Edens, J. F., Peters, R. H., & Hills, H. A. (1997). Treating prison inmates with co-occurring disorders: An integrative review of existing programs. *Behavioral Sciences and the Law, 15,* 439-457.

Federal Bureau of Prisons. (2001). *Substance abuse treatment programs in the Federal Bureau of Prisons: Report to Congress.* Washington, DC: Author.

Finkelstein, K. E. (2000, June 23). New York to offer addicts treatment instead of prison. *New York Times,* p. A1.

Florida Department of Corrections. (1995). *Substance Abuse Program Services Office: Comprehensive report, 1995.* Tallahassee: Author.

Florida Department of Corrections. (2000). *Community corrections and institutional substance abuse program services.* Tallahassee: Author.

Griffin v. Coughlin, 673 N.E.2d 98 (N.Y. 1996).

Griffith, J., Hiller, M., Knight, K., & Simpson, D. (1999). A cost-effectiveness analysis of in-prison therapeutic community treatment and risk classification. *The Prison Journal, 79,* 352-368.

Haas, A. L., & Peters, R. H. (2001). Development of substance abuse problems among drug-involved offenders: Evidence for the telescoping effect. *Journal of Substance Abuse, 12,* 241-253.

Henderson, D. J. (1998). Drug abuse and incarcerated women: A research review. *Journal of Substance Abuse Treatment, 15,* 579-587.

Hiller, M., Knight, K., & Simpson, D. (1999). Prison-based substance abuse treatment, residential aftercare, and recidivism. *Addiction, 94,* 833-842.

Huddleston, C. W. (1998). Drug courts and jail-based treatment. *Corrections Today, 60*(6), 98-101.

Hughey, R., & Klemke, L. W. (1996). Evaluation of a jail-based substance abuse treatment program. *Federal Probation, 60*(4), 40-44.

Inciardi, J. A. (1993). *Drug treatment and criminal justice.* Newbury Park, CA: Sage.

Inciardi, J., Martin, S., Butzin, C., Hooper, R., & Harrison, L. (1997). An effective model of prison-based treatment for drug-involved offenders. *Journal of Drug Issues, 27,* 261-278.

Justice Policy Institute. (2001). *Poor prescription: The costs of imprisoning drug offenders in the United States* [Online]. Available: www.cjcj.org/drug/pp.html

Kerr v. Farrey, 95 F.3d 472 (7th Cir. 1996).

Knight, K., Simpson, D., Chatham, L., & Camacho, L. (1997). An assessment of prison-based drug treatment: Texas's in-prison therapeutic community program. *Journal of Offender Rehabilitation, 24,* 75-100.

Knight, K., Simpson, D., & Hiller, M. L. (1999). Three-year reincarceration outcomes for in-prison therapeutic community treatment in Texas. *The Prison Journal, 79,* 337-351.

Leukefeld, C. G., & Tims, F. M. (1992). *Drug treatment in prisons and jails* (Research Monograph Series, Vol. 118). Rockville, MD: National Institute on Drug Abuse.

Leukefeld, C. G., Tims, F. M., & Farabee, D. (Eds.). (in press). *Clinical and policy responses to drug offenders.* New York: Springer.

Lipton, D. S. (1995). *The effectiveness of treatment for drug abusers under criminal justice supervision.* Washington, DC: National Institute of Justice.

Lockwood, D., McCorkel, J., & Inciardi, J. A. (1998). Developing comprehensive prison-based therapeutic community treatment for women. *Drugs & Society, 13,* 193-212.

Lurigio, A. J. (2000). Drug treatment availability and effectiveness: Studies of the general and criminal justice populations. *Criminal Justice and Behavior, 27,* 495-528.

Marshall v. United States, 414 U.S. 417 (1974).

Martin, S., Butzin, C., Saum, C., & Inciardi, J. (1999). Three-year outcomes of therapeutic community treatment for drug-involved offenders in Delaware: From prison to work release to aftercare. *The Prison Journal, 79,* 294-320.

Martinson, R. (1974). What works? Questions and answers about prison reform. *The Public Interest, 35,* 22-54.

McLaughlin, P., & Pepper, P. (1991). Modifying the therapeutic community for the mentally ill substance abuser. *New Directions for Mental Health Services, 50,* 85-93.

Messina, N. P., & Prendergast, M. L. (2001, July-August). Therapeutic community treatment for women in prison: Some success, but the jury is still out. *Offender Substance Abuse Report,* pp. 49-50, 54-56.

National Center on Addiction and Substance Abuse. (1998). *Behind bars: Substance abuse and America's prison population.* [Online]. Available: www.casacolumbia.org/pubs/jan98/summary.htm

National Center on Addiction and Substance Abuse. (2001). *Shoveling up: The impact of substance abuse on state budgets.* New York: Columbia University, National Center on Addiction and Substance Abuse.

National Commission on Correctional Health Care. (1996). *Standards for health services in jails.* Chicago: Author.

National Commission on Correctional Health Care. (1997). *Standards for health services in prisons.* Chicago: Author.

National GAINS Center. (1997). The prevalence of co-occurring mental and substance abuse disorders in the criminal justice system. *Just the Facts.* (Delmar, NY)

National GAINS Center. (1998). *Jail diversion: Knowledge development and application program.* Rockville, MD: Substance Abuse and Mental Health Services Administration.

National Institute of Justice. (2000). *1999 annual report on drug use among adult and juvenile arrestees* (Arrestee Drug Abuse Monitoring Program). Washington, DC: U.S. Department of Justice.

Office of National Drug Control Policy. (2000). *Drug-related crime* (Drug Policy Information Clearinghouse fact sheet). Washington, DC: U.S. Department of Justice.

Office of National Drug Control Policy. (2001). *Drug treatment in the criminal justice system* (Drug Policy Information Clearinghouse fact sheet). Washington, DC: U.S. Department of Justice.

Pace v. Fauver, 479 F. Supp. 456 (D. N.J. 1979).

Palmigiano v. Garrahy, 443 F. Supp. 956 (D.R.I. 1977).

Pearson, F. S., & Lipton, D. S. (1999). A meta-analytic review of the effectiveness of corrections-based treatments for drug abuse. *The Prison Journal, 79,* 384-410.

Pedraza v. Meyer, 919 F. 2d 317, 318-319 (5th Cir. 1990).

Pelissier, B., Rhodes, W., Saylor, W., Gaes, G., Camp, S. D., Vanyur, S. D., & Wallace, S. (2000). *TRIAD drug treatment evaluation project: Final report of three-year outcomes—Part 1.* Washington, DC: Federal Bureau of Prisons, Office of Research and Evaluation.

Peters, R. H. (1993a). Drug treatment in jails and detention settings. In J. Inciardi (Ed.), *Drug treatment and criminal justice* (pp. 44-80). Newbury Park, CA: Sage.

Peters, R. H. (1993b). Substance abuse services in jails and prisons. *Law and Psychology Review, 17,* 85-116.

Peters, R. H., Greenbaum, P. E., Edens, J. F., Carter, C. R., & Ortiz, M. M. (1998). Prevalence of DSM-IV substance abuse and dependence disorders among prison inmates. *American Journal of Drug and Alcohol Abuse, 24,* 573-587.

Peters, R. H., & Hills, H. A. (1993). Inmates with co-occurring substance abuse and mental health disorders. In H. J. Steadman & J. J. Cocozza (Eds.), *Providing services for offenders with mental illness and related disorders in prisons* (pp. 159-212). Washington, DC: National Coalition for the Mentally Ill in the Criminal Justice System.

Peters, R. H., Kearns, W. D., Murrin, M. R., Dolente, A. S., & May, R. L. (1993). Examining the effectiveness of in-jail substance abuse treatment. *Journal of Offender Rehabilitation, 19*(3/4), 1-39.

Peters, R. H., & Matthews, C. O. (2002). Jail treatment for drug abusers. In C. G. Leukefeld, F. M. Tims, & D. Farabee (Eds.), *Clinical and policy responses to drug offenders* (pp. 186-203). New York: Springer.

Peters, R. H., May, R. L., & Kearns, W. D. (1992). Drug treatment in jails: Results of a nationwide survey. *Journal of Criminal Justice, 20,* 283-297.

Peters, R. H., & Steinberg, M. L. (2000). Substance abuse treatment services in U.S. prisons. In D. Shewan & J. Davies (Eds.), *Drugs and prisons* (pp. 89-116). London: Harwood Academic.

Peters, R. H., Strozier, A. L., Murrin, M. R., & Kearns, W. D. (1997). Treatment of substance-abusing jail inmates: Examination of gender differences. *Journal of Substance Abuse Treatment, 14,* 339-349.

Peugh, J., & Belenko, S. (1999). Substance-involved women inmates: Challenges to providing effective treatment. *The Prison Journal, 79,* 23-44.

Prochaska, J. O., DiClemente, C. C., & Norcross, J. C. (1992). In search of how people change: Applications to addictive behaviors. *American Psychologist, 47,* 1102-1114.

Regier, D. A., Marmer, M. E., Rae, D. S., Locke, B. Z., Keith, S. J., Judd, L. L., & Goodwin, F. K. (1990). Comorbidity of mental disorders with alcohol and other drug abuse: Results from the Epidemiological Catchment Area (ECA) Study. *Journal of the American Medical Association, 264,* 2511-2518.

Rhodes, W., Pelissier, B., Gaes, G., Saylor, W., Camp, S., & Wallace, S. (2001). Alternative solutions to the problem of selection bias in an analysis of federal residential drug treatment programs. *Evaluation Review, 24,* 331-369.

Robins, L. N., & Regier, D. A. (1991). *Psychiatric disorders in America: The Epidemiologic Catchment Area Study.* New York: Free Press.

Ruiz v. Estelle, 503 F. Supp. 1265 (S.D. Tex. 1980).

Sacks, S., & Sacks, J. (1995). *Recent advances in theory, prevention, and research for dual disorder.* Paper presented at the Middle Eastern Institute on Drug Abuse, Jerusalem.

Santiago, L., Beauford, J., Campt, D., & Kim, S. (1996). *SISTER Project final evaluation report: Sisters in Sober Treatment Empowered in Recovery, San Francisco County Sheriff's Office Department.* San Francisco: University of California, San Francisco, Clearinghouse for Drug-Exposed Children.

Siegal, H., Wang, J., Carlson, R., Falck, R., Rahman, A., & Fine, R. (1999). Ohio's prison-based therapeutic community treatment programs for substance abusers: Preliminary analysis of re-arrest data. *Journal of Offender Rehabilitation, 28,* 33-48.

Simpson, D. D., Knight, K., & Pevoto, C. (1996). *Research summary: Focus on drug treatment in criminal justice settings.* Fort Worth: Texas Christian University, Institute of Behavioral Research.

Stevens, S., Arbiter, N., & Glider, P. (1989). Women residents: Expanding their role to increase treatment effectiveness in substance abuse programs. *International Journal of the Addictions, 24,* 425-434.

Substance Abuse and Mental Health Services Administration. (2000). *Substance abuse treatment in adult and juvenile correctional facilities: Findings From the Uniform Facility Data Set 1997 Survey of Correctional Facilities.* [Online]. Available: www.samhsa.gov/oas/ufds/correctionalfacilities97/correctionalfacilities97.pdf

Swartz, J. A., & Lurigio, A. J. (1999). Final thoughts on IMPACT: A federally funded, jail-based, drug-user-treatment program. *Substance Use & Misuse, 34,* 887-906.

Swartz, J. A., Lurigio, A. J., & Slomka, S. A. (1996). The impact of IMPACT: An assessment of the effectiveness of a jail-based treatment program. *Crime & Delinquency, 42,* 553-573.

Tauber, J., & Huddleston, C. W. (1999). *Reentry drug courts: Closing the gap* (Monograph Series No. 3). Alexandria, VA: National Drug Court Institute.

Taxman, F. S., & Spinner, D. L. (1996). *The Jail Addiction Services (JAS) Project in Montgomery County, Maryland: Overview of results from a 24-month follow-up study.* College Park: University of Maryland.

Teague, G. B., Schwab, B., & Drake, R. E. (1990). *Evaluating services for young adults with severe mental illness and substance use disorders.* Arlington, VA: National Association of State Mental Health Program Directors.

Teplin, L. A. (1990). The prevalence of severe mental disorder among male urban jail detainees. *American Journal of Public Health, 80,* 663-669.

Teplin, L. A., Abram, K. M., & McClelland, G. M. (1996). Prevalence of psychiatric disorders among incarcerated women: I. Pretrial jail detainees. *Archives of General Psychiatry, 53,* 505-512.

Tucker, T. C. (1998). *Outcome evaluation of the Detroit Target Cities Jail Based Substance Abuse Treatment Program.* Detroit, MI: Wayne County Department of Community Justice.

Tunis, S., Austin, J., Morris, M., Hardyman, P., & Bolyard, M. (1996). *Evaluation of drug treatment in local corrections.* Washington, DC: National Institute of Justice.

United States ex rel. Walker v. Fayette County, Pennsylvania, 599 F.2d 573, 575-576 (3d Cir. 1979).

U.S. Department of Justice. (1997a). *Defining drug courts: The key components.* Washington, DC: U.S. Department of Justice, Office of Justice Programs Office, Drug Courts Program Office.

U.S. Department of Justice. (1997b). *Grant programs for 1995* [Online]. Available: http://gopher.usdoj.gov/crime/ojp.brf.html

U.S. Department of Justice. (1997c). *Violent Crime Control and Law Enforcement Act of 1994* [Online]. Available: http://gopher.usdoj.gov/crime/crime.html

U.S. Department of Justice. (1998). *Looking at a decade of drug courts.* Washington, DC: U.S. Department of Justice, Office of Justice Programs, Drug Courts Program Office.

Wechsberg, W. M., Craddock, S. G., & Hubbard, R. L. (1998). How are women who enter substance abuse treatment different than men? A gender comparison from the Drug Abuse Treatment Outcome Study (DATOS). *Drugs & Society, 13,* 97-115.

Wellisch, J., Anglin, M. D., & Prendergast, M. L. (1993a). Numbers and characteristics of drug-using women in the criminal justice system: Implications for treatment. *Journal of Drug Issues, 23,* 7-30.

Wellisch, J., Anglin, M. D., & Prendergast, M. L. (1993b). Treatment strategies for drug-abusing women offenders. In J. Inciardi (Ed.), *Drug treatment and criminal justice* (pp. 5-29). Newbury Park, CA: Sage.

Wellisch, J., Prendergast, M. L., & Anglin, M. D. (1994, October). Drug-abusing women offenders: Results of a national survey. *Research in Brief,* pp. 1-19. Washington, DC: National Institute of Justice.

Wexler, H., DeLeon, G., Thomas, G., Kressel, D., & Peters, J. (1999). The Amity prison TC evaluation: Reincarceration outcomes. *Criminal Justice and Behavior, 26,* 147-167.

Wexler, H. K., Falkin, G. P., & Lipton, D. S. (1990). Outcome evaluation of a prison therapeutic community for substance abuse treatment. *Criminal Justice and Behavior, 17,* 71-92.

Wexler, H. K., & Lipton, D. S. (1993). From reform to recovery: Advances in prison drug treatment. In J. Inciardi (Ed.), *Drug treatment and criminal justice* (pp. 209-227). Newbury Park, CA: Sage.

Wexler, H., Melnick, G., Lowe, L., & Peters, J. (1999). Three-year reincarceration outcomes for Amity in-prison therapeutic community and aftercare in California. *The Prison Journal, 79,* 321-336.

CHAPTER 6

Managing and Treating Mentally Disordered Offenders in Jails and Prisons

Shelia M. B. Holton

C hapter 1 provided an excellent historical context for understanding the current situation of mentally ill persons in prison. It is clear that the mentally ill have been isolated from the rest of society throughout America's history. Although treatment and rehabilitation were once primary objectives in prison systems, these goals have been subordinated to other missions in corrections such as retribution, incapacitation, and deterrence. This shift in correctional thinking is pervasive throughout the prison systems in America. In their review of prison policy during the past quarter century, Haney and Zimbardo (1998) describe it as follows:

> Almost overnight the concept that had served as the intellectual cornerstone of corrections policy for nearly a century—rehabilitation—was publicly and politically discredited. The country moved abruptly in the mid-1970s from a society that justified putting people in` prison on the basis of the belief that

AUTHOR'S NOTE: Opinions expressed in this chapter are those of the author and do not necessarily represent the opinions of the Federal Bureau of Prisons or the U.S. Department of Justice.

their incarceration would somehow facilitate their reproductive reentry into the free world to one that used imprisonment merely to disable criminal offenders (incapacitation) or to keep them far away from the rest of society (containment). (p. 712)

Current Issues, Problems, and Trends

Mental Illness: Movement From Hospitals to Prisons and Jails

The result of this law-and-order trend has been an increase in the number of individuals incarcerated in America's prisons. Lengthier sentences, fewer diversion options, and changes in competency and responsibility standards have contributed to the growth in the number of incarcerated individuals with mental illnesses. As noted in Chapter 1, there is a higher percentage of mental illness found among incarcerated individuals than in the general population. Although the reported rates vary, the trend is well documented (James, Gregory, Jones, & Rundell, 1980; Jordan, Schlenger, Fairbank, & Caddell, 1996; Powell, Holt, & Fondacaro, 1997; Teplin, 1990).

While incarcerating mentally ill individuals has been a practice since this country began, the number of mentally ill individuals housed within American correctional systems began a sharp increase at approximately the same time as the passage of the Mental Retardation Facilities and Community Mental Health Centers Act of 1963. This event is commonly considered the beginning of the deinstitutionalization movement because of its emphasis on releasing the mentally ill from traditional psychiatric institutions. Although the goal of mainstreaming large numbers of the mentally ill back into society was certainly laudable, many legislatures failed to provide adequate funding for the community agencies charged with caring for mentally ill individuals (Lovell & Jemelka, 1998; Severson, 2000; Teplin, 1990). This led not only to inadequate mental health services but also to inadequate support services such as vocational training and housing assistance. As a result, the mentally ill are now at risk for all sorts of problems in daily living. For example, many of these individuals ended up homeless and/or unable to obtain or maintain employment. Poverty and accompanying mood instability set the stage for criminal behavior such as theft, vandalism, trespassing, and the use of drugs and alcohol. After passage of this act, many mentally ill individuals who would otherwise have been referred for mental health care after causing disturbances or engaging in criminal acts were instead remanded to the criminal justice system.

To complicate the picture, researchers began to discover that individuals with serious mental illness were more likely than nondisordered offenders to be arrested for the same crimes (Kilborn, 1999; Teplin, 1984). Kupers (1999) commented that our society has even passed laws that are biased against the mentally ill and set them up for run-ins with the law. For example, in many areas, homelessness and crimes related to it, such as sleeping in a public place and asking pedestrians for money, are now against the law (Bumiller, 1999; Herszenhorn, 1999). Researchers have documented that homelessness is much more prevalent among mentally ill individuals than among the general population (Lamb & Weinberger, 1998; Ditton, 1999).

In addition, the courts are more apt to lock up the mentally ill due to the public's beliefs about the potential for violence on the part of seriously mentally ill persons. In a recent study examining attitudes about mental illness, researchers noted an "unrealistically elevated fear of violence about persons with mental illness and a strong desire to maintain social distance from these individuals" (Link, Phelan, Bresnahan, Stueve, & Pescosolido, 1999, p. 1332).

Another current correctional trend that is having a great impact on the incarcerated mentally ill is that of their placement within "supermax" facilities. Supermax facilities are prisons or correctional units that are characterized by solitary housing, including eating and exercising alone. Inmates in these units are not allowed contact visits and are provided with limited, if any, educational, vocational, and treatment programs. At least 36 states and the federal prison system have adopted some form of supermax facility (Harrington, 1997). In many of these units, even opening the cell doors and listening to inmate complaints have become completely automated. Some researchers say that mentally ill inmates are overrepresented in these isolation units (Harrington, 1997; Jemelka, Trupin, & Chiles, 1989; Toch & Adams, 1986). Mentally ill offenders are placed in these facilities after being repeatedly found guilty of various prison infractions despite the fact that some of the infractions were inextricably linked to symptoms of their mental illness (e.g., being in an unauthorized area while reality testing was impaired, being insolent to staff while in a paranoid state) (Harrington, 1997; "Ohio Super-Max," 1998; "Security Housing," 1998). In addition, several researchers (Grassian, 1983; Haney & Lynch, 1997; Harrington, 1997) also argue that the extreme isolation and sensory deprivation created by extended periods in segregation or placement in one of these supermax facilities contribute more directly to mental illness. For example, Grassian (1983) observed that some isolated inmates could become floridly psychotic. Others could develop psychotic-like episodes in which they experience free-floating anxiety, hypersensitivity to external stimuli, perceptual distortions (including hallucinations), acute confusion, difficulty with concentration and memory, primitive aggressive fantasies, persecutory ideation, motor excitement, and outbursts of violence or self-mutilation. Although these cases are not the normative segregation experience, it is reasonable to assume that individuals with mental illness are more vulnerable to the detrimental effects of solitary confinement than are those not so afflicted. Many systems have recognized this possibility by carefully screening and diverting mentally ill offenders from supermax placements (Harrington, 1997; "Ohio Super-Max," 1998).

Obstacles to Effective Treatment in Prisons and Jails

Incarcerated individuals who experience mental illness face many of the same obstacles in obtaining treatment as do nonincarcerated mentally ill individuals, but there are other variables that are unique to correctional settings. Many of these can be classified into one of three categories: systemic variables, staff variables, or inmate variables. All of these must be considered when designing, choosing, and assessing effective treatment interventions for inmates with mental illness.

Systemic Variables. One of the most pervasive problems in providing quality mental health treatment is the lack of resources within the correctional environment. In particular, financial resources are allocated differently across correctional settings. In some systems, there are budgetary assignments that are specifically designated for mental health treatment, and these monies cannot be used for other activities or materials aside from mental health care. However, it is far more common that the money used in providing mental health care comes from the general fund of money assigned to the prison or jail. It has been this author's experience that money initially assigned for mental health services can be reallocated by the warden, sheriff, or other chief executive to another department or non-mental health project. This is especially true when monies are tight and security needs are not being adequately met with existing funds.

Privatization of correctional facilities and services has also had a tremendous influence on the resources allotted to mentally ill offenders. Although the data are mixed (U.S. General Accounting Office, 1996) regarding the cost-effectiveness of private prisons as opposed to public facilities, it makes economic sense that the introduction of privatization into corrections pressures state and federal agencies to reduce their budgets so as to compete. Given that rehabilitation is a secondary mission in corrections, it is reasonable to expect that mental health and other rehabilitative programs are particularly vulnerable to having their funding reallocated.

The climate of the institution can influence not only the types of treatment modalities used but also the types of inmates who receive mental health services (Toch, Adams, & Grant, 1989). Factors defining the climate of the institution include inmate space, privacy, and the predictability of daily activities. In an institutional climate that supports treatment, one typically observes some interdisciplinary collaboration (e.g., between medical and mental health staff, between mental health and custody staff) that contributes to improved quality of care for mentally ill inmates. The relationship between custody and mental health can be a tenuous one. It is not uncommon for a mentally ill inmate to receive a conduct or disciplinary report for inappropriate behavior, even though the behavior demonstrated was actually the product of a mental illness. For example, an inmate may be charged with disrupting an institutional count because he or she is talking, even though he or she is doing so in response to auditory hallucinations. If the institutional climate is supportive of treatment for the mentally ill, then the inmate may be referred to mental health services for an evaluation of his or her symptoms and the ability to cope with living in the general population. If the climate is punitive or invalidating of the experience of mental illness, then the inmate may simply be routed through the disciplinary process without any regard for the motivation of his or her behavior.

Inmate classification is another critical aspect of corrections that is often inconsistent with, or even counter to, the best clinical interests of an inmate. During classification, determinations are made regarding inmate placement within a particular institution or unit. These decisions are typically and primarily based on security or management aspects of behavior (e.g., assault history, escape risk) rather than on clinical need (Lovell, Allen, Johnson, & Jemelka, 2001). Furthermore, some treatment modalities may not be available at all security levels, so an inmate may be unable to receive optimal care due to his or her security rating. Although many correctional systems have some type of moderator or "override" variable that can be assigned to an inmate in need of a certain type of treatment, often the decision to apply such a variable is made by a nonclinical staff member, or factors such as the inmate's criminal or disciplinary history are given more weight than the inmate's need for treatment. For example, a clinician working with a mentally ill inmate at a maximum-security prison may deem that the inmate could benefit from a residential mental health program offered at a medium-security prison. However, given the fact that the inmate has become assaultive in the past (even if this was related to a psychotic episode), the inmate has worked his or her way up to a maximum-security facility due to past disciplinary problems. The clinician's recommendation may be in direct conflict with the recommendation of custody staff, that is, to retain the inmate at the higher security level due to past assaultive behavior. In this author's experience, this is further complicated by the fact that there is a great deal of variability across correctional systems in how much input mental health professionals have in the designation process.

Although this is the most common scenario, it is important to point out that there are some inmate classification systems that take mental health factors into account. In fact, they emphasize the importance of the environment-inmate match not only for the purpose of maximizing mental health treatment but also for the purpose of reducing management problems (Levinson, 1995). The most widely used psychological classification systems are personality or problem driven. For example, the Megargee Offender Classification System (Megargee, 1994) uses data generated by the second revision of the Minnesota Multiphasic Personality Inventory (MMPI-2), a well-researched personality instrument. From the normative data, Megargee established 10 categories of inmate types that include predictions of how inmates in the various categories are most likely to adjust to their incarceration. For example, "Charlie" inmates (as specified by certain elevations on the MMPI-2) are described as alienated, aggressive, and antisocial, with extensive histories of poor adjustment, criminal conduct, and mixed substance abuse (Megargee, 1994). Members of this group are most likely to come into contact with mental health professionals while in segregation. This is in contrast to "Baker" inmates, who are described as inadequate and anxious (Megargee, 1994). This group frequently seeks out mental health services. Drawbacks of this system are the need for every inmate to complete an MMPI-2, the instability of the categories over time, and low generalizability (Zager, 1988).

Another psychological classification system, Quay's (1984) Adult Internal Management System (AIMS), does not require an inmate's written or verbal response and is more behaviorally based. With the AIMS, data are obtained through two objective instruments completed by staff. The results yield scores on five dimensions that are typically categorized into one of three categories or types: Aggressive/Manipulators, Normal/Situationals, or Neurotic/Dependents, sometimes referred to as Heavies, Moderates, or Lights, respectively. One of the primary uses of the types is to separate the more predatory inmates (Heavies) from inmates most likely to be victimized (Lights).

Other psychological classification systems include the Jessness Inventory (Jessness, 1988), which attempts to classify inmates according to interpersonal maturity or social skills, and Hunt's (1971) Conceptual Level Matching Model (see also Reitsma-Street & Leschied, 1988), which classifies inmates based on cognitive ability in social domains. Although each of these systems uses a different method, they all have the common goals of identifying which inmates are in need of psychological services and which ones will most likely cause management problems or require special housing considerations. Unfortunately, although these systems may provide useful information, they are limited in their use due to cost-benefit issues. For example, most of these systems require a psychological assessment instrument, a thorough review of an inmate's history, a clinical interview, or some combination of these procedures. This is simply not feasible within prisons where a population may range from 400 to 1,500 inmates and the mental health staff is comprised of two to five professionals.

The actual physical design of the facility may impede optimal mental health treatment as well. For example, although many people think of inmates as being housed all alone in separate cells for a good majority of the day, very few inmates are typically so isolated. In fact, it is much more common to see inmates housed in two-, three- or four-person rooms. In lower security facilities, the housing may be even more public, with inmates housed in open areas or dormitory settings. Typically, in these environments, 50 to 200 inmates live in one area without any separating walls. It is easy to see how this environment could be threatening to a mentally ill inmate, particularly one suffering from paranoia. Several authors have discussed the difficulty that mentally ill individuals have in adjusting to traditional correctional settings (Lovell et al., 2001; Morgan, Edwards, & Faulkner, 1993; Toch, 1993) due to an inability to understand the rules, poor social skills, or conflicts with other inmates.

Staff Variables. Correctional staff attitudes toward mentally ill inmates have a critical impact on the outcome of treatment programs. Although most correctional staff, regardless of their positions, are trained in security issues, such as handling of keys, inmate accountability, and emergency situations, there is a great deal of variability in the training they receive regarding mental illness. Nearly all agencies provide training on suicide prevention because it is of greatest concern from the standpoint of both patient well-being and risk management. However, training in basic psychopathology and symptoms, conflict deescalation, and behavioral documentation is essential for effective interactions with mentally ill inmates. Without such training, staff are vulnerable to working on false assumptions about the mentally ill, with the most common assumption being that inmates with mental illness are more violent than other inmates in the general population. Some believe that inmates fake most mental illnesses in prison or that mentally ill inmates try to avoid responsibility for deliberate misbehavior because of their mental illness. Certainly, some mentally ill inmates are violent, some healthy inmates manufacture symptoms, and a few mentally ill inmates exaggerate their symptoms. However, to adopt these as normative viewpoints leads to cynicism with respect to programming. Assistance from officers and other frontline staff is vital in the identification, monitoring, and treatment of incarcerated offenders with mental illness.

Another important staff variable is cultural diversity. It has been documented that when the racial and ethnic makeup of the staff does not approximate that of the inmate population, there can be greater tension between the inmates and the staff within the prison or jail (Powell et al., 1997). In turn, this can contribute to an unwillingness on the part of the inmates to participate in treatment or to a lack of sensitivity among staff regarding the impact of an inmate's cultural background on the treatment process.

Inmate Variables. Variables specific to the inmate may serve as obstacles to the treatment process. One of the most common of these is mental health treatment history. An inmate's compliance pattern during incarceration can be quite different from that on the street, where there was less structure and supervision as well as easier access to alcohol and illegal drugs. Similarly, even when inmates do agree to comply with treatment, whether it is psychotherapy or a medication, they often show a slower or less complete response to medications than do individuals in the community given inmates' previous lifestyles (e.g., risk-taking behavior that may have led to head injuries, extreme and prolonged drug abuse, poor nutrition) (Lovell & Jemelka, 1998).

Inmates' vulnerability to and experience with peer pressure in the correctional environment also can affect treatment. For example, other inmates may advise inmates with mental illness against taking psychotropic medication. This may result from the other inmates' beliefs about the effects of psychotropic medications or from their own negative experiences with them. Peer pressure can take a different form. Stronger or more psychopathic inmates may pressure mentally ill inmates to surrender their psychotropic medications, particularly those that produce a more pleasurable subjective experience (e.g., benzodiazepines), so that the predators can sell the medications to other inmates or use the medications themselves.

A third inmate variable is related to the actual physiological side effects produced by some psychotropic interventions. For example, some inmates complain that they feel as though their reaction times are slowed when they are taking certain medications or certain doses of medications. This sense of decreased awareness or physical or mental slowness can contribute to the experience of feeling less safe or less able to defend oneself should the need arise, a concern that might be quite realistic. Another side effect, less openly talked about but even more aversive to some inmates, is the fact that some medications can decrease libido or interfere with a male inmate's ability to achieve an erection. Although some staff have argued with this author that this factor is irrelevant in correctional settings, the fact remains that the sex drive is an inherent aspect of human nature. Sexual self-gratification is one of the few pleasures that inmates have at their disposal, and many are reluctant to take medications that interfere with it.

In addition to psychotropic interventions, inmates may be reluctant to be seen going to visit a mental health professional. Although the dynamic may be similar to taking medications (i.e., inmates may fear that others view them as weak), there can also be a fear that other inmates will perceive the inmate seeking treatment as a staff informant or snitch. Among the inmate population, this can be a common belief about inmates who talk at length with staff.

Finally, the issue of institutionalization can affect an inmate's response to mental health treatment. Some inmates with lengthy mental health histories can become comfortable either with their status quo medications or with the familiarity of the correctional routine. Even when this routine may be a revolving door between segregation and the general population (Kupers, 1999), it can be difficult for an inmate to see that his or her quality of life could be improved beyond the expected pattern. Thus, although it is essential that mental health professionals be familiar with an inmate's mental health history and disciplinary pattern, there must also be a focus on the current presenting symptoms and a willingness to encourage the inmate to consider alternative interventions (Dvoskin & Steadman, 1989).

Serious Mental Health Disorders Found in Prisons and Jails: Management and Treatment Issues

Although incarceration is certainly a stressful experience for most inmates, those with mental illness find the experience especially challenging. In turn, these inmates create special challenges for the staff who work with them. The purpose of this section is to review some of the issues related to selected psychiatric disorders, that is, those more serious in terms of their impact on the individual and their potential for disrupting security in correctional settings.

Psychotic Disorders

This group of disorders includes schizophrenia, schizoaffective disorder, and delusional disorder and incorporates most of the disorders commonly associated with the term *seriously mentally ill*. Symptoms characteristic of these disorders include some type of reality impairment such as hallucinations (the false perception of [usually auditory] sensory stimuli, e.g., voices), bizarre beliefs, paranoid thoughts, disorganized behavior, poor personal hygiene, and weak interpersonal skills (American Psychiatric Association, 1994). Given the nature of these symptoms, it is easy to understand why this group has difficulty in adjusting to prisons and jails. Correctional environments are highly controlled and restrictive for purposes of both punishment and management. Individuals displaying psychotic symptoms can quickly become disruptive to the routine operation of the prison or jail. Management issues with this group include paranoid inmates making comments that are judged to be disrespectful or threatening to staff and disoriented inmates being in unauthorized areas. Psychotic inmates are also often viewed as management problems due to their not showering or eating as their mental status deteriorates. In this case, their symptomatic withdrawal may be mistaken for, and treated as, a form of defiance.

Furthermore, as a result of their unusual or disorganized behavior, some of these inmates run the risk of problems with other inmates, who may fear their labile behavior or view the illness as a weakness. Thus, in some cases, peers may isolate psychotic inmates, while in other instances, psychotic inmates may become easy targets for predatory behavior. All of these problems can lead to psychotic inmates receiving disciplinary sanctions for disruptive behavior or needing to be removed from the general population for their own safety. This leads to the larger question of where to place inmates with mental illness, especially those with psychotic disorders, whose mental status may vary considerably as a function of treatment compliance.

Mainstreaming Psychotic Inmates Into the General Population. Placement considerations for inmates with serious mental illness have generated considerable controversy. At one extreme, the British psychiatrist Tony Maden suggested in the preface to his book, *Women, Prisons, and Psychiatry,* that "women [and men] with a serious psychiatric disorder should not be in prison" (Maden, 1996, p. vii). At or near the other extreme are those who maintain that individuals with mental illness need to be housed in the general prison population, maintaining that inmates should not be excused from serving their prison sentences or from rule violations due to their mental illness. The latter viewpoint clearly reflects the goals of punishment and retribution. However, when mentally ill inmates are mainstreamed, they may end up being isolated in either of two ways.

Withdrawal. In the first scenario, a mentally ill inmate withdraws into the cell out of concern for "catching a charge," for predatory inmates, or for other reasons more directly related to his or her mental illness such as acute paranoia ("How Are Problems," 2000). In any event, self-isolation is certainly not likely to help the inmate to develop a coping repertoire or social skills or to maintain general self-care. Of greater concern to mental health professionals is the probability that when a seriously mentally ill inmate withdraws, it is likely that no one is adequately monitoring his or her psychological functioning. Thus, by the time the decompensation is noticed, the individual may be in an acute and severe depressive or psychotic episode, increasing the risk of harm to self or others.

The Segregation Cycle. A second scenario involves the mentally ill inmate who becomes a casualty of the segregation cycle. Often, an inmate is initially placed in segregation because of an overreaction to a stressor or an impulsive act of defiance. Once in segregation, the isolation can exacerbate the inmate's mental health difficulties ("Security Housing," 1998). The opportunities to participate in any type of treatment or programming, aside from taking psychotropic medication, are greatly reduced if not eliminated. Morgan et al. (1993) observed that psychotic inmates were sent to segregation more frequently and for longer periods of time than were other inmates, suggesting that the segregation from the general population did not provide much in the way of a behavioral deterrent. Some correctional systems, such as that in Wisconsin, have experimented with segregation step-down units, which are designed to allow an inmate to participate in meaningful treatment while in segregation status. However, it has been this author's experience that this practice remains uncommon and controversial, especially with custody staff, who often view the step-down process as "coddling" inmates. In any event, once in segregation, it can be difficult for a mentally ill individual to get out because his or her mental health has begun to deteriorate and people view him or her as insufficiently stable to return to the compound. Thus, the inmate may be placed in segregation for behaviors that were actually symptoms of a mental illness and then be unable to get out to receive more intensive services for that same illness. The point is not that seriously mentally ill inmates should never be accountable for their behavior but rather that their current mental status should be considered in assessing responsibility, as it is (or should be) during trials and in sentencing.

However, there seems to be a similar trend occurring within prisons that mirrors the criminal justice system in general. Specifically, some correctional systems are opting to remove the mental status defense from their disciplinary procedures. For example, the Wisconsin Department of Corrections recently removed the mental status defense, or the not guilty by reason of insanity defense, from its disciplinary process. When this author presented to correctional administrators the fact that many of the mentally ill inmates received charges for behavior that reflected or were a direct function of their mental illness, she was informed that the disciplinary committee would consider mental status as a mitigating factor when deciding the punishment. In this author's viewpoint, however, it appears that this remedy misses the point; mentally ill individuals will continue to accumulate a high number of incident reports for nonconforming behaviors that are related to mental illness if their mental status is not considered when determining whether they should be charged with misconduct. In the absence of an interruption to this cycle, this could result in an increase in security levels and placement at higher security facilities where treatment opportunities might not exist. A lack of mental health intervention will likely lead to sustained or increased problematic behaviors that result in another segregation placement. In this scenario, the process can continue until the decompensation reaches a point necessitating an inpatient hospitalization within the correctional system.

So far as treatment for inmates with psychotic symptoms is concerned, the most likely course is similar to the recommended treatment in the community. Psychotropic interventions are the primary mode of treatment, with additional emphasis on social skills training, cognitive-behavioral modification of delusional beliefs, and limited supportive individual therapy (Maxmen & Ward, 1995; Roth & Fonagy, 1996). However, although some inmates may participate in psychoeducational groups that stress medication compliance or social skills training, these services are quite limited in their availability in correctional settings. Furthermore, most members of this diagnostic class prefer to blend into the correctional framework without calling attention to themselves or their illness. Thus, aside from medication checks, they are often seen only once they have come to the attention of staff either due to deterioration in self-care or because they have been charged with disciplinary infractions. Given this pattern, it is essential that mental health professionals and correctional staff communicate and cooperate to monitor and intervene with these individuals. For example, educating officers about initiating routine social interactions rather than unknowingly reinforcing an inmate's withdrawal could set the foundation for interventions in the future.

This type of isolative behavior is of particular note given the relatively high risk of suicide in individuals with schizophrenia. In the U.S. general population, approximately 20% of individuals with schizophrenia attempt suicide, and 10% are successful in their efforts to take their lives (Maxmen & Ward, 1995). It should be noted that the risk is actually highest within the 3 months following an acute episode of psychosis, not during the actual episode. Thus, clinical monitoring and crisis intervention need to be increased, rather then scaled back, when symptoms begin to abate.

Mood Disorders

Although the primary issue with psychotic disorders is the inmate's interface with the reality of the correctional environment, the main concern for inmates with mood disorders is the inmate's ability to cope with strong affective states and accompanying symptoms. Mood disorders encompass both ends of the affective spectrum: depression and mania. At their most severe, affective disorders can involve psychosis. However, due to space limitations, this discussion addresses nonpsychotic affective states. Depression is characterized by the presence of a number of the following symptoms: intense sadness nearly every day, diminished interest in daily activities, weight loss or gain, insomnia or hypersomnia, fatigue, feelings of hopelessness, and suicidal ideation (American Psychiatric Association, 1994). Although it is normal to expect an inmate to be at a higher risk than the general population for experiencing feelings of loss and sadness, not all inmates develop clinical depression. However, when depression does become an issue, the behavioral concomitants cause management problems. For example, many depressed inmates may be unwilling to work or may be rendered incapable of working. They may sleep through educational or vocational programming or simply present as disinterested. Their irritability may make them less able to cope with the daily stresses of correctional life, making more frequent conflict with staff likely.

Although a manic presentation is less common than a depressed one, it too causes management difficulties. Symptoms of mania include grandiosity in self-esteem and self-perception, pressured speech, a decreased need for sleep, racing thoughts, distractibility, psychomotor agitation, and excessive involvement in risk-taking or self-destructive behaviors (American Psychiatric Association, 1994). Inmates are most likely to display manic behaviors after discontinuing or receiving changes in their mood-stabilizing medication. Manic episodes may be precipitated in those so genetically predisposed through discontinuation of medication, disruption of sleep patterns, use of stimulants, or the cyclical nature of the disorder. The clinical presentation of mania in the correctional environment may manifest itself through hypersexual behavior, a lower threshold of agitation, and a sense of grandiosity that may lead the manic inmate to perceive that he or she is above the rules of the institution, all of which increase the likelihood of conflict with staff.

Although depressive and manic episodes are distinct and generally opposing states within the mood disorder spectrum, many individuals with bipolar illnesses vacillate between the two ends of this mood continuum. However, even when individuals shift drastically, or cycle rapidly, between mania and depression, there is typically a maximum of four episodes per year (American Psychiatric Association, 1994). Thus, if a staff member is observing rapid mood shifts within minutes or hours, then it is more likely that the lability is due to a personality disorder, substance use, an organic condition associated with head trauma, malingering, or situational stressors.

The treatment of inmates with mood disorders is generally the same as the treatment offered to nonincarcerated individuals. Psychotropic interventions are used for both bipolar and major depressive disorders. Although psychoeducation about one's illness is certainly helpful, there is less support for the value of individual expressive psychotherapy for bipolar disorder (Roth & Fonagy, 1996). However, cognitive-behavioral and interpersonal modalities of psychotherapy are effective both independently (for lower intensity depression) and in tandem with psychotropic interventions (Roth & Fonagy, 1996).

Another essential element of care for individuals with mood disorders is suicide assessment and prevention. In the U.S. general population, approximately 15% of individuals with severe major depression or bipolar disorder commit suicide (Maxmen & Ward, 1995). This rate increases for incarcerated individuals with mood disorders (Hayes, 1995). During recent years, correctional standards and practices have addressed this fact more directly.

Borderline Personality Disorder

Probably as disruptive to the orderly operation of a correctional facility as a suicide watch, and perhaps more so, is the self-destructive behavior of an individual diagnosed with borderline personality disorder. This disorder is characterized by instability in self-esteem and interpersonal relationships, impulsivity, frantic efforts to avoid perceived abandonment, difficulty in controlling anger, feelings of emptiness, and recurrent suicidal or self-mutilating behavior (American Psychiatric Association, 1994). Although all of these symptoms can contribute to chaos in a correctional environment, it is the last one that often places the greatest strain on institutional resources.

When inmates harm themselves through suicidal gestures/attempts or self-mutilation, all institutional staff are likely to be involved. When inmates make repeated suicide attempts or threats, the potential for staff frustration or burnout is high. Although mental health treatment in corrections should always involve interdisciplinary cooperation, it is especially vital in treating and managing inmates with borderline tendencies. Proper treatment and management are often made more difficult due to time pressure and the need for intensive staff involvement, which are functions of the frequency, severity, and unpredictability of some of these inmates' self-injurious acts. The ethical and liability issues are complex and extend beyond mental health staff to other employees, who may be called on to prevent or treat potentially life-threatening self-injuries.

In addition to self-injury, other behaviors by this group of inmates may also contribute to management problems and stress. For example, individuals with borderline tendencies may place a strain on staff resources through their constant need to be reassured that they will not be abandoned. This may manifest itself by playing one staff member against another. Known as "staff splitting," this form of manipulation is often so ingrained among borderline patients that they might not be conscious of engaging in particular acts. It often results in conflicts among groups of staff members, particularly between mental health and custody employees. Other manifestations include creating crises to test staff responses (e.g., will staff adjust treatment interventions or punish the inmate through the disciplinary process?) and engaging in impulsive reckless behaviors (e.g., breaking simple institutional rules) to see whether staff will rescue them.

Of all the mental illnesses seen in corrections, it is borderline personality disorder that most requires the use of an integrated multidisciplinary treatment strategy to reduce an inmate's symptoms and suffering as well as to minimize the disruptive impact on the correctional environment. After accurately diagnosing the disorder, a clearly written treatment plan that articulates the responsibilities of all parties involved, including the inmate and specified staff, is the next necessary element for a successful treatment outcome with a borderline patient. It is essential that custody and mental health staff agree on what course of action should be taken in given circumstances and that all parties follow through with what they have agreed to do in the treatment plan.

Sometimes, despite the best efforts of staff, staff turnover rates, routine post/shift changes, the lack of clinical resources, and the inherently punitive aspects of correctional environments interfere with the treatment of borderline individuals. They may also move frequently from institution to institution as staff become burned out or frustrated with these inmates' continuous needs. These frequent moves contribute to borderline patients' fear of being abandoned, thus reinforcing the cycle and leading to a recurrence of symptoms. However, some institutions are trying some creative alternatives to transfers with this population, a point that is addressed later in the chapter.

Antisocial Personality Disorder and Psychopathy

Just as inmates with borderline personality disorder disrupt the orderly running of an institution due to the intensity of their self-destructive behaviors, inmates with antisocial personality disorder certainly do as much damage to the routine through their repeated inability to conform to social norms and their drive to challenge authority. By definition, the individual with antisocial personality disorder has repeatedly used deceit in one form or another for personal gain; tends to be impulsive, irritable, and aggressive; is reckless with regard for the well-being of others; lacks remorse; and consistently displays irresponsibility in financial or vocational obligations (American Psychiatric Association, 1994). Although antisocial personality disorder is technically very common in correctional populations, with about 75% of the incarcerated population meeting the criteria on average (Hare, 1996b), this is really not as informative as it might seem. Many inmates meet the diagnostic criteria through the nature of their crimes despite the fact that individuals who commit crimes often have very different attitudes and motivations for doing so (Hare, 1996a).

It is useful to distinguish one subset of individuals within this diagnostic class who are characterologically distinct. These are known as psychopaths. Although the terms *antisocial personality disorder* and *psychopath* are often used interchangeably, this is erroneous (Hare, 1996a). Psychopaths display the same behavioral markers found in individuals with antisocial personality disorder, but psychopaths also possess affective and interpersonal deficits such as glibness, superficial charm, impaired empathy, a high need for stimulation, proneness to boredom, pathological lying, and shallow affect (Hare, 1996a). Put simply, while most psychopaths (especially those in prison) also meet the criteria for antisocial personality disorder, only about one third of individuals with antisocial personality disorder also meet the criteria for psychopathy. Hare (1996a) estimated that 15% to 25% of the prison population meet the criteria for psychopathy. He also stated that this group of individuals is responsible for a disproportionate amount of crime and social distress in all societies.

Many career criminals or individuals with antisocial personality disorder seem to burn out or slow down once they reach middle age. These individuals may remain somewhat impulsive and more argumentative, but they are capable of responding to structured interventions geared at "resocialization" (Hare, 1996a). However, psychopathic individuals show less promise in terms of their response to clinical interventions. In one study with an intensive therapeutic community, the researchers found that treated psychopaths were actually more likely to commit crimes after release than were a nontreated group of psychopaths (Ogloff, Wong, & Greenwood, 1990). Rice, Harris, and Cormier (1992) found similar results. They observed that rates of violent recidivism for psychopathic inmates treated in a therapeutic community were higher than those for untreated psychopathic inmates. Since these studies first appeared, it has become clear that most insight-oriented programs, which typically involve empathy training, merely assist psychopaths in becoming more skilled in manipulation and exploitation of others (Hare, 1996a). Even from this brief discussion, it is easy to understand how psychopathic individuals can disrupt the orderly running of an institution and how the effects can be devastating if these individuals are placed in a treatment program with mentally ill or other vulnerable individuals (see Chapter 14 for a more detailed discussion of psychopaths and of research focusing on psychopaths in treatment).

Substance Abuse Disorders

Substance abuse and dependence disorders are another category of mental disorders that may cause significant disruption within the correctional environment. While issues of substance abuse were covered in more depth in Chapter 5, substance abusers or those dependent on substances typically display some of the following symptoms: exhibiting tolerance to and/or withdrawal from a given substance; repeatedly attempting to cut down on the use of the substance; using more than one initially expected to use; spending an excessive amount of time in obtaining, using, or recovering from substance use; neglecting social, occupational, or peer activities due to substance use; and continually using despite knowledge that one has a problem with a given substance (American Psychiatric Association, 1994).

While the majority of individuals diagnosed with substance abuse or dependence are clinically stable (although many mentally ill individuals are dually diagnosed with a substance abuse/dependence disorder and another mental disorder), it is not their mental status that makes them management problems in correctional environments. The problem lies in the fact that many of these individuals continue to seek, obtain, produce, and use illegal substances during their incarceration. These substances may be smuggled in or produced with a few ingredients found within the dining hall of any facility. Drug-seeking inmates may pressure inmates taking medications for legitimate conditions to give up or sell their medications. They also often use the resources of the medical or psychiatric departments in attempts to obtain medication for fabricated symptoms. In any event, although there is certainly an inherent risk in consuming a homemade product or someone else's medication, there is also another management problem associated with drug use in correctional settings: violence. Just as violence becomes intertwined with supply and demand and turf issues on the street, the same dynamics can play out in correctional settings.

Best Practices

Mental Health Treatment Units

In response to the problems that mainstreaming mentally disordered inmates can cause within a correctional facility, correctional systems have begun to develop different specialty units or programs designed to accommodate inmates with mental illness. However, often these programs or units are designed to be only temporary, usually for stabilization or transitioning purposes, rather then places where inmates reside instead of returning to the general population. For example, there are inpatient programs (these may be located in a specialty unit within a prison or in a separate secure facility), acute care units (often inmates are locked in their cells with nursing staff on the units), transitional care units (inmates moving from inpatient or acute care back to the general population), residential units (usually long-term residency after inmates are stabilized on medication in lieu of returning immediately to the general population), and outpatient services (Lovell et al., 2001; Lovell & Jemelka, 1998). Bed space in these units is usually quite limited because the supply is never near enough for the demand. In addition, most of these units are designed to serve inmates with psychotic disorders or major mood disorders, thereby often excluding individuals with personality disorders. Given the importance of coordination among the disciplines, the majority of the treatment units are staffed in a multidisciplinary manner, including staff such as psychologists, psychiatrists, nurses, social workers, correctional counselors, and correctional officers.

Within these units, the focus of treatment is usually biopsychosocial in nature. The biopsychosocial perspective involves integrating mind and body and employs pharmacological, psychotherapeutic, and milieu interventions, separately or in combination, as appropriate. Many correctional systems have adopted a community mental health model around which their services are designed (Dvoskin & Steadman, 1989). For example, correctional institutions may be divided into geographical clusters that operate similarly to a community mental health catchment area. Each cluster provides the full continuum of mental health care, ranging from inpatient to outpatient services. Other systems with fewer resources may ensure that they have one type of specialty unit at each level of security. For example, a state correctional system may provide a residential unit at its high-, medium-, and low-security facilities. Yet other systems may rely almost entirely on one or two facilities to provide the majority of mental health treatment (Lovell & Jemelka, 1998).

Although different correctional systems have different programs in place, it is clear that there is a generally greater need for step-down units, residential treatment, and partial hospitalization programs within prisons. Without continued development of such programs and units, the number of mentally ill inmates who deteriorate in segregation cells or who rotate through civil commitment procedures will remain high. In addition, the literature suggests that residential mental health programs within prisons are effective. One recent study found that inmates who had participated in residential care displayed more psychiatric stability, better disciplinary records, and improved self-management of symptoms on their return to the general population (Lovell et al., 2001). This confirmed past results suggesting that intermediate care facilities could reduce the rate of disciplinary infractions and segregation time for mentally ill inmates (Condelli, Dvoskin, & Holanchock, 1994). Another advantage of treatment units is that they can be staffed with correctional officers who are knowledgeable about and interested in the symptoms of mental illness. They may be more attuned to changes in inmate functioning, thereby allowing earlier and less intensive clinical interventions before symptoms become problematic.

Mobile Assessment Teams

As mentioned previously, inmates with mental illness can place a tremendous strain on already scarce resources within the correctional environment. This is especially true in cases where tension among the disciplines (e.g., custody and mental health) is already high due to philosophical differences regarding how best to manage particularly disruptive inmates such as those who engage in self-destructive behaviors. Staff may begin to lose their perspective on, or their willingness to work with, inmates who constantly rotate through the general population, specialized programs, and segregation. A creative solution for these situations is the use of a mobile assessment team (Lovell & Rhodes, 1997).

A mobile assessment team is a multidisciplinary group of individuals drawn from several different types of facilities or programs within a correctional system. The team is typically made up of medical and mental health staff, administrative staff, and frontline correctional staff. The institutional backgrounds of the team are also purposely heterogeneous, including members from medium-security facilities, residential or inpatient programs, and both women's and men's institutions. Once in place, the team serves as a consultation group for challenging cases throughout the correctional system, with the hope being that such a team will stimulate not only creative therapeutic and management options but also empathy and validation for staff working with the inmates. The team is usually composed of members drawn from a larger pool of staff also trained to work on the team. One study examined the effectiveness of mobile assessment teams in the state of Washington (Lovell & Rhodes, 1997). The researchers found that mobile assessment teams were successful in providing practical and useful consultation at a lower cost to the institutions and that these teams were successful in reducing tensions between institutions (e.g., regarding which institution had to take a difficult inmate). It has been the experience of this author, both as a team member and as a recipient of such a team consultation, that a fresh integrated perspective can often break the stalemate that has developed between an inmate and staff. This intervention can sometimes lead to meaningful and lasting behavior change, but even at a minimum, it can interrupt the problem behavior long enough to provide staff members with an opportunity to rest and regroup their resources and restore their perspective. Lovell and Rhodes (1997) further recommended better promotion and normalization of such programs as a way of lessening the resistance and defensiveness of staff who believe that they should be able to handle all cases without such consultation.

Suicide Prevention and Interventions

The National Commission on Correctional Health Care (NCCHC) and the American Correctional Association (ACA) both require that correctional facilities have suicide prevention plans in place (Hayes, 1995). NCCHC's (1992) standards address several specific characteristics of a suicide prevention plan, including identification, training, assessment, communication, notification, monitoring, housing, referral, intervention, and review. Although professional groups such as the ACA and the American Medical Association have called for improved standards in correctional health care for years, it was not until the landmark U.S. Supreme Court case of *Estelle v. Gamble* (1976) that the court found that *deliberate indifference* to the serious needs of prisoners constitutes unnecessary and wanton infliction of pain, as proscribed by the Eighth Amendment. The concept of deliberate indifference became the legal means by which arguments for suicide prevention programs gained credibility. Because the opposite of deliberate indifference, and thereby the best protection against suicide, is appropriate action, staff training is a key variable in any suicide prevention program. Important elements of strong suicide prevention programs include the education of all correctional staff about warning signs and predisposing factors relevant to suicide and about the importance of taking all suicidal threats seriously, accurate evaluations of suicidal potential by mental health providers, and the availability of a multilevel suicide prevention protocol (Hayes, 1995).

A typical intervention for suicidal ideation is through the use of the suicide watch. The institution psychologist, psychiatrist, or other mental health professional usually initiates a suicide watch, but in some systems, any staff member can initiate a suicide watch. The observation aspect of a suicide watch can take many forms. For example, should the suicidal inmate be observed via video monitor or face-to-face? Although a video monitor may allow for more regular observation or observation of a greater number of cases, important interpersonal data may be lost without face-to-face observation such as whether the inmate being watched makes eye contact or speaks with observers. In addition, some institutions use inmate companions instead of staff observers. When selecting inmates to serve as suicide observers or companions, staff should select inmates with enough prosocial qualities and self-assurance that they do not mind being viewed by other inmates as aligned with staff. In addition, when training suicide watch companions, it is important to stress the importance of sticking rigidly to the watch schedule and of seeking help without hesitation (M. Frenzel, personal communication, July 2001).

Related to the liability issues associated with inmate companions, there are ethical issues to be considered. Specifically, an inmate companion is not bound by any ethical code to maintain confidentiality surrounding the suicide watch. Although many of the institutions that use companions may issue a disciplinary report to a companion who breaks confidentiality (the companion signs an agreement to maintain confidentiality as part of the companion process), this may be of little consolation to the inmate whose confidentiality was breached (M. Frenzel, personal communication, July 2001). In addition, it may be difficult to prove that an inmate companion broke confidentiality. In addition to liability, there is the issue of safety. Although an inmate companion is very unlikely to have direct physical access to the inmate on the watch, there needs to be a system in place so that the inmate companion can immediately notify staff with access to the watch room if the suicidal inmate begins to engage in self-harm behaviors. Consequently, it is important that all of these issues be addressed in an organized policy or program before inmate suicide watch companions are used within correctional settings.

Another consideration when placing an inmate on suicide watch is the frequency of the observation. In general, there are two levels: intermittent and continuous (Hayes, 1995). An intermittent watch (most commonly observed in 15-minute intervals) is for those inmates who are not actively suicidal but who have expressed suicidal ideation. A continuous watch involves one-on-one observation of an inmate who is actively suicidal by threatening or engaging in self-injurious behaviors.

Telehealth

Although "telehealth" is an efficient means of delivery for all types of health services in a variety of settings, this technology is especially promising for treatment with inmates with serious mental illness because it can be difficult to get psychiatric and other highly credentialed providers into institutions. Practically speaking, telehealth is simply using technology such as telephones, fax machines, computers, and videoconferencing to provide a "virtual" appointment or consultation across distance (Nickelson, 1998; Stamm, 1998). Even in the prisons and jails where health resources are geographically readily available, the elimination of transporting an inmate out into the community is often more cost-effective (Brunicardi, 1998) and presents less risk to the community (Magaletta, Fagan, & Ax, 1998; Zincone, Doty, & Balch, 1997). In addition, from a mental health standpoint, the ability to use professionals from around the country, or even from around the world, increases the likelihood of providing services with professionals more familiar with inmates' ethnic backgrounds. This can be invaluable in bridging language and other cultural differences.

As more mental health services are delivered via telehealth technology, the literature regarding its clinical effectiveness continues to expand. In addition to the references for safety and financial benefits just cited, researchers are beginning to explore the more experiential aspects for inmate clients (Magaletta, Fagan, & Peyrot, 2000). Overall, it appears that many inmates' concerns are related to technological issues (e.g., audio quality) as opposed to the medium itself as a means for service delivery. (See Chapters 2 and 15 for additional discussions of telehealth in corrections.)

Future Trends in the Treatment of the Mentally Ill in Corrections

Although most jails and prisons have standard mental health screening and crisis intervention procedures in place, there is still much room for improvement regarding intervention. There is certainly a great need for more beds in residential or step-down units, but creating these units alone is not enough. A more critical issue regarding inmates with serious mental illness is that of staff perception and training. Without greater understanding of mental illness and its accompanying treatment, any program introduced into a correctional environment will be limited in its success. Mental health professionals working in corrections need to become and remain more actively involved in educating staff about mental illness and its relationship to the correctional environment. Furthermore, this training must include everyone, from the administration to the frontline staff. (See Chapter 12 for a more detailed discussion of this issue.) Although education and support are important, these factors alone will not carry a program during this era of managed care and cost containment. Mental health professionals will need to take a more active role in program outcome assessment to demonstrate the treatment value and institutional benefits derived from mental health programs and services.

In addition to staff education, there must be greater collaboration among the disciplines. It is all too easy to work within one's own niche in a prison, but from the preceding discussion of common disorders, it is clear that intervening with mental illness on one front alone can have only limited success. Thus, programs or units for the mentally ill should be staffed in a multidisciplinary fashion. Such a perspective strives to balance the inmates' mental and physical health needs with the institution's need for security so that all parties benefit. Interdisciplinary relationships may sometimes be strained due to the differing missions of the various departments, but without collaboration, any correctional treatment program is destined to fail. The importance and value of each discipline must be communicated from the top down within the correctional environment. Mobile assessment teams are fine examples of correctional systems' use and integration of valuable staff resources.

Although this chapter has focused on the needs of incarcerated individuals with mental illness, it is important to note that many of these offenders might have benefited from diversion programs rather than requiring incarceration, at least from a mental health standpoint. Although diversion programs are not new, only within the past few years has the effectiveness of such programs in facilitating access to mental health treatment been documented (Lamb, Shaner, Elliot, DeCuir, & Foltz, 1995; Lamb, Weinberger, & Reston-Parham, 1996). If these programs were better used, then there would likely be less strain on the treatment resources available to individuals who need incarceration.

References

American Psychiatric Association. (1994). *Diagnostic and statistical manual of mental disorders* (4th ed.). Washington, DC: Author.

Brunicardi, B. O. (1998). Financial analysis on savings from telemedicine on Ohio's prison system. *Telemedicine Journal, 4,* 49-54.

Bumiller, E. (1999, November 20). After attack, Giuliani plans crackdown on homeless. *The New York Times,* pp. A1, A11.

Condelli, W., Dvoskin, J., & Holanchock, H. (1994). Intermediate care programs for inmates with psychiatric disorders. *Bulletin of the American Academy of Psychiatry and Law, 22,* 63-70.

Ditton, P. (1999). *Mental health and treatment of inmates and probationers* (Bureau of Justice Statistics special report). Washington, DC: U.S. Department of Justice.

Dvoskin, J. A., & Steadman, H. J. (1989). Chronically mentally ill inmates: The wrong concept for the right services. *International Journal of Law and Psychiatry, 12,* 203-210.

Estelle v. Gamble, 429 U.S. 97 (1976).

Grassian, S. (1983). Psychopathological effects of solitary confinement. *American Journal of Psychiatry, 140,* 1450-1454.

Haney, C., & Lynch, M. (1997). Regulating prisons of the future: A psychological analysis of supermax and solitary confinement. *New York Review of Law and Social Change, 23,* 101-195.

Haney, C., & Zimbardo, P. (1998). The past and future of U.S. prison policy: Twenty five years after the Stanford prison experiment. *American Psychologist, 53,* 709-727.

Hare, R. D. (1996a). Psychopathy: A clinical construct whose time has come. *Criminal Justice and Behavior, 23,* 25-54.

Hare, R. D. (1996b). Psychopathy and antisocial personality disorder: A case of diagnostic confusion. *Psychiatric Times, 13*(2). [Online]. Available: www.mhsource.com/pt/960239.html

Harrington, S. P. M. (1997). Caging the crazy: Supermax? confinement under attack. *The Humanist, 57,* 14-20.

Hayes, L. M. (1995). *Prison suicide: An overview and guide to prevention.* Washington, DC: National Institute of Corrections.

Herszenhorn, D. M. (1999, December 6). 1,000 in park denounce Giuliani's policy of arresting homeless. *New York Times*, p. A31.

How are problems of mental illness being handled in the prison system? (2000, July). *Harvard Mental Health Letter*, p. 8.

Hunt, D. (1971). *Matching models in education: The coordination of teaching methods with student characteristics*. Toronto: Ontario Institute for Studies in Education.

James, F. J., Gregory, D., Jones, R. K., & Rundell, O. H. (1980). Psychiatric morbidity in prisons. *Hospital and Community Psychiatry, 31,* 674-677.

Jemelka, R., Trupin, E., & Chiles, J. (1989). The mentally ill in prisons: A review. *Hospital and Community Psychiatry, 40,* 481-491.

Jessness, C. (1988). Jessness Inventory Classification System. *Criminal Justice and Behavior, 15,* 78-91.

Jordan, B. K., Schlenger, W. E., Fairbank, J. A., & Caddell, J. M. (1996). Prevalence of psychiatric disorders among incarcerated women. *Archives of General Psychiatry, 53,* 513-519.

Kilborn, P. (1999, December 25). Gimme shelter: Same song, new tune. *New York Times*, p. D5.

Kupers, T. (1999). *Prison madness: The mental health crisis behind bars and what we must do about it*. San Francisco: Jossey-Bass.

Lamb, R. H., Shaner, R., Elliot, D. M., DeCuir, W. J., & Foltz, J. T. (1995). Outcome for psychiatric emergency patients seen by an outreach police-mental health team. *Psychiatric Services, 46,* 1267-1271.

Lamb, H. R., & Weinberger, L. E. (1998). Persons with severe mental illness in jails and prisons: A review. *Psychiatric Services, 49,* 483-492.

Lamb, H. R., Weinberger, L. E., & Reston-Parham, C. (1996). Court intervention to address the mental health needs of mentally ill offenders. *Psychiatric Services, 47,* 275-281.

Levinson, R. B. (1995). Evaluating the Federal Prison System's inmate classification model [comment]. *Criminal Justice and Behavior, 22,* 195-196.

Link, B. G., Phelan, J. C., Bresnahan, M., Stueve, A., & Pescosolido, B. A. (1999). Public conceptions of mental illness: Labels, causes, dangerousness, and social distance. *American Journal of Public Health, 89,* 1328-1333.

Lovell, D., Allen, D., Johnson, C., & Jemelka, R. (2001). Evaluating the effectiveness of residential treatment for prisoners with mental illnesses. *Criminal Justice and Behavior, 28,* 83-104.

Lovell, D., & Jemelka, R. (1998). Coping with mental illness in prisons. *Family and Community Health, 21,* 54-60.

Lovell, D., & Rhodes, L. A. (1997). Mobile consultation: Crossing correctional boundaries to cope with disturbed offenders. *Federal Probation, 61,* 40-45.

Maden, T. (1996). *Women, prisons, and psychiatry*. Oxford, UK: Butterworth-Heinemann.

Magaletta, P. R., Fagan, T. J., & Ax, R. K. (1998). Advancing psychology services through telehealth in the Federal Bureau of Prisons. *Professional Psychology: Research and Practice, 29,* 543-548.

Magaletta, P. R., Fagan, T. J., & Peyrot, M. F. (2000). Telehealth in the Federal Bureau of Prisons: Inmates' perceptions. *Professional Psychology: Research and Practice, 31,* 497-502.

Maxmen, J. S., & Ward, N. G. (1995). *Essential psychopathology and its treatment* (2nd ed.). New York: Norton.

Megargee, E. (1994). Using the Megargee MMPI-based classification system with MMPI-2's of male prison inmates. *Psychological Assessment, 6,* 337-344.

Morgan, D., Edwards, A., & Faulkner, L. (1993). The adaptation to prison by individuals with schizophrenia. *Bulletin of the American Academy of Psychiatry and the Law, 21,* 427-433.

National Commission on Correctional Health Care. (1992). *Standards for health services in prisons* (2nd ed.). Chicago: Author.

Nickelson, D. W. (1998). Telehealth and the evolving health care system: Strategic opportunities for professional psychology. *Professional Psychology: Research and Practice, 29,* 527-535.

Ogloff, J., Wong, S., & Greenwood, A. (1990). Treating criminal psychopaths in a therapeutic community program. *Behavioral Sciences and the Law, 8,* 81-90.

Ohio super-max diverts inmates with serious mental illness. (1998, September 28). *Mental Health Weekly,* pp. 1-3.

Powell, T. A., Holt, J. C., & Fondacaro, K. M. (1997). The prevalence of mental illness among inmates in a rural state. *Law and Human Behavior, 21,* 427-438.

Quay, H. (1984). *Managing adult inmates: Classification for housing and program assignments.* College Park, MD: American Correctional Association.

Reitsma-Street, M., & Leschied, A. (1988). The conceptual matching model in corrections. *Criminal Justice and Behavior, 15,* 199-212.

Rice, M. E., Harris, G. T., & Cormier, C. A. (1992). An evaluation of a maximum security therapeutic community for psychopaths and other mentally disordered offenders. *Law and Human Behavior, 16,* 399-412.

Roth, A., & Fonagy, P. (1996). *What works for whom? A critical review of psychotherapy research.* New York: Guilford.

Security housing for inmates generates growing mental health problem. (1998, August 24). *Mental Health Weekly,* pp. 3-4.

Severson, M. E. (2000). The impact of a state hospital closure on local jails: The Kansas experience. *Community Mental Health Journal, 36,* 571-587.

Stamm, B. H. (1998). Clinical applications of telehealth in mental health care. *Professional Psychology: Research and Practice, 29,* 536-542.

Teplin, L. A. (1984). Criminalizing mental disorder: The comparison arrest rate of the mentally ill. *American Psychologist, 39,* 794-803.

Teplin, L. A. (1990). Detecting disorder: The treatment of mental illness among jail detainees. *Journal of Consulting and Clinical Psychology, 58,* 233-236.

Toch, H. (1993). Mainstreaming disturbed offenders in the prison. *Journal of Psychiatry and the Law, 21,* 503-514.

Toch, H., & Adams, K. (1986). Pathology and disruptiveness among prison inmates. *Journal of Research in Crime and Delinquency, 23,* 7-21.

Toch, H., Adams, K., & Grant, J. D. (1989). *Coping: Maladaptation in prisons.* New Brunswick, NJ: Transaction Books.

U.S. General Accounting Office. (1996). *Private and public prisons: Studies comparing operational costs and/or quality of service* (GAO Publication No. B-261797). Washington, DC: Author.

Zager, L. (1988). MMPI-based criminal classification system: A review, current status, and future directions. *Criminal Justice and Behavior, 15,* 39-57.

Zincone, L. H., Jr., Doty, E., & Balch, D. C. (1997). Financial analysis of telemedicine in a prison system. *Telemedicine Journal, 3,* 247-253.

CHAPTER 7

Managing and Treating Female Offenders

G. Lane Wagaman

The management and treatment of female offenders has followed a historical course similar to that of male offenders (see Chapter 1) and in many ways has reflected contemporary attitudes and beliefs about females and their roles in society. Very early beliefs about the causation of criminality, both male and female, involved supernatural explanations, including possession by evil spirits. Subsequent theories focused more on biological or innate characteristics. Lombroso (1911/1968), for example, asserted that inborn tendencies resulted in engagement in criminal behavior and in differences between male and female offenders. Societal responses to such beliefs were reflected in females being incarcerated in the same or similar asylums, almshouses, or custodial institutions as men for purposes of isolation and punishment.

During the late 1800s, societal attitudes concerning offenders began to change once again. Early social reformers and emerging psychological and sociocultural explanations of human behavior heavily influenced this shift in societal thinking. Theorists argued that the behaviors of offenders, especially those of females, were more significantly influenced by social and psychological forces over which individuals had little voluntary control and that efforts should be made to rehabilitate rather than punish.

Because of the pervasive societal belief of the time that men were better suited for productive work outside the home and women were better intended for child care and other household activities and for working cooperatively with other women, the establishment of women's reformatories and rehabilitation programs became widespread. The emphasis on domesticity was reflected in the architectural and program design of the new female institutions that included small cottage-style accommodations with individual rooms and small family-style dining facilities in each cottage. Training programs emphasized household, clerical, and farm skills and the reinforcement of appropriate feminine decorum.

This rehabilitative emphasis with concurrent focus on differential treatment of male and female offenders continued until the 1970s, when societal changes once again created a resurgence of focus and insistence on equality of treatment for incarcerated men and women. This renewed interest in equal correctional treatment was in part a result of the women's movement of the late 1960s and early 1970s that rekindled interest in women's issues and societal conditions, including conditions of confinement for women. Women's and equality advocates began to demand correctional education and training programs beyond traditional domestic, clerical, and farm activities. They demanded programs that would better enable women released from incarceration to enter, compete, and be successful in the modern workplace and be able to provide adequate financial support for themselves and their families.

The renewal of arguments for equal treatment was furthered by litigation over the issue of differential correctional care and programs. *Glover v. Johnson* (1979), a case based on Fourteenth Amendment arguments, was the first of several court actions that resulted in improved conditions of confinement as well as expanded and enhanced programs for female offenders. Other research and litigation have continued to challenge sentencing laws and biases that make women liable for longer prison terms than men with similar offenses and criminal records and that address inequities in availability of correctional programs and services for female offenders (Bershad, 1985; Raeder, 1993; Wikler, 1990).

Current approaches to correctional management and treatment of female offenders have attempted to combine the best elements of both equal and differential treatment approaches to form the basis for a unique, more efficacious, and more productive intervention model. This newly evolving way of developing and implementing systems and programs for female offenders has begun to take several factors into account. These factors include an attempt to identify and understand the demographic and psychosocial descriptors of female offenders in general, a careful assessment of specific offender needs and responses to incarceration, consideration of the social and vocational environments from which offenders came, and a thorough review of the persons and circumstances to which offenders will return after incarceration. This chapter discusses these and other factors in some detail.

Characteristics of Female Offenders

Demographic Data

Although the number of incarcerated women in the United States remains considerably less than that of incarcerated men, the rate at which women are arrested, convicted, and sentenced to incarceration has increased steadily over the past two decades. Women accounted for only 4.1% of prison populations in 1980. By 1998, that figure had risen to 6.5% (Camp & Camp, 1998; Greenfeld & Snell, 1999). The mean annual increase in female incarceration through the 1980s was 8.3% (Curry, 2001). This trend is likely to continue in view of a 24% increase in female arrests through the mid-1990s compared with a 13% increase in arrests of men during the same period (Curry, 2001). By 1998, more than 950,000 women, or about 1 in every 109 women in the United States, were under some form of correctional supervision. Jails, state prisons, and federal prisons held approximately 15% of that number. Accompanying this steady rise in female imprisonment has been a concomitant interest in the identification of, and attention to, the characteristics, historical experience, and unique needs of female offenders.

Considerable demographic data have been collected on women involved in the criminal justice system. Following is a sampling of the general demographic data that have been found:

- Women incarcerated in state and federal prisons tend to be older than those housed in jails or under probation supervision.
- Minority women (African American, Hispanic, and other races) constitute more than two thirds of the incarcerated female population. Approximately 62% of women on probation and 33% of women in prison are white.
- Adult incarcerated females are significantly more likely than nonincarcerated females to have never married or to be separated or divorced (Glick & Neto, 1976; Greenfeld & Snell, 1999). Less than 10% of female offenders were residing with a spouse at the times of their incarceration (Glick & Neto, 1976).
- Approximately 65% of incarcerated women are parents of minor children, with an average of more than two children per woman (Greenfeld & Snell, 1999), and 72% of women on probation are the mothers of children under 18 years of age. Fully 1.3 million children have mothers who are under correctional supervision, and more than one quarter million of those are children with currently incarcerated mothers. Approximately 2% of the country's 72 million minor children had at least one imprisoned parent in 1999 (Curry, 2001), and 22% of these children were under 5 years of age (Temin, 2001). The number of children with incarcerated parents increased 60% during the 1990s.
- State and federal female offenders who have completed high school comprise 56% and 73% of the female offender populations, respectively, while 55% of jail inmates and 60% of probationers are high school graduates. Approximately one third of female inmates have attended some college. In general, female inmates have histories characterized by more limited financial and economic resources that do male inmates.
- Many incarcerated women have received little or no medical, dental, or mental health care prior to their incarceration. Although 5% to 8% of women were pregnant at the times of their incarceration (Curry, 2001; Kauffman, 2001), only a small percentage of those women received prenatal health care before their imprisonment. An estimated 3.5% to 4.0% of

incarcerated women are HIV-seropositive, while only about 2.0% of imprisoned males are similarly infected (Greenfeld & Snell, 1999). The number of HIV-infected women in prison has risen steadily since 1980 (DeGroot, 2001). Female offenders also have elevated rates of diagnosis of other sexually transmitted diseases, tuberculosis, and hepatitis (Curry, 2001; DeGroot, 2001; Greenfeld & Snell, 1999; Lawson & Fawkes, 1992), which is not surprising in view of their higher rates of involvement in drug abuse, prostitution, and physical and/or sexual abuse.

■ There is a higher incidence of psychiatric disorders among female offenders, a rate nearly twice that found among male offenders (Curry, 2001). An estimated 14% to 22% of incarcerated women report having experienced some form of psychiatric impairment (Curry, 2001; Temin, 2001; Warren, 1979).

■ Approximately one half of imprisoned women had engaged in alcohol and/or other drug use around the times of the offenses for which they were incarcerated (Greenfeld & Snell, 1999). Fully 75% to 86% of female jail inmates also reported being substance abusers (Curry, 2001; Temin, 2001).

■ A noticeable majority of incarcerated women report histories of physical, psychological, or sexual abuse and/or domestic violence. An estimated 50% to 80% of female offenders report such abuse experience prior to incarceration (Belknap, 1996; Bloom, Chesney-Lind, & Owen, 1994; Browne, Miller, & Maguin, 1999; Herman, 1992; Curry, 2001; DeGroot, 2001; Marcus-Mendoza, Sargent, & Chong Ho, 1994; Pollock-Byrne, 1990; Walker, 1994).

■ While female involvement in drug use and female convictions for drug offenses have increased dramatically over the past decade, so too have female convictions for burglary, larceny, and fraud. These offenses are often related to the need to maintain drug use.

■ Female offenders constitute only 14% of all offenders incarcerated for violent offenses (Bureau of Justice Statistics, 2001). Female offenders perpetrate violence against intimates nearly two times as often as against other relatives (Snell & Morton, 1994).

Responses to Incarceration

Correctional professionals who have worked with both male and female offenders historically and consistently report significant observable differences between these two populations, including variations in socialization and social learning, expression of emotion, behavior patterns, perception of interpersonal role, use of institution services and programs, and general experience of incarceration (Morash, Bynum, & Koons, 1998). This section discusses several of these differences, as observed by this author and others over the course of their correctional careers.

Perceptions of Confinement. Incarcerated males report several typical consequences of imprisonment that are most discomforting or debilitating (Sykes, 1958). The loss of freedom, social rejection, and the loss of status are generally the most troublesome.

The loss of access to familiar and preferred material goods and services creates a loss of perceived worth and personal control. Deprivation of heterosexual relationships with resultant changes in physical, social, and psychological expression often affects individual perceptions of masculinity and social standing. The imposed rules and structure of correctional institutions, where all activities are observed, supervised, or monitored and occur among groups of other offenders, contribute to a loss of independence and self-direction. This limited sense of autonomy and self-control is closely related to a loss of sense of security and safety in an environment populated by others who perceive the same losses, limitations, and frustrations and who might respond in irrational or violent ways.

In a seminal study of the needs, roles, and behaviors of incarcerated women, Ward and Kassebaum (1965) found that female offenders experienced similar losses as did imprisoned males but prioritized these losses differently and reported other unique deprivations. Of principal importance to female offenders was separation from, and loss of contact with, family members, especially children, parents, spouses, and lovers. The enforced absence of contact with intimates and family was reported to be significantly and negatively experienced throughout the course of incarceration for female offenders.

Females more often perceive imprisonment as a significant and negative change in their continuing lives. Males instead tend to perceive incarceration as an interruption after which they will return to and resume their lives. Because women are more likely to express the need for continuity and attempt to maintain as many of their pre-incarceration relationships and activities as possible, the impact of separation from important others, the markedly diminished availability of social and emotional support, and the relative absence of freedom, personal property, and privacy are typically significant. Females' adjustment to incarceration, both initially and throughout their sentences, is often characterized by anxiety, depression, withdrawal, irritability, negative changes in self-perception, and frequent and less predictable loss of emotional and behavioral control.

The second most frequently reported difficulty for female offenders was the constant stress and demands of living in close proximity and contact with other women who shared the same sense of loss and diminished self-concept. Incarcerated women reported significant deprivation as a result of the loss or disruption of social relationships and friendships of a nonsexual nature with both men and women. Persistent difficulty was reported during the entire period of incarceration as a result of the lack of privacy. For women, this included privacy of property, about which women are often very territorial and possessive; privacy of interpersonal space, which is frequently violated both intentionally and unintentionally; and modesty about their bodies and bodily functions and care.

In general, then, it would appear that male offenders are concerned more with issues of control, power, and personal capability and determination during incarceration, while female offenders often are more focused on relationships, support, and social and personal intimacy.

Differential Socialization Experiences. The socialization experiences of women reared in Western societies may help to explain some of these findings. Historically,

Western women have been taught to be more cooperative, submissive, nurturing, dependent, and emotionally expressive than men, who are reinforced for more competitive, aggressive, independent, and stoic behaviors (Flynn, 1963). Female preferences to both give and receive support and nurturance can be clearly seen among incarcerated women, who tend to be quite social and group oriented, express interest in and concern for fellow offenders, and demonstrate relatively infrequent other-directed violent behaviors. Female offenders prefer to form or re-create close extended groups that resemble and function much like family units. Tittle (1969) suggested that incarcerated females tend to initiate relatively long-standing principal relationships, while male offenders establish "an overall symbiotic structure." Although the development and organization of family-like groups may differ across correctional institutions, the delineation of gender roles and functions among female offenders is demonstrated consistently (Heffernan, 1972). Such roles provide avenues for mutual protection and assistance, and dependable relationships offer affection, care, and respect in an environment noticeably lacking in these characteristics (Sykes, 1978). Incarcerated females frequently engage in physically close behaviors with each other, including touching, hand holding, and hugging. Homosexual relationships among female offenders are typically more open and of longer duration than those among males. Such female relationships are based on the need for social and emotional support and on the need to express and share nurturing behaviors.

Male homosexual relationships, on the other hand, are based more on instrumental gain, power, coercion and control. For male offenders who tend to attempt to remain independent, self-protective, and self-concerned, group affiliation is principally instrumental and based on hierarchies of power and coercion.

Violent behavior demonstrated by male offenders is typically intended to gain or express control. Violent behavior demonstrated by female offenders is more often an expression of perceived loss of control and an effort to regain personal identity and/or maintain survival. Female offenders employ more covert, and often quite sophisticated, means of satisfying personal needs, including social manipulation, seduction, sexuality, and passive-aggressive activities.

Special Management, Treatment, and Program Considerations

All incarcerated individuals, whether male or female, have basic needs, and correctional systems must be aware of and attend to these needs. While providing settings for the service of court-imposed sanctions and the protection of society at large, correctional institutions are obliged to provide offenders with medical and mental health care, opportunities for religious expression, access to appropriate legal services, avenues of communication with families, and assistance in planning for release to the community after incarceration—all in an environment that must ensure offender safety and security.

Beyond these basic needs, however, specific offender populations have unique needs based on particular characteristics, including age, sex, history, and personal abilities. Female offenders, by virtue of physiological characteristics and psychosocial experiences and roles, consistently have specific and unique needs within the correctional environment. To the extent that these needs directly or indirectly affect the delivery of correctional mental health services, they are discussed here.

Use of Health and Mental Health Services

Women in Western cultures in general are more frequent and consistent consumers of medical and behavioral health care. It is often noted that a majority of patients in community medical and mental health settings are females who report illnesses, seek medical attention, and are prescribed medicines more frequently than are males. Not surprisingly, female correctional institutions experience higher rates of use of medical and dental care (on both scheduled and as-needed bases) and more frequent repeat clinic and practitioner visits than do male institutions. Similarly, the demand for and participation in mental health and religious services and programs are consistently higher among female offenders than among their male counterparts. This difference in the use of medical and mental health services might be related to a generally held belief among female offenders and correctional staff that because of inherently diminished personal capabilities or female dependency, women require more care and assistance than do men. Other possible influences might include cultural conditioning, which allows females to express emotion, apprehension, and pain and to seek assistance more quickly and frequently than do males (Ditton, 1999).

Obstetric and Gynecological Needs

In addition to the more frequent use of general medical and mental health services, female offenders have other needs for specialized care. Estimates are that 1 in 20, or even as many as 1 in 12, female offenders are pregnant at the times of their incarceration (Curry, 2001; Kauffman, 2001). Because a significant number of these women have received little or no prenatal care prior to incarceration, there are obvious increases in needs for prenatal, at-risk pregnancy, obstetric, and postnatal care. Related needs include medical and psychological counseling and care involving safe sex, reproductive choice, miscarriage and abortion, and family planning.

Gynecological care of both a routine and a nonroutine nature is frequently requested. Preventive examination and postpartum and post-surgical follow-up treatment are provided regularly. Nonroutine care for anatomical and physiological abnormalities and infections, often related to sexual abuse, drug use and addiction, and lack of prior preventive health care, is commonly required. As is true among nonincarcerated women, the increasing rates of breast, lung, and colon cancer and coronary artery disease are of considerable concern for incarcerated women and correctional health care professionals.

In large measure as a result of pre-incarceration high-risk behaviors, such as prostitution and drug abuse, and limited economic resources, imprisoned women also have higher rates of infection with tuberculosis, hepatitis, HIV, and sexually transmitted diseases than do imprisoned males and nonincarcerated females (Campbell, 1993). Of course, the presence of such diseases results in a higher need for institutional preventive medical procedures and lifestyle education as well as extended individual patient care.

Dietary and Nutritional Needs

Another medically related issue of concern for incarcerated women is the difference in female nutritional needs. Incarcerated women are often provided diets similar or identical to those prepared for male offenders. The levels of carbohydrates, fats, and sodium, as well as frequently limited nutrition options, in many prison diets are typically planned for the more physically active male lifestyle. DeBell (2001) found that female offenders imprisoned for longer that 18 months reported average weight gains of 20 pounds during their incarceration.

Another nutritional concern involves the actual nutritional intake of many female offenders. Although adequate quantities of food are typically provided in female institutions, many women frequently do not avail themselves of meals or eat very little of those they do take, citing lack of tasteful preparation, aesthetic presentation, and familiarity with the method of food preparation. Nutritionally inappropriate offerings and self-limited nutritional intake by offenders may often contribute to female health problems, including Type II diabetes, hypertension, obesity, and eating disorders. These and related disorders also contribute significantly to diminished self-esteem and confidence, as well as to increased depression and anxiety, among affected offenders.

Related to diet and nutritional issues among female offenders are increased demands for specialized dermatological, cosmetic, and behavioral and medical weight management interventions. Such requests are associated with women's increased concern about and attention to their physical appearances that is closely related to levels of self-esteem and confidence. Not only do these medical service needs and requests directly affect correctional medical service resources, they directly and indirectly affect institutional security, mental health, counseling, and commissary resources and operations.

Sleep Disturbance

Sleep disturbances and disorders are quite common among female offenders. During early phases of incarceration, imprisoned women typically report difficulty in falling asleep (i.e., initial insomnia). Frequent awakening throughout the night, also quite common during the initial periods of incarceration, is reported during the entire course of incarceration. Both initial and middle insomnia are also reported to increase during the last few weeks or months of incarceration and are viewed as related to pre-release anticipation and anxiety. Early morning awakening with an inability to return to sleep is more often reported during the middle and latter phases of imprisonment. Such sleep disturbances are most often associated with situational apprehension, diminished subjective sense of security, adjustment difficulties, anxiety or depressive disorders, and drug or medication withdrawal. Women often seek medical assistance for sleep problems, typically via requests for medications, more frequently and earlier in the pattern of disturbed sleep than do men.

Pain and Pain Management

The experience of pain is an important component of medical and mental health practice and has received increased attention over the past decade. Although pain is often related to biological conditions or processes, it is inextricably related to psychological, social, and environmental factors as well. Thus, the experience of pain is best understood as an interaction among physical, psychological, situational, and social influences (Holtzman & Turk, 1986). Physical or biological factors that contribute to the experience of pain include tissue or organ pathology or destruction as a result of disease, physiological malformation or dysfunction, procedural and post-procedural effects, and the efficacy of biochemical processes and responses. A wide range of psychological processes have been noted to affect the interpretation and experience of pain, including cognitive perception (Beecher, 1959; Blitz & Dinnerstein, 1968; Brock & Buss, 1962; Festinger, 1957; Johnson, 1973; Merskey, 1978; Reesor & Craig, 1988; Zimbardo, Cohen, Weisenberg, Dworkin, & Firestone, 1966), locus of control (Davison & Valins, 1969; Weisenberg, 1977), dependency (Sternbach, 1974), self-esteem (Atkinson, 1976; Elton, Stanley, & Burrows, 1978; Engel, 1958; Sternbach, 1974; Timmermans & Sternbach, 1974), and hypochondriasis (Nabilof, Cohen, & Yellin, 1982). Clear relationships among anxiety, situational apprehension, adjustment difficulty, and acute pain have also been reported (Blitz & Dinnerstein, 1968; Bowers, 1968; Glynn, Lloyd, & Folkhard, 1981; Tan, 1982). Depressive disorders are more often implicated in the experience of chronic pain (Barg, Perez, Main, & Bond, 1981; Sternbach, 1975, 1978). The integration of depression and pain is often so pervasive that it is sometimes difficult to determine which represents the principal difficulty.

As noted previously, females experience depressive disorders, situational anxiety, diminished self-esteem, externally focused perception of control, and dependency more often than do males. These factors are exaggerated and exacerbated by incarceration and separation from familiar caregivers and interpersonal support systems. Consequently, the frequency, intensity, and duration of acute and chronic pain are heightened by these additional factors among incarcerated females.

Alcohol and Other Substance Abuse Treatment Needs

Just as females have distinct and specific medical, mental health, and social needs, so too are their substance abuse treatment needs different from those of males (Amaro, 1994; Reed, 1994). Although issues in the management and treatment of incarcerated substance abusers have been a historical concern, approaches have traditionally been based on the needs and behaviors of male substance abusers (Blume, 1990; Wilke, 1994). As a result of this gender emphasis, the causative factors, consequences, and treatment needs of substance-abusing females were infrequently investigated until the mid-1970s (Mondonaro, 1989; Roth, 1991; Wells & Jackson, 1992; Woodhouse, 1992).

Since the 1975 passage of Public Law 94-371 and its requirement for the development of specialized treatment services for females, there has been increased attention to women's treatment programs (Wilsnack & Wilsnack, 1990). Research indicates that because of significantly different physiological responses to alcohol, nicotine, and other drugs, women develop harmful health consequences from substance abuse more quickly and with lower consumption levels than do men (Blume, 1990; Nespor, 1990; Reed, 1987; Urbano-Marquez et al., 1995). Women who report infertility or pelvic pain related to menstrual distress have higher rates of substance abuse problems than does the general female population (Blume, 1994; Lex, 1994). Sexual dysfunction and a wide range of menstrual cycle disruptions have been linked to excessive alcohol and nicotine abuse (Beckman, 1994; Blume, 1994; Teoh, Lex, Mendelson, Mello, & Cochin, 1992; Wartenberg, 1994). Abuse of alcohol and nicotine among women has been associated with osteoporosis (Center for Substance Abuse Treatment, 1994; Korsten & Lieber, 1994; Wartenberg, 1994) and breast cancer (Blume, 1994; Reichman, 1994) as well as cirrhosis, coronary artery disease, chronic obstructive pulmonary disease, lung and bladder cancer, and HIV infection (Blume, 1994).

Research has also demonstrated the co-occurrence of alcohol and other drug abuse with mental health difficulties. Estimates are that up to two thirds of substance-abusing females have a comorbid psychiatric disorder (Beckman, 1994; Helzer & Pryzbeck, 1994; Schuckit & Hesselbrock, 1994). The most frequently cited psychiatric disturbances are anxiety and mood disorders, including panic, post-traumatic stress disorder, and major depression (O'Hare, 1995). Women who abuse substances experience anxiety disorders three to four times more often than do nonabusing females (Helzer & Pryzbeck, 1994). It has been estimated that depression is an antecedent of alcohol abuse among women in more than two thirds of all cases. Diagnosed antisocial personality disorders occur 12 times more frequently among alcohol-dependent women than among those who are not alcohol dependent. Female substance abusers have also been shown to be at increased risk for self-destructive and suicidal behaviors (Anthenelli & Schuckit, 1994; Blume, 1994; Evans & Lacey, 1992; Lex, 1994). Last, research has suggested that women also develop cognitive deficits related to alcohol use over shorter periods of time and with less drinking than do men (Gomberg, 1994; Nixon, 1994).

The coexistence of substance abuse disorders with several other psychiatric and medical disorders, many of which are clearly influenced by social and environmental factors, suggests the appropriateness of considering a comprehensive, multi-faceted biopsychosocial approach to treating females with substance abuse problems. (Chapter 5 provided a detailed discussion of substance abuse treatment programs for both male and female offenders.)

Trauma and Abuse

As noted earlier, a significant proportion of female offenders have experienced physical, emotional, or sexual abuse and/or domestic violence. Abuse suffered during childhood is reported by 19% to 40% of incarcerated females, while adulthood abuse is reported by 24% to 80% (Belknap, 1996; Bloom et al., 1994; Browne et al., 1999; Curry, 2001; DeGroot, 2001; Herman, 1992; Marcus-Mendoza et al., 1994; Pollock-Byrne, 1990; Walker, 1994). Incarcerated women report physical and sexual abuse more than twice as often as do nonincarcerated women and report it three to six times more often than do incarcerated men (Snell & Morton, 1994).

The relationship between physical and/or sexual abuse and a wide range of medical, mental health, and substance abuse problems is marked for women (Richie & Johnson, 1996; Stevens et al., 1995). Physical and sexual abuse has been identified as an antecedent and/or consequence of alcohol and other drug abuse among women (Amaro & Hardy-Fanta, 1995; Beckman, 1994; Wilsnack, Wilsnack, & Hiller-Sturmhofel, 1994; Woodhouse, 1992). Estimates suggest that drug use among abused females is four times that among nonabused women (Martin, 1995). Childhood abuse and trauma have also been related to diagnoses among women of anxiety disorders (e.g., panic attacks, generalized anxiety disorder, post-traumatic stress disorder) as well as substance-related anxiety, mood (especially major depression), adjustment, dissociative, sleep, eating, and identity disorders (Miller, Downs, & Testa, 1993; Wilsnack et al., 1994). Browne and Finkelhor (1986) reported additional psychosocial effects of childhood abuse and sexual assault, including social isolation, lack of development of interpersonal trust and meaningful relationships, tendency toward revictimization in later life, sexual dysfunctions and adjustment difficulties, and self-mutilation. The incidence of recurrent or persistent suicidal ideation and attempts is also heightened among female victims of physical and/or sexual abuse (Browne & Finkelhor, 1986).

Although different correctional treatment programs have provided interventions for many consequences of abuse and for certain aspects of the trauma response, specifically defined and organized programs that consider the overall female experience of abuse and trauma are a relatively recent addition to most correctional systems. Morrow (1993) proposed an early outpatient model that included program areas addressing childhood physical and sexual abuse, domestic violence, parenting values and skills, and the development of effective relationships. According to Morrow, program areas can be accessed via four different levels of intervention intensity. At the lowest level, a single-session workshop is offered, with a primary focus on increasing awareness and interest and on providing introductory information. The second level consists of multiple-session class experiences for relatively smaller numbers of participants. Classes consider specific topics, involve didactic instruction, and encourage general class discussion. The third intervention level includes group psychotherapy for a limited number of participants who have completed appropriate workshops and classes, are carefully screened for group inclusion, and express a commitment to personal disclosure commensurate with the group process. Co-therapists guide the integration of personal and social content and process building on cognitive frameworks learned in classes. The fourth level of intervention involves intensive individual psychotherapy, including conditions and goals specified in a treatment plan developed jointly by the clinician and the offender. This model provides a useful basic structure on which more comprehensive abuse and trauma intervention programs can be developed. Several state and federal correctional institutions have implemented similar abuse programs. Still other facilities have initiated more structured residential programs that include more clearly defined components, activities, and sequential organization.

Regardless of the specific program parameters, the author believes that effective abuse and trauma programs must be multifaceted and include careful screening and assessment of potential program participants, individual needs assessments, a meaningful range of program content and activities, a variety of educational and learning approaches and opportunities, clearly defined and sequentially progressive organizational structure, allowances for participant review and repetition of particular program areas as appropriate, and an effective method of measuring program success.

Family Relationship and Parenting Issues

Another vital aspect worth considering with incarcerated women is the centrality of children and family systems in their lives. While an estimated 5% to 10% of female offenders are pregnant at the time of their admission to prison, an additional 15% have given birth within the year prior to their incarceration (Curry, 2001; Kauffman, 2001). Wooldredge and Masters (1993) reported, however, that fewer than 50% of state prison systems have written guidelines for medical care of pregnant offenders, and less than half of these institutions provide prenatal care. Of those facilities providing such services, 21% offer prenatal counseling, 15% provide infant placement counseling and assistance following birth, and 15% have provisions for appropriate institutional work assignments during pregnancy.

Approximately 60% to 80% of incarcerated females have children, the majority of which are under 10 years of age (Kauffman, 2001; Snell & Morton, 1994). While only 44% of incarcerated males resided with their minor children prior to incarceration, nearly two thirds of female offenders lived with their children before imprisonment (Greenfeld & Snell, 1999; Snell & Morton, 1994). Although 28% of children reside with their fathers following their mothers' incarceration, the great majority of minor children reside with grandparents. Approximately 10% to 15% of children of incarcerated parents are placed in foster homes or agency care (Snell & Morton, 1994; Temin, 2001).

The fact that the majority of female offenders are mothers of, and primary caregivers to, minor children underscores the importance of parenting and family services and programs for incarcerated women. Imprisoned females are more likely to maintain contact both during and following incarceration with their children than are incarcerated males. Approximately 90% of female offenders have contact with their children via mail, telephone, or personal visitation (Snell & Morton, 1994). This figure may be somewhat misleading, however, given that more than half of imprisoned mothers report never having personal visits with their children during incarceration (Temin, 2001). Such limited personal contact is often the result of a number of factors, including the distance between the site of incarceration and the location of the offender's children. In view of the significantly greater number of state and federal prisons that house male offenders compared with those designated for females, women are typically incarcerated much farther from family and other social support systems than are men. In addition, the limitations of economic and social resources experienced by many female offenders markedly diminish the availability of adults and reliable transportation to bring children for institution visits (Snell & Morton, 1994; Temin, 2001).

Early correctional institutions and programs designed and constructed for women emphasized socially traditional, feminine family values and practices, including development and continuation of family and parenting relationships. For example, the Federal Correctional Institution at Alderson, West Virginia, and the New York State Institution at Bedford Hills have operated institution hospitals and nurseries where children born at the institutions remain until they reach 1½ to 2 years of age. This opportunity for children to remain with their birth mothers for the first 2 years of their lives continued at the Alderson facility from its opening during the late 1920s until the early 1970s, when it was discontinued at the urging of social theorists and service agencies. These theorists and agencies regarded correctional institutions as inappropriate places for the healthy development and well-being of children. As a result of these views, offenders began to deliver their babies at community hospitals, and their infants were immediately taken into the care of family or friends of the mothers or social service agencies. The Bedford Hills institution continues to operate an on-site nursery and parent education program (Gwinn, 1992; Kauffman, 2001).

The dramatic increase in incarceration of females over the past several years and a contemporaneous societal resurgence of interest in parent-child relationships and the identification, learning, and reinforcement of effective parenting attitudes and skills have led to renewed consideration of the potential advantages and appropriateness of services and programs for female offenders and their children. Although the numbers remain relatively small, there has been a noticeable increase over the past decade in the establishment of programs that focus on the specific concerns and issues facing incarcerated mothers and their children. These programs include enhanced visitation opportunities and facilities that emphasize continuity of family relationships as well as specific programs sponsored by community agencies and organizations such as the Girl Scouts of America. Other programs designed to build and maintain relationships between offenders and their children include week-long summer camps in which children participate in daily organized activities at the correctional institutions with their mothers and stay at night with selected families in the local community. Other facilities encourage several overnight visits annually at the institutions between offenders and their children (Kauffman, 2001). More structured and extensive programs, such as Linking Inmate Families Together (LIFT) and Mothers With Infants Together (MINT), combine educational components addressing prenatal care, child and family nutrition, communications and parenting skills, and the use of community resources with parent-child interaction, practical parenting experience, and family relationship counseling.

Some correctional systems have established or reestablished institutional nurseries in which children born therein can remain with their mothers for up to 18 months. These programs allow opportunities not only for the development and strengthening of children's relationships with their mothers but also for parent education and release preparation. The criteria for participation in these programs typically include consideration of date of release from incarceration, history of violent behavior, intention of being the child's or children's primary caregiver on return to the community, and participation in appropriate educational, parenting, and/or substance abuse treatment programs.

An extremely comprehensive and innovative program for incarcerated mothers and their children is operated in Frankfurt, Germany, where the correctional administration acknowledges primary parenting as a viable and important occupation and consequently as an appropriate and productive work release placement. Although higher security offenders may keep their children with them in the institution until 3 years of age, the children of low-security offenders may remain with their mothers until 5 years of age. Infants remain with their mothers during the day. Offenders whose children are older but still of preschool age work within the prison or in the community during the day while their children are cared for by certified child care workers. On return from their assigned places of work, offenders again assume primary responsibility for their children. School-age children of offenders do not reside in the institution but may live in the surrounding area. The mothers of these children may be placed on work release to assume parenting responsibilities and related homemaking duties for their families and children during the day and then return to the prison at night after their children have been put to bed.

Such programs, which emphasize the importance of parenting and family relationships both to the individuals involved and to the society at large, provide an extensive variety of educational and pragmatic experiences. Many of these activities or programs focus on the attainment of information necessary for the understanding of the needs, development, and behaviors of children; appropriate self-assertion and decision making; situational coping strategies; the development of positive relationships; family health care and budgeting; the use of legal and support services; and other needs unique to the offenders.

Although it is important to consider the family and parenting needs of incarcerated mothers, it is critical not to ignore the effects of parental incarceration on children. The imprisonment of mothers, who are frequently the primary child caregivers and sources of social, emotional, and financial support within the family, often results in serious disruption within, or dissolution of, their families. Separation from parents or primary caregivers, especially during early developmental periods, can be traumatic for and have long-lasting effects on children (Bowlby, 1982). In addition to impaired development of trusting and stable interpersonal relationships and psychiatric or behavior disorders, these effects can include the increased likelihood that children of incarcerated parents will become involved in illicit activities and in criminal justice systems as compared with children whose parents have not been imprisoned (Kauffman, 2001; Temin, 2001). By providing program opportunities for female offenders (both with and independent of their children) for the development, implementation, maintenance, and reinforcement of effective communications, parenting, and relationship skills, the negative effects of separation between offenders and their children may be reduced and the likelihood of the children of those offenders engaging in the same behaviors and experiencing the same personal and social difficulties as their mothers may well be diminished.

Mental Health Services

Integrally related to the general and specialized medical, substance abuse, trauma and abuse intervention, and parenting and family support needs of female offenders are specific mental health concerns and needs. As noted previously, incarcerated women are generally more likely to express emotion, to behave more passively and dependently, and to seek assistance with little or no hesitation or embarrassment. This typically results in consistently large numbers of female offenders requesting and participating in a wide variety of mental health services from crisis intervention through long-term therapeutic programs.

The psychological components and consequences of medical disorders and concerns are not insignificant among female offenders who are facing the uncertainties and stresses of new or ongoing medical disorders without the support of family and friends. The relationship of mood and anxiety disorders with diseases such as diabetes, coronary artery disease, cancer, HIV, persistent and recurrent eating disorders, and major mental illnesses must be addressed with immediacy and efficacy. The physical and psychological effects of miscarriage, abortion, and sexual assault can be significant for the individual as well as for other offenders within an institution. The significant co-occurrence of psychiatric disorders and substance abuse was already noted earlier.

For a large proportion of female offenders who enter prison with preexisting psychiatric disorders, the demands of incarceration can quickly—and often dramatically—exacerbate affective, cognitive, and behavioral difficulties. For those without preexisting mental health concerns, admission to prison can contribute to adjustment disorders and to the development of other initial mood, anxiety, and psychophysiological disorders.

Because of the perceived multitudinous losses and absence of support that many women experience in response to incarceration, suicidal behavior is a constant and serious concern within female correctional settings. It is the author's belief that many of the suicidal thoughts, gestures, and attempts by female offenders are in response to family disruption and other effects of incarceration as well as to continuing or exacerbated psychiatric disturbance.

Correctional mental health programs that have established close working relationships with medical, pastoral care, and substance abuse treatment programs and with institution administrative, security, and case management staff can provide consultation and direct offender care services that result in improved institution operations and offender safety and care. Significant positive impact can be demonstrated by reported decreases in areas such as subjective pain, anxiety, depression, and adjustment difficulty; requests for medications; housing changes; institution transfers; and disruptive or violent outbursts.

Conclusions

The population of female offenders and their needs and characteristics have long been ignored, underestimated, misunderstood, and maligned. Reasons for this have included the small numbers of incarcerated females relative to those of males; the relatively low visibility of incarcerated women due to infrequent acts of violence, disruptions, and disturbances within correctional institutions; the perceptions, beliefs, and preferences of correctional professionals and the society at large; and the consequent allocation of significantly limited resources for female offender services and programs. Communities often forget females incarcerated far from their homes, families, and friends. Correctional workers often express dissatisfaction, hesitancy, and ambivalence with respect to working with female offenders. Increased interest in the needs, characteristics, and rights of females, both in society in general and within incarceration settings, has emerged as a result of the evolution of social and correctional perceptions, beliefs, and practices.

The long-accepted correctional practice of approaching offenders in a firm, fair, and consistent manner provides an appropriate and productive basis for the safe, secure, and effective management of both male and female offenders. It has also been demonstrated, however, that provision of the same environment, services, and programs for males and females does not necessarily result in equality of treatment. As this chapter has described, female offenders have unique characteristics, needs, and responses to incarceration that are distinctly different from those of incarcerated males. Clear and significant differences were discussed in the areas of medical and mental health care, problematic substance use, trauma and abuse, and family and parenting relationships. Efficacious and meaningful responsiveness to the particular needs of female offenders, although perhaps requiring reevaluation and reprioritization of resource allocations, need not necessarily demand additional resource expenditures. Ensuring effective services for incarcerated women requires that the specific characteristics, priorities, and psychological and sociocultural attributes of female offenders continue to be accurately identified, understood, and addressed in the development of programs and services. Continuing or returning to attempts to provide female offenders with services and programs developed for males is clearly ineffective and unjust to society, to correctional professionals who must manage and treat offenders, and to female offenders themselves.

The basis for future female offender services must include, as a beginning, those procedures, programs, and priorities that have been demonstrated to be currently the most effective, responsive, and heuristically promising. In view of the consistent importance of relationships to females, especially female offenders separated from families and friends, it appears reasonable to conceptualize and implement new best practices with this significant factor in mind. Review of current best practices in the areas of medical services and mental health services suggests that those programs must go beyond provision of basic services to programs that specifically and directly address the unique needs of female offenders. The most efficient service delivery systems are those that provide care in an integrative and inclusive manner that conceptualizes and actualizes conjoint comprehensive medical and mental health care.

The most productive and promising current substance abuse treatment approach, as noted in Chapter 5, appears to be a comprehensive and adaptable model that simultaneously addresses biological, psychological, and sociocultural aspects of participants' lives and addiction processes. Treatment programs that employ biopsychosocial aspects as a foundation, then, provide additional emphases on longitudinal perspectives of individuals' lives; the importance of gender role and relationships; a holistic approach to prevention, intervention, and post-intervention treatment efforts; and the particular assets of each individual program participant. As such, they offer increased potential for female offenders.

Programs that address issues of trauma and abuse will be most effective when they provide a needs-based range of intervention intensity and involvement across an appropriate variety of treatment experiences. Included in this multilevel and multifaceted approach must be access to brief inpatient psychiatric services as needed as well as comprehensive outpatient programs. As with optimal intervention strategies in other program areas, the basic emphasis must be on continued awareness of and attention to the participant's total life experience and unique needs, particularly with respect to the development and maintenance of effective relationships. Staff who provide trauma and abuse program services should be well grounded and experienced not only in the treatment of the range of clinical presentations but also in the identification and treatment of processes such as acute and post-traumatic stress and self-destructive behaviors and suicidality.

Female offender programs that address parenting and family relationship concerns must also involve multiple educational and experiential components at a variety of levels of personal intensity and involvement. Again, principal consideration of the importance of relationships across the lives of participants is vital. Beyond the effective formation of meaningful relationships, program emphasis must include aspects of relationship continuity and resumption and of the dynamic nature and characteristics of interpersonal relations. The programs that are most productive are those that involve sequential learning activities that form a solid basis for subsequent and contemporaneous applied learning, parenting, and family relationship experiences with maximal opportunity for rehearsal and feedback as well as transition services to ensure compatibility and continuity on return to the community.

The conceptualization, development, and implementation of correctional services and programs for female offenders have evolved from archaic and punitive practices, to those that were generally a secondary adjunct to male offender programs, to recognition of female offender programs as a beneficial and necessary component of proactive correctional management. It now appears clear that the unique needs and gender and cultural expectations and experiences of female offenders significantly affect correctional management as well as results of correctional services and programs. In view of such influence, these specific female offender characteristics and experiences should be viewed as potential assets, strengths, and foundations for further personal development and skills enhancement rather than as problems or inconveniences. Correctional programs and services for female offenders must involve a comprehensive and holistic approach that provides sensitivity to and understanding of female offender needs, opportunities for meaningful and reasonable decisions, respect, dignity, and empowerment in an environment that is safe, secure, supportive, and appropriately structured.

References

Amaro, H. (1994). *The social context of being a girl: Implications for prevention of substance abuse.* Paper presented at the Conference Link III meeting of the Center for Substance Abuse Prevention, Washington, DC.

Amaro, H., & Hardy-Fanta, C. (1995). Gender relations in addiction and recovery. *Journal of Psychoactive Drugs, 27,* 325-327.

Anthenelli, R. M., & Schuckit, M. A. (1994). *Genetic influences in addiction.* In N. S. Miller (Ed.), *Principles of addiction medicine* (sec. 1, chap. 6, pp. 1-14). Chevy Chase, MD: American Society of Addiction Medicine.

Atkinson, L. (1976). The management of intractable pain. *Medical Journal of Australia, 1,* 786-788.

Barg, J., Perez, A., Main, C., & Bond, M. R. (1981). Personality traits and the chronic pain population comparatively to neurotic and control groups. *Pain, Suppl. 1,* S71 (Abstract 83).

Beckman, L. J. (1994). Treatment needs of women with alcohol problems. *Alcohol Health and Research World, 18,* 206-211.

Beecher, H. K. (1959). *Measurement of subjective response.* New York: Oxford University Press.

Belknap, J. (1996). *The invisible woman: Gender, crime, and justice.* Belmont, CA: Wadsworth.

Bershad, L. (1985). Discriminatory treatment of the female offender in the criminal justice system. *Boston College Law Review, 26,* 289-438.

Blitz, B., & Dinnerstein, A. J. (1968). Effects of different types of instruction on pain parameters. *Journal of Abnormal Psychology, 73,* 276-280.

Bloom, B., Chesney-Lind, M., & Owen, B. (1994). *Women in California prison: Hidden victims of the war on drugs.* San Francisco: Center on Juvenile and Criminal Justice.

Blume, S. B. (1990). Chemical dependency in women: Important issues. *American Journal of Drug and Alcohol Abuse, 16,* 297-307.

Blume, S. B. (1994). Women and addictive disorders. In N. S. Miller (Ed.), *Principles of addiction medicine* (sec. 16, chap. 1, pp. 1-16). Chevy Chase, MD: American Society of Addiction Medicine.

Bowers, K. S. (1968). Pain, anxiety, and perceived control. *Journal of Consulting and Clinical Psychology, 32,* 596-602.

Bowlby, J. (1982). *Attachment and loss* (2nd ed.). New York: Basic Books.

Brock, T. C., & Buss, A. H. (1962). Dissonance, aggression, and evaluation of pain. *Journal of Abnormal and Social Psychology, 65,* 197-202.

Browne, A., & Finkelhor, D. (1986). Initial and long-term effects: A review of the research. In D. Finkelhor (Ed.), *A sourcebook on child sexual assault.* Beverly Hills, CA: Sage.

Browne, A., Miller, B., & Maguin, E. (1999). Prevalence and severity of lifetime physical and sexual victimization among incarcerated women. *Journal of Law and Psychiatry, 22,* 301-322.

Bureau of Justice Statistics. (2001). *Criminal offenders statistics.* Washington, DC: U.S. Department of Justice.

Camp, G. M., & Camp, C. (1998). *The corrections yearbook, 1998.* Middletown, CT: Criminal Justice Institute.

Campbell, M. K. (1993). Infection control: Managing exposure to communicable diseases. In *The state of corrections.* Lanham, MD: American Correctional Association.

Center for Substance Abuse Treatment. (1994). *Practical approaches in the treatment of women who abuse alcohol and other drugs.* Rockville, MD: U.S. Department of Health and Human Services, Public Health Service.

Curry, L. (2001). Tougher sentencing, economic hardships, and rising violence. *Corrections Today, 63*(1), 74-76.

Davison, G. C., & Valins, S. (1969). Maintenance of self-attributed and drug-attributed behavior change. *Journal of Personality and Social Psychology, 11,* 25-33.

DeBell, J. (2001). The female offender: Different, not difficult. *Corrections Today, 63*(1), 56-61.

DeGroot, A. S. (2001). HIV among incarcerated women: An epidemic behind the walls. *Corrections Today, 63*(1), 77-81.

Ditton, P. M. (1999). *Mental health and treatment of inmates and probationers* (Bureau of Justice Statistics special report). Washington, DC: U.S. Department of Justice.

Elton, D., Stanley, G., & Burrows, G. (1978). Self-esteem and chronic pain. *Journal of Psychosomatic Research, 22,* 25-30.

Engel, G. L. (1958). Psychogenic pain. *Medical Clinics of North America, 42,* 1481-1496.

Evans, C., & Lacey, J. H. (1992). Multiple self-damaging behavior among alcoholic women: A prevalence study. *British Journal of Psychiatry, 161,* 643-647.

Festinger, L. (1957). *A theory of cognitive dissonance.* Evanston, IL: Row, Peterson.

Flynn, E. G. (1963). *My life as a political prisoner.* New York: International Publishers.

Glick, R. M., & Neto, V. V. (1976). *National Study of Women's Correctional Programs.* Sacramento: California Youth Authority.

Glover v. Johnson, 478 F. Supp. 1075, 1077 (E.D. Mich. 1979).

Glynn, C. J., Lloyd, J. W., & Folkhard, S. (1981). The effect of reported arousal, anxiety, aggression, and depression on the diurnal variation of reported intractable pain. *Pain, Supplement 1,* S74 (Abstract 89).

Gomberg, E. L. (1994). Risk factors for drinking over a woman's life span. *Alcohol Health and Research World, 18,* 220-227.

Greenfeld, L. A., & Snell, T. L. (1999). *Women offenders: Bureau of Justice Statistics special report* (NJC 175688). Washington, DC: National Criminal Justice Research Service.

Gwinn, B. (1992). Linking inmate families together. *Federal Prison, 3*(1), 37-39.

Heffernan, E. (1972). *Making it in prison: The straight and cool life.* New York: John Wiley.

Helzer, J. E., & Pryzbeck, T. R. (1994). The co-occurrence of alcoholism and other psychiatric disorders. In N. S. Miller (Ed.), *Principles of addiction medicine* (sec. 6, chap. 2, pp. 1-6). Chevy Chase, MD: American Society of Addiction Medicine.

Herman, J. L. (1992). *Trauma and recovery.* New York: Basic Books.

Holtzman, A. D., & Turk, D. C. (Eds.). (1986). *Pain management: A handbook of psychological treatment approaches.* New York: Pergamon.

Johnson, J. E. (1973). Effects of accurate expectations about sensations of sensory and distress components of pain. *Journal of Personality and Social Psychology, 27,* 261-275.

Kauffman, K. (2001). Mothers in prison. *Corrections Today, 63*(1), 62-65.

Korsten, M. A., & Lieber, C. S. (1994). Organ pathology. In N. S. Miller (Ed.), *Principles of addiction medicine* (sec. 5, chap. 5, pp. 1-14). Chevy Chase, MD: American Society of Addiction Medicine.

Lawson, W. T., & Fawkes, L. S. (1992). HIV, AIDS, and the female offender. *Federal Prisons, 3*(1), 27-32.

Lex, B. W. (1994). Alcohol and other drug abuse among women. *Alcohol Health Research World, 18,* 212-220.

Lombroso, C. (1968). *Crime and its causes and remedies.* Montclair, NJ: Patterson-Smith. (Original work published 1911)

Marcus-Mendoza, S. T., Sargent, E., & Chong Ho, Y. (1994). Changing perceptions of the etiology of crime: The relationship between abuse and female criminology. *Journal of the Oklahoma Justice Research Consortium, 1,* 13-23.

Martin, S. L. (1995, November). *Domestic violence and substance abuse among pregnant adolescents.* Paper presented at the annual meeting of the American Public Health Association, San Diego.

Merskey, H. (1978). Pain and personality. In R. A. Sternbach (Ed.), *The psychology of pain.* New York: Raven.

Miller, J. B., Downs, W. R., & Testa, M. (1993). Interrelationships between victimization experiences and women's alcohol use. *Journal of Studies on Alcohol, Suppl. 11,* 109-117.

Mondonaro, J. (1989). *Chemically dependent women: Assessment and treatment.* Lexington, MA: D. C. Heath.

Morash, M., Bynum, T. S., & Koons, B. A. (1998). *Women offenders: Programming needs and promising approaches* (NIJ Research in Brief). Washington, DC: National Institute of Justice.

Morrow, D. E. (1993). *Special issues program for female offenders.* Unpublished proposal, Federal Correctional Institution, Alderson, WV.

Nabilof, B. D., Cohen, M. J. , & Yellin, A. N. (1982). Does the MMPI differentiate chronic illness from chronic pain? *Pain, 13,* 333-341.

Nespor, K. (1990). Treatment needs of alcohol-dependent women. *International Journal of Psychosomatics, 37,* 50-52.

Nixon, S. J. (1994). Alcohol and female sexuality: A look at expectancies and risks. *Alcohol and Research World, 18,* 197-205.

O'Hare, T. (1995). Mental health problems and alcohol abuse: Co-occurrence and gender differences. *Health and Social Work, 20,* 207-214.

Pollock-Byrne, J.M. (1990). *Women, prison, and crime.* Pacific Grove, CA: Brooks/Cole.

Raeder, M. S. (1993). The forgotten offender: The effect of the sentencing guidelines and mandatory minimums on women and their children. *Pepperdine Law Review, 20,* 905-991.

Reed, B. G. (1987). Developing women-sensitive drug dependency treatment services. Why so difficult? *Journal of Psychoactive Drugs, 19,* 151-164.

Reed, B. G. (1994). Women and tobacco, alcohol, and other drugs: The need to broaden the base within EAPs. *Employee Assistance Quarterly, 9*(3), 179-201.

Reesor., K. A., & Craig, K. D. (1988). Medically incongruent chronic back pain: Physical limitations, suffering, and ineffective coping. *Pain, 32,* 35-45.

Reichman, M. E. (1994). Alcohol and breast cancer. *Alcohol Health and Research World, 18,* 182-184.

Richie, B. E., & Johnson, C. (1996). Abuse histories among newly incarcerated women in a New York City jail. *Journal of the American Medical Women's Association, 51,* 111-114, 117.

Roth, P. (1991). *Alcohol and drugs are women's issues.* Metuchen, NJ: Scarecrow Press/Women's Action Alliance.

Schuckit, M. A., & Hesselbrock, V. (1994). Alcohol dependence and anxiety disorders: What is the relationship? *American Journal of Psychiatry, 151,* 1723-1734.

Snell, T. L., & Morton, D. C. (1994). *Women in prison* (Bureau of Justice Statistics bulletin). Annapolis Junction, MD: Bureau of Justice Statistics Clearinghouse.

Sternbach, R. A. (1974). *Pain patients: Traits and treatments.* New York: Academic Press.

Sternbach, R. A. (1975). Psychological aspects of pain and the selection of patients. *Clinical Neurosurgery, 21,* 323-333.

Sternbach, R. A. (1978). Clinical aspects of pain. In R. A. Sternbach (Ed.), *The psychology of pain.* New York: Raven.

Stevens, J., Zierler, S., Cram, V., Dean, D., Mayer, K. H., and DeGroot, A. S. (1995). Risks for HIV infection in incarcerated women. *Journal of Women's Health, 4,* 569-577.

Sykes, G. M. (1958). *The society of captives.* Princeton, NJ: Princeton University Press.

Sykes, G. M. (1978). *Criminology.* New York: Harcourt Brace Jovanovich.

Tan, S. Y. (1982). Cognitive and cognitive-behavioral methods for pain control: A selective review. *Pain, 12,* 201-228.

Temin, C. E. (2001). Let us consider the children. *Corrections Today, 63*(1), 66-68.

Teoh, S. K., Lex, B. W., Mendelson, J. H., Mello, N. K., & Cochin, J. (1992). Hyperprolactinemia and macrocytosis in women with alcohol and polysubstance dependence. *Journal of Studies on Alcohol, 53,* 176-182.

Timmermans, G., & Sternbach, R. A. (1974). Factors in human chronic pain: An analysis of personality and pain reaction variables. *Science, 184,* 806-807.

Tittle, C. R. (1969). Inmate organization: Sex differentiation and the influence of criminal subcultures. *American Sociological Review, 34,* 492-505.

Urbano-Marquez, A., Estruch, R., Fernandez-Sola, J., Nicolas, J., Pare, J. C., & Rubin, E. (1995). The greater risk of cardiomyopathy and myopathy in women compared with men. *Journal of the American Medical Association, 274,* 149-154.

Walker, L. E. A. (1994). *Abused women and survivor therapy.* Washington, DC: American Psychological Association.

Ward, D., & Kassebaum, G. G. (1965). *Women's prisons.* Chicago: Aldine.

Warren, M. (1979). The female offender. In H. Toch (Ed.), *Psychology of crime and criminal justice* (pp. 444-469). New York: Holt, Rinehart & Winston.

Wartenberg, A. A. (1994). TB, HIV, and other comorbidities. In N. S. Miller (Ed.), *Principles of addiction medicine* (sec. 5, chap. 4, pp. 1-7). Chevy Chase, MD: American Society of Addiction Medicine.

Weisenberg, M. (1977). Pain and pain control. *Psychological Bulletin, 84,* 1008-1044.

Wells, D. V., & Jackson, J. F. (1992). HIV and chemically dependent women: Recommendations for appropriate health care and drug treatment services. *International Journal of Addictions, 27,* 191-207.

Wikler, N. J. (1990). Gender and justice: Navigating curves on the road to equality. *Trial, 26*(2), 36-37.

Wilke, D. (1994). Women and alcoholism: How a male-as-norm bias affects research, assessment, and treatment. *Health and Social Work, 19,* 29-35.

Wilsnack, S. C., & Wilsnack, R. W. (1990). Women and substance abuse: Research directions for the 1990s. *Psychology of Addictive Behaviors, 4*(1), 46-49.

Wilsnack, S. C., Wilsnack, R. W., & Hiller-Sturmhofel, S. (1994). How women drink: Epidemiology of women's drinking and problem drinking. *Alcohol Health and Research World, 18,* 173-181.

Woodhouse, L. D. (1992). Women with jagged edges: Voices from a culture of substance abuse. *Qualitative Health Research, 2,* 262-281.

Wooldredge, J. D., & Masters, K. (1993). Confronting problems faced by pregnant inmates in state prisons. *Crime & Delinquency, 39,* 195-203.

Zimbardo, P. G., Cohen, A. R., Weisenberg, M., Dworkin, N. L., & Firestone, I. (1966). Control of pain motivation through cognitive dissonance. *Science, 151,* 217-219.

CHAPTER 8

Treating and Managing Sexual Offenders and Predators

Andrea Fox Boardman and David DeMatteo

S exual crimes generate tremendous media attention and public outrage. Sexual crimes tear at the fabric of society, regardless of whether committed against adults or children or whether singular or serial in nature. The incidence of sex crimes is notoriously difficult to measure. Ellis (1989) described the low rate at which sexual crimes against adults are reported to police and the even lower rate at which such crimes result in legal consequences for the offenders. Salter (1992) called attention to much higher rates of sexual offending against children than are detected and prosecuted.

A recent Bureau of Justice Statistics report (Greenfield, 1997) integrated the data from more than two dozen statistical databases, including crime rates and victim surveys, to highlight current trends in sexual offending. According to that report, a 1995 survey of individuals age 12 years or over revealed approximately 260,300 rapes and nearly 95,000 other sexual assaults that year. However, crime rate data from 1995 revealed only 97,460 forcible rapes reported to police nationwide, the lowest number since 1989. Approximately half of all reported rapes result in arrests. Once arrested, about half of all rape defendants are released on bond prior to trial.

AUTHORS' NOTE: Opinions expressed in this chapter are those of the authors and do not necessarily represent the opinions of the Federal Bureau of Prisons or the U.S. Department of Justice.

Two thirds of convicted rapists are ultimately sentenced to prison, with an average sentence length of 14 years. The average convicted sex offender is 35 years old, 99% of convicted sex offenders are male, and 60% of convicted sex offenders are white.

In this chapter, current trends in the legislature pertaining to sexual offenders and predators are highlighted. Types of sexual offenders are described, and administrative issues affecting the housing of sexual offenders in correctional settings are considered. The chapter concludes with a review of sex offender treatment strategies, including best practices in the field today. Directions for future inquiry and research are suggested.

Legislative Trends

During the past 10 years, a considerable number of state legislatures have become acutely aware of the risk presented by individuals who engage in repetitive acts of sexual violence (Feldman, 1997; Freeman-Longo & Knopp, 1992). In response to recent tragedies highlighting the recidivistic tendencies of sex offenders, many state legislatures have proposed various legislative tools in an effort to address the recidivism problem among sex offenders (Freeman-Longo, 1997; Teir & Coy, 1997). Two relatively recent types of legislation—sexually violent predator laws and sex offender registration and notification laws—have become the centerpiece of states' efforts to reduce recidivism among sex offenders. A third type of legislation dealing with the consumption and transmission of child pornography over the Internet highlights another recent trend in the prosecution, conviction, and incarceration of sexual offenders.

Sexually Violent Predator Laws

The state of Washington enacted the first sexually violent predator law in 1990 (Bodine, 1990), and subsequently, at least 15 other states have followed Washington's lead by enacting similar legislation.[1] Sexually violent predator laws differ from state to state, but they generally provide for the civil commitment and long-term care of certain sex offenders on completion of a term of incarceration (Feldman, 1997; Teir & Coy, 1997).

Commentators, researchers, practitioners, and legal scholars have recently devoted considerable attention to the sexually violent predator law enacted by the state of Kansas, primarily because it was the first legislation of this type to be challenged, reviewed, and upheld as constitutional by the U.S. Supreme Court (see *Kansas v. Hendricks,* 1997; McAllister, 1997; Morris, 1997; Teir & Coy, 1997). The Kansas legislature enacted the Sexually Violent Predator (SVP) Act of 1995 (Kansas SVP Act, 1993) after the highly publicized kidnapping, rape, and murder of Stephanie Schmidt, a Kansas college student, by a convicted rapist who had recently been released from prison. The Kansas legislature expressly designed the SVP Act to address the specific dangers posed by repeat sex offenders by providing a statutory scheme for the post-sentence, involuntary civil commitment of individuals who have a "mental abnormality" or "personality disorder" that makes them more likely to engage in "predatory acts of sexual violence."

The SVP Act defines a *sexually violent offense* as one of the following: rape, indecent liberties with a child, aggravated indecent liberties with a child, criminal sodomy, aggravated criminal sodomy, indecent solicitation of a child, aggravated indecent solicitation of a child, sexual exploitation of a child, or aggravated sexual battery. Also included in the definition is conviction for a felony offense in effect prior to the effective date of the SVP Act that is comparable to a sexually violent offense as defined in the act as well as any attempt, conspiracy, or criminal solicitation of a sexually violent offense or any act that, either at the time of sentencing or subsequently during civil commitment proceedings, has been determined beyond a reasonable doubt to have been sexually motivated.

The SVP Act defines *mental abnormality* as a "congenital or acquired condition affecting the emotional or volitional capacity which predisposes the person to commit sexually violent offenses in a degree constituting such person a menace to the health and safety of others." The act defines the term *predatory* as "acts directed towards strangers or individuals with whom relationships have been established or promoted for the primary purpose of victimization."

Under the SVP Act, the state agency with authority over the release of a potential sexually violent predator is required to notify the local prosecutor, who in turn may file a petition invoking the involuntary civil commitment procedures of the SVP Act. If a petition is filed, then a federal district court must determine whether there is probable cause to conduct a trial to determine whether the person is a sexually violent predator.

The SVP Act provides several procedural safeguards for the sexual offender. First, the burden of proof is placed on the state. Second, the state may be required to provide the assistance of counsel and an examination by a mental health professional. Finally, the individual subject to the SVP Act has the right to present and cross-examine witnesses. If an individual is judicially declared to be a sexually violent predator, then he or she will be committed to the "custody of the Secretary of Social and Rehabilitation Services for control, care, and treatment until such time as the person's mental abnormality or personality disorder has so changed that the person is safe to be at large."

Individuals confined pursuant to the SVP Act are afforded three avenues of review. First, the committing court is required to conduct annual reviews of the mental condition of the sex offender to determine whether continued detention is still warranted. Second, if the secretary of social and rehabilitative services decides that a change in the individual's status makes release appropriate, then the secretary can authorize the individual to petition for release. Finally, the confined individual, even without the secretary's authorization, can petition for release at any time.

Sexually violent predator laws, such as the SVP Act, have generated considerable controversy. For example, several individuals confined pursuant to sexually violent predator legislation have challenged these laws on numerous legal grounds. In two recent cases, *Kansas v. Hendricks* (1997) and *Seling v. Young* (2001), the U.S. Supreme Court addressed the constitutionality of sexually violent predator laws. In *Hendricks,* the court upheld the constitutionality of the SVP Act, concluding that it comports with substantive due process and does not violate the Ex Post Facto Clause or the Double Jeopardy Clause of the U.S. Constitution.[2] Similarly, in *Seling*, which was decided in January 2001, the court upheld Washington State's sexually violent predator law.

Sex Offender Registration and Notification Laws

Another type of legislation that states have implemented in an effort to reduce recidivism among sex offenders is sex offender registration and notification (DeMatteo, 1998; Hacking, 1997; Teir & Coy, 1997). In response to several highly publicized acts of repetitive violence committed by previously convicted sex offenders, all 50 states have enacted laws requiring persons convicted of certain statutorily designated sex offenses to register with local law enforcement authorities on release from incarceration.[3] In May 1996, Congress enacted a federal sex offender registration law, called the Jacob Wetterling Crimes Against Children and Sexually Violent Offender Registration Program Act, as part of the Violent Crime Control and Law Enforcement Act of 1994 (otherwise known as the 1994 Omnibus Crime Bill) (Center for Sex Offender Management [CSOM], 1999; Hacking, 1997; Martin, 1996; Stacy & Dayton, 1997; Violent Crime Control and Law Enforcement Act, 1994). The general goals of sex offender registration laws include deterring sex offenders from committing future crimes, providing law enforcement with an additional investigative tool, and increasing public protection (CSOM, 1999).[4]

Several states, however, require more than just the registration of sex offenders (Gibeaut, 1997). For example, in response to the abduction, rape, and murder of 7-year-old Megan Kanka by a twice-convicted sex offender, New Jersey became the first state to add a notification component to the legislation (DeMatteo, 1998; Goodman, 1996). Specifically, in addition to a registration requirement, "Megan's Law" provides for community notification to statutorily designated entities and members of the local community (New Jersey Registration and Community Notification Law, 1997). Subsequently, a majority of states followed New Jersey's lead by enacting some form of community notification program (Gibeaut, 1997; Teir & Coy, 1997). Because sex offender registration and notification laws differ from state to state, both in terms of requirements and in terms of scope, this section focuses primarily on the New Jersey legislation—Megan's Law—which served as the model for similar legislation enacted in other states and in the federal jurisdiction (Martin, 1996).

The fundamental premise of Megan's Law is that the registration of sex offenders, when combined with a carefully tailored notification plan, will prevent sex offenders from reoffending by alerting certain parties to the potential danger posed by repeat sex offenders in their communities (Freeman-Longo, 1997). Specifically, Megan's Law was designed to identify potential recidivists through registration, to alert the public through notification when necessary for public safety, and to help prevent and promptly resolve incidents involving sexual abuse and missing persons (New Jersey Registration and Community Notification Law, 1997). To accomplish these goals, Megan's Law provides for both mandatory registration and a three-tier notification system.

The registration provisions of Megan's Law require all individuals who have completed sentences for certain sex offenses to register with local law enforcement authorities on their release from incarceration.[5] Each registrant is required to provide the following information to the chief law enforcement officer of the municipality in which the registrant resides: name, social security number, age, race, sex, date of birth, height, weight, hair color, eye color, address of legal residence, address of any current temporary legal residence, and date and place of employment. After registration is complete, the information is forwarded to the Division of State Police, where it is incorporated into a central registry. The registrant's information is also provided to the prosecutor of the county in which the registrant plans to reside. Noncompliance with the registration requirements of Megan's Law constitutes a fourth-degree offense in New Jersey, but in some states it is treated as a felony; penalties range from reincarceration to civil penalties of up to $5,000. The Megan's Law registration requirement continues for 15 years from the date of conviction or release, whichever is later. Once the 15-year period lapses, the registrant may petition the Superior Court of New Jersey to terminate his or her obligation to register.

The information gathered from the registrant during the registration phase is used in the subsequent notification phase of Megan's Law. Prior to disseminating information about the registrant, the local authorities must first assess the registrant's risk of reoffending. To assess the registrant's risk of reoffending, the prosecutor of the county in which the registrant resides and the prosecutor of the convicting county use the registration information to jointly determine whether the registered sex offender poses a low (Tier 1), moderate (Tier 2), or high (Tier 3) risk of reoffending. These determinations are made using a Registrant Risk Assessment Scale created by the attorney general of New Jersey.

The registrant's designated tier classification determines the scope of the subsequent notification, with Tier 1 having the smallest scope and Tier 3 having the largest scope. Under the Tier 1 notification scheme ("law enforcement alert"), which is imposed on every registrant, information about the registrant is provided only to local law enforcement authorities. Under the Tier 2 notification scheme ("law enforcement, school, and community organization alert"), information about the registrant is provided to registered schools, day care centers, summer camps, and community organizations that care for children or provide support to women. Finally, under the Tier 3 notification scheme ("community notification"), information about the registrant is provided to members of the public who are likely to encounter the registered sex offender (New Jersey Registration and Community Notification Law, 1997).

The ethicality and impact of Megan's Law and other similar legislation have been the source of much discussion and debate. Spencer (1999) provided an overview of the potential advantages and apparent disadvantages of community notification practices. Under ideal conditions, advantages of community notification could include alerting members of the community that they may be living in the presence of a sex offender, providing a context in which parents can alert children to potentially dangerous members of the community, creating a "feeling of safety" among community residents who can look out for themselves and each other, and promoting understanding by disseminating information about the nature of sexual offending and how to protect oneself and one's children. Other potential advantages include reducing the anonymity of the offender and creating an informed group of relatives, friends, and neighbors who could not only protect themselves and each other but also provide support to the offender to lessen the risk of reoffending.

Spenser (1999) summarized potential disadvantages of community notification practices as well. That community notification creates a new form of punishment for persons who have already served their sentences for sexual crimes has raised questions about the civil rights of sexual offenders. However, legal challenges to various aspects of the Megan's Law tier classification and notification schemes have been largely unsuccessful (see *Doe v. Poritz*, 1995; *In re Registrant C.A.*, 1996). That community notification legislation may serve to decrease reports of juvenile sex offenses and incest offenses by individuals who wish to avoid subjecting themselves and their family members to the stigma of community notification (Freeman-Longo, 1996) is another potential disadvantage. Other potential disadvantages include the possibility of violence and/or discrimination against sex offenders by members of the community, increased public awareness not only of sex offenders but also of their victims, the promotion of a false sense of security among members of the community (or, alternatively, of the community living in fear), and the likelihood of driving sex offenders "underground," that is, out of contact with supervised release officers and community treatment programs. It has been suggested that community notification procedures may have the unintended obverse impact of promoting rather than reducing recidivism by hampering the likelihood of effective community reintegration for sex offenders.

Internet Child Pornography

A third area of legislative development affecting sexual offenders is that of addressing the consumption and transmission of child pornography using the Internet. Title 18 of the U.S. Criminal Code defines as criminal "any person who knowingly mails, or transports, or ships in interstate or foreign commerce by any means, *including by computer,* any child pornography" (emphasis added). In addition, it defines as criminal "any person who knowingly receives or distributes" child pornographic materials, "including by computer."

To crack down on the growing number of individuals using the Internet as a source of child pornographic material as well as of those who use the Internet to lure child victims for sexual crimes, the Federal Bureau of Investigation (FBI) established a large-scale operation known as "Innocent Images" (FBI, 2001). According to the FBI's online report, the Internet has become one of the most prevalent sources of child pornographic materials as well as a primary vehicle to target children for sexual victimization. The Innocent Images National Initiative (IINI), a component of the FBI's Crimes Against Children Program, is defined as "an intelligence-driven, proactive, multi-agency investigative initiative to combat the proliferation of child pornography/child sexual exploitation facilitated by an online computer." IINI was enacted in 1995 with an initial emphasis on Internet service providers that facilitated teen "chat rooms" used by pedophiles to lure children into sexually exploitative situations. Currently, IINI focuses on individuals who express, via the Internet, a willingness to travel across state lines to engage in sexual activity with children as well as on producers and distributors of child pornography. Since the inception of IINI, there has been a 1,200% increase in the number of cases identified for prosecution.

The identification, investigation, and prosecution of Internet child pornography and other computer sex crimes have led to an increased number of incarcerated sex offenders who claim no history of in-person offending. Often, individuals convicted of Internet child pornography crimes report that they unknowingly received or transmitted child pornographic materials while using the Internet to seek adult pornography, a First Amendment right recently upheld in *ACLU v. Reno II* (2000). The presence of these individuals in prison settings, their treatment needs, and their risk of in-person offending are issues yet to be fully explored.

Sexual Offenders in Prisons and Jails: Clinical Descriptions

Nearly a quarter of a million sex offenders are under the "care, custody, or control" of correctional agencies on any given day in the United States (Greenfield, 1997). More than half (60%) of these offenders are on some form of supervised release in the community. Within correctional facilities, sex offenders account for less than 5% of the total inmate population. However, the number of inmates sentenced for violent sexual assaults has increased by an average annual rate of nearly 15% during recent years, faster than all other categories of crime except drug trafficking. Understanding this population is the first step toward developing effective correctional management and treatment strategies.

Rapists

Groth (1979), Knight and Prentky (1990), and Hazelwood (1995) have developed rapist typologies. Studying a population of incarcerated sex offenders, Groth (1979) theorized that aggression and sexuality are components of every rape. He developed a clinical typology based on three apparent psychological motivations for rape: anger, power, and sadism. Kercher (1998) summarized Groth's typology as follows.

Rapists motivated by *anger* commit sexual assaults to release feelings of rage stemming from various facets of their lives. They use tremendous force and often know their victims. According to Groth (1979), angry rapists comprise approximately one third of incarcerated sex offenders.

Rapists motivated by *power* commit sexual assaults to compensate for feelings of incompetence and insecurity. They use intimidation and threats but little physical violence. Their crimes are planned, and rehearsal fantasies include themes of mastery and control. Groth (1979) divided power rapists into two subtypes: assertive and reassurance. *Power-assertive rapists* are motivated by a desire to exploit victims for psychological satisfaction, whereas *power-reassurance rapists* are motivated by a desire to impress women sexually. Power rapists were estimated by Groth (1979) to be the most common group of incarcerated sex offenders.

For rapists motivated by *sadism*, "aggression itself has become eroticized" (Kercher, 1998). Sadistic rapists are thought to be gratified by the suffering and traumatization of their victims. Sadistic rapes are characterized by bondage, physical torture, and the use of objects or weapons to penetrate their victims. Groth (1979) estimated that sadistic rapists comprise only 5% to 6% of the incarcerated sex offender population.

Elements of Groth's model can be found in the rapist typology developed by Knight and Prentky (1990). As described by Kercher (1998), Knight and Prentky's model identifies four types of rapist: those acting on *opportunity,* those who are *pervasively angry,* those seeking *sexual gratification,* and those acting on *vindictiveness.*

Opportunistic rapists engage in unplanned, impulsive, predatory acts of sexual violence. Kercher (1998) described these rapists as acting out of undersocialization and poor behavioral control. They use only the force necessary to gain submission of their victims, and they appear to be motivated by immediate sexual gratification rather than the discharge of rage.

Pervasively angry rapists are distinguished by their use of violence, even in the absence of victim resistance. Kercher described these rapists as exhibiting aggressive behavior in a variety of contexts. Thus, their sexual crimes are another form of expression of rage but are not typically driven by aberrant sexual fantasies.

Rapists seeking *sexual gratification* comprise the third component of the overall typology and are subdivided into four types: *overtly sadistic, muted sadistic, nonsadistic/high social competence,* and *nonsadistic/low social competence.* Overtly *sadistic rapists* are most like the sadistic rapist described by Groth (1979), with an emphasis on sexual humiliation and torture as an outlet for rage. They are distinguished from pervasively angry rapists by the degree of planning and torture in their crimes. For *muted sadistic rapists,* sadistic fantasies are moderated by high social competence such that they are not acted out behaviorally during rape. *Nonsadistic rapists* are characterized by rape fantasies involving sexual prowess.

For *vindictive rapists,* "women are the central and exclusive focus of their anger" (Kercher, 1998). Sexual assaults committed by vindictive rapists include degradation and humiliation of victims, although the aggression does not appear to be eroticized as it is for sadistic rapists.

In 1995, Hazelwood borrowed from the work of Groth (1979) and Knight and Prentky (1990) to develop a rapist typology for law enforcement use. Hazelwood's six-part typology, as described by Cunning and Buell (1997), is as follows. *Power-reassurance rapists* seek reassurance of their sexual competence, do not intend to degrade or traumatize their victims, and do not use more force than necessary. *Power-assertive rapists* use rape to assert control and dominance over women but do not use extreme physical force; they may repeatedly rape the same victims, remove or destroy the victims' clothing, and/or leave the victims in a remote area. *Anger-retaliatory rapists* experience generalized anger toward women and use rape to degrade, humiliate, and punish; they use excessive force, often incapacitating their victims with violence so that they are unable to resist rape, and their rapes are triggered by rage and occur quickly and randomly. *Anger-excitement rapists,* most like sadistic rapists described previously, enjoy the suffering of their victims and are sexually stimulated by fear and submission; these rapes are vicious and result in significant emotional and physical trauma to the victims. *Opportunistic rapists* commit sexual assaults spontaneously during the commission of other crimes; an example might be finding a woman home alone during a burglary. Finally, *gang rapists* perpetrate sexual assaults with two or more offenders; in these situations, there is often a leader and sometimes a reluctant participant who is described by the victim as more protective and helpful than the leader).

Child Molesters

Typologies of child molesters all find their roots in the work produced by Groth (1978), who distinguished between "fixated" and "regressed" pedophiles. *Fixated pedophiles* have a primary sexual preference for children, with pedophilic interests beginning during adolescence and continuing persistently through adulthood. Offenses committed by fixated pedophiles are characterized by forethought and planning, targeting young males. Fixated pedophiles have little sexual contact with same-age peers and are immature with poor interpersonal skills. Alcohol and drug abuse is considered uncommon for this group.

In contrast, *regressed pedophiles* have a primary sexual preference for similar-age peers. Pedophilic interests are manifest during adulthood, due in part to some type of precipitating stress. For the regressed type, pedophilic urges are episodic rather than persistent, and offenses involve less premeditation. Whereas fixated pedophiles target young males, regressed pedophiles target young females. Unlike fixated pedophiles, who have little or no sexual contact with similar-age peers, regressed pedophiles engage in sexual contact with peers and are often married. Regressed pedophiles have a more traditional lifestyle than do fixated pedophiles, but with underdeveloped peer relationships. Alcohol abuse and drug abuse were considered more prevalent for this group.

Dietz (1983) further delineated Groth's model by renaming the two major components (*fixated* to *preferential* and *regressed* to *situational*) and subdividing each category. *Preferential child molesters* are seductive, introverted, and/or sadistic. *Situational child molesters* are regressed, morally indiscriminate, sexually indiscriminate, and/or inadequate. According to Kercher (1998), Dietz's model has clinical utility in its description of the personality characteristics, motivations, victim preferences, and methods of operation for each type of child molester. However, it is primarily considered to be a "prosecution-focused" model rather than a "clinically focused" one in that it emphasizes how child molesters operate rather than the psychological dynamics of their behavior.

Finkelhor and Araji (1983) posited a multifactorial model of sexual offending against children. The four factors are *emotional congruence* (child molesters seek emotionally satisfying relationships with children due to their own immaturity, low self-esteem, and poor peer relations), *sexual arousal* (the early sexual experiences of pedophiles explain their sexual attraction to children), *blockages* (developmental factors interrupt offenders' progression through normal developmental stages, and situational factors such as marital disintegration create crises propelling pedophiles to seek sexual gratification through children), and *disinhibitors* (these include poor impulse control, senility, alcohol and/or drug abuse, mental illness, etc.).

A fourth pedophile typology was developed by Knight and Prentky (1990) and integrates Groth's (1978) construct of fixation with other factors deemed relevant to the understanding of pedophilic behavior. Included in the model are constructs defining the degree of social competence of the offender, the amount of contact with children, the meaning of such contact (interpersonal or narcissistic), the presence of physical injuries, and the sadistic quality of such injuries.

Offender Typologies: A Cautionary Note

The sex offender typologies just outlined are useful in that they provide a framework for describing and understanding the characteristics, motivations, and behaviors of rapists and child molesters. However, Cunning and Buell (1997) noted that typologies should be used cautiously so as to avoid oversimplification. To illustrate this point, Cunning and Buell cited two studies (Abel et al., 1987; Becker & Coleman, 1988) that examined the heterogeneity of sexual offending behavior.

Abel et al. (1987) found that nearly half of nonincarcerated sexual offenders admitted to multiple types of sexual offending. Specifically, of the 89 rapists in the study, 51% admitted to child molestation, 29% admitted to exhibitionism, 20% admitted to voyeurism, 12% admitted to frotteurism, and 11% acknowledged sexually sadistic acts. Of the 232 pedophiles in the study, 30% admitted to exhibitionism, 17% admitted to rape, 14% admitted to voyeurism, 9% admitted to frottage, and 6% acknowledged sexually sadistic acts.

Becker and Coleman (1988) found that among incest offenders, 44% had molested unrelated female children, 11% had molested unrelated male children, 18% had committed rape, 18% had committed exhibitionism, 9% had committed voyeurism, 5% had committed frottage, and 4% had committed sexually sadistic acts. Given the heterogeneity of sex crime behavior, it is useful to review the types of sexual activity that may themselves be crimes or that may be enacted in the course of a rape or other sexual assault.

Other Sexual Acts

Paraphilias are defined as fantasies, behaviors, or sexual urges focusing on unusual objects, activities, or situations. They are not, by definition, crimes. To the extent that these types of sexual acts are limited to fantasies and urges that are not translated into behaviors, they remain in the realm of clinical intervention rather than criminal prosecution. Not all paraphilias, even when acted out, would constitute criminal activity. The fourth edition of the *Diagnostic and Statistical Manual of Mental Disorders* (American Psychiatric Association, 1994) identifies eight paraphilias, which are defined as follows:

- *Fetishism:* Sexually arousing fantasies, urges, or behaviors in which an individual uses a nonhuman object in a sexual manner and generally cannot become aroused in the absence of that object
- *Transvestic fetishism:* Sexually arousing fantasies, urges, or behaviors involving cross-dressing
- *Sexual masochism:* Sexually arousing fantasies, urges, or behaviors in which the individual himself or herself is humiliated or made to suffer
- *Sexual sadism:* Sexually arousing fantasies, urges, or behaviors in which an individual is sexually stimulated by causing humiliation or suffering to another
- *Exhibitionism:* Sexually arousing fantasies, urges or behaviors in which an individual exposes his or her genitals to another person
- *Voyeurism:* Sexually arousing fantasies, urges or behaviors in which an individual observes an unsuspecting other who is naked, disrobing, or engaged in sexual activity
- *Frotteurism:* Sexually arousing fantasies, urges, or behaviors in which an individual touches or rubs against a nonconsenting person in a sexual manner, usually in a crowded public place
- *Pedophilia:* Sexually arousing fantasies, urges, or behaviors involving sexual activity with a child

Of these eight paraphilias, the first three (fetishism, transvestic fetishism, and sexual masochism) seem least likely to bring an individual into contact with the law because they generally do not involve an infringement on the rights of others. Sexually sadistic acts would be considered criminal when perpetrated against a nonconsenting victim. Exhibitionism, voyeurism, frotteurism, and pedophilia, when expressed behaviorally, clearly represent violations of the law. However, statistics identifying the frequency of criminal complaints or convictions for these actions are difficult to establish. This is true in part because these acts may be committed in the context of a rape or other sexual assault and might not be prosecuted independently. Furthermore, the statutory definitions of sex crimes vary from state to state. In some jurisdictions, terms such as *exhibitionism, voyeurism, frotteurism,* and *sadism* might not appear in the criminal code and instead might be subsumed under nondescript, general sexual offense categories.

Despite the difficulties associated with identifying the prevalence of sexually aberrant acts that may be committed by sexual offenders, it is not surprising that their presence in correctional settings poses a host of problems for correctional workers and administrators. In the next section, issues affecting the management of sexual offenders in correctional settings are reviewed.

Sexual Offenders in Prisons and Jails: Management Considerations

Popular and media portrayals of prisons display images of extreme violence. They also contribute to the public perception that prison culture is stratified in such a way that sex offenders are targeted for both physical and sexual violence in prison. To the extent that this is so, important administrative management considerations arise from this cultural phenomenon within prisons and jails. Correctional administrators are concerned with the safety of both staff and inmates. Sexual offenders not only may be at increased risk for physical and sexual violence by other inmates, they also may themselves pose a danger to inmates and staff (Fagan, Wennerstrom, & Miller, 1996). In light of these concerns, correctional administrators must contend with a variety of issues to ensure the safety, security, and orderly running of their institutions. Because sexual violence is considered by correctional workers to be related to other types of violence in prison, it seems particularly important to examine the problem of sexual assault in prison in more depth.

Sexual Assault in Prison

Much is hypothesized but little is actually known about the frequency and nature of sexual assaults in prison. Portrayals in the popular media suggest high rates of such behavior. Unfortunately, a number of complications prevent accurate assessment of this problem. Fagan et al. (1996) summarized these complications as (a) reluctance on the part of victims to report instances of sexual assault, (b) lack of data collection by correctional systems, (c) lack of awareness among correctional personnel of the indicators of sexual assault in their facilities, (d) inconsistent operational definitions of sexual assault and questionable methodologies across existing studies, and (e) lack of generalizability of findings from jails, to prisons, to other correctional systems. As a result of these complications, estimates of the rate of sexual assault in prison have ranged from just a few each year to as many as 18 per minute (Fagan et al., 1996). Based on their review of studies considered methodologically sound, Fagan et al. concluded that (a) the number of inmates reporting actual sexual assaults is relatively low, (b) the number of inmates reporting being pressured to engage in unwanted sexual behavior is much higher, and (c) staff are not aware of many instances of sexual assault and sexual coercion that occur in correctional facilities.

Despite the lack of firm empirical data regarding the incidence and prevalence of sexual assault in prison, those familiar with the problem have theorized about the characteristics, behavioral strategies, and psychological motivations of inmates who commit such acts. Fagan et al. (1996) reviewed the literature and concluded that inmates who perpetrate sexual assaults in prison (a) tend to be older and larger in stature than their victims, (b) identify themselves as heterosexual, (c) may have histories of childhood physical and/or sexual abuse, (d) may have poor anger management and problem-solving skills, and (e) may demonstrate exhibitionistic and voyeuristic tendencies as well as overt sexual assault.

Groth and Burgess (1980) described the behavioral strategies and psychological motivations of inmates who commit sexual assault in prison. With respect to strategies, some inmates appear to use *conning and manipulation* to ensnare other inmates into sexually exploitative relationships. This technique may manifest itself initially as attempts at ingratiation with younger, more naive inmates through offers of cigarettes, snacks, and protection. A second strategy involves *threats and intimidation* in which the perpetrators may stalk and threaten intended victims to gain sexual compliance. A final strategy is simply to take by *force* whatever sexual objects are desired, sometimes without prior interaction.

What drives inmates to engage in sexually exploitative and aggressive behavior in prison? Groth and Burgess (1980) identified five motivational patterns offered by inmates to explain their behavior. The first was *conquest and control* so as to assure the perpetrator of his or her power and authority and to compensate for feelings of insecurity. The second was *revenge and retaliation* so as to repay another inmate for a perceived wrong. The third was *sadism or degradation,* in which aggressive behavior has become eroticized and sexually stimulating. The fourth was *sexual conflict,* in which the perpetrator acts on homosexual urges despite a general heterosexual orientation. The fifth was *status or affiliation,* or participation in gang rapes, so as to ensure one's status among a dominant peer group.

Clearly, the problem of sexual offending extends from the community into our prisons and jails. It is conceivable, then, that treatment of sexual offending behavior could, if effective, affect the rate of sexual assault not only in the community but also in correctional settings.

Sexual Offender Treatment Programs

Over the past two decades, the number of incarcerated sex offenders in both state and federal correctional facilities has increased dramatically (Becker & Murphy, 1998). For example, the number of sex offenders in state prisons more than quadrupled during a 14-year span, from 20,500 in 1980 to 88,100 in 1994 (NCMEC Sex Offender Policy Task Force, 1998). As a result, state and federal correctional facilities have been confronted with difficult decisions regarding the treatment of incarcerated sex offenders.

The empirical literature regarding the treatment of incarcerated sex offenders differs greatly in terms of accepted treatment methods and demonstrated treatment effectiveness. The majority of sex offender treatment programs in the United States use some form of cognitive therapy in conjunction with psychopharmacological or behavioral techniques (State of Minnesota, 1994). Currently, however, there is no universally accepted treatment approach for the treatment of incarcerated sex offenders.

Despite the lack of universal agreement regarding a treatment approach for sex offenders, one particular treatment approach has gained wide acceptance. Specifically, the most widely accepted treatment approach for incarcerated sex offenders is cognitive-behavioral therapy within a relapse prevention model, which may also include a pharmacological component (Becker & Murphy, 1998). Each of the components of this comprehensive treatment approach—cognitive-behavioral therapy, relapse prevention techniques, and pharmacological interventions—is briefly discussed next.

The cognitive-behavioral component of this comprehensive treatment approach is generally provided in both group and individual formats. A primary focus of cognitive-behavioral treatment is reducing denial and cognitive distortions (e.g., minimization, rationalization). This is particularly important because it is believed that sex offenders use denial and cognitive distortions to justify and maintain their offending behavior. In addition, cognitive-behavioral treatment enables sex offenders to identify individual risk factors that may trigger recidivistic sexual crimes. Treatment also focuses on identifying sex offenders' deviant arousal patterns and fantasies. Through the use of both cognitive and behavioral techniques, sex offenders learn how to decrease the intensity and frequency of these urges. Cognitive-behavioral treatment also typically includes anger management, social skills training, problem-solving, and decision-making components. An essential aspect of cognitive-behavioral treatment is helping sex offenders to develop victim empathy; it is believed that victim empathy will inhibit offenders from committing future sexual crimes.

The relapse prevention model within which cognitive-behavioral therapy is ideally applied is based on the model first used with substance abusers (Alaska Department of Corrections, 1996). The relapse prevention model is predicated on the premise that, although sex offenders may never be "cured" in the traditional sense, treatment can help offenders to manage and cope with their aberrant sexual desires (Becker & Murphy, 1998). This approach ostensibly enables sex offenders to identify cognitive and behavioral patterns that are precursors to their sexual offending behavior, and it also helps them to develop self-management strategies to deal effectively with these patterns.

A final component of the comprehensive model described here is the adjunctive use of pharmacological interventions. Certain medications, such as antiandrogens and antidepressants, have been shown to be moderately effective with sex offender populations (Becker & Murphy, 1998). Antiandrogens, used for what is commonly termed "chemical castration," limit circulating testosterone, thereby reducing sexual urges and desires. Antidepressants, particularly selective serotonin reuptake inhibitors such as Prozac, Paxil, and Zoloft, have been shown to assist sex offenders in controlling compulsive behaviors that are believed to contribute to repeat sexual offending (Kafka, 1991).

Sex Offender Treatment Outcome Studies

The effectiveness of treatment with sex offenders, both incarcerated and non-incarcerated, has been the subject of considerable debate. A review of the relevant empirical literature reveals that treatment outcome studies report widely differing conclusions regarding the effectiveness of treatment for sex offenders. Part of the difficulty in assessing the efficacy of sex offender treatment lies in the lack of uniformity and poor methodology in many sex offender treatment studies. For example, researchers often use different definitions of key terms such as *sex offender, treatment, recidivism,* and *cured.* As a result, there is inherent difficulty in drawing conclusions across studies. Accordingly, some researchers have expressed the view that definitive conclusions regarding the effectiveness of treatment with sex offenders cannot be drawn at the current time (see, e.g., State of Minnesota, 1994).

Given the difficulty in assessing the effectiveness of treatment approaches and programs for incarcerated sex offenders, it is difficult to reach firm conclusions regarding the efficacy of these treatments. Nonetheless, research suggests that treatment is effective in some cases. For example, in a meta-analysis of 12 sex offender treatment outcome studies, Hall (1995) found a significant treatment effect with a mean recidivism rate of 19% for the treatment group and 27% for the comparison group. Based on his review, Hall concluded that cognitive-behavioral and pharmacological approaches are more effective than purely behavioral interventions. Similarly, Marshal, Jones, Ward, Johnston, and Barbaree (1991) concluded that cognitive-behavioral treatment programs are the most effective treatment approach for child molesters.

In light of these findings, a key concern is whether treatment programs for incarcerated sex offenders are employing treatment approaches that have empirical support. A review of the literature addressing various corrections-based treatment programs reveals significant variability in the types of programs being offered. In the next section, we discuss a treatment program that is viewed as representing the state of the art in corrections-based sex offender treatment.

Best Practices

As discussed in the previous section, the most widely accepted treatment method for incarcerated sex offenders is cognitive-behavioral therapy within a relapse prevention framework, often with a pharmacological component. In light of the demonstrated empirical support for this comprehensive treatment approach, it is only logical that any state-of-the-art program should contain these components. One such corrections-based program is the Sex Offender Treatment Program (SOTP) offered by the Federal Bureau of Prisons.

In 1990, the Federal Correctional Institution at Butner, North Carolina, established the SOTP, a 112-bed residential treatment program for male sexual offenders within the federal prison system. Consistent with the empirical literature discussed previously, the SOTP uses a cognitive-behavioral approach within a relapse prevention context. The SOTP's underlying philosophy is that although sexual offending cannot be "cured" per se, criminal sexual behavior can be effectively managed through comprehensive treatment and intensive supervision. The SOTP recognizes that criminal sexual behavior is influenced by a variety of factors, including biological, social, and psychological conditions. The stated goal of the SOTP is to help sex offenders manage their sexual thoughts and behaviors so as to reduce recidivism.

Inmates may be referred to the SOTP from any federal prison if they are serving sentences for sexual offenses or if they have had previous convictions for sexual offenses. The program is voluntary, and potential treatment candidates must express personal motivation for treatment. Acknowledgment of responsibility for a sexual crime is a prerequisite. The program seeks to provide services to those inmates who appear determined to engage genuinely in the treatment process. Recently, there has been some discussion about mandating treatment for federal inmates convicted of sexual crimes.

Once accepted into the program, the length of participation in treatment is usually between 18 and 36 months depending on several factors, including the length of the inmate's sentence, the date of referral to the program, the number of beds available, and the date of the inmate's arrival at the Butner facility. The SOTP regimen consists of four phases: pretreatment and orientation, psychosexual assessment, treatment, and release planning.

The pretreatment and orientation phase is designed to introduce inmate clients to the various aspects of the program and the therapeutic community. During this phase, inmates participate in a series of informational sessions to learn about the program itself, the benefits of treatment, staff expectations, and the required standards of conduct for program participants.

The psychosexual assessment phase is designed to provide a comprehensive examination of each participant across several different domains. Specifically, through the use of questionnaires, psychological test batteries, and physiological assessment tools (including penile plethysmography and polygraphy), the inmates are evaluated in three areas: intellectual and cognitive functioning, personality and psychopathology, and psychosexual characteristics.

The treatment phase consists of several modalities, including milieu therapy, individual and group psychotherapy, structured psychoeducational programs, therapeutic community meetings, and discussion groups. Treatment may include a pharmacological component based on individual offender needs as identified in each participant's specific treatment plan. General goals for each program participant include complete acceptance of responsibility for sexual crimes, expression of remorse for sexual crimes, recognition of deviant sexual arousal and offense patterns, control of deviant sexual arousal and offense patterns, improved management of negative emotional states, genuine expression of empathy for victims, improvement in social skills and interpersonal functioning, and knowledge of relapse prevention skills, including development of a specific individualized relapse prevention plan.

The release planning phase of the SOTP is designed to help program participants translate and maintain therapeutic gains in the community after their release from prison. Attention is given to several key concerns, including appropriate post-release housing, employment, ongoing treatment, and community supervision.

Future Directions

This chapter began with an introductory review of sex crime statistics; continued with a discussion of legislative trends affecting sexual offenders; provided a clinical description of rapists, child molesters, and paraphiliacs; addressed issues pertaining to sexual assault in prison; described various approaches to sex offender treatment; and highlighted best practices in sex offender treatment today. The information and issues outlined in the chapter answered some questions but also raised many others. We conclude this chapter with a discussion of directions for future research. This task is made easier by the Center for Sex Offender Management. Established in 1997 with the goal of enhancing public safety by improving the management of adult and juvenile sex offenders, CSOM is a joint effort of the Office of Justice Programs, the National Institute of Corrections, and the State Justice Institute. CSOM approaches its goals through research, policy analysis, implementation of model programs, and technical assistance to the field.

A review of research initiatives adopted by CSOM (1999) sheds light on future directions in the field of sex offender management and treatment that follow the format of this chapter. To further hone what is known about sex crime statistics, CSOM has developed two programs. The first, titled "Learning About Crime and Criminals From Criminal History Records," will track approximately 300,000 inmates released from prisons in 15 states. They will be followed for a 3-year period to determine (a) what can be learned from criminal history records about the impact of a particular sanction, intervention, or treatment on the subsequent behavior of convicted sex offenders; and (b) what can be learned from criminal history records about the reinvolvement of convicted sex offenders in crime. A second project focusing on sex crime statistics, titled "National Crime Victimization Survey," has been conducted continually since 1972. This project addresses the sociodemographic characteristics of offenders involved in violent crime, including rape and sexual assault, as well as the rate at which victims report crimes to police and the self-defense measures used by victims.

Regarding legislative trends affecting sex offenders, CSOM is affiliated with a study that will explore the impact of sex offender notification on Wisconsin communities, with an emphasis on improving law enforcement and correctional responses. Specifically, this study will examine the manner of implementation of sex offender notification laws, the impact of community notification on law enforcement and corrections (e.g., with respect to resources, time, workload, and cost), the community's satisfaction with the notification process, and the impact of community notification on sex offenders.

Additional research pertaining to legislative trends affecting sex offenders is being conducted in the area of risk assessment. Risk assessment research has a direct link to sexually violent predator laws, which seek to detain convicted sex offenders beyond their period of incarceration based on the presumption that their crimes are habitual in nature. Risk assessment studies currently associated with CSOM include the development of diagnostic instruments to classify adult and juvenile sex offenders for treatment and future risk by examining sociodemographic, clinical, and actuarial variables.

With respect to the clinical description and treatment of sex offenders, research is being conducted on both adults and juveniles. One study, aimed at examining the utility of rapist classifications for criminal justice applications, will determine whether a typology developed on samples of incarcerated rapists is generalizable to other groups of aggressive sexual offenders. The efficacy of various treatment approaches for incarcerated adult sex offenders is currently being examined in the Colorado and Illinois Departments of Corrections.

Other studies will address important questions concerning the classification and treatment of juvenile sex offenders. CSOM's research initiatives pertaining to juvenile sex offenders include examinations of procedures in the juvenile justice system, the utility of juvenile sex offender typologies, and risk profiling of juvenile sex offenders with an eye toward predicting success in community-based treatment programs.

To date, there are no known studies of the clinical, sociodemographic, or criminal history characteristics of individuals convicted of Internet child pornography crimes or their risk of in-person offending against children. Given the growing number of such cases in the United States, research in this area is needed. Another topic addressed in this chapter, but largely excluded from the professional literature, has to do with the management of sex offenders in correctional settings. For correctional administrators and treatment providers, questions regarding the safest and best options for housing sex offenders in prison remain largely unanswered. Research examining the relative rates of physical and sexual violence against inmates and staff in sex offender-only prisons compared with general population facilities is recommended.

Although much is known about sex offenders, their crimes, and modes of intervention to reduce recidivism, there remain many areas of controversy and uncertainty. This chapter was intended to provide an overview of the existing literature on sex offenders and to identify areas of doubt and debate that may be appropriate topics for future study.

Notes

1. For a survey of recently enacted sexual offender commitment statutes, see Ariz. Rev. Stat. Ann. §§ 13-4601 to 13-4613 (West Supp. 1996 & 1997); Cal. Welf. & Inst. Code §§ 6600-6609.3 (West Supp. 1997); Colo. Rev. Stat. § 16-11.7-101 et seq. (Supp. 1996); Conn. Gen. Stat. § 17a-566 et seq. (1992 & Supp. 1996); 725 Ill. Comp. Stat. § 205 et seq. (1994); Iowa Code Ann. §§709C.1 to 709C.12 (West Supp. 1997); Kan. Stat. Ann. § 59-29a01 to 59-29a17 (1994 & Supp. 1996); Mass. Gen. Laws ch. 123A (Supp. 1997); Minn. Stat. Ann. § 253B.01 to 253B.23 (1994 & West Supp. 1997); Neb. Rev. Stat. § 29-2923 et seq. (Supp. 1996); N.J. Stat. Ann. § 30:4-82.4 (West Supp. 1997); N.M. Stat. Ann. § 43-1-1 et seq. (1993); Oreg. Rev. Stat. § 426.510 et seq. (1995); Tenn. Code Ann. § 33-6-301 et seq. (1984 & Supp. 1996); Utah Code Ann. § 77-16-1 et seq. (1995); Wash. Rev. Code Ann. §§ 71.09.010 to 71.09.230 (West 1993 & Supp. 1997); Wisc. Stat. Ann. §§ 980.01 to 980.13 (West Supp. 1997).

2. The Ex Post Facto Clause of the U.S. Constitution expressly prohibits the following: (a) a law that punishes a previously committed act as a crime if the act was not a crime at the time it was committed, (b) a law that makes a crime more serious than it was at the time it was committed, (c) a law that retroactively inflicts a greater punishment for the crime than the law originally provided for at the time the crime was committed, and (d) a law that alters the legal rules of evidence that existed at the time the crime was committed. See *Collins v. Youngblood* (1990). The Double Jeopardy Clause of the Fifth Amendment to the Constitution protects against the following: (a) a second prosecution for the same offense after acquittal, (b) a second prosecution for the same offense after conviction, and (c) multiple punishments for the same offense. See *United States v. Ursery* (1996).

3. For a survey of the sex offender statutes enacted in all 50 states, see Ala. Code § 13A-11-200 (1994); Alaska Stat. §§ 12.63.010, 18.65.087 (Michie 1996); Ariz. Rev. Stat. Ann. §§ 13-3821, 41-1750(B) (West 1996); Ark. Code Ann. § 12-12-901 (Michie 1995); Cal. Penal Code § 290 (West 1996 & Supp. 1997); Colo. Rev. Stat. § 18-3-4123.5 (1996); Conn. Gen. Stat. Ann. § 54-102r (West 1997); Del. Code Ann. tit. 11, § 4120 (1995); Fla. Stat. Ann. § 775.21 (West 1997); Ga. Code Ann. § 42-1-12 (1997); Hawaii Rev. Stat. §§ 707-743 (1995); Idaho Code §§ 18-8301 to 18-8311 (1997); 730 Ill. Comp. Stat. §§ 730-150/1 to 730-150/10 (West 1995); Ind. Code Ann. §§ 5-2-12-1 to 5-2-12-12 (West 1996); Iowa Code Ann. §§ 692A.1-.13 (West 1997); Kan. Stat. Ann. §§ 22-4902 to 22-4097 (1996); Ky. Rev. Stat. Ann. § 17.510 (Michie 1996); La. Rev. Stat. Ann. §§ 15:540 to 15:549 (West 1997); Maine Rev. Stat. Ann. tit. 34-A, §§ 11003-11004 (West 1996); Md. Ann. Code art. 27, § 792 (1996 & Supp. 1997); Mass. Gen. Laws Ann. ch. 22, § 37 (West 1994); Mich. Comp. Laws Ann. §§ 28.721-.730 (West 1997); Minn. Stat. Ann. § 243.166 (West 1997); Miss. Code Ann. § 45-33-1 (1997); Mo. Ann. Stat. § 566.600 (West 1997); Mont. Code Ann. §§ 46-23-501 to 46-23-507 (1995); Nebr. Rev. Stat. §§ 29-4001 to 29-4013 (1996); Nev. Rev. Stat. Ann. §§ 207.151 to 207.157 (Michie 1997); N.H. Rev. Stat. Ann. § 651-B:1 to 651-B:9 (1996): N.J. Stat. Ann. §§ 2C:7-1 to 2C:7-5 (West 1995 & Supp. 1997); N.M. Stat. Ann. §§ 29-11A-1 to 29-11A-8 (Michie 1996); N.Y. Correct. Laws § 168 (McKinney 1997); N.C. Gen. Stat. §§ 14-208.5 to 14-208.13 (1996); N.D. Cent. Code § 12.1-32-15 (1995); Ohio Rev. Code Ann. §§ 2950.01-.08 (Anderson 1996); Okla. Stat. Ann. tit. 57, §§ 581-587 (West 1997); Oreg. Rev. Stat. §§ 181.594-.600 (1996); 42 Pa. Cons. Stat. Ann. §§ 42-9791 to 42-9798 (West 1997); R.I. Gen. Laws §§ 11-37-16 to 11-37-19 (1996); S.C. Code Ann. §§ 23-3-400 to 23-3-490 (Law Co-op. 1996); S.D. Codified Laws §§ 22-22-39 to 22-22-41 (Michie 1997); Tenn. Code Ann. §§ 40-39-101 to 40-39-108 (1996); Texas Civ. Prac. & Rem. Code Ann. § 4413(51) (West 1997); Utah Code Ann. § 77-27-21.5 (1997); Vt. Stat. Ann. tit. 13, §§ 5401-5413 (1997); Va. Code Ann. §§ 19.2-298.1-3, 19.2-390.1 (Michie 1997); Wash. Rev. Code Ann. § 9A.44130 (West Supp. 1997); W.Va. Code §§ 61-8F-1 to 61-8F-10 (1994 & Supp. 1997); Wis. Stat. Ann. § 175.45 (West 1996); Wyo. Stat. Ann. §§ 7-19-301 to 7-19-306 (Michie 1997).

4. It is interesting to note that 27 states also provide for the registration of some or all juvenile sex offenders (CSOM, 1999).

5. Megan's Law defines a "sex offense" as including "aggravated sexual assault, sexual assault, aggravated criminal sexual contact, kidnapping, . . . or an attempt to commit any of these crimes if the court found that the offender's conduct was characterized by a pattern of repetitive, compulsive behavior, regardless of the date of the commission of the offense or the date of conviction" (Megan's Law § 2C:7-2b(1)).

References

Abel, G., Becker, J., Mittelman, M., Rathner-Cunningham, J., Rouleau, J., & Murphy, W. (1987). Self-reported sex crimes of nonincarcerated paraphiliacs. *Journal of Interpersonal Violence, 2,* 3-25.

ACLU v. Reno II, 99-1324 (2000).

Alaska Department of Corrections. (1996). *Sex offender treatment program: Initial recidivism study.* Juneau: Alaska Department of Corrections, Offenders Program.

American Psychiatric Association. (1994). *Diagnostic and statistical manual of mental disorders* (4th ed.). Washington, DC: Author.

Becker, J., & Coleman, E. (1988). Incest. In V. Van Hasselt, R. Morrison, A. Bellack, & M. Hersen (Eds.), *Handbook of family violence.* New York: Plenum.

Becker, J., & Murphy, W. D. (1998). What we know and do not know about assessing and treating sex offenders. *Psychology, Public Policy, & Law, 4,* 116-137.

Bodine, B. G. (1990). Washington's new violent sexual predator commitment system: An unconstitutional law and an unwise policy choice. *University of Puget Sound Law Review, 14,* 105.

Center for Sex Offender Management. (1999). *Compendium of OJP-sponsored projects related to sex offenders.* Silver Spring, MD: Author.

Collins v. Youngblood, 497 U.S. 37 (1990).

Cunning, G., & Buell, M. (1997). *Supervision of the sex offender.* Brandon, VT: Safer Society Press.

DeMatteo, D. S. (1998). Welcome to Anytown, U.S.A.—Home of beautiful scenery (and a convicted sex offender): Sex offender registration and notification laws in *E.B. v. Verniero. Villanova Law Review, 43,* 581-635.

Dietz, P. E. (1983). Sex offenses: Behavioral aspects. In S. H. Kadish (Ed.), *Encyclopedia of crime and justice* (pp. 1489-1490). New York: Free Press.

Doe v. Poritz, 662 A.2d 367 (N.J. 1995).

Ellis, L. (1989). *Theories of rape.* New York: Hemisphere.

Fagan, T. J., Wennerstrom, D., & Miller, J. (1996). Sexual assault of male inmates: Prevention, identification, and intervention. *Journal of Correctional Health Care, 3*(1), 49-65.

Federal Bureau of Investigation. (2001). *Online child pornography: Innocent Images National Initiative* [Online]. Available: www.fbi.gov/hq/cid/cac/innocent.htm

Feldman, D. L. (1997). The "Scarlet Letter laws" of the 1990s: A response to critics. *Alabama Law Review, 60,* 1081-1125.

Finkelhor, D., & Araji, S. (1983). *Explanations of pedophilia: A four factor model.* Durham: University of New Hampshire Press.

Freeman-Longo, R. E. (1996). Prevention or problem. *Sexual Abuse: A Journal of Research and Treatment, 18*(2), 91-100.

Freeman-Longo, R. E. (1997). Reducing sexual abuse in America: Legislating tougher laws or public education and prevention. *New England Journal on Criminal & Civil Confinement, 23,* 303-331.

Freeman-Longo, R. E., & Knopp, F. H. (1992). Sex offender recidivism: Issues and outcomes. *Annals of Sex Research, 5,* 142-160.

Gibeaut, J. (1997). Defining punishment: Courts split on notification provisions of sex offender laws. *American Bar Association Journal, 3,* 36.

Goodman, E. A. (1996). Megan's Law: The New Jersey Supreme Court navigates uncharted waters. *Seton Hall Law Review, 26,* 764.

Greenfield, L. A. (1997). *Sex offenses and offenders: An analysis of data on rape and sexual assault.* Washington, DC: U.S. Department of Justice, Office of Justice Programs, Bureau of Justice Statistics.

Groth, A. N. (1978). Guidelines for the assessment and management of the offender. In A. W. Burgess, A. N. Groth, L. L. Holmstrom, & S. M Sgroi (Eds.), *Sexual assault of children and adolescents* (pp. 25-42). Lexington, MA: Lexington Books.

Groth, A. N. (1979). *Men who rape: The psychology of the offender.* New York: Plenum.

Groth, A. N., & Burgess, A. W. (1980). Male rape: Offenders and victims. *American Journal of Psychiatry, 137,* 806-819.

Hacking, J. O. (1997). Won't you be my neighbor? Do community notification statutes violate sexual offenders' rights under the Constitution's ban on the passage of ex post facto laws? *St. Louis Law Journal, 41,* 761-807.

Hall, G. C. N. (1995). Sexual offender recidivism revisited: A meta-analysis of recent treatment studies. *Journal of Consulting and Clinical Psychology, 63,* 802-809.

Hazelwood, R. (1995). Analyzing the rape and profiling the offender. In R. Hazelwood & A. Burgess (Eds.), *Practical aspects of rape investigation: A multidisciplinary approach* (pp. 155-181). New York: CRC Press.

In re Registrant C.A., 679 A.2d 1153 (N.J. 1996).

Kafka, M. P. (1991). Successful antidepressant treatment of nonparaphilic sexual addictions and paraphilias in men. *Journal of Clinical Psychiatry, 52,* 60-65.

Kansas Sexually Violent Predator Act, Kan. Stat. Ann. §§ 59-29a01 to 59-29a17 (1995).

Kansas v. Hendricks, 117 S. Ct. 2072 (1997).

Kercher, G. A. (1998). *Supervision and treatment of sex offenders.* Holmes Beach, FL: Learning Publications.

Knight, R. A., & Prentky, R. A. (1990). Classifying sexual offenders: The development and corroboration of taxonomic models. In W. L. Marshall, R. Laws, & H. E. Barbaree (Eds.), *Handbook of sexual assault: Issues, theories, and treatment of the offender* (pp. 25-52). New York: Plenum.

Marshall, W. L., Jones, R., Ward, T., Johnston, P., & Barbaree, H. E. (1991). Treatment outcome with sex offenders. *Psychology Review, 11,* 465-485.

Martin, R. J. (1996). Pursuing public protection through mandatory community notification of convicted sex offenders: The trials and tribulations of Megan's Law. *Boston University Public International Law Journal, 6,* 29-56.

McAllister, S. R. (1997). The constitutionality of Kansas laws targeting sex offenders. *Washburn Law Journal, 36,* 419-467.

Morris, D. L. (1997). Constitutional implications of the involuntary commitment of sexually violent predators: A due process analysis. *Cornell Law Review, 82,* 594-643.

NCMEC Sex Offender Policy Task Force. (1998). *A model state sex-offender policy.* Alexandria, VA: National Center for Missing and Exploited Children.

New Jersey Registration and Community Notification Law, N.J. Stat. Ann. 2C:7-1 to 2C:7-5 (West 1995 & Supp. 1997).

Salter, A. (1992). Epidemiology of child sexual abuse. In W. O'Donohue & J. H. Greer (Eds.), *The sexual abuse of children: Vol. 1. Theory and research* (pp. 108-138). Hillsdale, NJ: Lawrence Erlbaum.

Seling v. Young, 99-1185 19 2 F.3d 870 (2001).

Spencer, A. (1999). *Working with sex offenders in prisons and through release to the community: A handbook.* London: Jessica Kingsley.

Stacy, T., & Dayton, K. (1997). The underfederalization of crime. *Cornell Journal of Law & Public Policy, 6,* 247-324.

State of Minnesota. (1994). *Sex offender treatment programs.* Minneapolis: State of Minnesota, Office of the Legislative Auditor, Program Evaluation Division.

Teir, R., & Coy, K. (1997). Approaches to sexual predators: Community notification and civil commitment. *New England Journal on Criminal & Civil Confinement, 23,* 405-426.

United States v. Ursery, 116 S. Ct. 2135 (1996).

Violent Crime Control and Law Enforcement Act, 42 U.S.C. §§ 13701-14223 (1994).

Identifying Juvenile Offenders With Mental Health Disorders

Lisa Melanie Boesky

The purpose of this chapter is to provide correctional workers with a workable understanding of the mental health issues of juvenile offenders, including identification of the mental health disorders most commonly seen among youth involved with the justice system. This chapter addresses issues related to the prevalence of mental health problems among juveniles in corrections, the job-related implications for correctional workers, the training needs for correctional workers regarding mentally ill juveniles, and the role of correctional workers in helping to identify mental health problems among the youth they supervise.

There are a significant number of juveniles with mental health disorders involved with the corrections system. Although many juvenile offenders have some type of mental health *issue* (e.g., childhood abuse, inability to control anger, poor interpersonal skills, low frustration tolerance, poor coping skills) and could benefit from some form of individual or family counseling, not all of these youth suffer from a mental health *disorder*. According to the most widely used resource on mental health disorders, the text-revised fourth edition of the *Diagnostic and Statistical Manual for Mental Disorders* (*DSM-IV-TR;* American Psychiatric Association [APA], 2000), symptoms of mental health disorders must cause a juvenile significant distress and/or significantly interfere with the juvenile's ability to function in important areas of his or her life (e.g., interpersonal relationships, school, work).

The exact number of juvenile offenders with mental health disorders is currently unknown because there are no national prevalence studies on this population of youth. In addition, the small number of studies that have investigated mentally ill youth involved within the justice system have typically been methodologically flawed. However, despite these issues, it is still clear that the prevalence of mental health disorders is higher among youth in juvenile justice than among their peers in the general population (Edens & Otto, 1997). Because accessing comprehensive quality mental health care in the community can be a challenge for some adolescents, particularly those involved with the justice system (e.g., lack of finances/insurance, minimal or no family support, transportation issues, language barriers, shortage of clinicians trained to work with youth), correctional facilities are often the default placement for youth with mental health disorders who are not receiving appropriate mental health treatment in the community.

Many correctional workers who supervise juveniles report that young offenders with mental health disorders add to the stress of their job and can be challenging, both physically and emotionally. Part of the reason for this is that most correctional workers receive little or no training on mental illness, particularly on how mental health disorders manifest among child and adolescent offenders. Misunderstanding a juvenile's mental health symptoms can result in correctional workers feeling ineffective and frustrated when they interact with a juvenile, which can add to feelings of staff burnout and eventually high rates of staff turnover. Supervising and managing juvenile offenders with mental health disorders is challenging enough when one is educated about a juvenile's emotional and/or behavioral difficulties; without this knowledge, effective interventions are unlikely if not impossible.

To run safe and secure living units within a correctional facility, as well as to effectively supervise youth on probation/parole (which typically translates into public safety), correctional workers need to be able to identify young offenders with mental health disorders. Correctional officers (COs), in particular, are in a key position to make referrals to appropriate mental health professionals when mental illness is suspected among youth under their supervision. COs are often the first to notice a change in a young offender's behavior and can provide critical information to the clinicians who evaluate these youth. Furthermore, if psychotropic medication is prescribed to a juvenile, COs can provide feedback as to whether the medication appears to have a positive, a negative, or no impact on the juvenile's behavior. They can also report various medication side effects they observe. In addition, the likelihood of developing positive interpersonal relationships, engaging in constructive interactions, and using effective management strategies with youth are significantly increased when COs increase their ability to recognize a young offender's mental health symptoms as signs of a psychiatric disorder as opposed to oppositional or manipulative behavior.

Identification of Juveniles With Mental Health Disorders

The identification of mental health disorders among juvenile offenders can be challenging. Some youth are eager to inform staff that "I can't do that because I have bipolar disorder" or to scream throughout an entire living unit that they are going to kill themselves. However, there are a significant number of mentally ill youth that never notify staff of their psychiatric diagnoses, current mental health symptoms, or thoughts of wanting to end their lives. Because most correctional workers have not been trained on mental health disorders, it is easy for them to overlook subtle signs and symptoms of a juvenile's mental illness. Furthermore, many staff misinterpret a young offender's mental health symptoms as an attempt by the juvenile to avoid unpleasant tasks, to be intentionally resistant toward adult requests, or to manipulate others into getting whatever it is the juvenile wants. When mentally ill juvenile offenders are not correctly identified, they are typically viewed as "troublemakers" or "bad" kids in need of sanctions instead of "sick" kids in need of assistance or treatment. Some juvenile offenders with mental health disorders remain unidentified throughout their adolescent years and even into adulthood. The criminal justice system is filled with a considerable number of mentally ill adult offenders—some appropriately diagnosed and treated, but many continuing to remain unidentified and without therapeutic services.

Self-Report Information

There are many ways in which to identify young offenders with mental health disorders. One of the most common ways is to ask a juvenile if he or she has ever received a mental health evaluation or mental health treatment (e.g., individual therapy, psychotropic medication, psychiatric hospitalization) in the past. However, this is not always an accurate method of distinguishing mentally ill from non-mentally ill juveniles. Because adolescent offenders typically do not refer themselves for mental health evaluations or treatment, the adults in their lives play a significant role as to which youth are referred for mental health services and which are not. Parents/caretakers, teachers, COs, probation/parole officers, child welfare staff, and the like who have a low tolerance for behavior that is outside the norm for most youth (e.g., overly active, sad much of the time, complaints of fatigue, idiosyncratic thinking) might be more likely to refer a juvenile for mental health services. On the other hand, some families/caretakers, teachers, COs, community supervisions staff, child welfare workers, and the like have a higher tolerance for these types of symptoms and might not even notice that a juvenile is displaying unusual behaviors or, if they do, might perceive the juvenile as "energetic" or as a "creative thinker." In addition, adults from various cultural backgrounds hold different views regarding what types of behaviors indicate mental illness or maladaptive functioning, and this can significantly influence if and when an adult decides to seek mental health services for a juvenile.

Family History

Family history of mental illness may also provide some insight into the mental health symptoms of juveniles. Many serious mental health disorders (e.g., schizophrenia, bipolar disorder, major depression, dysthymic disorder, attention deficit/hyperactivity disorder [ADHD]) are more common among first-degree biological relatives than among individuals in the general population. Twin and adoption studies have also provided evidence of a genetic influence for some mental health disorders (APA, 2000). Therefore, having a biological parent or another relative who is mentally ill can increase a juvenile's risk of having the same or a similar mental health disorder. However, mental illness in a juvenile's family does not automatically imply that the juvenile will definitely manifest a mental health disorder, but it may be more likely than in someone without this type of family history. The manifestation of mental health disorders is typically a culmination of a juvenile's inherited biological or psychological vulnerabilities, environmental stressors, and particular abilities and coping skills. Youth who have significant mental illness in their families, exposure to a variety of psychosocial stressors (including incarceration), and poor coping skills are usually at highest risk for developing a mental health disorder. A significant number of juvenile offenders fit into this category.

Screening and Assessment Instruments

Some criminal justice agencies use mental health screening tools to help identify which young offenders are suffering from mental illness. Two instruments designed specifically for screening mental health symptoms among juvenile offenders are the second edition of the Massachusetts Youth Screening Instrument (MAYSI-2) (Grisso & Barnum, 2000) and the Mental Health Juvenile Detention Admission Tool (MH-JDAT) (Washington State Detention Managers Association & Boesky, 2000). Both are brief self-report measures that can be administered by nonclinical staff. These instruments were developed to distinguish those juveniles who may be suffering from mental health disorders and who may be in need of more in-depth mental health assessments by trained mental health professionals.

Although mental health screening tools can be extremely helpful in the identification of juveniles with mental illness, the possibility of acquiring inaccurate information also exists. Most screening instruments rely on juvenile offenders' self-reports of mental health symptoms, so the juveniles themselves are typically the gatekeepers as to what information is conveyed. Adolescents, particularly older ones, can provide fairly accurate descriptions of their thoughts, feelings, and behaviors. Clearly, they are the only ones who truly know what they are thinking and feeling. In general, most youth experiencing mental health symptoms, including strange or unusual thoughts and behavior, will answer honestly if asked about them directly (Herjanic & Reich, 1982; Verhulst & van der Ende, 1992). However, there are some juvenile offenders who may inaccurately report their thoughts, feelings, and behaviors during both mental health screenings and more in-depth mental health assessments. This may or may not be done intentionally. Youth may inadvertently provide erroneous information if they are intoxicated, do not have good memories, or are unable to describe their internal experiences verbally. Other youth may deliberately provide false information; they may purposely minimize their mental health symptoms, or they may manufacture or exaggerate them.

Potential reasons why a juvenile offender may *minimize* mental health symptoms include the following:

- Does not want to be seen as "weird" or "crazy"
- Does not want to be seen as weak or vulnerable by peers
- Does not want to talk to a mental health professional, nurse, doctor, correctional supervisor, or the like
- Does not want to take psychotropic medication
- Does not want to participate in additional mental health assessments
- Does not want to attend specialized treatment groups
- Does not want to be sent to a psychiatric hospital
- Does not want to be placed on a specialized treatment unit or in a special "safe" room
- Does not want to be placed on any type of precautionary levels with staff intensively observing him or her
- Does not want anything to lengthen the amount of time he or she has to reside in a correctional facility
- Does not want staff to intervene with his or her suicide plan
- Wants the screening/assessment to be over as quickly as possible

Potential reasons why a juvenile offender may *exaggerate or fabricate* mental health symptoms include the following:

- Wants mind-altering psychotropic medication
- Wants to talk to and spend time with as many staff members as possible
- Wants to be sent to a psychiatric hospital (e.g., co-ed, less restrictive, less security)
- Wants to be placed on specialized treatment unit (e.g., co-ed, different programming)
- Wants to be placed in a special room (e.g., no roommate, located near staff)
- Wants to attend treatment groups (e.g., time out of his or her room, activities)
- Wants staff to pay as much attention to him or her as possible
- Wants peers to think he or she is "crazy" or "weird" so that others will stay away from him or her

It is not difficult for a juvenile to "fake mental illness" or to "fake non-mental illness" on most self-report mental health tools if the juvenile is motivated to do so. Many mental health screening and assessment tools contain items in which it is obvious what is being measured. This is particularly true for screening tools that criminal justice agencies develop themselves. Some standardized mental health instruments, such as the Minnesota Multiphasic Personality Inventory–Adolescent (MMPI-A) (Butcher et al., 1994), have tried to address this issue. On this tool, youth are unable to determine which way they should answer a question (e.g., to appear mentally ill or not to appear mentally ill) just by viewing the wording of an item. It also has special items and scales to detect whether a juvenile is answering the test questions honestly or whether he or she is minimizing problems, exaggerating problems, or answering questions in a random fashion. These types of mental health tools are fairly lengthy, and trained mental health professionals are required for interpretation of the results.

Some juvenile offenders may actually appear *worse* on self-report measures of mental heath symptoms when reassessed at a later time. Once they feel more comfortable in a particular setting and/or with certain staff members, they may be more willing to reveal personal information on a screening or assessment tool that they were unwilling to disclose when they were initially asked the questions.

Improving the Accuracy of Self-Reported Information

Most youth answer self-report questions as truthfully as they are able. However, there are some steps that staff can take to increase the chances of obtaining accurate self-report information from juvenile offenders:

- Conduct all mental health screenings/interviews in a private environment where interruptions are unlikely.
- Preface the screening with a discussion about what will be done with the results.
- Discuss limits of confidentiality *before* beginning the screening.
- Review any documentation or records on the juvenile to guide questioning.
- Ask questions in a matter-of-fact tone.
- Portray a nonjudgmental attitude, regardless of the juvenile's answers.
- Do not confront the juvenile during the screening if he or she reports engaging in negative behaviors.
- If possible, have someone the juvenile knows and trusts conduct the screening.
- If the juvenile has difficulty in remembering exactly when certain symptoms, experiences, or behaviors occurred, develop a time line with important events from his or her life (e.g., birthday, Christmas, last time incarcerated, concert attended) so as to provide some historical anchors and help the juvenile to be more specific.

Collateral Sources of Information

The potential limitations of self-reported mental health information from juvenile offenders make it important for staff to supplement screening and assessment results with additional sources of data. Reviewing previous records (including prior mental health evaluations) can provide essential information, as can observing a juvenile's behavior. Gathering information from individuals who are familiar with a juvenile (e.g., family/caretakers, arresting officers, correctional facility staff, teachers, treatment staff, case managers, community supervision staff) is often beneficial as well. These collateral sources can often provide valuable and fairly accurate information about a juvenile (Abikoff, Courtney, Pelham, & Koplewicz, 1993; Herjanic & Reich, 1982; Verhulst & van der Ende, 1992). However, the accuracy of their reports diminishes if these sources are questioned about ambiguous symptoms or behavior that is not readily observed or when oppositional behaviors co-occur with a juvenile's mental health symptoms.

Observation

An important way for corrections staff to identify juvenile offenders with mental health disorders is to *observe* youth behavior. Within correctional facilities, adults have the opportunity to continuously interact with youth as they supervise them. In addition, staff have the unique opportunity to observe the behavior of these juveniles when they are not under the influence of drugs and/or alcohol. Because community supervision staff (probation and parole) interact with particular youth over a period of weeks, months, or years, they may notice deterioration in functioning within one or more important areas of a juvenile's life (e.g., home, school, work, peers). Also, because juveniles have greater access to drugs and alcohol when residing in the community, probation and parole staff may see the emergence or worsening of juveniles' mental health symptoms if they resume their use of substances.

Behavior or Symptom Checklists

Using standardized checklists of mental health symptoms and behaviors can be a time-efficient and cost-effective way of gathering important behavioral observations from correctional workers. Correctional agencies can design their own checklists based on the diagnostic criteria listed in the *DSM-IV-TR* (2000), the standard resource for describing mental health disorders. Alternatively, agencies may prefer to use published checklists that already exist (Conners, Sitarenios, Parker, & Epstein, 1998). Most behavioral checklists take no more than 5 to 15 minutes for a correctional worker to complete, and the resulting information can provide valuable information to a clinician evaluating a young offender.

Common Mental Disorders Found Among Juvenile Offenders

The following are brief descriptions of some of the most common mental health disorders seen among youth involved with the criminal justice system. All of the symptoms listed are from the *DSM-IV-TR* (2000). If a juvenile exhibits the following signs and symptoms of mental illness, staff should refer the juvenile to a mental health professional for evaluation.

Oppositional Defiant Disorder

Juvenile offenders diagnosed with oppositional defiant disorder exhibit a pattern of negative, hostile, and defiant behaviors that lasts at least 6 months. These youth typically argue repeatedly with adults, defy or refuse to comply with rules or adult requests, frequently lose their temper, regularly annoy others in a deliberate fashion, often are spiteful and vindictive, frequently are easily annoyed by those around them, and often are angry and resentful.

Although many adolescents (offenders and nonoffenders alike) engage in the preceding behaviors, they do not all have oppositional defiant disorder. Youth receive this diagnosis when they engage in these behaviors more often than do peers of the same age and developmental levels, and only when these behaviors significantly interfere with their ability to function (e.g., in relationships, at school/work). If left unidentified and untreated, many youth with oppositional defiant disorder progress into developing conduct disorder. Although a significant number of juvenile offenders have received the diagnostic label of oppositional defiant disorder, many of these youth also suffer from one or more additional mental health disorders (e.g., major depression, ADHD, learning disorder).

Conduct Disorder

Conduct disorder is one of the most commonly diagnosed mental health disorders among youth involved with the justice system. These youth display a recurring and enduring pattern of behavior in which the basic rights of others or major age-appropriate societal norms/rules are violated. Juveniles with conduct disorder typically are aggressive toward others (e.g., physical fights, intimidation, robbery, rape, weapon use, physical cruelty), are destructive with property (e.g., deliberate fire setting, property defacing), engage in theft or deceitfulness (e.g., lies, forgery, shoplifting, car/house/building break-ins), and violate important rules (e.g., school truancy, curfew violations, running away from home).

The diagnosis of conduct disorder is given to a juvenile who is under 18 years of age when the preceding behaviors significantly interfere with the juvenile's ability to function in school, work, and/or interpersonal relationships. Although many juveniles experiment with these behaviors during their pre-adolescent and/or adolescent years, youth with conduct disorder engage in these behaviors on a repetitive basis. Delinquency is not the same as conduct disorder; just because a juvenile commits a crime or is involved with the justice system does not indicate that he or she meets all of the diagnostic criteria to receive this label. In comparison with the general population of teenagers, the negative and problematic behaviors of juveniles with conduct disorder tend to be more intense, frequent, and chronic. Youth diagnosed with conduct disorder usually exhibit a multitude of these behaviors, and their symptoms are typically not a reaction to a short-term stressor (e.g., breakup of a romantic relationship, moving to a new neighborhood) but instead reflect a persistent *pattern* of behavior. To receive the diagnosis of antisocial personality disorder as an adult, an individual must have met diagnostic criteria for conduct disorder before 18 years of age.

Although conduct disorder is frequently diagnosed among juvenile offenders, these youth often suffer from one or more additional mental health disorders as well. Mental health professionals should conduct comprehensive evaluations when assessing a juvenile exhibiting behaviors indicative of conduct disorder because there is often something underlying a juvenile's continual cruelty to others, repeated running away from home, deliberate destruction of others' belongings, and so on. It is often too convenient for professionals to focus primarily on a juvenile's delinquent behavior and assign him or her a label of conduct disorder without asking the critical question, "What else is going on?" Solely diagnosing a juvenile offender with conduct disorder provides minimal information to guide treatment plans and effective management strategies for a particular juvenile. It is not uncommon for some of these youth to suffer from an additional mental health disorder such as ADHD, major depression, post-traumatic stress disorder, substance abuse, learning disorder, or bipolar disorder.

Attention Deficit/Hyperactivity Disorder

Juvenile offenders with ADHD display a continual pattern of difficulties related to inattention and/or hyperactivity/impulsivity that causes them significant problems. Their symptoms of inattention and/or hyperactivity/impulsivity are more frequent and severe than those of other youth who are the same age or at the same level of development.

Youth who have difficulty with *inattention* tend to be easily distracted, have difficulty with organization, lose things, find it difficult to pay attention to one task or activity for a significant period of time, forget things, appear as if they are not listening, avoid tasks requiring sustained mental effort, often do not follow through on instructions, and make careless mistakes. These juveniles frequently have difficulty in completing chores or responsibilities. Although it may appear that they are behaving in an intentionally disobedient manner, this is often not the case; it is common for these youth literally to forget what it is they have been instructed to do. In addition, juveniles with ADHD may attempt to avoid written assignments in a classroom or on a living unit because it is too hard for them to pay attention long enough to complete them. These youth frequently misplace their belongings, including trivial objects as well as items that are important to them.

Youth who primarily have difficulty with hyperactivity/impulsivity tend to move around excessively, fidget with their hands or feet, have difficulty in remaining seated for long periods of time, have difficulty in quietly engaging in play activities, talk constantly, appear "revved up" and full of energy, interrupt others, call out answers before questions are finished, and have difficulty in waiting for their turn. These youth often touch and take things that do not belong to them, and it is not unusual for them to damage items or knock things over because they move around so quickly. They are often disruptive in school and/or on a living unit within a correctional facility because they are typically noisy and overly energetic and have difficulty in sitting still.

Youth with ADHD fall into one of three types: ADHD, predominantly *inattentive* type; ADHD, predominantly *hyperactive/impulsive* type; and ADHD, *combined* type (if youth are exhibiting significant behaviors from each of the first two areas).

Many youth with ADHD become involved with the justice system (Davis, Bean, Schumacher, & Stringer, 1991). Difficulty in thinking ahead to potential consequences of their behavior may lead some of these youth to place themselves in high-risk or dangerous situations. Juveniles with ADHD may be more likely than their non-ADHD peers to get *caught* for the crimes they commit because they frequently have poor planning and organizational abilities. For some youth with ADHD, it may be a combination of these factors, or neither factor may play a role.

The majority of young people occasionally struggle with inattention and/or hyperactivity/impulsivity, but that does not mean they all qualify for a diagnosis of ADHD. Children and adolescents are not expected to follow directions or control their behavior to the same degree as are adults. To receive a diagnosis of ADHD, a juvenile must exhibit *many* of the previously described behaviors for a minimum of 6 months, and the behaviors must be severe enough that they interfere with the juvenile's functioning. Also, difficulties associated with a juvenile's behaviors must be evident in two or more settings (e.g., home, school, work, correctional facility, group home), and some of these behaviors must have been evident and caused some impairment before the juvenile was 7 years of age. If a juvenile's difficulties with attention or hyperactivity are due to another mental health disorder or are directly related to the effects of drugs or alcohol, then a diagnosis of ADHD would not be warranted.

It is common for corrections staff to dismiss the diagnosis of ADHD on the grounds that it is too frequently diagnosed among the juvenile offender population. However, when trained clinicians use diagnostic criteria in the manner in which they were developed, the diagnosis of ADHD is not easy for a juvenile to receive. To ascertain whether ADHD symptoms are present to a significant degree and interfere with a juvenile's functioning, a comprehensive mental health evaluation should be conducted. Information gathered from a variety of sources (e.g., family/caretakers, teachers, correctional staff, previous mental health professionals, medical professionals, psychological tests, behavioral checklists) improves the accuracy of assigning this mental health diagnosis. Correctional workers can play an important role in the diagnosis of ADHD by communicating their behavioral observations of a juvenile to the mental health/medical professional who is assessing the juvenile for ADHD.

Symptoms of inattention and hyperactivity can be caused by a variety of factors other than ADHD (e.g., high levels of stress, traumatic experiences, physical or sexual abuse, parental neglect, drug or alcohol use, anxiety, chaotic home environment, medical disorders). So, although it is true that many juvenile offenders demonstrate problems in the areas of attention and impulsivity, only a subset of them truly meet the diagnostic criteria for ADHD. However, for those youth experiencing difficulty with inattention and impulsivity due to factors other than ADHD, mental health services might still be necessary and intervention strategies should be specifically responsive to the juveniles' underlying issues (e.g., substance use, trauma). When a juvenile exhibits considerable difficulty with inattention or hyperactivity, a referral should be made to a mental health/medical professional so that the underlying cause can be determined.

Major Depression

Juvenile offenders with major depression experience several of the following symptoms for a period of at least 2 weeks. The symptoms represent a change from a juvenile's typical functioning, and at least one of the juvenile's symptoms is either a depressed/irritable mood or diminished interest or pleasure in most activities. Depressed youth frequently display a significant change in sleep patterns (e.g., sleeping too much, being unable to sleep), a significant change in appetite (e.g., weight loss, weight gain), noticeable restlessness or slowed body movements, loss of energy/feelings of fatigue, feelings of worthlessness/excessive or inappropriate feelings of guilt, indecisiveness/difficulties with thinking and concentrating, and repeated thoughts of death and/or a suicide attempt.

During an episode of major depression, a juvenile typically suffers from the preceding symptoms nearly every day, and these difficulties result in significant distress or impairment in his or her ability to function in school, work, and/or relationships with others. To be diagnosed with depression, a juvenile's symptoms must not be directly related to the effects of drugs and/or alcohol, a medical condition, or the recent death of a loved one.

Major depression is one of the most misunderstood mental health disorders among youth involved with the justice system and is often challenging to diagnose. For example, most adults associate depression with sadness, crying, social withdrawal, and appetite and sleep disturbances. Although these are common symptoms of depression, there are a variety of reasons why incarcerated youth may experience a change in their eating and sleeping behavior that have nothing to do with depression. For example, they might not like the taste of the food, might not be used to eating institution food, might be withdrawing from drugs, might be overeating to comfort themselves, might be overeating because they have not had a hot meal in days or weeks, and so on. Incarcerated youth might have difficulty in sleeping because the beds are uncomfortable or because they fear their roommate(s). In addition, the sleeping environment in correctional institutions is often noisy, the youth might not be used to going to sleep sober, they are typically asked to go to sleep 4 or 5 hours earlier than their usual bedtimes (9 p.m. vs. 1 a.m.), they might intentionally oversleep so that time will pass more quickly, and so on.

Furthermore, many adolescents (particularly males) manifest major depression in an *irritable* mood instead of a sad and gloomy mood. Juvenile offenders suffering from major depression often appear agitated, angry, and aggressive. Because many adults do not recognize these symptoms as signs of major depression, these irritable youth can be misdiagnosed with oppositional defiant disorder or conduct disorder. This can result in a depressed juvenile receiving numerous sanctions within a correctional facility in relation to his or her aggressive behavior, and he or she might never be identified as in need of mental health services and referred for treatment. If correctional staff notice a change in a juvenile's functioning that includes extreme irritability or aggression as well as a lack of interest and pleasure in things the juvenile used to enjoy (e.g., basketball, watching videos, family visits, phone calls from girlfriend/boyfriend, gossiping with peers), then depression is a possibility and should be further explored.

Social withdrawal is common among individuals with major depression, and corrections staff should be alert to the ways in which depressed youth may try to isolate themselves from others. Whereas incarcerated youth with sad and gloomy moods may withdraw into the corner of the day room, aggressively depressed youth may intentionally engage in behaviors they know will result in room confinement/seclusion. One of the best ways for an irritable and agitated depressed juvenile to withdraw from staff, peers, responsibilities, and activities is to get locked down for a significant period of time. While in room confinement/seclusion, many juvenile offenders try to pass the time sleeping as many hours as possible during the day and night. Because this is often how depressed individuals want to spend their time, room confinement/seclusion may actually be appealing to a young offender suffering from major depression.

Depressed youth with a predominantly irritable mood are also at high risk for serious suicide attempts. Because corrections staff do not always recognize the symptoms of aggressive juveniles suffering from major depression, they often do not take this type of juvenile's threats of suicide as seriously as those of a youth who is crying and visibly upset. Room confinement/seclusion is one of the most high-risk periods for these offenders to engage in suicidal behavior, as they often have little to occupy their minds other than all of the things about which they are depressed.

Dysthymic Disorder

Juvenile offenders diagnosed with dysthymic disorder also suffer from a depressed or irritable mood. These mood states are typically less intense than those found among individuals suffering from major depression, but they last for a significantly longer period of time (at least 1 year). There is also the presence of fatigue/low energy, feelings of hopelessness, indecisiveness/concentration difficulties, lack of appetite or overeating, sleeping too little or too much, and/or low self-esteem. These symptoms must cause a juvenile considerable distress and/or interfere with his or her ability to function in relationships, school, or work. The symptoms cannot be the direct result of substance use or a medical condition.

Rather than being a *change* from how a juvenile usually appears (as with major depression), the irritability and sadness typical of a youth with dysthymic disorder *is* how a youth usually appears. Dysthymic youth with a predominantly irritable mood seem to be easily annoyed by everyone and everything around them. Those with a predominantly sad mood usually walk around looking mildly depressed all of the time, rarely getting excited about anything.

Bipolar Disorder

Juvenile offenders diagnosed with bipolar disorder suffer from severe changes in mood that cause them significant distress and/or interfere with their ability to function. This disorder has been referred to as "manic-depressive disorder" in the past because individuals tend to experience episodes of *mania* as well as episodes of *depression*. The typical features of depression were listed earlier under the "Major Depression" section of the chapter.

Juveniles suffering from mania experience a discrete period of time (at least 1 week) when their mood is abnormally and consistently overly joyous, extroverted, or irritable. Their manic mood state is so extreme and excessive that these youth sometimes require psychiatric hospitalization. During their intense mood state, juveniles with mania also suffer from some of the following symptoms: more talkative than usual/rapid and pressured speech, increased activity/physical agitation, grandiosity/inflated self-esteem, racing thoughts/accelerated speech with abrupt topic changes, distractibility, excessive involvement in pleasurable activities that have a high potential for painful consequences, and a decreased need for sleep (e.g., able to go several nights without sleep, feeling rested after only 3 to 4 hours of sleep).

Some juvenile offenders exhibit the preceding symptoms after ingesting particular types of drugs (e.g., methamphetamines, cocaine). If a juvenile's abnormal behavior were due primarily to the direct effects of substance use, then he or she would not be diagnosed with bipolar disorder.

The pattern of mood changes among youth with bipolar disorder is very individualized. Some juveniles may experience a manic episode that is followed immediately by an episode of depression. Other youth may experience a significant time period between episodes of mania and episodes of depression (e.g., weeks, months, years) in which their mood states are fairly stable. Intense emotions and a wide variation of moods are not uncommon among youth during their adolescent years; these should not be confused with bipolar disorder. Bipolar disorder is a serious, often disabling disorder that interferes with a juvenile's ability to function in important daily activities.

Over the past few years, this author has noticed a significant increase in the number of juvenile offenders receiving the diagnosis of bipolar disorder. It is not clear whether the disorder has become more widely recognized or whether many of these youth are being misdiagnosed. There is still much that remains unknown about how bipolar disorder manifests itself among adolescents, particularly those involved with the justice system. Because juvenile offenders often have histories of abuse, trauma, drug use, and extreme stress, their changes in mood could be associated with a variety of factors other than suffering from bipolar disorder. Before assigning this major mental health diagnosis to a juvenile, it is critical for clinicians to conduct a comprehensive mental health evaluation to ensure that the juvenile possesses the specific symptoms required to qualify for bipolar disorder as well as to make certain that the juvenile's symptoms are not due to factors other than this particular form of mental illness.

Suicidal Behavior

Suicide is the third leading cause of death among adolescents and is a national health care problem (Centers for Disease Control, 1997). Although there are currently no national data available on the extent of suicidal behavior among incarcerated youth, national studies of adults within the criminal justice system have found the annual rate of suicide in prisons to be double the rate of suicide in the general population (Hayes, 1995; Hayes & Rowan, 1988). The rate within jails was nine times higher. One study of youth in juvenile detention found that more than one third (34%) of the juveniles had thought about killing themselves at some point in their lives and that 14% had thought about killing themselves within the past week. Nearly one fifth (19%) of the juveniles had made at least one suicide attempt in the past, and 10% of the youth had made two or more suicide attempts (Rhode, Seeley, & Mace, 1997). Another study found that 21.0% of the juvenile offender population had made suicidal threats and that 13.5% had engaged in actual suicidal behaviors by trying to hang, drown, poison, or strangle themselves (Davis et al., 1991).

The Office of Juvenile Justice and Delinquency Prevention published a report on various conditions of confinement within juvenile correctional facilities (Parent et al., 1994). With regard to suicide prevention practices, lower rates of suicidal behavior were found within facilities that trained their staff in suicide prevention as well as within facilities that conducted suicide screening at admission. Rates of suicidal behavior increased for youth who were housed in isolation. When comparing different types of juvenile justice facilities, juvenile *detention* centers had the highest number of youth suicidal behaviors. Reception centers had the next highest rate, followed by training schools and then ranches. Similar to adults in jails, the highest number of suicidal behaviors among detention and reception centers may reflect the fact that youth residing in these types of facilities are often admitted directly off of the street, immediately on arrest. This can be stressful for youth, particularly if it is their first time in one of these facilities. They may be unclear as to what is going to happen to them, how long they will remain in the facility, and what norms exist in a juvenile correctional environment. In addition, some of these juveniles are still intoxicated and/or high on drugs. Although juveniles typically engage in fewer suicidal behaviors in long-term residential facilities than in short-term detention centers, youth within long-term justice programs can still be at high risk for suicide.

There are a variety of risk factors associated with suicidal behavior among adolescents (Berman & Jobes, 1994; Brent & Perper, 1995; Brent et al., 1993; Ladely & Puskar, 1994; Marttunen, 1994; Shaffer et al., 1996; Shafii, Carrigan, Whittinghill, & Derrick, 1985). When correctional staff work with youth who possess any of the following risk factors, they should be alert to the possibility of suicidal behavior: previous suicidal behavior, mental health disorders (particularly mood disorders such as major depression and bipolar disorder as well as conduct disorder), substance use disorder, aggressive and violent behavior, gay or lesbian sexual orientation, parental psychopathology, negative family factors (e.g., conflict, parental absence, parental abuse/neglect, negative communication patterns, lack of support, suicide of family member), poor social skills/having few friends, stressful life events (e.g., interpersonal conflict/breakup of romantic relationship, school suspension/expulsion, sexual assault, suicidal behavior of friend/family member, incarceration). Because these risk factors are common among youth involved with the justice system, a significant number of them (particularly incarcerated youth) are at high risk for suicidal behavior. However, this does not necessarily imply that all juvenile offenders will make suicide attempts. In fact, despite having several of the preceding risk factors, the majority of youth involved with the justice system do not engage in suicidal behavior, thereby making the identification of those youth who will make actual suicide attempts even more complex. It is important for corrections staff to be aware of each juvenile's risk factors, to document these risk factors, and to use them when making decisions about a juvenile's risk for suicide. Although special safety measures should be taken for youth who are thinking about or planning to kill themselves, threatening to kill themselves, and/or engaging in suicidal behavior, corrections staff also need to continue monitoring the other high-risk juveniles under their care in case one of them suddenly becomes suicidal.

It is dangerous (and potentially lethal) for correctional staff to worry only about sad and withdrawn juveniles who are crying in the corner of a living unit or those who publicly make suicidal statements about wanting to kill themselves. Staff need to be just as concerned about depressed youth who do not talk about their suicidal thoughts as well as about depressed youth who are angry, aggressive, and repeatedly getting into fights. These youth are just as likely to make serious suicide attempts as are youth who appear more obviously distressed. If there are any indications that incarcerated juveniles are considering harming themselves, then these youth should be referred to medical/mental health professionals for evaluations.

Impulsive juvenile offenders who are extremely angry with staff or who feel rejected/emotionally hurt by a staff member might make a suicide attempt to "pay the staff member back." The combination of impulsivity and an intense focus on retaliation can interfere with a juvenile offender's realization that such suicidal behavior will be most harmful to the juvenile himself or herself. This type of juvenile can make a serious and potentially lethal suicide attempt in a matter of minutes. This is why it is essential that *all statements about suicidal behavior be taken seriously*. Regardless of a juvenile's intention or motive, his or her behavior could result in death.

It is critical for every correctional agency to have clear written policies and procedures in place regarding how staff should respond to youth at high risk for suicide. At a minimum, issues related to screening for suicide risk, intensive monitoring of suicidal juveniles, immediate access to mental health/medical professionals, potential transfer of youth to a hospital environment, and any special housing requirements all should be addressed.

When identifying a suicidal juvenile, correctional staff should avoid making determinations about underlying motivations for suicidal behavior (e.g., eliciting attention from staff, avoiding placement in seclusion, avoiding certain responsibilities, wishing to be housed on a special unit, superficially wounding oneself solely to frighten staff, truly trying to end one's own life). There is no way for correctional staff to be absolutely sure of the intention behind a juvenile's suicidal behavior, so they should focus on the juvenile's objective observable *behavior* (e.g., saying he or she wanted to die, saying he or she would kill himself or herself if placed in a seclusion room, tying a T-shirt around his or her neck, cutting his or her wrist with a plastic fork during dinner, making a noose with his or her sheet in room).

When a juvenile offender engages in suicidal behavior, he or she is trying to meet some need. This need could be related to ending unbearable psychological distress, escaping an intolerable situation, trying to influence correctional staff, and so on. Distinguishing between juveniles who are "serious" about suicide and those who are "manipulative" or "attention seeking" is difficult and dangerous. There are a variety of ways in which a juvenile can get attention and/or influence staff behavior other than making suicidal statements or engaging in a suicide attempt. Youth who choose this type of behavior to meet their needs should always be evaluated by a medical/mental health professional.

Mental Retardation

Juvenile offenders with mental retardation have significantly sub-average general intellectual functioning (intelligence quotient [IQ] of approximately 70 or less) *and* deficits in their ability to cope with the everyday demands of life and ability to function independently. Mentally retarded youth are typically unable to function in a manner expected for their age or developmental level in areas related to taking care of themselves, interacting with others, communicating, and/or keeping themselves safe, and so on. The onset of this disorder must occur prior to 18 years of age, and the severity of mental retardation is based on the level of a juvenile's intellectual impairment (mild, moderate, severe, or profound).

The majority of mentally retarded juvenile offenders fall into the mild range of mental retardation and typically function at about a sixth-grade level. These youth tend to need more guidance and supervision than do their peers. Juveniles whose IQs and levels of adaptive functioning place them in the moderate range of mental retardation function at close to a second-grade level and need a tremendous amount of adult supervision and support. Even with additional support and structure, these youth often have a difficult time adjusting to a correctional environment. The majority of youth in the severe and profound range of mental retardation reside with their families or in specialized residential facilities.

Juvenile offenders with mental retardation constitute a heterogeneous group of youngsters. Some juveniles with mental retardation are gentle, compliant, and dependent on adults; others are aggressive, impulsive, and oppositional; and still others will display a combination of these behaviors. It is not uncommon to see juvenile offenders with mental retardation become hostile or aggressive when they are having difficulty with communicating their wants and needs to those around them. These youth might not always understand the rules of a correctional facility or how certain consequences are related to specific behaviors. Although the majority of juvenile offenders who self-injure are not mentally retarded, there are some youth with mental retardation who bang their heads against walls and doors or slap their faces and other parts of their bodies. Supervising juveniles with mental retardation can be frustrating for correctional staff, particularly when staff do not understand the motivation underlying the juveniles' behavior. It is often difficult to determine whether a juvenile's negative behavior is purposefully oppositional or whether it is associated with the juvenile's cognitive limitations.

Many youth with mental retardation have difficulty with successfully participating in rehabilitation or treatment programs provided within the justice system. A large component of many treatment programs focuses on helping offenders gain insight into their behavior (e.g., offense cycle, anger), including understanding the connection among their thoughts, feelings, and behavior. Youth with significantly low IQs might not be able to fully participate in treatment that is cognitive in nature because they may be unable to think abstractly or gain insight into why they behave as they do.

Many youth with mental retardation experience interpersonal difficulties when incarcerated. Most of these youth do not understand the peer culture of a juvenile correctional facility, and they are often teased because their interests and behaviors may be childlike and immature. Mentally retarded juveniles are also likely to be victimized by peers. Because of their low intellectual functioning, these youth frequently have poor judgment and are unable to distinguish between those whom they should and should not trust. It is not uncommon for cognitively impaired youth to be "set up" by peers so that they are left to take the blame for something they did not do. In addition, if not appropriately supervised, these youth can be physically or sexually victimized by peers. Although some peers will try to exploit cognitively limited youth, others will do just the opposite and will provide extra support and protection as a way to help mentally retarded youth adjust to the environment.

The diagnosis of mental retardation relies heavily on the evaluation of a juvenile's cognitive functioning. One of the most common ways in which to measure a juvenile's intellectual functioning is to *individually* administer a standardized IQ test. Juveniles should receive IQ testing by clinicians with specific training and experience in these types of tests. Due to a variety of factors (e.g., hunger, intoxication, anxiety, lack of motivation, distractibility, stressors, mental illness), a juvenile offender's IQ score may be an underestimate of his or her true level of intellectual functioning. Therefore, some juvenile offenders diagnosed with mental retardation may be inaccurately diagnosed. On the other hand, there are some juvenile offenders who suffer from mental retardation but who have never been so identified. This is more likely to occur when youth appear "street smart" or act tough and intimidating so as to avoid having others discover their intellectual and functional difficulties.

In addition to assessing a juvenile's intellectual abilities, clinicians must assess his or her level of adaptive functioning. This is typically done by using a variety of behavioral observations and often includes the use of a standardized instrument, such as the Vineland Social Maturity Scale (Sparrow, Balla, & Cicchetti, 1984), that assesses the juvenile's ability to perform the daily activities required for personal and social sufficiency.

Learning Disorders

Juvenile offenders with learning disorders demonstrate a significant discrepancy between how they *should* perform on standardized academic tests (given their intellectual ability and education) and how they *actually* do perform on these tests. For example, if youth have IQs in the above-average range and they have received adequate schooling, then one would expect them to perform fairly well on a test of reading, written expression, or mathematics. It would be unexpected for these youth to perform poorly given their above-average intellectual ability and educational experience. A learning disorder is typically diagnosed when this discrepancy is substantial. Juveniles with average, above-average, or below-average IQs can be diagnosed with a learning disorder so long as a major discrepancy exists between the intellectual ability (IQ) and scores on individually administered, standardized school-based tests. The difficulties must also interfere with academic achievement or everyday activities that require reading, writing, or mathematical skills. A juvenile offender can have a learning disorder in reading, mathematics, or written expression, and many youth involved with the justice system suffer from more than one learning disorder simultaneously.

Problems related to information processing are common among juveniles with learning disorders. These juveniles are often bright, and many are of at least average intelligence. However, transferring what is in their brains onto a piece of paper can be difficult, especially when they are under time constraints. Some youth have difficulty in learning information solely by hearing it aloud and need to see information in written form. Others know what they want to say but may have difficulty in translating their thoughts into words when they are speaking aloud. Still others do not comprehend what someone is saying in the same way the speaker intended it. Not surprisingly, incidents of miscommunication are commonplace when interacting with these youth.

Information processing difficulties can interfere with a juvenile's ability to be successful within interpersonal relationships, and many juvenile offenders with learning disorders have poor social skills. Many of these youth do not understand the "give and take" of relationships, may be slow to pick up on subtle social cues, and may misinterpret what peers or adults are saying to them. Because of this, their interpersonal style can inadvertently irritate or offend others.

Because of problems related to academic achievement and social relationships, many juveniles with learning disorders have a negative view of themselves. They often feel stupid and do not understand why schoolwork is so difficult for them and why they have difficulties in getting along with others. Over the years, adults may have accused these youth of being "lazy" or of "not applying themselves." By the time they reach adolescence, many juveniles with learning disorders are tired of struggling academically, so they stop trying to achieve in school; a significant percentage drop out before high school graduation. Because school is such an integral part of childhood and adolescence, repeated failure in the academic setting can result in these juveniles feeling continually discouraged and demoralized.

Post-traumatic Stress Disorder

Post-traumatic stress disorder (PTSD) is an anxiety disorder. To receive the diagnosis of PTSD, a juvenile must be exposed to a *traumatic* event in which he or she witnessed or experienced an event involving threatened or actual serious injury or death. At the time of the trauma, the juvenile's response typically involves intense fear, horror, and/or helplessness.

Youth with PTSD repeatedly *reexperience* the traumatic event with frequent intrusive and upsetting thoughts and memories of the event and/or repeated nightmares about the event. They may actually experience flashbacks, feeling as though the traumatic event is happening all over again. Juvenile offenders with PTSD avoid things that remind them of the trauma and become less responsive in general. They typically avoid places, people, or activities associated with the traumatic event and often do not want to talk about what happened to them. They may lose interest in activities they used to enjoy and often display a restricted range of emotions (e.g., unable to feel joy). It is common for youth with PTSD to describe feeling "different" and separate from others because of the negative event that has happened to them, and many have a sense of a foreshortened future (e.g., do not expect to live past 21 years of age).

Because PTSD is an anxiety disorder, juveniles suffering from this disorder typically experience symptoms of increased arousal, including an exaggerated startle response, problems falling or remaining asleep, concentration difficulties, irritability or outbursts of anger, and a need to be excessively attentive or watchful regarding what is going on around them.

A significant number of juvenile offenders have witnessed or directly experienced one or more traumatic events in their lives (Cauffman, Feldman, Waterman, & Steiner, 1998; Steiner, Garcia, & Matthews, 1997). Physical abuse, sexual abuse, and parental abandonment and neglect are common among youth involved with the criminal justice system. Some juvenile offenders have been sold into pornography or prostitution at very early ages, and some have been raped numerous times. Sadly, witnessing the death of a parent, relative, or close friend is not an infrequent occurrence in the lives of these youth. Some of these young people have been shot or severely beaten. In fact, some young offenders suffer from lead poisoning, not necessarily from lead-based paints but instead from bullets that remain lodged in their bodies. Some juveniles have watched one of their parents murder the other parent, beat one or more of their siblings, or overdose on drugs. Some female offenders have been forced to kill their babies immediately after giving birth. Because the rate of traumatic experiences is so high among this population of youth, it is not surprising that many juvenile offenders suffer from PTSD. However, just because a juvenile experienced a traumatic event does not automatically imply that he or she is suffering from PTSD. This diagnosis is given only when a juvenile is experiencing several of the preceding behaviors. In addition, the symptoms of PTSD must be present for more than 1 month and must cause significant distress or impairment in the juvenile's ability to function in the important areas of his or her life (e.g., school, work, relationships).

Many juvenile offenders with PTSD have significant difficulty in regulating their emotions. They may experience severe mood swings (e.g., becoming angry and hostile with minimal provocation), impulsivity, and the perception that they are constantly being threatened in some way. Once emotionally upset, juvenile offenders with PTSD often find it difficult to calm themselves down. Stomachaches, headaches, and vague muscle or joint pain are not uncommon among youth with anxiety disorders such as PTSD. Juvenile offenders, particularly male offenders who are concerned about looking tough and appearing to be in control, may be reluctant to report feelings of anxiety or fear related to a traumatic incident. For some of these youth, anxiety manifests itself in more physical, health-related symptoms.

Juveniles with PTSD have varied reactions to the trauma they have experienced. Some may suffer from "survivor guilt" because they survived traumatic incidents that others did not survive. They may feel guilty for being unable to "save" their friends or family members when traumatic incidents occurred, especially if they were incarcerated at the time when the traumatic incidents occurred to their loved ones. Many youth who have been sexually abused report feelings of shame, as if they are now damaged in some way; they may perceive themselves as "dirty" and "bad." Male juvenile offenders who have been molested by men or older boys may experience guilt in relation to having had sexual activity with someone of the same sex, with some now wondering whether they are homosexual. Depending on their beliefs about homosexuality, this may result in feelings of guilt and shame and can lead these youth to question their own sexual orientation.

Some youth with PTSD experience episodes of *dissociation*. When experiencing something incredibly painful and overwhelming (e.g., sexual abuse, rape, gang beating, being shot), the mind may try to separate the experience from consciousness. It is as if the mind shuts down so as not to process the terrible thing that is happening. Some youth have reported that during traumatic incidents, they tried to "disconnect" from their bodies so that they did not have to emotionally experience the pain their physical bodies were going through. They sometimes describe these situations as if they were "watching themselves from above." Even after a traumatic incident is over, juveniles with PTSD may still experience symptoms of dissociation. In the past, this may have been their bodies' way of helping them to survive horrific incidents, serving as a coping mechanism during periods of extreme stress. But for some juveniles, this way of coping may become so automatic that whenever they are faced with highly charged or stressful situations, their minds begin to shut down. During periods of dissociation, these youth may appear as if they are "spacing out" and can actually lose track of time (e.g., unable to recall what happened for several minutes or hours).

Feelings of *derealization*, in which youth feel as though the world around them is not real, can also occur. They may feel detached from their peers and/or as if they are walking around in a dream-like state.

Because it can be difficult to identify juvenile offenders with PTSD, many of these youth remain undiagnosed. Some juvenile offenders have never told anyone about the significant symptoms of anxiety they experience; this can be particularly true in a correctional facility, where youth typically want to appear strong and in control of their emotions. Youth with PTSD may feel as though they are going crazy and cannot understand why they are unable to stop thinking or dreaming about horrible things that happened to them in the past or about violent things they have done to others in the past. They usually do not know why they feel tense or on edge much of the time, and they may feel as though they cannot control their angry reactions even when making a conscious effort to do so. From the outside, these juveniles may appear as strong and tough to correctional staff and peers, but inside, these youth often feel frightened and uneasy. They may be unable to shake a general sense of feeling "different" from those around them, as if they are broken in some way. Sometimes, these juveniles are aware of how they avoid certain places, situations, and/or people but might not link their apprehension and avoidance behavior to previous traumatic events.

Many juvenile offenders do not want to talk about the traumatic incidents they have experienced, even when directly asked to do so. Some do not see the point in discussing agonizing issues that happened in the past and that no one can do anything about. In addition, they often do not want to reexpose themselves to the painful emotions they have already experienced. Fear of retribution from family members, peers, or other individuals may also prevent juveniles from revealing terrible things that have happened to them.

A small number of juvenile offenders with PTSD report hearing voices that other people do not hear. These experiences tend to occur during periods of increased stress and anxiety. Juvenile offenders with PTSD often report that they know the voices are not real but that they are unable to make them stop. Any juvenile who reports hearing voices should be immediately referred for a mental health evaluation.

Self-injury/self-mutilation is a behavior frequently linked to youth suffering from PTSD. These youth are often very anxious, and self-injury can serve as a way in which to release built-up tension. When these youth are anxious, they often cut themselves or burn themselves in an attempt to help them relax.

Self-Injury

Self-injury is becoming an all-too-common behavior in juvenile corrections. Although known by various names—self-injury, self-mutilation, cutting, and so on—this type of behavior reflects a juvenile's deliberate attempt to harm his or her own body in a non-life-threatening manner. The majority of self-injurers in corrections engage in superficial cutting and carving, but some young offenders engage in more serious and dangerous self-harm behaviors. Regardless of the severity of their self-injury, self-injurers pose a safety and security risk in a juvenile facility and can be extremely disruptive for the rest of the milieu. Self-mutilating juvenile offenders can be frightening for staff as well as for the other youth, and both administration and line staff can end up feeling hopeless and frustrated when trying to supervise these juveniles.

Self-injury tends to begin during the adolescent years and can continue into early adulthood without appropriate intervention. The most common form of self-injury among juvenile offenders is cutting, carving, or burning of the skin. Juvenile offenders with cuts, scratches, burns, or bruises on their arms and other parts of their bodies as a result of accidents, physical altercations, or abuse by others would not fit the description of self-injury. Self-injurious behavior is done purposefully and voluntarily.

Tattoos and trendy piercings are becoming more common among today's teenagers, and many juvenile offenders have pierced ears, eyebrows, tongues, belly buttons, or other body parts. These behaviors, in and of themselves, do not constitute self-injury. Neither does youth burning their skin as part of a cultural or ritualistic tradition or as part of an initiation into or identification with a certain group or gang. Burning or carving of the skin as part of a contest or game to see which juvenile is the toughest (most "macho") and who can take the most pain is not uncommon among some juvenile offenders and does not typically fit into the category of self-injury.

One of the primary ways in which self-injury differs from the preceding behaviors is that self-mutilation is usually done for the purpose of regulating a youth's emotions or getting his or her emotional needs met in some way. Whereas youth who self-injure often engage in self-harming behavior as a coping strategy during stressful or emotionally laden situations, the current popularity of piercings and tattoos among adolescents is typically related to youth wanting to look a certain way, express their identity, or fit in with a certain group or culture. For juveniles who have multiple piercings or tattoos, there can be a fine line between fashion and self-injury, and it is important to explore their motives if they continue to obtain a significant number of piercings or tattoos.

Self-injury occurs among both male and female juvenile offenders. Although all self-injurers are different and present with their own set of issues, many of these youth are impulsive, repulsed by their bodies or disgusted by how they look, perfectionistic ("all-or-none" thinking), unable to form stable interpersonal relationships, and/or unable or unwilling to appropriately care for their health or hygiene (Walsh & Rosen, 1988). Self-injurers often have low self-esteem, use drugs or alcohol, and/or suffer from an eating disorder. Many of these youth have experienced trauma in their lives (e.g., physical or sexual abuse) and/or have experienced excessive violence or neglect in their family homes. Loss of a parent, childhood illness or surgery, and inhibition of emotional expression as a child are not uncommon. In addition, a considerable number of self-injurers are confused over their own sexuality and may have gender identity issues.

Many youth in the justice system who have engaged in self-injurious behavior have been identified and treated as if they were suicidal. The intention behind these behaviors is quite different. Suicidal youth typically want to die or escape an unbearable situation. They are usually engaging in specific self-harm behavior in hopes that it will end their lives and/or end their psychological pain. Youth engaging in self-injury typically have no intentions of killing themselves, and their behavior is not related to wanting to die. Self-injurers are often in a great deal of emotional pain, and they want their distress to diminish. However, many of these juveniles describe cutting or carving as a way of coping with their problems, with some saying that they would become suicidal if they did not engage in self-injurious behavior. These adolescents often see self-injury as a *life-sustaining* behavior. Although they are not the same, suicidal behavior and self-injurious behavior are not mutually exclusive. Engaging in self-injury can increase a juvenile's risk of suicidal behavior. Self-injuring juvenile offenders can become suicidal and make serious suicide attempts. However, once these suicidal crises are resolved and the self-injuring youth no longer want to die, they are likely to return to their self-mutilating behavior as a coping strategy.

Correctional facilities are designed to be highly safe and secure settings; however, there are still many ways in which self-injurious youth can harm themselves while incarcerated (and even more ways when the youth are released back into the community). Incarcerated juveniles have used the following items for self-mutilation purposes (and some of these items were obtained while correctional personnel were closely supervising the youth): staples, thumbtacks, paper clips, pencils, pens, erasers, safety pins, combs, brush bristles, barrettes, earrings/nose rings, eyeglasses, teeth, fingernails, eating utensils, snaps/zippers on uniforms/clothing, eyelets on tennis shoes, belt buckles, metal mattress handles, rocks/gravel, fists against wall, heads against doors, playing cards, paint chips, corn/potato chips, tops of soda cans, toxic cleaning chemicals, pieces of floor tile, and chicken bones. This list is certainly not exhaustive, and anyone working with self-injurious juvenile offenders knows that nearly *anything* can be used for self-mutilation purposes if a juvenile is creative.

There are a variety of reasons why juvenile offenders may engage in self-injurious behavior. Self-injury typically relates to youth not being able to express their thoughts and emotions in words, so instead they rely on actions to express themselves. Strong feelings of sadness, anger, anxiety, disappointment, frustration, and embarrassment are often experienced as intolerable, and self-injuring juveniles may cut, carve, or burn themselves to reduce these emotional experiences. Some self-injurious juveniles describe feeling "pent-up" and tense much of the time; they describe feeling as though they are going to "explode." Once a juvenile cuts or carves himself or herself and observes blood oozing out of the skin, he or she typically experiences a sense of relief and relaxation. Feelings of tension eventually return, and the juvenile may again self-injure so as to return to a sense of calm. Some self-injurers believe that they deserve to be punished, and they feel exonerated after harming themselves; it is as if their "badness" flows out of them with the blood from their cuts or with the fluid from their burns. Other self-injurers (particularly those with PTSD) begin to feel "fuzzy" and as though things are "unreal" when they are extremely anxious or stressed. They describe self-harming behavior as being "grounding" and that it helps them to feel "whole" again. Some self-injurers involved with the criminal justice system have more interpersonal reasons associated with their mutilation, including wanting to communicate their emotions (e.g., sadness, anger, frustration) to others and attempting to elicit attention, nurturance, or support from those they care about.

Even though self-injurious behavior appears to be more common among today's youth than it was in the past, self-injury is not a normal part of adolescence and should be evaluated whenever it becomes apparent. Even if staff believe that a juvenile is engaging in self-injurious behavior as a strategy to solicit extra attention from adults, the self-harming juvenile should be evaluated by a medical/mental health professional. There are a variety of ways in which to obtain staff attention in a correctional facility; it is not normal for youth to cut their skin or to rely on other self-harming behavior as a means to that end.

Psychotic Disorders

The term *psychosis* typically refers to impairment in reality testing. Individuals who are psychotic tend to have difficulty in differentiating what is real from what is not real. Psychotic individuals typically experience and exhibit hallucinations, delusions, disorganized speech, disorganized behavior, and "negative" symptoms.

Hallucinations are false sensory perceptions that are not associated with real external stimuli. Although youth can experience hallucinations with any of the five senses (auditory, visual, gustatory, olfactory, and tactile), the type of hallucination most commonly reported among juveniles is auditory—hearing voices that other people cannot hear. Psychotic youth may report that these voices are coming from inside or outside of their heads; regardless, they perceive these voices not as their own thoughts but rather as other people talking to them or about them. Some juveniles report recognizing the voices they hear (e.g., a brother, an uncle, God, the devil), while others report that they do not. Some psychotic youth can decipher exactly what the voices are saying, while for others the voices may be more muffled and vague. In addition, the voices may tell juveniles to behave in certain ways such as killing themselves or killing staff. Sometimes, when youth hear voices, the voices are commenting on the youth or their behavior (e.g., telling them they are stupid or ugly, ridiculing them for something they have done). Although less common, some psychotic juveniles will see things that others cannot see (e.g., people or animals in their room). Others may feel spiders or other bugs crawling on their skin, or they may feel that they have some type of object or creature moving inside their bodies. Some juveniles may even smell things that no one else can smell.

Delusions are personal beliefs that individuals rigidly hold on to despite obvious proof that the beliefs are false or irrational. Examples of delusional beliefs held by psychotic juveniles include thinking that other people are plotting against them, are talking negatively about them, are trying to steal or control their thoughts, and are trying to read their minds. Persecutory delusions are not uncommon, with some juveniles believing that staff are trying to poison them or that all law enforcement and corrections staff are in a conspiracy against them. Some psychotic female juvenile offenders are convinced that they are pregnant despite the fact that they are virgins and multiple pregnancy tests were negative. Some psychotic youth believe that parts of their body are diseased, decayed, or rotting away even though all medical tests are normal. In addition, some psychotic juveniles have grandiose delusions, believing that they have been "chosen" in some way (e.g., by someone famous, by God) or have special/magical gifts or talents. Religious themes are not uncommon among individuals suffering from delusional thinking.

Disorganized thinking and speech is also common among youth suffering from psychotic disorders. These youth may speak in sentences that do not make sense or are only loosely related, use words that do not make sense, talk in rhymes or with a singsong tune, or repeatedly parrot back what others have said. Some psychotic juveniles are quite talkative, but what comes out of their mouths is often strange and confusing. Correctional staff often feel as though they are not listening closely enough to a psychotic juvenile because they do not understand what he or she is trying to convey; however, the reality is that the juvenile is not making much sense.

He or she may put words or sentences together that are not logical (e.g., "I hate my school because cats eat birds and rats when they are hungry"). Or, a psychotic juvenile may put words and sentences together that are not really related (e.g., "My mom is coming to visit. The dinosaur book is too long. My roommate is driving me crazy. I did the extra credit portion of the last assignment."). Some youth with psychotic disorders may use words they have made up themselves that are typically meaningless to a listener (e.g., "Whenever I used to go to the blarly, I would always have the greatest time"). Or, juveniles' words may make no sense at all (e.g., "Come over here and books no go"). These youth may repeat certain words over and over, or they may completely stop talking in the middle of a sentence for no apparent reason. Some psychotic youth will take a very long time to answer questions asked of them, or they may have little or no speech at all. Even when asked to elaborate, psychotic juveniles might provide only one- or two-word answers or sentences.

Youth with disorganized behavior usually exhibit a messy appearance, restless or agitated behavior, bizarre movements or posturing, pacing, and rocking. Poor hygiene is also common. Psychotic youth may appear odd or strange to correctional staff. These youth may repeatedly engage in unusual and stereotypical movements with specific parts of their bodies, or they may sit on their bed or in a corner of a room and rock back and forth for hours. Within correctional facilities, some psychotic youth like to crawl into tight spaces when in their room, including under their bed, in between their toilet and the wall, and in between their toilet and any type of cabinet. These juveniles may appear to be extremely tense and nervous, wringing their hands and walking back and forth in the small space of their dorm room or in one particular segment of the living unit. Whereas some psychotic youth may be unable to remain still and may feel as though they have to constantly keep moving, others will remain still, without any movement, for extended periods of time.

Juveniles from different ethnic, racial, and socioeconomic backgrounds, as well as youth with lower levels of intellectual functioning, may report experiences that can be *misinterpreted* as psychotic symptomatology. For example, some young children and cognitively impaired adolescents talk about interacting with imaginary friends; these youth may also report seeing or hearing the voices of superheroes they have watched on television. It may be standard (and completely acceptable) in some cultures for individuals to see visions of deceased relatives or religious figures. Depending on the context of the situation, it can sometimes be difficult to determine whether a juvenile is telling the truth or suffering from delusional thinking. For example, some juvenile offenders are adamant that someone is trying to kill them or that law enforcement officials are arresting them more often than they are arresting their peers. Depending on the juvenile's lifestyle or the community in which he or she lives, the juvenile's beliefs may be entirely accurate and not a reflection of "paranoid" thinking. Developmental, cultural, and lifestyle issues should always be considered when working with juveniles who could potentially be suffering from psychotic disorders.

Symptoms of psychosis can be associated with a variety of different mental health disorders. Youth with schizophrenia commonly exhibit psychotic symptoms, but youth suffering from major depression or bipolar disorder can experience symptoms of psychosis as well. In addition, juveniles who use large amounts of drugs (e.g., methamphetamines, LSD, PCP) may also experience symptoms of psychosis.

In general, juvenile offenders with mental health disorders are typically no more violent than youth without mental health disorders; however, there is a small subgroup of mentally ill individuals who are significantly more likely to engage in violent and assaultive behavior (Monahan, 1996). These youth typically cannot be distinguished by their mental health diagnosis but can be distinguished by the particular mental health symptoms they experience and exhibit. For example, youth experiencing specific types of psychotic symptoms are significantly more likely to engage in interpersonal assaults than are youth not experiencing these symptoms, and this risk is even higher when combined with alcohol and/or drug use. Psychotic youth experiencing *paranoid delusions* can be at higher risk for assaultive behavior than other youth because these psychotic youth may believe that correctional staff are trying to harm them in some way. These particular youth can react aggressively to benign actions on the part of adults due to misperceiving the intent underlying social interactions.

Comorbidity

Most mentally ill juvenile offenders suffer from more than one of the preceding mental health disorders simultaneously. In fact, it is not uncommon for a juvenile involved with the justice system to be diagnosed with three or four mental health disorders at the same time. For example, a juvenile may have ADHD, a learning disorder, and conduct disorder. He or she may then develop major depression while incarcerated. If the juvenile has been raped or severely beaten in the community or in a correctional facility, then he or she may also develop PTSD. As one can imagine, the assessment and treatment of a mentally ill juvenile becomes more clinically complex with each additional diagnosis.

Co-occurring Mental Health and Substance Use Disorders

The term *co-occurring disorders* typically describes the simultaneous presence of a mental health disorder (e.g., major depression, ADHD, PTSD) *and* a substance use disorder (e.g., alcohol abuse, cannabis abuse, cocaine abuse, heroin dependence). Although there are many youth involved with the justice system who have a mental health disorder *or* a substance use disorder, some juvenile offenders have *both* types of disorders. The notion that some mentally ill juveniles also have a substance use disorder or that some youth with a substance use disorder also suffer from a mental health disorder is not new. Over the years, there have been a variety of terms used to describe this complicated subset of youth with coexisting disorders including, but not limited to, dually diagnosed, double jeopardy, and mentally ill chemically addicted (MICA) youth.

Identifying juvenile offenders with co-occurring disorders can be challenging because they are such a diverse group of adolescents. There are no *typical* juveniles with co-occurring disorders because their clinical presentation is related to each juvenile's particular combination of mental health and substance abuse symptoms. In addition, juveniles may present themselves differently at different time periods due to the level of stress they are experiencing, the degree of access they have to alcohol or drugs, and the potentially changeable nature of both of these types of disorders. The assessment, treatment, and management needs of youth with co-occurring mental health and substance use disorders are different from the needs of youth who have only one of these types of disorders.

Mental health and substance use disorders can interact in a variety of different ways (Peters & Bartoi, 1997) such as those that follow.

Set Off. Substance use can *set off* or trigger the emergence of a mental health disorder if a juvenile is biologically/genetically predisposed to mental illness. For example, a juvenile whose grandfather has bipolar disorder may never have experienced symptoms of mania until the juvenile started using cocaine.

Produce. Substance use can *produce* psychiatric symptoms. For example, alcohol is a depressant. If a juvenile ingests large enough amounts of alcohol and/or ingests alcohol for a long enough period of time, then he or she could develop depressive symptoms. If a juvenile's heavy alcohol use continues for a significant time period, then he or she could eventually meet diagnostic criteria for major depression.

Worsen. Symptoms of mental illness may *worsen* when a juvenile uses alcohol and/or other drugs. For example, a juvenile with schizophrenia can experience a significant worsening of psychotic symptoms when using hallucinogenic drugs. Alcohol and drugs can intensify feelings of depression, lower inhibitions, or raise a juvenile's feelings of courage. Therefore, a juvenile who has thought about killing himself or herself but never made an attempt may take action on these thoughts while he or she is drunk or high.

Imitate. Substance use can look very *similar* to the symptoms of a mental health disorder. For example, a juvenile who uses cocaine or amphetamines regularly can appear as though he or she has ADHD or mania. Some heavy users of methamphetamines develop significant paranoid delusions about their friends, family, and neighbors.

Cover Up. Symptoms of a mental health disorder may be *covered up* or hidden by a juvenile's drug and alcohol use. For example, a juvenile who has ADHD may use cocaine so often that others attribute his or her hyperactive behavior solely to the use of drugs, completely overlooking a possible mental health disorder. Only when the juvenile is clean and sober does it become evident that symptoms of overactivity remain without substance use.

Unrelated. A juvenile may have both a mental health disorder and a substance use disorder, but the two disorders might *not be causally related* to one another; however, a common factor may underlie both of them. For example, a juvenile's genetic makeup may result in an increased vulnerability for the development of mental illness and/or substance abuse.

The onset of mental health and substance use disorders appears to vary among different youth (Deykin, Buka, & Zeena, 1992). For some adolescents, symptoms of mental illness may precede the onset of significant substance abuse. For others, mental illness appears to occur secondary to a juvenile's substance use disorder. A third group of adolescents may experience the simultaneous onset of mental health and substance use disorders. At this time, the *exact* relationship between mental illness and substance use is uncertain. However, one thing that is clear is that juveniles with co-occurring mental health and substance use disorders are at significant risk for multiple problems, including an increased risk for a completed suicide (Brent et al., 1993).

Cultural Issues

Care should be taken to keep cultural issues at the forefront when identifying juvenile offenders with mental health disorders. Youth from various racial and ethnic backgrounds can manifest symptoms of mental health disorders differently (e.g., headaches and stomachaches vs. sad mood and crying). Some cultures are more open about the expression of mental health symptoms than are others. Certain minority youth may be reluctant to discuss their mental health symptoms with correctional or mental health staff because they fear it will bring shame to their families. In addition, some minority families have already sought mental health assistance for youth from individuals other than mainstream mental health professionals (e.g., extended family, clergy, tribal healer, *curandero*); therefore, from mainstream standards, it may appear that these youth have not received mental health services when in fact they have.

A juvenile's race can influence the mental health diagnosis he or she is given (Flaskerud & Hu, 1992; Kilgus, Pumariega, & Cuffe, 1995) as well as where the juvenile is referred for services. African American youth suffering from psychopathology and violent behavior are more likely to be incarcerated within the justice system, and Caucasian youth suffering from psychopathology and violent behavior are more likely to be hospitalized within the mental health system (Lewis, Balla, & Shanok, 1979). Even after youth have been incarcerated, this type of racial bias appears to exist within juvenile correctional facilities as well. Caucasian girls are more likely to be referred to mental health professionals and/or transferred to "treatment" units within a correctional facility than are African American girls displaying similar behaviors (Lewis, Shanok, & Pincus, 1982). When African American girls engaged in the same types of troublesome behaviors that initiated referral or transfer to a treatment unit for their Caucasian counterparts, the African American girls were more likely to receive punishments (e.g., placement in a seclusion room). Both Caucasian and African American correctional staff sought more mental health assistance for the Caucasian girls and less mental health assistance for the African American girls. It seems that minority juvenile offenders have to exhibit more dramatic and extreme behaviors reflective of mental illness than do their Caucasian peers to be perceived as having a mental health disorder and in need of treatment (Lewis et al., 1982).

Conclusions

This chapter has presented a review of some of the critical issues related to the identification of mental health disorders among juvenile offenders. Identifying mental illness among this clinically complex group of youth can be challenging. However, it can be done and should be done. Correctional workers and probation/parole officers can play a critical role in the identification of mentally ill youth. The ability to recognize key mental health symptoms among the youth in their care, as well as to refer juveniles who are potentially mentally ill for evaluation and services, makes the appropriate treatment of these youth more likely. Documenting and reporting the specific youth behaviors that staff *observe* (as opposed to staff's opinions or informal assessments of what is occurring or the juveniles' underlying motivations) can be of great value to clinicians working with juvenile offenders who have mental health disorders. Many staff members have "hunches" or "gut feelings" about certain youth being mentally ill and/or in danger of harming themselves, although they might be unable to pinpoint exactly on what they are basing their judgments. These individuals should trust their feelings, err on the side of caution, and refer these youth to medical/mental health professionals, describing the specific behaviors of concern that they observed. Because relying solely on a juvenile's self-report of psychiatric symptoms and previous mental health treatment has some limitations, the importance of staff observation is critical. As corrections staff are trained and become more educated about what symptoms are indicative of mental illness, they will be less likely to view youth behaviors that are "different" or unusual as oppositional or manipulative behavior on the part of mentally ill juveniles and more likely to make appropriate referrals to mental health/medical professionals. Having a relationship with one significant adult figure (e.g., parent, relative, neighbor, correctional staff member, probation/parole officer, teacher, coach, mentor) can serve as a protective factor against a juvenile's future negative behavior. Many juvenile offenders look up to and get emotionally attached to the staff with whom they interact. Developing a better understanding of a juvenile's mental health symptoms can help these types of relationships to develop and remain strong, which in turn can lessen the effects of some of the negative occurrences in the juvenile's life (Werner & Smith, 1992).

When unidentified or misclassified, juvenile offenders with mental health disorders often receive a significant amount of sanctions and are not referred for appropriate mental health treatment. Because some symptoms of mental illness appear similar to youth behavior that is defiant and intentionally oppositional (e.g., disruptions during treatment groups, disruptions during school, repeated conflict with staff, not following adult directives, not following through on assignments and responsibilities, feces smearing, irritability, aggression, repeated self-harm behavior, inability to advance within the point/level system on a living unit), it is common for correctional staff to misinterpret much of this type of behavior and to respond by becoming more restrictive or punitive with youth. However, some mentally ill youth may be so impaired that they do not have the capability to meet all of the expectations placed on them by the correctional program. In addition, youth who have experienced trauma to their brains from accidents, injuries, and/or drug use also may suffer impairment in their ability to fully participate in a facility's daily programs and to meet all of the expectations of supervision plans. This is not to imply that mentally ill juvenile offenders should not be held accountable. Other than rare cases in which a young offender has been found incompetent or legally insane at the time of the crime, juveniles with mental health disorders should receive consequences for engaging in negative behavior. However, they also require treatment or services for their mental health disorders as well as any substance abuse disorders and neuropsychiatric factors that are causing them distress or interfering with their ability to function. The proper identification of mentally ill juveniles is the first step in the referral and treatment process.

The role of correctional staff should not be overlooked in the continuum of care for juvenile offenders with mental health disorders. Their particular role places them in an ideal position to serve as a positive role model, observe youth behavior, and refer juveniles in possible need of treatment to mental health/medical professionals. Providing these valuable staff with education and training on the identification and management of juvenile offenders with mental health disorders increases the likelihood of them carrying out these critical functions in a more strategic and effective manner.

References

Abikoff, H. A., Courtney, M., Pelham, W. E., & Koplewicz, H. D. (1993). Teacher's ratings of disruptive behaviors: The influence of halo effects. *Journal of Abnormal Child Psychology, 21,* 519-533.

American Psychiatric Association. (2000). *The diagnostic and statistical manual of mental disorders* (4th ed., text rev.). Washington, DC: Author.

Berman, A. L., & Jobes, D. A. (1994). *Adolescent suicide: Assessment and intervention.* Washington, DC: American Psychological Association.

Brent, D. A., & Perper, J. A. (1995). Research in adolescent suicide: Implications for training, service delivery, and public policy. *Suicide and Life-Threatening Behavior, 25,* 222-230.

Brent, D. A., Perper, J. A., Moritz, G., Allman, C., Friend, A., Roth, C., Schweers, J., Balach, L., & Baugher, M. (1993). Psychiatric risk factors for adolescent suicide: A case control study. *Journal of the American Academy of Child and Adolescent Psychiatry, 32,* 521-529.

Butcher, J., William, C., Graham, J., Archer, R., Tellegen, A., Ben-Porath, V., & Kaemmer, B. (1994). *Manual for administration, scoring, and interpretation: MMPI-A.* Minneapolis: University of Minnesota Press.

Cauffman, E., Feldman, S. S., Waterman, J., & Steiner, H. (1998). Posttraumatic stress disorder among female juvenile offenders. *Journal of the American Academy of Child and Adolescent Psychiatry, 37,* 1209-1216.

Centers for Disease Control and Prevention. (1997). *Deaths and death rates: All races, both sexes, 15-24 years old.* Hyattsville, MD: U.S. Department of Health and Human Services.

Conners, C. K., Sitarenios, G., Parker, J. D., & Epstein, J. N. (1998). The Revised Conners Parent Rating Scale (CPRS-R): Factor structure, reliability, and criterion validity. *Journal of Abnormal Child Psychology, 26,* 257-268.

Davis, D. D., Bean, G. J., Schumacher, J. E., & Stringer, T. L. (1991). Prevalence of emotional disorders in a juvenile justice institutional population. *American Journal of Forensic Psychology, 9*, 5-17.

Deykin, E. Y., Buka, S. L., & Zeena, T. H. (1992). Depressive illness among chemically dependent adolescents. *American Journal of Psychiatry, 149*, 1341-1347.

Edens, J. F., & Otto, R. K. (1997). Prevalence of mental disorders among youth in the juvenile justice system. *Focal Point, 11*, 1-8.

Flaskerud, J. H., & Hu, L. (1992). Relationship of ethnicity to psychiatric diagnosis. *Journal of Nervous and Mental Disease, 180*, 296-303.

Grisso, T., & Barnum, R. (2000). *Massachusetts Youth Screening Instrument-2: User's manual and technical report.* Worcester: University of Massachusetts Medical School.

Hayes, L. M. (1995). *Prison suicide: An overview and guide to prevention.* Washington, DC: U.S. Department of Justice, National Institute of Corrections.

Hayes, L. M., & Rowan, J. R. (1988). *National Study of Jail Suicides: Seven years later.* Washington, DC: U.S. Department of Justice, National Institute of Corrections.

Herjanic, B., & Reich, W. (1982). Development of a structured psychiatric interview for children: Agreement between child and parent on individual symptoms. *Journal of Abnormal Child Psychology, 10*, 307-324.

Kilgus, M. D., Pumariega, A. J., & Cuffe, S. P. (1995). Influence of race on diagnosis in adolescent psychiatric inpatients. *Journal of the American Academy of Child and Adolescent Psychiatry, 34*, 67-72.

Ladely, S. J., & Puskar, K. R. (1994). Adolescent suicide: Behaviors, risk factors, and psychiatric nursing interventions. *Issues in Mental Health Nursing, 15*, 497-504.

Lewis, D. O., Balla, D. A., & Shanok, S. S. (1979). Some evidence of race bias in the diagnosis and treatment of the juvenile offender. *American Journal of Orthopsychiatry, 49*, 53-61.

Lewis, D. O., Shanok, S. S., & Pincus, J. H. (1982). A comparison of the neuropsychiatric status of female and male incarcerated delinquents: Some evidence of sex and race bias. *Journal of the American Academy of Child Psychiatry, 21*, 190-196.

Marttunen, M. (1994). Psychosocial maladjustment, mental disorders, and stressful life events precede adolescent suicide. *Psychiatria Fennica, 25*, 39-51.

Monahan, J. (1996). *Mental illness and violent crime.* Washington, DC: U.S. Department of Justice, National Institute of Justice Research Preview.

Parent, D. G., Leiter, V., Kennedy, S., Livens, L., Wentworth, D., & Wilcox, S. (1994). *Conditions of confinement: Juvenile detention and correction facilities.* Washington, DC: U.S. Department of Justice, Office of Justice Programs, Office of Juvenile Justice and Delinquency Prevention.

Peters, R. H., & Bartoi, M. G. (1997). *Screening and assessment of co-occurring disorders in the justice system.* Tampa: University of South Florida, Louis de la Parte Florida Mental Health Institute, GAINS Center.

Rhode, P., Seeley, J. R., & Mace, D. E. (1997). Correlates of suicidal behavior in a juvenile detention population. *Suicide and Life-Threatening Behavior, 27*, 164-175.

Shaffer, D., Gould, M. S., Fisher, P., Trautman, P., Moreau, D., Kleinman, M., & Flory, M. (1996). Psychiatric diagnosis in child and adolescent suicide. *Archives of General Psychiatry, 53*, 339-348.

Shafii, M., Carrigan, S., Whittinghill, J. R., & Derrick, A. (1985). Psychological autopsy of completed suicides in children and adolescents. *American Journal of Psychiatry, 142*, 1061-1064.

Sparrow, S. S., Balla, D. A., & Cicchetti, C. V. (1984). *Vineland Adaptive Behavior Scales.* Circle Pines, MN: American Guidance Service.

Steiner, H., Garcia, I. G., & Matthews, Z. (1997). Posttraumatic stress disorder in incarcerated juvenile delinquents. *Journal of the American Academy of Child and Adolescent Psychiatry, 36*, 357-365.

Verhulst, F. C., & van der Ende, J. (1992). Agreement between parents' reports and adolescents' self-reports of problem behavior. *Journal of Child Psychology and Psychiatry, 33*, 1011-1023.

Walsh, B. W., & Rosen, P. M. (1988). *Self-mutilation: Theory, research, and treatment.* New York: Guilford.

Washington State Detention Managers Association & Boesky, L. M. (2000). *The Mental Health Juvenile Detention Admission Tool (MH-JDAT).* Seattle: Washington State Detention Managers Association.

Werner, E., & Smith, R. (1992). *Overcoming the odds: High risk children from birth to adulthood.* Ithaca, NY: Cornell University Press.

CHAPTER 10

Other Special Offender Populations

Linda Richardson

The explosion in the population of jails and prisons in the United States has resulted in a concomitant explosion in the number of incarcerated persons with special health and/or mental health care needs. As Gondles (2000) pointed out, the correctional system is a reflection of our society, and because society includes persons with special needs, so does the correctional system. Moreover, jails and prisons typically have a higher proportion of persons with special needs than does the general population. Given that the lives of many offenders are characterized by poor health habits—including unhealthy living environments, limited or nonexistent health care, and heavy use of tobacco, alcohol, and drugs—their vulnerability to physical and mental health problems is high.

Prisons and jails have increasingly become primary treatment sites for serious physical and mental health problems, in part because our society has chosen to ignore the needs of persons with these problems, looking instead to the government to bear the responsibility (Gondles, 2000). Care for individuals with special health and mental health needs is specialized and intensive as well as difficult and expensive. Yet from both a humanitarian stance and a legal stance, correctional systems have no choice but to provide it (Gondles, 2000). The growth of these special needs groups and their increasingly costly and complex care, however, threatens to overwhelm correctional systems, which were initially designed to provide safety and security rather than health and mental health care. Not only do individuals in these groups have needs requiring specialized programs and services, but in some cases they also may have more difficulty in coping with the correctional environment, often resulting in more rule infractions and a disproportionately large amount of time spent in segregation and other highly secure and more costly types of housing.

Correctional systems vary widely in the staffing they provide to care for these special needs groups. An American Correctional Association (ACA) survey of mental health staffing in state and federal prisons found a considerable range in mental health staffing patterns, with several state prison systems employing no psychiatrists, others employing no psychologists, and still others employing no mental health therapists (ACA, 1999a). A few departments did not employ any mental health professionals from any of these three categories, either internally or on a contractual basis (ACA, 1999a). Thus, such systems are likely to have limited or no ability to respond to the mental health needs of their special offender groups. Moreover, the level of mental health staffing did not appear to be directly related to the size of the correctional systems. For example, North Dakota reported having fewer than 1,000 inmates, who were cared for by four psychiatrists and one psychologist. New York, on the other hand, reported housing nearly 70,000 inmates but had no psychiatrists, psychologists, or mental health therapists.

Until recently, most jails and prisons made limited efforts to identify inmates with special needs. Because the focus of correctional work was primarily on deterrence and punishment and not on rehabilitation (Lovell, Allen, Johnson, & Jemelka, 2001), there was little justification for identifying such individuals because they would be treated the same as other inmates. However, as legal cases were brought against jail and prison systems because of their limited health/mental health care to these groups, and as case law developed supporting increased services, it became clear that jails and prisons would be held to the community standard of care. To meet this standard required the expansion of services. As a result, medical and mental health services and programs in jails and prisons experienced rapid growth and development. To meet this community standard of care, it was necessary to first identify those offenders with special needs so as to provide them with appropriate care. Therefore, methods of screening inmates to identify those with special needs were developed, focusing especially on those offenders with serious mental illness, developmental disabilities, and significant medical problems.

Typically, the assessment process used in prisons (see Chapters 1 and 4 for additional information on inmate screening and assessment) occurs in two phases. During the first phase, all inmates entering the correctional system undergo a brief screening process for the purpose of identifying significant programmatic and/or treatment needs. Assessment methods during this phase are likely to include structured interviews, questionnaires, and/or objective psychological tests. If any significant findings emerge from this initial screening process (e.g., a health problem, mental illness, mental retardation), then a second, more detailed evaluative phase is warranted. More extensive assessments target the particular deficits and treatment needs of these individuals and often result in the development of specific treatment plans and recommendations. There is considerable variation across correctional systems in the depth of these assessments, the instruments employed, and how the results are interpreted and used to make decisions. For instance, staff in many correctional systems assess intellectual/cognitive functioning with brief screening measures developed in the community, while others administer very comprehensive measures to all incoming inmates. Many of these standard psychometric measures may have varying degrees of applicability and predictive value in a correctional environment. Ideally, empirically based assessment devices should be developed, or existing devices should be adapted for use in correctional settings. The content of this more extensive evaluation may relate, in part, to the nature of the programming and services available within the facility because the results may be used for placement purposes. In general, then, screening is the first step in the identification and management of offenders with special needs in jails and prisons. However, if an institution does not intend to provide special programming for specific subgroups of the inmate population, then there is little need for an elaborate screening process.

Although there are many special needs groups in jails and prisons, this chapter focuses on the following six groups and their particular mental health needs: military prisoners, foreign-born inmates, offenders with HIV/AIDS, geriatric offenders, terminally ill inmates, and offenders with mental retardation. Each of these groups is discussed in terms of its numbers within the correctional setting, its unique characteristics, its mental health needs, and how these needs might be addressed within the correctional environment. The chapter addresses the concerns of these special offender groups in jails and prisons. However, because the average length of incarceration for inmates in jail is brief and so therapeutic/programmatic opportunities are often limited, the chapter's primary focus is on the prison setting.

Military Offenders

Although military inmates are not, strictly speaking, a special needs group, they represent a small and somewhat unusual group of inmates. In 1997, there were 2,772 prisoners under military jurisdiction (Bureau of Justice Statistics, 2000). The subset of this group with special needs is extremely small. One reason for the relatively low number of military inmates with special needs is the military selection process. Recruits are assessed to determine their fitness for military duty. Those individuals found to have serious physical or mental health problems are screened out and thus never enter the military. A member of the military who develops a special need at a later time (i.e., a serious physical or mental illness) is likely to be given a medical discharge due to the inability to carry out military duties. Those with less serious illnesses are provided care while remaining in the military. The very old are not found in the military due to limitations on length of service and mandatory retirement. Persons with developmental disabilities are not found in the military because such persons are screened out during the initial recruitment assessment. Military personnel must be U.S. citizens, thus eliminating illegal aliens. Screening cannot rule out those who may commit crimes, although persons with felony records are not accepted. In the military, a small number of individuals are found guilty of crimes and sentenced to serve time in military prisons. If the sentence is for a year or longer, then the military has the option of transferring the offender to a federal prison to serve the time (A. Beeler, personal communication, April 26, 2001). Once transferred to the federal prison system or the Bureau of Prisons (BOP), the military offender is treated like any other inmate. The only aspect of the federal prison experience that is different for an inmate from the military is that a military offender can earn "good time." Military inmates may prefer serving their time in BOP because the size of the BOP system and its various institutions allows for more programming than is feasible in the much smaller military prison system.

In the military, both military personnel and civilians provide mental health assessment and treatment services to offenders. On entering the military prison system, each military offender receives psychological testing to assess mental health needs. Test results determine whether the inmate receives a more extensive individual evaluation by a psychologist. If there is evidence suggestive of mental illness, then the individual is assessed in greater depth. Once the evaluation by mental health staff is completed, a treatment plan is formulated. Typically, the inmate is offered individual or group counseling. Some specialized treatment programs are also offered by the military. For example, sex offenders are placed in a 2-year sex offender treatment program, substance abusers are placed in a 9-month treatment program, and assaultive offenders are placed in a 6-month treatment program. These targeted programs are modeled after similar programs in Canada. Once the inmate serves the sentence and completes the appropriate treatment program, the individual may be considered for return to active duty. If not found appropriate to return to duty, the person is discharged from military service. Because the incidence of crime in the military is low, there are only a few correctional facilities for military offenders. All female military offenders are housed at one institution in San Diego. Male military offenders are housed in several facilities, with the highest security unit located in Fort Leavenworth, Kansas. Individuals from all branches of the military are housed together in military prisons and in these specialized treatment programs.

The mental health needs of military inmates generally parallel those of persons in nonmilitary correctional settings. However, in comparison with inmates in nonmilitary prisons, military offenders at least initially seem to be more disciplined and thus are better able to follow rules, presumably due to their military training (A. Beeler, personal communication, April 26, 2001).

Foreign-Born Offenders

A significant number of persons incarcerated in the United States are foreign born, and some of these are in the country illegally. In 1991, it was estimated that approximately 4% of all state inmates were not U.S. citizens (Bureau of Justice Statistics, 2001). BOP also houses a large number of foreign-born individuals, who are most commonly arrested for illegal entry into the United States, drug smuggling, or smuggling people into the country illegally. For the past several years, this group has represented approximately 30% of the federal prison system's total inmate population. Although this group includes individuals from more than 90 nationalities, more than half of them are from Mexico. This population is concentrated in several institutions but can be found throughout the system.

Illegal aliens are persons who are citizens of foreign countries and reside in the United States without appropriate visas, passports, or permits. In some instances, they enter the United States legally but remain here illegally following the expiration of their visas. In other instances, they enter the United States illegally, lacking the proper documentation that permits residence in this country. Although these individuals have not committed crimes in the United States, their presence in this country is unlawful. In the United States, there is no known state or federal correctional institution that focuses exclusively on serving inmates who are illegal aliens.

Criminal aliens are persons living in the United States, either legally or illegally, who have been convicted of crimes that may cause them to be deported (Draper & Reed, 1995). The Immigration and Naturalization Service (INS) is responsible for determining whether a person is a criminal alien. Criminal aliens can be found in jails, state prisons, and federal prisons as well as in INS detainment facilities. Within the federal prison system, certain prisons have been designated to house criminal aliens serving sentences. This assists INS staff greatly in that they are able to conduct INS deportation hearings on-site at these institutions. This process helps to expedite deportation and eliminates the extra cost of funding and scheduling these hearings in various community locations after the persons are released from prison. It also eliminates the chances of the person's fleeing after release.

Many foreign-born inmates do not speak English. Correctional staff or fellow inmates who speak the primary language of the individual may provide translation. If none is available, then translator services are employed or the AT&T phone translation service is used. Language capability in the correctional environment is an enormous challenge given the large number of nationalities and languages represented.

In most cases, foreign-born individuals are mainstreamed in the general prison population. At this time, there are no known mental health treatment programs specific to this group in correctional settings. However, one federal prison offers a therapy group for immigrant violators (A. Beeler, personal communication, April 26, 2001). In general, it has been found that the mental health needs of this population are no different from those of native-born individuals. However, the physical health needs of immigrant violators are sometimes different. For example, they may bring health problems from their countries that are rarely, if ever, encountered in the United States. Regardless of the service provided, staff must be sensitive to the languages and cultures of these individuals.

Given the high cost of delivering health services, it has been proposed that service delivery to this group be considered from a cost-benefit point of view. Draper and Reed (1995) suggested that it might make more sense to target services to U.S. citizens, given that they will return to the community when released, rather than to criminal aliens, who might be deported.

One illegal alien group that has been particularly difficult to manage in prison is the Mariel Cuban detainees. In 1980, Fidel Castro tried to rid Cuba of "undesirable" people—including persons with mental illness, mental retardation, and physical illness, as well as criminals—by sending them out to sea. More than 125,000 came to the United States in what has been referred to as the "Mariel boat lift." Of these, less than 20% reported histories of criminal convictions. The U.S. attorney general ordered BOP to house those Mariel detainees with histories of mental illness or criminal histories if they could not be safely detained in resettlement camps or detention centers (BOP, 2001). Not surprisingly, they quickly came to represent an unusually high percentage of the inpatient psychiatric population in BOP (C. Mack, personal communication, January 24, 2001). This group also had a relatively high rate of escapes and a high rate of participation in riots as compared with the general inmate population.

At this time, if Mariel detainees are serving sentences, then INS must be notified 16 months prior to their expected release dates, allowing INS enough time to decide whether or not to detain them. Today, a large percentage of Mariel detainees are in prison because they committed crimes in the United States, served their sentences, and are now in INS custody. Typically, they are not eligible for repatriation. BOP limits each institution to 55 Mariel detainees, presumably to lower the risk of riots and other potential problems that may arise from a larger group (Bureau of Prisons, 2001). Within BOP, these individuals are housed with convicted inmates. They are not required to work, but they must meet the mandatory educational requirements. Each year, they are reviewed by the INS Cuban Review Panel to determine whether they need continued detention or are ready for release. To be considered for release, a person must have a community sponsor or a release program in the community. Those with known substance abuse histories may be required to attend a residential substance abuse treatment program prior to release.

Although Mariel Cuban detainees are not given any special programming in BOP, they are tracked closely. These individuals receive the same mental health services as do other inmates, including individual and group counseling as needed and substance abuse treatment if indicated. Because they are typically non-English speaking, services must be provided in a culturally sensitive manner in their native language (i.e., Spanish). Every 3 years during incarceration, each detainee undergoes a psychological evaluation that provides updated information on the individual's mental health status.

Another subgroup of foreign-born inmates of growing concern to BOP is Mexican aliens, most of whom are male (C. Mack, personal communication, January 24, 2001). Many are arrested for illegal entry into the United States. An unusually high proportion of this group are mentally ill. There has been speculation by corrections experts that Mexico and several other underdeveloped countries may be trying to dump their citizens with mental illness in the United States because of the problems these individuals create in their home countries, their acute need for care, the high cost of this care, and its limited availability.

In addition to BOP, many state prisons house a significant number of foreign-born persons. In a report issued by New York State in 1999, it was noted that between April 1, 1985, and December 31, 1998, the number of native-born inmates in the Department of Correctional Services in New York grew by 94%, while the number of foreign-born inmates grew by 249% (Clark, 1999). At the time of the report, the New York State prison population numbered approximately 70,600, with foreign-born inmates accounting for 13% of that number. Of this group, 89% were Hispanic. About three fourths of these foreign-born inmates were from the Caribbean or South America, and 60% were specifically from the Dominican Republic, Jamaica, Colombia, or Cuba. As a group, they were more likely to be convicted of drug offenses and more serious felonies. Although they tended to receive longer sentences, they served the same amount of time on average as did native-born inmates.

Texas also reported having a significant population of foreign-born inmates. In June 1995, there were 115,145 inmates in the Texas prison system, and 10,698 (more than 9%) were foreign born (Draper & Reed, 1995). INS identified 46% of the foreign-born inmates as criminal aliens, of whom 75% were from Mexico. Other states with the highest numbers of criminal aliens in their prison systems include California, Florida, and Illinois (Draper & Reed, 1995).

In 1988, the Institutional Hearing Program (IHP) was established for the purpose of allowing INS and the Executive Office for Immigration and Review to finish removal proceedings while aliens were incarcerated, thus ridding INS of the task of locating these persons after they are released and freeing up detention space for other persons (Rabkin, 1999). The law mandates that INS initiate and complete, if possible, removal proceedings against aggravated felons during their incarceration. Data indicate that INS has not been able to implement the IHP as planned, with the result that many deportable inmates are released from prison. If and when they are located and detained, they take up costly detention beds. Even with aggravated felons, INS has had limited success in completing their hearings while they are in prison. In addition to the expense, this failure to conduct detention hearings on aliens with aggravated felony convictions while they are incarcerated poses a danger to the community due to the nature of their offenses. INS has been strongly encouraged by Congress and others to correct these problems (Rabkin, 1999).

Elderly Offenders

In 1999, approximately 4.5% of the U.S. prison population was estimated to be elderly, that is, over 55 years of age (ACA, 1999b). Older offenders are the fastest growing population in state prisons, having increased more than 200% during the past 10 years (Ortiz, 2000). The "tough on crime" attitude of our society during recent years has resulted in harsher, often longer sentences and in an increase in the number of persons sentenced to life without parole. This phenomenon has resulted in a growing number of persons aging and dying in prison.

One difficulty encountered in discussing this population is the lack of a universal definition of what constitutes older, elderly, or aged. It is generally agreed that prison inmates tend to age faster than the general population due to their histories of poor health care, unhealthy lifestyles, and other factors. Thus, the traditional definitions of aging based solely on chronological age may be less appropriate for incarcerated persons. However, the simplicity of chronological age as a definitional criterion is attractive. Two ages have most frequently been cited as useful. One expert has suggested that 50 years of age be used as a cutoff for defining the elderly in prison (Morton, 1992). The Pennsylvania Department of Corrections (2001) designates inmates as geriatric offenders if they are age 55 years or over. A recent survey of U.S. prisons investigating their special provisions for older inmates used age 55 years or over as the definition for older offender (ACA, 1999b). Thus, there appears to be some consensus that elderly adults in prison are those who are somewhere between 50 and 55 years of age.

Gerontologists have divided older adults in the community into chronological age groups and have used these divisions to help study this population. In one classification scheme, older adults refer to those ages 55 to 64 years, elderly refers to those ages 65 to 79 years, and aged refers to those age 80 years or over (Florida Department of Corrections, 1994). In another classification system, the young-old are described as those adults ages 60 to 74 years, the middle-old are those ages 75 to 84 years, and the old-old are those age 85 years or over (Florida Department of Corrections, 1994). Applied within the correctional setting, these methods of grouping older offenders based exclusively on their age may assist correctional health/mental health providers in gaining a better understanding of this population as well as in planning and implementing services for them.

Elderly offenders are clearly a diverse group, due in part to variability in their heredity, socioeconomic status, lifestyles, and aging experiences (Morton, 1992). From a criminal perspective, some may be first-time offenders who were arrested for serious, usually violent crimes. These offenses may have occurred recently or when the offenders were much younger. In either case, they are likely to live out their lives in prison. These individuals might not identify themselves as criminals due to their limited histories of criminal activity (Goetting, 1983). Other elderly inmates may be multiple criminal offenders who view themselves, and who are seen by others, as career criminals.

Departments of correction are now being confronted with an increased demand for, and the associated growing costs of, health services for this aging population. A 1998 survey of health care budgets in state departments of correction found an enormous range in the dollar amount spent per inmate as well as in the percentage of the total corrections budget represented by health care (ACA, 1999a). Per inmate annual health care costs ranged from $53 in Wyoming to $4,150 in Michigan, with a nationwide average of $2,248. The percentages of the total departments of correction budgets represented by health care ranged from 4% in Wisconsin to 18% in Nevada; however, it should be noted that nine states, as well as the District of Columbia and BOP, did not respond to the survey. Contributing factors to the increasing heath care costs in prisons include the growing inmate population, the expense of treating inmates with HIV infection/AIDS, and the high cost of medications (ACA, 1999a). Although there was no data on the specific cost of caring for elderly inmates, given their high use of health care services, it can be assumed that a large portion of these health care dollars were spent on older inmates. In 1994, it was estimated that the average cost of incarcerating an older inmate was $60,000 per year (Florida Department of Corrections, 1994).

Little is currently known about the use and cost of mental health services for older offenders in correctional settings because service use and costs are not ordinarily tracked by age group. The ease of accessing older inmates and delivering mental health services to them may be related in part to the housing policy for older inmates in the specific prison system. Elderly inmates usually prefer to be housed together apart from other inmates. However, correctional experts are divided on the most appropriate housing for older inmates. Some advocate mainstreaming the elderly in general population housing because older inmates tend to be calmer, quieter, and more obedient than younger inmates and thus can serve as a stabilizing influence. Age-segregated housing can also be labeled discriminatory (Goetting, 1983). Other experts tout the benefits of age-segregated housing for older inmates along with the greater ease of delivering population-specific programming (Goetting, 1983). Segregated housing not only offers older offenders protection from younger, aggressive, more predatory inmates but also may enhance older offenders' sense of well-being, community, and belonging (Ortiz, 2000). More than half of all state prisons have some special provisions for inmates age 55 years or over, typically in the form of special housing, although in many instances, assignment to this housing may be based more on health status than on age (ACA, 1999b). BOP, however, does not house inmates according to age (A. Beeler, personal communication, April 26, 2001).

When designing and implementing programs for older adults, service delivery systems must take into account several significant characteristics of the aging process, including sensory changes, mobility changes, and developmental issues. Older adults are often uninterested in education and job training programs that entice the young. Although they want to work and enjoy working, they prefer stability in their work roles. They often take pride in the work they perform in prison. In most prison systems, older inmates tend to be given lighter duty assignments, which often are the more desirable jobs. When released to the community, if they have not reached retirement age, older offenders often are easiest to place in jobs, make the best adjustment to the community, and have the lowest rate of recidivism (Goetting, 1983). However, they may have more difficulty in obtaining parole in those states that grant good time for participation in educational, job training, and other rehabilitation programs because they are less likely to participate in such programs than are younger offenders (Florida Department of Corrections, 1994).

Few, if any, formal mental health programs or services in jails and prisons are focused specifically on elderly inmates. In most correctional systems, geriatric mental health services are typically provided on an individual basis rather than through a program specific to the population. In those instances where therapeutic groups are offered to older offenders, they are more likely to be found in correctional environments that have age-segregated housing because this arrangement facilitates the identification of suitable candidates as well as the provision of services. According to a survey of U.S. jails and prisons, the incidence of mental illness in inmates age 55 years or over, based on self-reports, ranges from 9% to 20% of the population (Ditton, 1999). The most common mental illnesses reported among older adults include anxiety, severe cognitive impairments, and mood disorders. Diagnoses of depression, schizophrenia, and dementia pose the greatest challenges (Administration on Aging, 2001). One issue of particular concern to correctional administrators is the expected increase in the number of inmates with Alzheimer's disease and other forms of dementia—disorders that are found primarily in older adults. Given the duration of these disorders and the high cost of treatment, there is concern about how this care will be provided in a correctional setting.

Adjusting to prison can be a significant issue, not only for first-time offenders who have entered the prison as older adults but also for those who have aged in prison.

Most people do not want to grow old in prison. Older offenders may also express concern about dying in prison. They do not worry about the process of dying, but they do not want to die while incarcerated. However, it cannot be assumed that all older inmates have a difficult adjustment to prison or to growing old in prison.

Goetting (1983) suggested that some older offenders may regard prison as a protective environment and may appreciate being taken care of. They may also enjoy the respect they receive from others, especially the young inmates, who may value their age and life experiences. In addition, because the basic necessities of food, clothing, shelter, and health care are provided for them, they are relieved of the burden of having to meet their own needs in these domains. They are likely to have healthier lifestyles in prison that may result in a slowing of the aging process.

For those older inmates who have spent most of their adult lives in prison, the prospect of returning to the community can be frightening. Through television and newspapers, they may be aware that the world has undergone many changes during their incarceration, and they may lack confidence in their ability to adapt. Most have few supports in the community, having lost contact with friends and family due to the passage of time, physical separation, and/or deaths. Concerns about finding housing, activities, and relationships, as well as financial worries, make the outside world seem like a scary place. Fear of discrimination in the community due to the status of ex-offender is a concern as well. If an elderly offender is considered for release, then the individual should be provided with information and support while in prison to assist him or her in making appropriate release plans.

Terminally Ill Offenders

Although mental health staff might not have frequent involvement with elderly inmates in the general population, they are likely to have contact with inmates who are dying, many of whom are elderly. Hospice programs are becoming more widely available in prisons, another indicator of the graying of the population. Such programs provide total health care to those who are dying, with an emphasis on pain management rather than on cure of illness. The most common criteria for hospice care in prison are a terminal illness and less than 6 months to live. More people are dying in prison today primarily because (a) the prison population is aging due to longer sentences and (b) younger inmates are dying of AIDS (National Institute of Corrections, 1998). In a National Institute of Corrections (1998) survey, 12 formal hospice programs were identified in the 53 departments of correction (47 states, BOP, Canada, Philadelphia, Guam, Virgin Islands, and Washington, DC) canvassed. In BOP, a hospice is located in each medical referral center. In addition, among the 53 departments of correction, 8 were starting hospice programs and 12 were considering starting hospice programs. In 5 states, there were multiple hospice sites. In 1997, a total of 824 inmates were identified as terminally ill and housed in infirmaries or hospital units, 152 were housed in formal hospice programs in departments of correction, and 96 were released on parole or another type of compassionate release. It should be noted that not all prison systems track their terminally ill inmates, so these data likely underestimate the size of this population.

Nearly all departments of correction have policies on humanitarian early releases, yet few inmates are released under these policies. Moreover, the decisions to grant these releases are more frequently based on an inmate's health status than on age. It has been estimated that 9% of all state prison inmates in 1999 had chronic or terminal illnesses (ACA, 1999b). However, only a small percentage of this group may have been eligible for a humanitarian release. Many older inmates are not candidates for such a release because of the serious and/or violent nature of their crimes, their lengthy sentences, and other factors.

In the federal prison system, an inmate can be considered for compassionate release without being terminally ill so long as the inmate has a serious illness that would prevent him or her from committing more crimes. Recently, there has been a rise in the number of compassionate releases granted in BOP as a result of the position taken by its director (A. Beeler, personal communication, April 26, 2001). Such releases are more likely to occur if inmates' families are involved given that families often work hard to locate the care that their relatives need in the community. Social service agency staff are often overworked and have little time to devote to finding placements for persons under consideration for release. BOP will not grant such a release without an appropriate plan of care.

In Texas, individuals who are convicted of nonaggravated offenses, require 24-hour skilled nursing care, and are not a danger to the public may be granted early parole reviews (Eisenberg, Munson, & Ygnacio, 2000). Those eligible include offenders who are elderly (over 60 years of age), those with terminal illnesses, and those with physical handicaps, mental illness, or mental retardation. The purpose of the program is to decrease the costs of incarceration (nearly $34,000/year for skilled nursing care in prison vs. nearly $7,000/year for skilled nursing care in the community), protect the public, and provide more humane care for these inmates with special needs. However, the number of referrals to this program has been low due to problems with the referral and screening methods and stricter parole criteria. An additional obstacle is the lack of skilled nursing facilities in the community that are willing to accept these offenders. Although those with mental disabilities are eligible, they are rarely referred. Mental health staff could play a key role in making such referrals.

In prison, terminally ill inmates in a hospice program are typically housed in single or double cells. If housed in an infirmary or prison hospital unit, they may be placed in a multiperson ward. Prison-based hospice programs often grant special privileges to the residents, including more liberal visiting and more flexible rules regarding personal property. An interdisciplinary team, which usually includes a mental health staff member and a chaplain, provides total health care to hospice participants, emphasizing quality of life rather than cure. Inmate volunteers typically play a key role in these programs by providing many caregiving services to inmate residents. They also offer emotional support, often functioning as surrogate family members. Counseling families of inmates in hospice programs is an important component of the care because of their relationships to the inmates and their role in the inmates' process of dying. The positive aspects of prison-based hospice programs include improved quality of medical and mental health care, enhanced quality of life, improved relations with families, and enhanced inmate and staff morale. There are many challenges encountered in these programs, including the slowness of staff (especially custody staff) to accept the concept (in contrast to nurses, who readily accept it), the lack of trust from inmates concerning terminal diagnoses and their hesitancy or refusal to sign living wills and "do not resuscitate" orders, and the large number of staff needed to operate the programs (National Institute of Corrections, 1998). Although less expensive than hospital care, these programs are still costly.

Mental health staff in hospice programs play a key role by providing mental health assessments, individual counseling, family counseling, and (occasionally) group counseling. In addition, they offer education and support to both inmates and staff working with hospice inmates. Death and dying is a major focus of this work. Both inmates and their families must face the fact that the inmates will likely die in prison, a reality that is difficult for most to accept. Counseling with families may continue after inmates' deaths to assist them in the grieving process. Hospice staff often benefit from participating in support groups, where they can discuss their thoughts and feelings about their emotionally demanding work with this population and come to terms with their own grief related to the inmates who have died. Work in hospice programs can be difficult and draining, but it can also be very rewarding.

HIV-Infected/AIDS Offenders

HIV/AIDS is one of the leading causes of death in adults ages 25 to 44 years in the United States. It was the number one cause of death in adults in this age group in 1995, but by 1998 it had dropped to number five (Murphy, 2000). In 1996, AIDS-related diseases were responsible for 29% of all inmate deaths (Hammett, Harmon, & Maruschak, 1999). Although the prevalence of HIV/AIDS in inmates has remained static since 1991 and the death rate among inmates has declined since 1995, the prevalence among inmates is higher than in the U.S. general population (Hammett et al., 1999). Moreover, female inmates have a higher prevalence than do male inmates, and Hispanic and African American inmates have a higher prevalence than do Caucasian inmates. There is also considerable geographic variation in prevalence, with the Northeast having both the largest number and highest percentage of inmates with HIV/AIDS. Among the 50 states, New York, Florida, Texas, and California have the highest numbers of HIV-infected inmates, with New York accounting for more than a third of the HIV-infected inmates in the United States. The increased public awareness about HIV/AIDS, and the concomitant rise in federal funding for research and treatment, has resulted in the development and expansion of medical and mental health services for inmates with HIV/AIDS in prison as well as in the community, and the high cost of treatment has contributed substantially to the skyrocketing health care costs in departments of correction.

Identification of persons with HIV/AIDS in a correctional setting can be difficult because testing for HIV/AIDS in prison is controversial. Some correctional systems test all inmates on entry, others test all inmates returning to the community, and still others test only when requested by inmates or when medically necessary (e.g., when there has been an exchange of body fluids in a fistfight). Early identification allows for early and aggressive treatment that may result in a more hopeful prognosis.

Although it is never easy to inform someone that the test results for HIV infection/AIDS are positive, this process can be even more difficult in prison. In BOP, the standard practice is to use a team consisting of a physician and a psychologist to jointly inform the inmate of the diagnosis and to discuss treatment and prognosis. Such a team can then address both the physical health and mental health aspects of the illness and care.

During the early years of the HIV/AIDS epidemic, many jails and prisons isolated individuals with HIV/AIDS to protect the inmate patients, other inmates, and staff. Attitudes toward those with HIV/AIDS were often very negative due to the assumption—often erroneous—that the infected persons must be homosexual. These individuals were seen as "bad" people, and their illness was considered their punishment. The negative attitudes of both staff and other inmates toward those with HIV/AIDS resulted in the ostracizing of these individuals. More recently, as people have become more knowledgeable about HIV/AIDS (including how it is transmitted), the associated stigma is slowly declining.

Today, most health personnel in corrections recommend mainstreaming HIV/AIDS inmates whenever possible, with the exceptions being those individuals who require skilled nursing care. Inmates are typically quite concerned that their diagnoses remain confidential. Although health care staff make every effort to protect these inmates' privacy, it is very difficult to prevent others from guessing the truth due to the nature of the treatment, which often includes extensive drug regimens, frequent physician visits, and trips outside the institution for consultation and care. In 1999, it was reported that two thirds of all jails and prisons offered support groups for HIV/AIDS inmates, typically led by staff from community-based programs (Hammett et al., 1999).

The mental health treatment provided to inmates with HIV/AIDS is primarily in the form of individual counseling. Groups, although very effective with this population, present concerns related to trust and confidentiality that might not be able to be overcome. In addition, given the small number of HIV/AIDS inmates in many institutions, there might not be a sufficient number of interested inmates to form a group. BOP does not offer a mental health treatment program specifically for this population, but individual counseling is offered to all HIV/AIDS inmates. Although groups are rarely conducted for this population in BOP, when they are held, they are typically given another name and identity, such as substance abuse group or adjustment group, to maintain confidentiality. In this author's experience, group counseling with HIV/AIDS inmates can be very powerful and effective because of the information the members exchange about their illness and its treatment as well as the support and understanding they offer each other. Although co-leaders rather than a sole leader enhance the facilitation of all therapy groups, the use of co-leaders in groups with HIV/AIDS inmates is especially recommended given the challenging and emotionally draining nature of these groups.

Issues in counseling HIV/AIDS inmates, whether seen individually or in a group, include how to handle the stigma of the illness both within the prison and in the community, how to inform family and friends and how to respond to their fears about the illness, concern about how others may react to the news, worries about the quality of health care in prison, fears about the physical and emotional effects of the illness, the treatment and its side effects, the fear of dying (including dying at a young age), and the fear of dying in prison. If an inmate is to be released from prison, then discharge planning becomes an important component of the treatment. Locating housing, medical care, and social support in the community is critical to the success of the inmate's release (M. Forbes, personal communication, February 21, 2001). Case managers can play a key role in the care of HIV/AIDS inmates by coordinating their care and discharge planning, monitoring their treatment, and advocating for them (Hammett et al., 1999).

For health care and custody staff to work effectively with inmates with HIV/AIDS, they first need to be provided with factual information about the illness to increase their understanding and decrease their misconceptions. In addition, their attitudes toward the illness and those with the illness warrant exploration and adjustment as needed. Many departments of correction include information and updates on HIV/AIDS in their new staff orientations as well as in their annual training. BOP and the Louisiana Department of Corrections are two examples of correctional systems that provide all staff training in HIV/AIDS each year. Including an HIV/AIDS patient from the community in staff training can be a powerful learning experience. The goal of training is to teach staff how to relate to HIV-infected/AIDS inmates with dignity and respect and how to maintain their confidentiality regarding their illness.

Offenders With Mental Retardation

Inmates with mental retardation are found in nearly all jails and prisons. Although many such offenders may be diverted from jails and prisons, those sent to prison have often been found ineligible for diversion because of the seriousness of their offenses and/or the lack of appropriate community-based services (Illinois Planning Council on Developmental Disabilities, 1990). Correctional systems differ in the degrees of effort made to identify and serve these individuals. The definitions of mental retardation employed in the intake screening process of correctional settings may vary as well. Although the text-revised fourth edition of the *Diagnostic and Statistical Manual of Mental Disorders* (American Psychiatric Association, 2000) defines mental retardation as significantly sub-average intelligence and significant limitations in two or more areas of adaptive functioning, departments of correction may use somewhat broader definitions of deficits in cognitive functioning and adaptive behavior. In general, corrections administrators are more concerned with inmates' prison adjustment than with their level of functioning. Individuals with mental retardation often come to the attention of prison personnel during intake because their responses on the screening measures trigger more extensive evaluations. Once identified, special programming may be offered if it is available.

Because mental retardation encompasses deficits in both cognitive/intellectual functioning and adaptive behavior, screening for mental retardation must focus on both domains. To identify those with mental retardation, cutoff scores on the assessment measures, the cognitive measure that provides an intelligence quotient (IQ) score, and the adaptive measure that addresses behavior deficits must be established. In some instances, professional judgment may play a role in borderline cases.

Some correctional administrators espouse the normalization view, claiming that persons with mental retardation are responsible and accountable for their actions just like other inmates. They advocate both that it is a disservice to segregate these inmates and that doing so constitutes discrimination (Glaser & Deane, 1999). Others disagree, claiming that the unique needs of this population are more effectively served if they are housed separately and provided with specific programming (Glaser & Deane, 1999). Inmates with mental retardation are typically weak and vulnerable to various forms of exploitation and thus need protection. Segregated housing can provide such protection. A study comparing mentally retarded inmates who were mainstreamed with those who were segregated in correctional settings found that segregated housing was more effective in meeting their needs (Glaser & Deane, 1999). A survey of state prisons found that 29 states provided special units for individuals with mental retardation, although sometimes they were co-located with other special needs groups such as those with physical or mental health problems (ACA, 2000). The Texas Department of Corrections segregates mentally retarded inmates, housing them together in one building within a large institutional complex. In contrast, BOP mainstreams persons with mental retardation, although their numbers are very small in this agency.

The typical inmate with mental retardation is a young single individual who is a member of an indigenous group and has a prior history of incarceration (Glaser & Deane, 1999). In this author's experience, individuals with mental retardation are often convicted of crimes planned by others. They are recruited to join in illegal activity and are rewarded with minimal compensation such as a pack of cigarettes. Because of their naïveté and their eagerness to be accepted by their peers, persons with mental retardation may agree to participate in illegal activities even though they may be aware that what they are doing is wrong. What they often do not appreciate are the possible consequences of their actions.

Mental health staff are responsible for designing and implementing services for this population. Although persons with mental retardation are usually better served by agencies in the community, mental health staff in correctional settings can provide quality care to this population. However, service delivery to this population might not be a high priority within an institution so long as the individuals do not create management problems.

Prison administrators typically assume—sometimes incorrectly—that inmates' behavior is under their control (Lovell et al., 2001). Nonetheless, behavior modification methods have often been successful in shaping the behavior of inmates with mental retardation to promote compliance with institutional rules and appropriate behavior. Inmate workers or buddies can be valuable as mentors to inmates with mental retardation by coaching them in the daily routine of the institution, ensuring that they follow the institutional rules and procedures and assisting them in their adjustment to prison life. They can also work alongside these inmates in job assignments. Individuals with mental retardation may function well in the prison environment because the structure and routine provides guidance and comfort in their daily lives. Including case managers in the treatment team is recommended because of their skill in coordinating services and pre-release or discharge planning (Texas Board of Pardons and Paroles, 1987).

Discharge planning is a critical aspect of service delivery to this population because the quality of these inmates' release plans may directly affect the probability that they will remain in the community or return to jail/prison. Once offenders with mental retardation have been involved in the criminal justice system, it may be difficult to locate services for them in the community due to ignorance and fear on the part of community agency staff. Many programs will not accept persons with histories of violence. Involving community agency personnel early in the discharge planning process and educating them about inmates and their needs should help to alleviate these concerns. Glaser and Deane (1999) suggested that the ideal treatment setting for mentally retarded offenders is a small, community-based facility with a range of individual programs and services. Such a program would seek to maximize offenders' potential for reintegrating into the community.

Correctional staff serving inmates with mental retardation should be trained in how to work effectively with this population. Many staff members are likely to have negative attitudes and prejudices toward this very needy and vulnerable group. Individuals with mental retardation may be viewed as stupid and untrainable. In fact, most persons with mental retardation are able to care for themselves in the community if given adequate instruction and support. Staff need to be educated about the learning style and typical behaviors of adults with mental retardation. For instance, mentally retarded individuals may be slow to learn new information, including rules and procedures, and they may be delayed in their response to commands due to slower processing of information. If custody and other staff can be taught to understand, tolerate, and work with such behavioral styles, then it will lead to fewer confrontations, and more harmonious relations will occur.

Conclusions

During the past three decades, jails and prisons have undergone enormous changes in both their size and their services. The explosion in the inmate population, coupled with the increase in recognized needs of inmates, has resulted in the construction of many jails and prisons and in the development and implementation of a wide variety of services. No area within the correctional environment has been more affected than that of health and mental health care. This chapter has attempted to describe some of the special populations with whom mental health staff work in jails and prisons, their unique needs, and how these needs may be addressed. It is expected that during the years to come, many more changes will be seen in the development and implementation of correctional health/mental health services. These changes are likely to be paralleled by research on the efficacy of these services to determine which services are most effective with which inmates and under what circumstances. Although it is often difficult for correctional mental health staff to find time to conduct research in general and to conduct research on special needs populations in particular, certain research designs, such as comparing "before" and "after" measures and using wait list controls, can be easily included in treatment regimens (Lovell et al., 2001). In the future, correctional mental health care is likely to be an increasingly exciting and challenging field in which to work.

References

Administration on Aging. (2001). *Older adults and mental health: Issues and opportunities.* [Online]. Available: www.aoa.gov/mh/report2001/default.htm

American Correctional Association. (1999a). Inmate health care: Part I—Survey summary. *Corrections Compendium, 24*(10), 8-15.

American Correctional Association. (1999b). Inmate health care: Part II—Survey summary. *Corrections Compendium, 24*(11), 12-20.

American Correctional Association. (2000). Survey summary: Special housing. *Corrections Compendium, 25*(6), 8-18.

American Psychiatric Association. (2000). *Diagnostic and statistical manual of mental disorders* (4th ed., rev. text). Washington, DC: Author.

Bureau of Justice Statistics. (2000). *Correctional populations in the United States, 1997.* Washington, DC: Author.

Bureau of Justice Statistics. (2001). *Criminal offender statistics.* [Online]. Available: www.ojp.usdoj.gov/bjs/crimoff/htm

Bureau of Prisons. (2001). *PS 5111.03 Mariel Cuban detainees.* [Online]. Available: www.bop.gov/progstat/5111_03 html

Clark, D. D. (1999). *The impact of foreign-born inmates on the New York State Department of Correctional Services.* Albany: New York State Department of Correctional Services, Division of Program Planning, Research, and Evaluation.

Ditton, P. M. (1999). *Mental health and treatment of inmates and probationers* (Bureau of Justice Statistics special report). Washington, DC: U.S. Department of Justice.

Draper, G., & Reed, M. (1995). *Criminal alien project for the state of Texas.* Austin: Texas Criminal Justice Policy Council.

Eisenberg, M., Munson, A., & Ygnacio, R. E. (2000). *Overview of special needs parole policy and recommendations for improvement.* Austin: Texas Criminal Justice Policy Council.

Florida Department of Corrections. (1994). *Status report on elderly inmates.* Tallahassee: Florida Department of Corrections, Youth and Special Needs Program Office.

Glaser, W., & Deane, K. (1999). Normalization in an abnormal world: A study of prisoners with an intellectual disability. *International Journal of Offender Therapy and Comparative Criminology, 43,* 338-356.

Goetting, A. (1983, August). *The elderly in prison: Issues and perspectives.* Paper presented at the annual meeting of the American Sociological Association, Detroit, MI.

Gondles, J. A., Jr. (2000). Special needs offenders: Everyone's concern. *Corrections Today, 62*(7), 6.

Hammett, T. M., Harmon, P., & Maruschak, L. M. (1999). *1996-97 update: HIV/AIDS, STDs, and TB in correctional facilities* (Issues and Practices in Criminal Justice). Washington, DC: National Institute of Justice.

Illinois Planning Council on Developmental Disabilities. (1990). *Progress report on the mentally retarded and mentally ill offender task report recommendations.* Springfield, IL: Author.

Lovell, D., Allen, D., Johnson, C., & Jemelka, R. (2001). Evaluating the effectiveness of residential treatment for prisoners with mental illness. *Criminal Justice and Behavior, 28,* 83-104.

Morton, J. B. (1992). *An administrative overview of the older inmate.* Washington, DC: National Institute of Corrections.

Murphy, S. (2000). Death: Final data for 1998. *National Vital Statistics Reports, 48,* 1-106.

National Institute of Corrections. (1998). *Hospital and palliative care in prisons. Special issues in corrections.* Washington, DC: Author.

Ortiz, M. (2000). Managing special populations. *Corrections Today, 62*(7), 64-66, 68.

Pennsylvania Department of Corrections. (2001). *Older inmates.* [Online]. Available: www.cor.state.pa.us/oldinma.htm

Rabkin, N. J. (1999). *Criminal aliens: INS's efforts to identify and remove imprisoned aliens continue to need improvement/Statement of Norman J. Rabkin.* Washington, DC: U.S. General Accounting Office.

Texas Board of Pardons and Paroles. (1987). *Special programs: Mentally retarded offenders.* Austin, TX: Author.

PART III

TRAINING
AND CONSULTATION

CHAPTER 11

Staff Services and Programs

Richard Ellis

> *Leave it at the gate, you hear time and again in corrections. Leave all the stress and bullsh__ at work; don't bring it home to your family. This was good in theory. In reality, though, I was like my friend who had worked the pumps at a service station: Even after she got home and took a shower, you could still smell the gasoline on her hands. Prison got into your skin, or under it. If you stayed long enough, some of it probably seeped into your soul.*
>
> —*New Jack* (Conover, 2000, p. 242)

As the opening quote implies, no review of correctional mental health can proceed without a discussion of the psychological needs of correctional staff. The correctional environment has been described as a chronically stressful setting with intermittent periods of acute stress (Finn, 1998). Inadequately addressed chronic and acute stress can have a negative emotional impact on staff and, consequently, on the overall functioning and safety of the correctional institution (Chenier, 1998; Miller-Burke, 1998).

AUTHOR'S NOTE: Opinions expressed in this chapter are those of the author and do not necessarily represent the opinions of the Federal Bureau of Prisons or the U.S. Department of Justice.

Staff often respond uniquely to the chronic and acute stressors to which they are exposed. Research suggests that the negative impact of these stressors on staff is mediated by several factors including the type, length, and magnitude of the stressor; individual staff members' coping repertoires, vulnerability, and resilience; the institution's mental health programs for staff and its contingency plans for addressing acute stressors; the actual institutional response to the situation and the individuals affected; and post-experience mediation variables such as preexisting life stressors and psychological problems, individuals' coping styles, the organizational response, community response and support, regional and cultural issues, and gender (Hyer et al., 1994).

As already noted, the correctional environment is a chronically stressful one. Each day, correctional workers must contend with offenders and, depending on the mission of the institution, may have little or no information about inmates' histories, degrees of violence, crimes, and so on. The less predictable the environment, the greater the potential for unpredictable inmate behavior and heightened levels of employee stress. The correctional environment obviously requires a heightened level of awareness. Each day, correctional workers face the potential of being assaulted, having urine or feces thrown on them, suffering needle pricks when pat-searching inmates, enduring verbal insults, continuing criminal activity, and being seriously injured or—in the most extreme circumstance—killed. On most days in any major correctional facility, there will be some sort of assault (e.g., food tray or food thrown at staff in segregated housing), some sort of continuing criminal activity, and some verbal insults, to name just a few of the potential stressors. Research has shown that failure to adequately deal with continuous levels of stress can have deleterious effects on the physical and emotional well-being of law enforcement personnel (Finn, 1998; Miller-Burke, 1998; Montey & Li-Ping Tang, 1992).

For these low levels of continuous stress, the most basic intervention an institution can offer is to institutionally acknowledge that the work is stressful, that is, that it is out of the ordinary realm of experience for most citizens and that emotional and physical responses to having food thrown at or verbal invectives delivered to staff are normal. Individual and institutional denial that the environment is stressful means that there is no way in which to explain the common feelings and physical responses that staff experience in regard to the stressful environment. It promotes the "John Wayne," tough cop, stand-alone attitudes of dealing with the environment, that is, toughing it out, sucking it up, and moving on. There is ample literature to suggest that this approach only exacerbates the problem and over time leads to a decline in attitude, motivation, health, and mental health (Moriarty & Field, 1990; Reiser, 1974a, 1974b, 1982).

This chapter first discusses employee assistance programs, designed to assist individual staff in dealing with the chronic and acute stressors to which they are routinely exposed. The chapter then highlights examples of workplace violence often experienced in the correctional setting and describes the debriefing and defusing programs commonly used to address the stressful, sometimes debilitating aftereffects of these incidents on staff.

Employee Assistance Programs: Intervention Models

When institutional acknowledgment of the stressful nature of correctional work is not enough to negate the stressful effects of this work, the next level of intervention for chronic staff stress is often the employee assistance program (EAP). The EAP can also be used to address the acute traumatic stress periodically faced by correctional staff (McWhirter & Linzer, 1994). As an outlet for individual employees who are not coping optimally with job-related stressors, the EAP has several advantages, including the ability to address physical, psychological, and organizational health by offering staff problem-solving strategies, confidential short-term counseling, management consultation, health and wellness training, and critical incident stress debriefing (CISD). Ideally, EAPs are available to staff 24 hours a day and can be set up in many different ways. The three most common EAP models are described next.

In-House Model

Many correctional agencies have in-house EAPs that are staffed by mental health professionals whose primary job is to provide mental health services to inmates. Although this is better than nothing at all, it does possess some inherent problems. For example, it is difficult for in-house mental health workers, who are co-workers of the correctional staff they are expected to counsel, to maintain the appearance of impartiality and confidentiality when they are part of the system. An EAP counselor cannot easily or effectively be a peer, co-worker, subordinate, or supervisor and also be perceived by staff as providing objective individual or institutional interventions. In-house EAPs often tend to be underused by staff due to this perceived and sometimes actual lack of confidentiality and objectivity of the program. Notwithstanding these perceptions, some correctional staff actually prefer in-house EAPs. These correctional staff are more willing to approach someone they know and feel more comfortable talking to, that is, someone within the system who knows what they are experiencing. Despite the benefit that this type of EAP may offer to some employees, this author does not recommend it because of the perceived and actual ethical dilemmas it imposes on its mental health providers.

Mixed Model

A second EAP model involves the use of both in-house and contractual services. This model usually has institution mental health staff providing interventions for the more typical employee problems and contracting out for fitness-for-duty evaluations and drug/alcohol interventions. Although this model takes the more serious cases out of the purview of institution mental health staff, it still does not address the multiple roles that institution mental health providers must serve as peers, co-workers, subordinates, and/or supervisors; consequently, it does not maintain the levels of objectivity and confidentiality needed for an effective EAP.

Imagine, for example, a situation in which an institution psychologist, in his or her EAP capacity, has just finished talking with the supervisor of education, Bill, in the psychologist's office. As the supervisor of education leaves the office, several staff see him. Later in the day, one of those staff members comments, "I see Bill is trying to get on the wagon again. He sure has a drinking problem." Later the same day, the warden calls the psychologist to his office and asks about the overall health of the staff and whether anyone in particular is having difficulty. The warden specifically mentions Bill as someone he is concerned about and asks the psychologist for comment. The problems here are obvious. It is difficult to provide confidential services to staff within the correctional setting, which in many ways is a very closed community. It is also hard for the psychologist to withhold information from the warden, his boss, about a staff member who may be experiencing some degree of psychological distress and who ultimately may become a management problem.

Similar to the in-house EAP, the mixed EAP model is also underused. A significant reason is the fact that managers are often hesitant to use this program. In most correctional agencies, managers are at a higher organizational level than the mental health staff and are often not comfortable with sharing personal concerns with someone who is subordinate to them in the organizational structure. In addition, they are concerned that their staff may see them leaving the psychologist's office and make assumptions about their mental health. These types of situations can be averted if the EAP is completely independent of institution mental health staff.

Independent Model

The completely independent EAP is one that is contracted out by the correctional agency to a community-based provider/organization that understands the agency's policies and needs. From this author's perspective, this is the program of choice. Contract EAPs offer a wide range of confidential services to all institution staff and avoid the ethical dilemmas of the other two types of EAPs. As such, staff typically use them at greater rates than they use in-house and mixed EAPs.

The independent EAP is paid for out of agency or institution funds. Typically, an annual flat fee per person is paid to the program by the agency. To arrive at the total contract amount, this flat fee is multiplied by the number of staff members in the agency. The agency and the program come to an agreement on the services to be provided. Often, EAPs have a package that includes family and employee access to short-term assessment and treatment services; management consultation; organizational development; customized training programs such as communication skills, supervisory skills, career development, team building, and smoking cessation; workplace violence prevention/intervention; fitness-for-duty evaluations; health and wellness programs; and CISD. An anonymous system to account for staff use is typically part of the contract. It is critical that the EAP have a solid understanding of the agency's limits on confidentiality. Typically, for example, the agency will have a need to know the outcome of fitness-for-duty evaluations. It may also have specific drug/alcohol abuse reporting requirements. Whatever the limits to confidentiality are, the staff participant must understand these before any intervention takes place. It is usually the responsibility of both the agency and the EAP counselor to convey these limits.

For an EAP to effectively intervene with a staff member, the stressor or stressors must be identified, and the employee's coping repertoire, vulnerability, and resilience in relationship to those stressors must be assessed. To accomplish these tasks, EAPs typically allow for four to six sessions per problem. For problems that cannot be addressed in this time frame, one commonly accepted solution is referral to a community mental health provider, health maintenance organization, or some other appropriate service that is insurance reimbursable. For this reason, EAPs should be familiar with agency or institution insurance policies as well as with all other insurance policies and third-party reimbursements. This is critical for a smooth transition from EAPs to community services.

Other EAP Considerations

Correctional facilities that have well-supported mental health programs for their staff and clearly defined, well-publicized contingency plans for crisis situations will tend to have generally healthier workforces and a greater breadth of participation in EAPs (Frolkey, 1996; Miller-Burke, 1998). These institutions will actively promote participation in preventive programs and in management and organization programs. Law enforcement personnel often attach a stigma to anything vaguely related to mental health services. If the agency or institution openly supports the EAP, then the stigma is lessened and individual participation is promoted. By the same token, if the agency does not proactively promote the EAP and does not support participation during times of individual acute stress or institutional crisis, then program participation will wane and individual and institutional health will suffer. An additional issue is the legal liability suffered by agencies that choose to ignore EAP issues (Brakel, 1998).

Workplace Violence: From the Individual to the Institution

Given the aggressive nature of the inmate population, the possibility of workplace violence is an ever-present source of acute stress for correctional workers. Episodes of workplace violence may involve just one individual or may affect the entire institution. In most workplace settings, the potential for violence comes from other employees and/or customers. In a correctional setting, the greatest potential for violence typically comes from the inmates, who may act violently toward each other or toward staff. In many ways, correctional workers are prepared for this possibility early in their careers. However, in less frequent circumstances, other staff may be the perpetrators of workplace violence.

Workplace violence perpetrated by staff includes any actual or attempted infliction of physical harm against a person or that person's property (personal or institutional). Examples of this type of workplace violence include bumping, slapping, hitting, stalking, or stabbing a co-worker; shooting or slashing tires; "keying" cars; and breaking a window, computer, or piece of furniture. Staff-on-staff workplace violence may also include written, verbal, or other behavior that a reasonable individual would interpret as a threat to inflict harm to person or property. Examples of this type of violence include leaving threatening notes; leaving a bullet with the inscription "this one's for you"; dry firing (i.e., firing without ammunition) a weapon at staff crossing the prison compound; making statements regarding the intention to harm or kill others (whether made directly or indirectly made to the intended victims); and making threats to blow up property, slash tires, or key cars.

Actual Examples of Correctional Workplace Violence

The following examples of workplace violence are actual correctional incidents that occurred. Specific circumstances, places, and names have been changed so that they no longer resemble the actual incidents but still convey the spirit of the events. Each example should be considered a critical incident worthy of formal CISD. How this is accomplished and how individual institutions responded to each event are discussed later in the chapter.

The Suicidal/Homicidal Tower Officer. At 11:00 a.m. on a Tuesday, a jail tower officer contacted the institution social worker indicating that he wanted to talk. It was the practice of the social worker to go see staff anytime they called. The social worker was identified as the EAP contact for the jail. Shortly after receiving the call, the social worker was negotiating the several hundred steps to the top of the guard tower. When she opened the floor door into the tower, she was confronted with the tower guard spinning the chambers of a revolver, placing the muzzle to his head, and pulling the trigger. The social worker's first thought was, "Do I enter or retreat?" She entered. After exchanging awkward greetings and another spin of the chamber and pull of the trigger, the intervention evolved to a tenuous yet more stable level. During the next several minutes, as the social worker began to ascertain the antecedents of the guard's behavior, he continually dry fired an M-1 rifle at staff as they crossed the yard. The social worker discovered that the guard was distraught over the potential for serious disciplinary action and was considering first killing those who might initiate that action against him and then killing himself. The implication was that the social worker might also be killed just because she was there.

The social worker was able to determine who the intended victims were and asked whether she could make a phone call to her supervisor so that she could state that she would not be back in the office for quite some time. The request for this call came only after she felt that a degree of trust had developed between herself and the guard. That supposition of trust was founded on the guard's initial desire to talk as well as behavioral and emotional changes (gun placed on the table, no more dry firing, and a desire to problem solve as opposed to self-destruct) that occurred during the course of the intervention. The astute supervisor asked some specific questions and, without creating suspicion on the guard's part, was able to discover who the intended victims were. Without the guard knowing, the yard was cleared and the risk for more widespread tragedy was averted.

After several hours of good crisis intervention and a degree of joining with the guard to build trust, validation, and problem solving, the social worker had gotten the guard to agree to be voluntarily hospitalized in a locked psychiatric hospital. At that point, the social worker asked for the gun, it was surrendered, and the guard was escorted to the hospital.

Workplace violence? Yes. There was a risk of immediate threat of death to more than one employee. The staff member's words, actions, plan, identified victims, and highly lethal means of implementation make this a high-risk situation.

The Angry, Emotionally Distraught Inmate. This workplace violence situation took place at a male medium-security facility in the northwestern United States. Through some unknown means, an inmate acquired a .38-caliber revolver. This inmate's father was terminally ill and was not expected to live more than another week. For purposes of this scenario, the inmate's name was John Smith. Smith had recently asked for an armed escorted furlough so that he might visit his father before he died in a neighboring state. The furlough request was denied for security reasons. Smith was informed of this denial by a guard at 10:00 a.m. At 11:30 a.m., Smith was seen in an out-of-bounds area near the inner perimeter fence by Lieutenant Jones. Jones approached Smith and asked what he was doing in an out-of-bounds area. Smith did not respond. Jones got within three feet of Smith, and the inmate pushed a gun under his cheek. Jones was now a hostage. Smith got behind Jones, placed the barrel of the revolver at the base of his skull, and instructed him to follow the path to the institution control center, where there was an exit to the parking lot. The lieutenant complied with every command along the way. As they rounded the corner of the education building, a counselor was checking some window bars. The startled inmate pointed the gun at him from three feet away and fired. The revolver misfired, and the guard was not physically injured. The inmate again placed the revolver to the lieutenant's head and ordered the counselor to leave the area. The inmate and the lieutenant proceeded to the institution exit. Manning the control center were a guard (Grant) and a correctional supervisor (Lieutenant Vasquez). Both knew Jones well. Jones was the guard's training officer and supervisor, and the correctional supervisor was Jones's best friend. Smith demanded that the gate to the institution be opened or he would kill Jones. Grant and Vasquez knew that institution policy states that no door will be opened for an inmate to exit the facility. Vasquez told the inmate that the door could not be opened. At that moment, a counselor who knew Smith arrived at the scene. He was unaware that Smith had a revolver but assumed that Smith had some type of weapon to control Jones. He approached the situation and talked to Smith. As he got within 15 feet of Smith and Jones, Smith turned and fired the revolver at the counselor. It again misfired. Jones seized the moment and tackled Smith. The counselor assisted, and the situation was resolved.

Murder of a Staff Member. Of all the potential workplace violence situations, those resulting in the deaths of co-workers or colleagues have the most devastating and lasting effects on staff (Stuart, 1992). For purposes of this example, let us assume that an inmate in a large state penitentiary had killed a correctional psychologist. It was a particularly brutal murder with a knife. The murder occurred in the psychologist's office. No suspect was identified. The psychologist was well liked by institution staff and had been seen by many staff that morning greeting fellow staff as they arrived at work. His secretary discovered his body. She immediately sounded an emergency alarm. The second person to respond was the physician, who had an office down the hall from the psychologist. She immediately started life-saving measures, including cardiopulmonary resuscitation (CPR). Several other staff members had arrived and were standing outside the psychologist's office. They could see pools of blood and the desperate look on the treating physician's face. An emergency medical team from the local hospital arrived and continued life-supporting efforts until the medical technicians reached the emergency room. The psychologist was pronounced dead 15 minutes after arriving at the hospital. The warden told staff about the psychologist's death at an institution recall a half hour before the end of the shift. Announcements were made at each roll call for the next two shifts.

Murder of an Inmate. For unknown reasons, an inmate was murdered outside the office of a correctional counselor. The inmate was stabbed more than 30 times. The correctional officer discovered the inmate outside his office door gasping for air and reaching up from the floor for the correctional counselor. The inmate attempted to say something and then expired in front of the counselor. A large pool of blood surrounded the inmate. The correctional counselor sounded the emergency alarm, and several staff members responded. The inmate was removed from the scene, a crime scene was set up, and mass inmate interviews were initiated to identify witnesses and the culprit(s).

Responses to Workplace Violence Examples

These four scenarios have one common theme: Several correctional employees were affected by these acts of workplace violence. In each of these situations, there are several key institutional responses that should be implemented. First, every (directly or indirectly) affected staff member, whether line, supervisory, or executive management, should be offered the opportunity for CISD (Everly, 1995; Mitchell & Everly, 1993). In general terms, CISD is an intervention that occurs following a traumatic event. Its purpose is to assist those affected in understanding what happened to themselves and others and to come to a more complete understanding of how this event has affected them, their families, and their peers. This early intervention has been shown in many instances to effectively prevent or lessen the negative emotional, physical, and social consequences of the traumatic event. Ideally, this intervention should occur no later than 72 hours after the traumatic event.

In the first scenario, each identified target, as well as the social worker, was debriefed. Because each victim was from a different management level and in a different place during the trauma, and because there were only a few identified victims, the victims were debriefed individually. A trained mental health worker who did not work at that particular institution debriefed each individual. All other institution staff were offered the opportunity to be debriefed as well. It was important for them to have the opportunity to understand the current situation and how it affected them so that they would not feel uncomfortable when walking by the towers in the future.

In the second scenario, each affected individual was debriefed and then the institution lieutenants and guards were debriefed in separate groups. All institution staff attended a staff recall. At the recall, the debriefing team gave an overview of typical responses to extreme life events. It also gave an overview of the chain of events and answered specific questions posed by staff. All staff who were directly affected by the hostage taking were given the option to speak about their experiences at the recall. All chose to do so.

In the third scenario, every staff member in the institution was debriefed. Family members also participated in debriefings. Several trained debriefers were brought in from around the country to participate in 3 full days of debriefing. All staff were debriefed within 96 hours of the staff murder.

In the fourth scenario, the counselor and responding staff were debriefed individually.

Other Examples of Workplace Violence

Workplace violence does not have to take on the dramatic and tragic proportions of the preceding examples to have a significant impact on staff. Other examples may involve significant verbal or minor physical abuse by inmates or staff, sexual harassment, racial inequities, and stalking, to name just a few. Again, it is important to note that no matter how major or minor the incident might appear from the outside, each individual tends to respond to incidents in a unique manner. With this in mind, the most important tenet for responding to an individual's perception of a threat is validating his or her experience while exploring and understanding the event from the individual's perspective.

Verbal Abuse. In a correctional environment, the potential for verbal abuse from inmates is high. Sexual, racial, ethnic, regional, and profession-related slurs are expected. These are most likely to occur anonymously from one or more inmates in a crowd or from inmates in disciplinary housing units. In each case, the staff member's personal history, his or her coping repertoire, and the type of slur all will interact to create an immediate, unique, and potentially long-term response. Mental health professionals and EAP counselors should be prepared to deal with these diverse situations, individuals, and responses. Without a degree of professional flexibility, intervention outcomes, individual learning, and adaptation will be less than optimal.

Minor Physical Abuse. Minor physical abuse, which may carry a major emotional impact, is also to be expected in the correctional environment. In the disciplinary housing units, staff can expect to have urine, feces, food, and food trays thrown at them. They can also expect to be spat on and to be involved in forced cell moves. The latter involves physically removing a resisting inmate from a cell with a trained team. Although this team is trained to effectively and safely immobilize and move an inmate, there is always the potential that a team member will be injured by the inmate. EAPs should be prepared to deal with these types of issues because they do arise in correctional settings. Lack of awareness may negatively affect the intervention and result in an unsatisfactory outcome for the correctional worker.

Sexual Harassment. Sexual harassment can come in many forms. When it has reached the level of workplace violence, several general criteria have been met. It is important that the EAP staff be aware of the sexual harassment thresholds for workplace violence, whether they be legal, agency, or professional thresholds. If the sexually harassed staff member feels threatened or in danger of physical harm, or if the staff member actually suffers physical harm, then it is generally considered a workplace violence issue. Once this has been established, other situational factors must be considered for an optimal intervention outcome. The factors leading up to the workplace violence incident need to be fully understood. A thorough understanding of the perpetrator's motivation must also be taken into account. Was the perpetrator a supervisor, peer, or supervisee? Did other sexually harassing behaviors occur prior to the workplace violence incident? If so, how were those dealt with? What legal and agency protections does the victim have from the perpetrator? Will the perpetrator be removed from duty until the judicial system has taken its course? How will the victim be protected from further victimization? It is important for mental health professionals to have an understanding of the legal, agency, and professional responses to sexual harassment as well as specialty training in assessing and treating victims and perpetrators of violent sexual harassment.

Stalking. Stalking is another form of workplace violence. Staff and inmates both can be guilty of stalking. As with sexual harassment, the threshold for workplace violence is the victim's perception of a threat of physical harm. Again, it is important for EAP counselors and mental health professionals to understand the legal, agency, and professional responses to allegations of stalking. Understanding these will affect the treatment course and outcome. In addition, a mental health worker who has specific training and experience in dealing with victims and perpetrators of stalking would be preferred to a general practitioner.

Racially Motivated Violence. Racially motivated violence may also be a form of workplace violence. Staff or inmates may use racial or ethnic prejudices as motivation for workplace violence. Similar to previous examples of workplace violence already reviewed, this also requires mental health professionals to understand the legal, agency, and professional responses to this particular form of workplace violence. Also, as with the aforementioned forms of workplace violence, there are additional specific intervention strategies that are particular to racially or ethnically motivated workplace violence.

Interventions for Workplace Violence: Defusing and Debriefing

For each of the workplace violence situations mentioned, the agency or institution should have a structure in place that outlines the general protocol for defusing and debriefing staff who have been directly or indirectly affected by the event (Dignam & Fagan, 1996; Mitchell & Everly, 1993; Raphael & Wilson, 2000; Robinson, 2000). The degree of victimization depends on the magnitude of the event, the individual's proximity to and involvement in the event, the individual's reaction to the event, and the individual's internal and external resources. A survivor of an airplane crash who is seriously injured and has a significant emotional reaction, but who possesses extensive internal and external emotional resources, will experience the trauma differently from an individual with similar injuries and responses but with poor internal and external resources.

The importance of organizational workplace violence protocols and interventions is manifold. First, the staff are aware that the institution or agency has their best interests in mind, that is, safety on the job, strategies for dealing with workplace violence, and strategies for dealing with the aftereffects of workplace violence. Knowing that the agency supports the staff in these ways can be a tremendous team, morale, and loyalty builder. Second, during and following a protracted workplace violence event (e.g., a hostage incident), the affected staff will be provided interventions to assist in their short- and long-term professional and personal adjustment (Leonard & Alison, 1999). Third, agency health, staff retention, and productivity are maximized by an emotionally well-adjusted and composed workforce (Frolkey, 1996; Stuart, 1992).

Debriefing: What to Do When the Workplace Goes Wrong

Crisis theory can be used to conceptualize an individual's response to workplace violence. Typically, when workplace violence occurs, the individual experiences an overload of stress in which typical problem-solving skills and attempts are no longer effective and the perception or experience of a threat of loss or actual loss is present. This means that the individual has, on a continuum of severity, experienced a crisis. All individuals who experience a crisis ultimately reach some resolution to the crisis. The resolution falls on a continuum from positive to negative. Factors contributing to resolution are the personal strengths of the individual, the magnitude and duration of the crisis, and the actions the individual takes to resolve the crisis. Debriefing takes all of these factors into consideration as it tries to maximize the individual's resolution of the crisis (Mitchell & Everly, 1993, 2000; Raphael & Wilson, 2000). Everly (1995) conducted a meta-analysis of research on the efficacy of CISD. The results of the analysis revealed a significant positive treatment effect across a wide range of traumatic events and a variety of subject groups.

Debriefing is an initial intervention for helping the workplace violence victim to better understand (a) the traumatic situation to which the victim has been exposed, (b) the loss or threat of loss that the victim has experienced, (c) the atypical as well as universal reactions (e.g., emotional, physical, behavioral, social) that the victim is experiencing, (d) the new personal and professional meaning of the victim's world as it has been affected by the violence, and (e) the new survival and coping strategies that will allow the victim to effectively negotiate his or her world subsequent to the workplace violence.

The primary goals of debriefing are to help the victim assess and understand his or her thoughts, emotions, and behaviors as they relate to the traumatic event; mitigate the impact of the critical incident; and accelerate the recovery process. Other objectives include education about stress and survival techniques, reassurance, forewarning about future reactions, reduction in fallacies of uniqueness and abnormality, discussion of common responses to trauma, and development of ways in which to normalize the experience (Mitchell & Everly, 1993, 2000).

One of the main foci of debriefing is the prevention of post-traumatic stress disorder (PTSD) (Everly, 1995). The fourth edition of the *Diagnostic and Statistical Manual of Mental Disorders* (American Psychiatric Association, 1994) provides the following description of the diagnostic features of PTSD:

> The essential feature of PTSD is the development of characteristic symptoms following exposure to an extreme traumatic stressor involving direct personal experience of an event that involves actual or threatened death or serious injury, or other threat to one's physical integrity; or witnessing an event that involves death, injury, or a threat to the physical integrity of another person; or learning about unexpected or violent death, serious harm, or threat of death or injury experienced by a family member or other close associate. . . . The person's response to the event must involve intense fear, helplessness, or horror (or in children, the response must involve disorganized or agitated behavior). . . . The characteristic symptoms resulting from the exposure to the extreme trauma include persistent re-experiencing of the traumatic event, . . . persistent avoidance of stimuli associated with the trauma and numbing of general responsiveness, . . . and persistent symptoms of increased arousal. The full symptom picture must be present for more than 1 month . . . and the disturbance must cause clinically significant distress or impairment in social, occupational, or other important areas of functioning. (p. 424)

Another important aspect of debriefing is screening for extreme responses to the workplace violence and referral for additional assessment and appropriate treatment. Emotional and behavioral reactions may be so extreme that the debriefing process is an inadequate intervention. Medication and hospitalization are higher level interventions for individuals who are having extreme responses to the event. Referral is also made for those individuals who wish to explore more long-term interventions but who are not in need of immediate intervention.

The Debriefing Process

The institution or agency should have a written policy regarding the implementation of the debriefing process. The agency should have identified a list of readily available trained debriefers. The debriefers may come from an outside EAP or be trained agency staff. Alternatively, a list of trained debriefers can be obtained from agencies such as the American Red Cross. Once the policy and procedures have been developed, the following protocol should be followed in the event of a workplace violence incident.

First, the debriefing team should be activated. There should be an institution or agency procedure for initiating the activation and a site where the team will meet to be briefed on the nature of the workplace violence. The team should assess the need for CISD. The agency should have a defined threshold for implementation of CISD. The CISD team should hold a strategy meeting to discuss who should be debriefed; whether there should be group, individual, or both forms of CISD; and whether a family service center (i.e., a center for family members of workplace violence victims to gather during the incident to receive information and support) needs to be implemented. CISD should occur 24 to 72 hours after the trauma in a private setting for greatest efficacy (Campfield & Hills, 2001). There should be no risk of interruption or breach of confidentiality.

Careful consideration should be given to the composition of the debriefing groups. The groups should be composed of persons of similar rank and trauma experience; for example, staff who were held hostage should be debriefed with each other (not with non-hostage victims), and lieutenants and sergeants should not be debriefed with direct line staff. At each debriefing site, there should be refreshments, an easily accessible bathroom, and tissues available. Large sheets of paper should be available for recording the debriefing process. One member of the debriefing team should record group member statements on these sheets of paper. This is a visual aid to assist the participants in identifying their reactions to the trauma. CISD groups should generally be composed of no more than 12 participants. In addition to the participants, there should be two group leaders and one standby leader to deal with participants needing immediate individual attention.

Debriefing Procedures and States

Debriefings can last from an hour to several hours. Duration depends on the needs of the group/individual, the magnitude of the experience, the size of the group, practical issues such as staff and family schedules, and institution/agency needs. Debriefing is a structured process, but it is not therapy and should never be treated as such. It is a systematic approach to addressing the individuals' response to a traumatic event and consists of a series of progressive stages: an introduction stage, a fact stage, a thought stage, a reaction stage, a symptom stage, a teaching stage, and a reentry stage (Mitchell & Everly, 1993). Debriefing stages are designed to cover in specific detail the individuals' cognitive, behavioral, and emotional reactions to the traumatic event while those reactions and the event are fresh. Making the connection between these reactions and the event early on will help to prevent the negative consequences of PTSD at a later date.

It is important to note that although debriefing stages are introduced sequentially in the text as well as in the debriefing, there is crossover between each stage. The main point to note is that the sequential method of introduction and review in the group is key to the overall efficacy of the intervention. In debriefing a traumatic event, it is often helpful to understand the facts, thoughts, emotions, and symptoms in that order (Everly, 1995; Mitchell & Everly, 1993).

The introduction stage lays the groundwork for all that follows. Specific rules for the group are established, and normalizing the process is accomplished. It is important to explain that a debriefing is a natural process. For example, after a near car accident, people often talk to others about what happened to them. They may explain the event in great detail. This is a natural process that victims go through to help them understand, accept, and carry on with their lives. It allows them to put things in perspective so that they can get back on the road without undue emotional or behavioral consequences. Debriefing is not therapy; rather, it is a place to talk about reactions and to learn from one another. It is not a place to assign fault or to attack others. It is important for participants to feel safe to explore their experiences without guilt or fear of attack. It is a place to get information. Information is knowledge, and knowledge provides perspective and understanding.

It is important to establish that the process is confidential during the introductory stage. Without that standard, the group will not be productive. With confidentiality comes the understanding that this process is not part of an investigative arm of the agency or institution. With that understanding, information can flow more freely and people can have a greater understanding of what happened to them and others. It is important to note that no record will be kept of the participants and that no tape-recordings or transcripts will be kept of the debriefing. These rules give the participants permission to explore all aspects of the event without fear of reprisal or public awareness. The bottom line is that this is a place to obtain information about personal responses to the workplace violence incident.

The fact phase involves a detailed review of each group participant's literal experience of the trauma. It requires a detailed review of what happened to each participant. The most important thing to convey during this phase is that facts often get attached to feelings regardless of whether those facts are clearly understood. Those who do not understand the facts have a greater incidence of negative symptoms than do those who understand the facts. In a debriefing, the "devil is in the details." It is important for the debriefing participant to understand who was involved, what specifically happened, when it happened, where it happened, and how it happened. During the fact phase, a debriefer might want to ask a physician's assistant, who was first to arrive at the scene of a staff member's death, about everything that happened from the moment he was first notified of the assault to every action taken thereafter. It is also important during this phase to discuss the thoughts that participants attach to the facts.

The emotional phase looks at the emotions participants attach to the thoughts and facts associated with the incident. Questions that can be asked of participants include the following: What was the worst thing about this situation? What bothers you the most? What causes you the most pain? How did you react to specific events? How are you currently reacting?

During the course of the debriefing, participants will talk about symptoms they are experiencing. It is important to normalize these symptoms, that is, to indicate that these are normal and typical reactions to an abnormal event. Others in the group may be having similar experiences. Seeing that others are experiencing similar symptoms is both validating and relieving. Participants recognize that they are not unique in their responses to the traumatic event. The standby facilitator can see individually any participant who has extraordinary reactions during the course of the debriefing.

Toward the end of the debriefing, when everyone has had the opportunity to explore his or her responses to the trauma, the facilitators can further validate the participants' experiences by describing typical symptoms and symptoms that may arise in the future. Survival strategies such as diet, rest, exercise, and talking with family and friends should be mentioned. Community resources and follow-up services should also be reviewed. A handout with available community resources should be provided.

As the debriefing begins to reach closure, facilitators want the participants to reflect on what they have learned during the debriefing. Questions such as "What have you learned from this experience that helps you deal with the episode?" leave people thinking about positive resolution. Closure of the meeting should involve a review of the material discussed. This is where the items written on those large sheets of paper will be used to summarize the entire process.

During the final part of the debriefing process, the debriefing team's responsibilities include answering questions, providing reassurance, offering further information, discussing feelings that have not been mentioned, distributing appropriate handouts, and making summary comments. The debriefing is ended and participants leave with newfound knowledge of what they have been through, knowledge of what might happen in the future, and resources for managing their reactions to the trauma.

The Defusing Process

Defusing is a limited form of debriefing that occurs immediately following a traumatic event (Mitchell & Everly, 1993). A good example is the contact with a hostage immediately after he or she has been released. The defuser can serve as a guide for the released hostage during an especially confusing transition and can also serve as an advocate and a protector. The defusing process is also a good time for the defuser to do a cursory mental status screening to assess mental stability and to assist the hostage in orienting to the present and to the immediate future. The defuser should explain where the released hostage is going next, discuss what will happen to him or her there (e.g., visit with family, interviews with internal affairs and law enforcement officials), and ask who he or she would like to see or contact first.

If time permits, it is advisable for the defuser to do his or her homework about multiple hostages prior to their release. Each defuser should know who he or she will be talking to, should know what their potential needs are ahead of time, and should research who they might want to see first. Defusers should discuss what they are going to say when they meet the hostages. It is important to lay the groundwork. Defusers should know where they would take hostages first and should arrange advance agreements with executive staff, other agencies, media, and the like about when, where, and how they can have contact with the hostages.

There are several things to do and say when the defuser first approaches a hostage. The defuser should introduce himself or herself and convey to the hostage that the defuser is there to help the hostage meet his or her immediate personal needs. Questions to ask might include "How are you?," "Is there anything you need to talk about right now?," "What do you feel you need most right now?," and "Where are you going to go after you leave here?" It is important for the defuser to inform the hostage of the services that will be provided in the immediate future (e.g., group defusing, debriefing, contact with law officials). If the hostage is experiencing severe emotional difficulty, then the defuser should arrange for immediate psychological and medical attention. This intervention will assess the need for medication, assess the need for hospitalization, and research and provide other community services to meet these immediate needs.

The final step in the defusing process is a limited form of group debriefing. The group defusing involves three main steps: introduction, exploration, and information (Mitchell & Everly, 1993, 2000). The introduction phase establishes the ground rules for the defusing. The exploration phase lets the participants briefly explain their involvement in broad terms. The information phase outlines the types of short-term reactions and symptoms the participants are likely to experience as a consequence of the traumatic event.

Conclusions

Without a doubt, the correctional environment is a stressful one. The mental health provider plays a critical role in helping the agency or institution and individuals to manage these stressors optimally. Agencies that fail to recognize this are doomed to have a greater incidence of staff misconduct, increased sick leave abuse, and decreased staff morale. As a consequence, the ability to manage a difficult population is compromised. This chapter has highlighted some of the day-to-day stressors of correctional work that require an organized agency response. Confidential EAPs meet this need. The most confidential and least compromised by role conflicts are the independent EAP service providers. Realistically, not all institutions have the financial resources to have a full-service EAP contract. These institutions can still provide adequate services through in-house EAPs, referrals to community mental health resources, or a combination of both. These might not be perfect responses, but the alternative (i.e., no services or policy at all) is not acceptable.

This chapter has also shown that the correctional environment has many of the workplace violence issues of other professional environments; however, the nature of the correctional environment and the concentration of potentially violent inhabitants compound the frequency and intensity of workplace violence. The concentration of violent inhabitants and the increased frequency and intensity of workplace violence add to the argument that the agency or institution must have a thorough mental health program for assisting staff in dealing with the correctional environment. The mission of mental health professionals is to sell the program in terms of better correctional management, better inmate management, and a safer and more secure correctional facility as a result of improved staff well-being. Educating correctional administrators about the benefits of EAPs and the value of critical incident debriefing and defusing programs and policies and then implementing quality EAPs and CISD programs should be the dual missions of all correctional mental health professionals interested in providing quality services to correctional staff.

References

American Psychiatric Association. (1994). *Diagnostic and statistical manual of mental disorders.* Washington, DC: Author.

Brakel, S. (1998). Legal liability and workplace violence. *Journal of the American Academy of Psychiatry and the Law, 26,* 553-562.

Campfield, K. M., & Hills, A. M. (2001). Effect of timing of critical incident stress debriefing (CISD) on posttraumatic symptoms. *Journal of Traumatic Stress, 14,* 327-340.

Chenier, E. (1998). The workplace: A battleground for violence. *Public Personnel Management, 27,* 557-568.

Conover, T. (2000). *New Jack: Guarding Sing Sing.* New York: Random House.

Dignam, J. T., & Fagan, T. J. (1996). Workplace violence in correctional settings: A comprehensive approach to critical incident stress management. In G. R. VandenBos & E. Q. Bulatao (Eds.), *Violence on the job* (pp. 367-384). Washington, DC: American Psychological Association.

Everly, G. S., Jr. (1995). The role of the critical incident stress debriefing (CISD) process in disaster counseling. *Journal of Mental Health Counseling, 17,* 278-290.

Finn, P. (1998). Correctional officer stress: A cause for concern and additional help. *Federal Probation, 62*(2), 65-74.

Frolkey, C. A. (1996). Trauma in the workplace. *Personnel Journal, 75*(11), 10-13.

Hyer, L., Bagge, R. W., Brandsma, J. F., Boudewyns, P. A., Gerrard, C., Hearst, D., Peralme, L., Shapiro, F., Sperr, E., & Summers, M. N. (1994). *Trauma victim: Theoretical issues and practical suggestions.* Muncie, IN: Accelerated Development.

Leonard, R., & Alison, L. (1999). Critical incident stress debriefing and its effects on coping strategies and anger management in a sample of Australian police officers involved in shooting incidents. *Work and Stress, 13*(2), 144-161.

McWhirter, E. H., & Linzer, M. (1994). The provision of critical incident stress debriefing services by EAPs: A case study. *Journal of Mental Health Counseling, 16,* 403-414.

Miller-Burke, J. A. (1998). The impact of traumatic events and organizational response. *Dissertation Abstracts International, 58*(9-B), 5177.

Mitchell, J. T., & Everly, G. S. (1993). Critical incident stress debriefing (CISD): An operations manual for the prevention of traumatic stress among emergency services and disaster workers. *Journal of the American Academy of Psychiatry and the Law, 26,* 553-562.

Mitchell, J. T., & Everly, G. S. (2000). Critical incident stress management and critical incident stress debriefings: Evolutions, effects, and outcomes. In R. Raphael & J. P. Wilson (Eds.), *Psychological debriefing: Theory, practice, and evidence* (pp. 71-90). New York: Cambridge University Press.

Montey, L., & Li-Ping Tang, T. (1992). The effects of hardiness, police stress, and life stress on police officers' illness and absenteeism. *Public Personnel Management, 21,* 493-511.

Moriarty, A., and Field, M. W. (1990). A new approach to police EAP programs. *Public Personnel Management, 19,* 155-161.

Raphael, B., & Wilson, J. P. (2000). *Psychological debriefing: Theory, practice, and evidence.* New York: Cambridge University Press.

Reiser, M. (1974a). Mental health in police work and training. *The Police Chief, 4*(1), 51-52.

Reiser, M. (1974b). Some organizational stresses on policemen. *Journal of Police Science and Administration, 4,* 51-52.

Reiser, M. (1982). *Police psychology.* Los Angeles: LEHI Publishing.

Robinson, R. (2000). Debriefing with emergency services: Critical incident stress management. In R. Raphael & J. P. Wilson (Eds.), *Psychological debriefing: Theory, practice, and evidence* (pp. 91-107). New York: Cambridge University Press.

Stuart, P. (1992). Murder on the job. *Personnel Journal, 71*(2), 72-82.

CHAPTER 12

Staff Training: Multiple Roles for Mental Health Professionals

Kathy J. Harowski

Correctional work is often stressful and challenging, as Chapter 11 indicated. Correctional workers are tasked with managing a difficult, sometimes violent, often volatile client population. To accomplish this task, correctional workers are provided with various policies and procedures aimed at creating an environment that will run smoothly and operate efficiently. In addition, many correctional systems expect their workers to form professional relationships with offenders and to serve as their mentors, parent surrogates, work supervisors, teachers, role models, protectors, disciplinarians, and so on. It is often through the strength and vitality of these professional relationships that institutions are able to manage their inmate populations on a daily basis. Staff are expected to provide routine guidance and support to offenders when things are going well and to assist with conflict resolution when problems arise.

It is readily apparent to anyone who spends time in a correctional facility that the proper preparation and training of new correctional workers is crucial if they are to function effectively in their multiple roles. The high turnover rates in corrections, especially among first-year employees (Conover, 2000), provide mute testimony to the difficulty and dissatisfaction of many who undertake this difficult but vital work. Ongoing training to refresh and supplement existing knowledge and skills is also crucial to the maintenance of employee satisfaction, effectiveness, and overall well-being. Certainly, mental health professionals, with their educational background in the behavioral sciences, are in an excellent position to provide much of the training that correctional workers need to function efficiently and effectively with the inmate population.

However, as Hawk-Sawyer (1997) noted, prison work is often ignored or dismissed by psychologists and other health/mental health care workers. Indeed, health care providers who choose to work in the public sector often face bias from peers and have to manage the concerns of family members who assume that such providers' careers have gone awry. For licensed health care providers, the potential for stigma is represented by headlines and articles such as "Prison Deaths Spotlight How Boards Handle Impaired, Disciplined Physicians" (Skolnick, 1998), which highlights the practice employed by some private contractors of hiring physicians with licensure restrictions that limit their practice to specific populations such as incarcerated individuals.

Many correctional mental health providers endure the negative comments of peers and also bear the fears and worries of family members because they believe that they can have a positive impact on the offender population through the provision of quality care and on the staff through the provision of quality training. Clearly, good correctional mental health care providers are desperately needed in a society that has such a large prison population, and the experience gained by working in this environment provides a valuable perspective on the training needed to survive and function effectively for the many individuals now working in corrections as well as for those who will join them in the next several years as the field continues to grow.

This chapter discusses three aspects of staff training informed by this author's 10 years of experience as a correctional psychologist. First, the chapter reviews current correctional trends and the implications these trends have for the training of correctional workers. Second, it discusses the various training roles that mental health professionals can provide for correctional workers, roles that serve to better prepare them for managing offenders more effectively and for inoculating them against some of the better known stressors inherent in their work. Last, the chapter describes roles that current correctional mental health providers can play in the training of future generations of correctional mental health professionals.

Correctional Trends and Their Training Implications

During the past 20 years, several trends have highlighted the importance of training and staff development in corrections. These trends are discussed in the following sections.

Rapid Growth in the Correctional Population

As federal and state governments acted to incarcerate American citizens at a higher rate than any other country in the world, the so-called prison-industrial complex emerged as a social, financial, and political force (Donziger, 1998). At the end of 1999, there were 1,366,721 adults incarcerated in the United States (Bureau of Justice Statistics, 2000). If juvenile facilities, Immigration and Naturalization Service facilities, and military and Indian jails are added, then this total rises to 2,026,596. The rate of incarceration in 1999, 476 sentenced inmates per 100,000 U.S. residents, was nearly double what it was in 1990, 292 per 100,000 (Bureau of Justice Statistics, 2000). The growth of prisons as a powerful industry in which more are incarcerated, are on parole, violate while on parole/probation and thus return to prison, or reoffend and return to prison, coupled with longer prison sentences for nonviolent drug-related crimes, has created a boom in correctional hiring, particularly at the entry level. For example, Camp and Camp (1998) reported that 239,299 individuals were employed as correctional officers in prisons nationwide in 1998 compared with 60,026 in 1982. Therefore, it is vital that correctional training, which initially introduces new employees to their agency and the field of corrections and later provides them with the ongoing skills they need to keep up with the ever-changing demands of the job, be effective enough to recruit, enable, and retain sufficient numbers of good workers to meet the high current demand for sound correctional workers.

An introductory training program offers an agency the single best opportunity to inculcate new employees into its organizational culture. In so doing, it may promote pride and enthusiasm in the agency. It can also assist in building support for the agency's cultural anchors. In the absence of effective introductory training, new employees are quickly exposed to the cynicism and disillusionment of inmates and more senior staff and may quickly develop similar attitudes and dysfunctional behavioral patterns. Despite the value of introductory training, fiscal concerns often constrain resources, and training budgets sometimes suffer as a result. There may be pressure to eliminate training or to provide "quick and dirty" training simply to indemnify the agency as inexpensively as possible.

Often, it is the attitudes and perspectives of top correctional administrators that set the tone for a positive training environment in an institution or agency. When top managers value new ideas and support training in these ideas, their enthusiasm often trickles down to staff and encourages them to seek new skills or to further develop existing skills. When correctional managers eagerly participate in training along with staff, they serve as excellent role models for their staff. Allowing staff to seek training in conventional (e.g., conferences, seminars) as well as innovative ways (e.g., Internet-based training programs) represents other ways for administrative staff to show their support for staff training.

Diversity in Both Offenders and the Workforce

Another trend that has significantly affected the need for training in corrections is the increasing diversity of incarcerated individuals. Prisons in the United States now house a global population (see Chapter 15 for a discussion of globalization), with female and juvenile populations growing at the fastest rates. As noted in Chapter 10, the Federal Bureau of Prisons (BOP) estimates that 30% of the individuals now incarcerated by the federal government are non-U.S. citizens.

With nearly all countries, as well as the many subcultures found within the United States, represented in the prison population, the potential is real for language, cultural, racial, and gender misunderstandings as well as for charges of discrimination to arise.

When correctional systems fail to provide adequate staff training regarding the management of these diverse populations, headlines and judicial interventions are the frequent outcomes. For example, as part of a lawsuit settlement (*Lucas v. Dublin*) alleging sexual assault and harassment of female offenders at the Federal Correctional Institution in Dublin, California, BOP was required to provide training on sexual harassment to all supervisory staff. In this instance, psychologists were designated as trainers. Clearly, proper training can do much to alter the organizational culture, thereby discouraging further behavior of this sort. Conversely, a failure to provide proper training exposes agencies to increased liability.

As correctional agencies hire more women and more culturally and racially diverse staff to manage this changing offender population, issues and conflicts among staff also emerge or are exacerbated. The integration of women and ethnic minorities into the paramilitary culture of corrections has created a need for training aimed at reducing harassment and workplace conflict and stress. Here again, training can alter the organizational culture so as to provide the context for more appropriate behavior as well as to remediate skill deficits that have led to prior problem interactions.

The lack of basic public health and mental health services in communities has led to the increased incarceration of individuals with medical conditions such as HIV (see Chapter 10), with infectious diseases such as tuberculosis (Berkman, 1995), and with mental illness (see Chapter 6). Staff concerns about exposure to infectious diseases, along with institutional and social priorities to limit staff exposure to these diseases, create a high staff training need. Conklin (1998) stated, "When the famous bank robber Willie Sutton was asked why he robbed banks, he answered because that's where the money is. . . . Well, jails are where infectious diseases are that most threaten public health" (p. 1).

High rates of HIV, tuberculosis, and sexually transmitted diseases such as syphilis are among those that move through America's jails and prisons. Staff education is necessary to increase awareness of safe management procedures and to prevent abuse and discrimination toward infected offenders. The correctional culture presents particular challenges for HIV treatment and prevention efforts in prison. Staff and offender fear of contagion, homophobia, a multicultural inmate population, and limited health care resources all are issues that must be addressed through training (Harowski, 1999).

Transinstitutionalization of the mentally ill is a reality. In many states, the correctional setting is a primary provider of mental health care (Butterfield, 1998). It is estimated that on any given day, 10% to 15% of the correctional population display active symptoms of a major mental illness (Lamb & Weinberger, 1998; Torrey, 1995). Staff concerns about contact with the mentally ill also put pressure on systems to provide appropriate training. Learning signs, symptoms, and the proper response techniques for identifying and managing mentally ill individuals, especially those with suicidal thoughts, can mean the difference between life and death.

Corrections and law enforcement administrators across the country have expressed high levels of concern about the numbers of individuals with mental illness flooding into prisons and jails as a result of deinstitutionalization and increased homelessness (Strandberg, 2000). Identification and management of the mentally ill and the diversion and provision of treatment thus become key areas for staff training (Strandberg, 2000). Highlighting this need is the fact that in 1997, 67 correctional facilities were under investigation by the Department of Justice, and another 46 correctional facilities were correcting deficits in mental health care to avoid lawsuits ("Allegations of Poor Psychiatric Care," 1997).

Changing Technology

As correctional environments become more technologically dependent and provide less and less human contact for both workers and offenders, another important training need emerges. The interface between people and technology creates a unique set of challenges, and the human factors involved in the appropriate and non-dehumanizing use of computer technology are an area just beginning to be explored in many work environments. New maximum-security prisons are now being built that rely less on human contact to manage offenders and more on the use of complex technology monitored by fewer and fewer staff. The new generation of "no human contact" segregation units and entire "super-max" prisons built on the noncontact model also represent an interesting real-life laboratory on the effects of this sterile environment on both staff and offenders.

Using video technology to monitor offenders who are mentally unstable often means that an officer managing a housing complex is also charged with observing up to 10 offenders on suicide watch. Staff placed in this untenable position are well aware of the real limits of technology when human factors are not considered. Most will readily admit that they do not believe the level of observation occurring under these conditions is adequate to meet current health care standards.

Training Roles for Mental Health Professionals

Trainer and Audience Issues

Correctional training roles for mental health professionals can be framed along several dimensions. For example, should mental health trainers come from within the institution (i.e., be full-time correctional employees), or should outside mental health consultants be used? In-house mental health trainers are likely to possess more credibility with other staff and are more likely to have firsthand understandings of the particular issues facing their institutions. However, outside mental health consultants may have more ready access to executive staff and a consequent ability to have a greater impact on institutional programs, policies, and training.

Roles played by mental health professionals may also vary across agencies or facilities. For example, in some institutions, mental health professionals may be asked to identify specific training needs, develop training programs, or measure specific training outcomes—in effect, functioning in the role of in-house consultants. In other institutions, mental health professionals may simply serve as trainers. They may be selected for this role because of their special knowledge of the areas selected for training or because of their particular training abilities. In this role, they may either train staff directly or train other staff who will ultimately provide the training to all correctional staff.

Who mental health professionals target as their audience is a variable that is often overlooked in correctional training. Line staff and middle management are typically seen as the correctional audience most in need of training because of their routine direct contact with inmates. However, two other audiences are worth mentioning. Institution executive staff are a training audience that is frequently overlooked, even though training this audience can result in more rapid system changes. Mental health professionals who are knowledgeable about the practices of functional and dysfunctional organizations or systems may also be helpful in assisting institution executive staff with "thinking outside the box" in ways that might ultimately assist their organizations in operating more efficiently and effectively. Mental health professionals may also play a vital role in training offenders to fulfill specific institution needs such as suicide watch monitors, inmate companions, and facilitators of psychoeducational programs (e.g., health promotion programs, smoking cessation programs).

Developing Mental Health Paraprofessionals

A wide variety of mental health paraprofessionals (e.g., correctional counselors, correctional treatment specialists, addictions counselors) are employed in correctional settings. These individuals are especially in need of training and supervision because they may function in a variety of roles (e.g., as direct service providers, as trainers) and their performance may well affect the general perception among both inmates and staff regarding the value of mental health services. These paraprofessionals are often trained by psychologists or other mental health providers to provide structured therapeutic programs or groups specifically designed for the correctional population and may provide many of the mental health services being offered within a facility (Morgan, Winterowd, & Ferrell, 1999).

The trend to hire less well-trained mental health providers means that most correctional systems are now using doctoral psychologists more in supervisory, program development, and administrative roles (Morgan et al., 1999). Training and supervision become especially important to assist less adequately prepared providers in attempting to effect change in the often "difficult to treat" correctional population. Initial on-the-job training for these staff obviously needs to include programs that address basic interpersonal communication skills, group dynamics, how to deal with resistant difficult clients, and management of special needs offenders.

Training in Particular Skill Areas

Correctional systems often use mental health professionals to design, implement, and evaluate a wide variety of training programs so as to better manage the volatile correctional environment. For example, mental health professionals can offer training programs that assist staff in interviewing and/or screening prospective new employees, in developing supervisory/leadership skills in correctional managers, or in managing their workloads and job-related stressors more effectively. However, training line staff in the use of particular skills currently forms the bulk of training provided by mental health professionals within most correctional agencies.

Often, when institution executive staff need a curriculum designed or training conducted to educate staff about a special organizational need, they turn to psychologists or other mental health staff for assistance. Mental health professionals can help to define and transform executive staff ideas into viable training curricula and implementation strategies. In the past, mental health professionals have been most helpful in developing curricula in vital correctional areas such as communications and interpersonal skills training, conflict resolution and confrontation avoidance training, training to assist staff in identifying and managing inmates with suicidal tendencies or mental illness, crisis/hostage negotiation training, hostage survival skills training, and sexual assault prevention and intervention training.

Trauma Inoculation/Individual Factors in Coping With Stress

Correctional work is stressful. Similar to other occupations, correctional work shares common work stressors such as shift work, difficult people, and a challenging physical work environment. And correctional workers, like other law enforcement personnel, face additional stressors such as exposure to direct and vicarious traumatization (e.g., responding to crisis/rescue scenes that may include severe injury or death) (see Chapter 11 for a detailed discussion of this topic). Correctional workers are also required to manage people in an interpersonal environment permeated by criminal thinking, false statements, and other forms of manipulation coupled with the constant threat of physical assault or even death (Sewell, 1993).

Because most correctional staff have exposure to at least some of these corrosive elements, they can expect to be negatively affected by them. Training designed to inoculate employees from the "normal" stressors of the correctional environment as well as to raise awareness of each individual worker's specific vulnerabilities to trauma and post-traumatic stress disorder is a role for which mental health professionals are particularly well suited. Psychologists and mental health workers who debrief and treat their correctional colleagues may also develop vicarious traumatization (Briere, 1996) and should be cognizant of their own need for stress reduction.

The growing body of literature regarding vulnerability to post-traumatic stress (Briere, 1997; Stamm, 2001), along with the documented higher incidence of alcoholism, domestic violence, family stress, and divorce among correctional personnel, underscores the need for training on how to survive in a stressful work environment. During recent years, Web sites (e.g., www.corrections.com, www.ojp.usdoj.gov/nij/lefs) have been created to assist correctional and law enforcement personnel and their families in coping with "the negative effects of stress." If staff are not properly prepared, trained, and supported, what Janik (1995) called correctional compassion fatigue can result and be manifested by dysfunctional coping mechanisms such as denial (concentrating on other things or withdrawal from people in the workplace), rationalization (overusing bleak humor or thinking about other aspects of life while at work), and sublimation/identification with the aggressor (working more, seeing only the negative in people, and being cynical). Although these mechanisms serve to control or manage internal pain, Janik noted that many correctional professionals cope with discomfort produced on the job by just "not feeling" or by becoming emotionally numb. This coping strategy has limits and costs for both the workplace and staff members' lives outside of work.

The case for correctional staff training and stress inoculation has never been more clearly defined. Judicial, political, and media attention is increasingly focused on corrections. A growing number of staff members, many of whom are naive about the potentially corrosive effects of the correctional environment, are being asked to manage a growing, more diverse, and more challenging offender population. Both initial and regular on-the-job training opportunities are clearly needed. Agencies and institutions should not ignore opportunities to work to reduce the stress level present in the correctional environment. Administrative staff will be key in noting the need for training to increase understanding and reduce stress in broad areas such as cultural diversity/sensitivity, sexual harassment, maintenance of boundaries, and stress management. When administrators make clear the need for this type of training, it communicates to staff at all levels that these areas are important and starts the process of education and change.

Training the Next Generation of Correctional Mental Health Professionals

As the correctional population has grown, so too has the number of mental health providers employed in prisons. Camp and Camp (1998) reported that there were a total of 10,167 mental health and counseling staff working in 51 different federal and state correctional agencies in 1998. Approximately 4.1% of these staff were psychiatrists, 22.9% were psychologists, 8.0% were social workers, 15.2% were caseworkers, 36.7% were counselors, and the remaining 13.1% represented other treatment staff (e.g., recreational therapists). In most prison systems, mental health workers are employed in job roles that often push the boundaries of traditional health care career expectations. Optimal functioning in these roles requires careful preparation, supervision, and training.

To assist correctional workers in managing offenders more effectively in the correctional environment, mental health providers must learn to successfully combine their specific training background in the behavioral sciences with the unique aspects and missions of the correctional environment. For example, a classic "culture clash" can easily occur between mental health providers and correctional management staff if the clinicians fail to recognize and address the primary correctional missions of safety and security when providing treatment services to mentally disordered or behaviorally disruptive offenders. If mental health providers can maintain the perspective that provision of services in correctional settings is subordinate to the primary missions of safety and security, then it will be easier for them to communicate effectively about therapeutic concepts such as mental illness, voluntary disruptive behavior by antisocial offenders, and least restrictive alternatives for those who are genuinely mentally ill.

Graduate course work in how best to deliver clinical service in a correctional setting is not commonly available in most professional training programs. A recent survey of psychology interns completing their predoctoral internship training in a correctional setting found that only 7% of them reported a course in correctional psychology prior to the clinical immersion of the internship training year (Pietz, DeMier, Dienst, Green, & Scully, 1998). Thus, the primary method of learning the practice of correctional mental health continues to be on-the-job training, work experience, and mentoring by more experienced mental health professionals.

For doctoral-level psychologists, completing the required clinical internship in a correctional setting begins to immerse the providers in clinical work with offenders as well as expose them to the unique features of the prison environment. Because the internship year is supervision intensive and includes didactic training as well as provision of direct service, it begins to shape the professionals for effective work with a correctional population. Learning about the common crises and clinical problems of offenders, receiving supervision on working with a culturally diverse population, being exposed to effective treatment models with offenders, and developing sensitivity to the unique role of mental health providers in prison occur in a supportive context.

BOP is a leader in the provision of accredited internship training for doctoral-level psychologists in the prison setting. Since the early 1980s, the bureau has provided training for approximately 40 interns each year. With internships placed in Federal Medical Centers as well as in general-population correctional institutions for both male and female offenders, trainees can choose from a wide variety of training opportunities, including working with seriously mentally ill offenders, HIV-positive/AIDS offenders, and substance abusers. Interns may also work 1 day a week in a placement outside of the correctional setting to round out their training experience. Interns with the bureau are exposed to the agency's culture at the beginning of their careers and with high levels of supervision/support, allowing them time to decide whether this setting is consistent with their long-term career goals and personal interests.

A survey of psychology interns completing this training in the correctional setting (Pietz et al., 1998) found that the majority of responding interns reported selecting internships in corrections due to the variety of training experiences that such a setting offers. Nearly half of the trainees responding planned to seek jobs in correctional facilities, many based on the perception that job availability is currently good. Of note, 59% of the trainees reported that coping with the bureaucracy and the paramilitary model used in corrections was a definite stressor around which they needed to adjust. The fact that many new psychologists seek institutional employment early in their careers emphasizes the importance of internship and training availability in the correctional environment.

Ax and Morgan (2002) conducted a more recent survey of psychology internships set in corrections. Internship training directors in the correctional setting reported strong support from mental health colleagues for the training function but less support from correctional administrators and other staff. A high level of diversity in the client population was noted, as was the opportunity to participate in multidisciplinary treatment with medically or biologically oriented treatment and training, such as HIV and managing those on psychotropic medication.

Because most mental health workers do not have the opportunity for course work or supervision in the correctional environment, on-the-job training and supervision become central in their adjustment to the correctional setting and in their development of correctional competencies. The supervisor is clearly the key in assisting new correctional mental health workers with acclimation, support, and maintenance of professional identity in corrections. Norton (1990) emphasized the need for supervision to assist mental health workers in their transition into careers as effective correctional practitioners. He noted that the range of treatment issues and the diversity of problems in a correctional population are unique both in terms of their complexity and in terms of their potential to traumatize. He also indicated that the challenges of treatment with the offender population are great and not often amenable to typical therapy models. Finally, he noted that the stressors of the environment (e.g., noise, chaos, risk to personal safety) are energy draining and distracting from the role of helping professionals. The unique approaches needed for successful work with inmates require a strong sense of professional identity and a strong awareness of where one is working so as to have the greatest impact possible. Again, as the number of mental health professionals new to the correctional environment continues to increase, the importance of on-the-job training becomes even more critical.

In adjusting to correctional work, Harowski, Norton, Schlak, and Allen (1993) described the following phases of adaptation in their peers and trainees:

- *Taking it all in:* Any newcomer to corrections spends a good deal of time initially acclimating to the language and attitudes of the environment. Learning prison slang and institution routine and lore, as well as monitoring one's own reactions to the stress and chaos of this unique environment, becomes the primary level of focus for a period of adjustment.
- *Fatigue/Denial:* Once the mental health practitioner "gets" the environment and its focus on controlling people, he or she often denies being a part of the system and begins to work on developing an identity separate from the larger system.

- *Awareness:* Beginning to feel part of the flow of the institution allows the mental health professional to communicate and intervene most effectively with other staff and offenders. Being part of the system, yet being different, is the adjustment that many successful correctional psychologists most typically describe. Reality therapy, interventions clearly in tune with what is safe and possible, and provision of support/advice to staff in a style that is effective represent optimal impact.

- *Managing stress/Avoiding burnout:* Even for mental health professionals, wellness and stress management can be challenging in the correctional environment. Both body and mind need attention, and an awareness of one's own tension/fear/anxiety level within the correctional environment is obviously an important first step in providing this attention. Depending on others to give realistic feedback about job performance is especially important in this type of work environment because reliance on denial as a personal defense against stress is a frequent event. This is particularly true for mental health professionals, who observe and connect with traumatizing events on a high-frequency basis and often have a limited support system within the correctional environment. They are further constrained in their ability to address personal stress by the perceptions of other staff who view them as providers—not consumers—of mental health services and by issues of confidentiality and ethics. On-the-job supervised training, particularly from experienced mentors well versed in correctional mental health practice, and strong team building across disciplines to allow for successful and appropriate management of difficult inmates are key factors in helping new mental health practitioners to integrate successfully into the correctional environment.

Two final points are worth mentioning in this section. First, correctional mental health workers, like other correctional workers, are faced with changing technologies that affect their work routine. For example, due to their remote locations and security concerns, many correctional systems have invested in technology for the provision of telehealth to enhance services, reduce costs, and minimize risk to staff tasked with providing health and mental health care and services (Magaletta, Fagan, & Ax, 1998). These technologies not only can enhance the types of services that may be provided to offenders but also can be of great assistance in making advanced training accessible to treatment providers. This type of technology may also reduce the level of isolation that many mental health providers experience in an agency or institution by increasing supervision and teleconferencing options for mental health professions throughout the agency at minimal cost.

Finally, correctional administrators, in consultation with mental health providers, can work to enhance services provided to offenders by developing new work and skill areas for mental health staff that might better integrate them into the correctional routine or increase their value to the correctional agency. For example, moving psychology into a primary care or case management role might allow for enhanced care overall and also assist special needs offenders at key transition points during their incarceration and community reentry. Some correctional systems have also begun to explore allowing psychologists prescription authority similar to the program used by the Department of Defense as a cost reduction measure for the agency and as a job enhancement strategy for psychologists. As of this writing, no correctional system has yet implemented this type of program.

References

Allegations of poor psychiatric care in county jails prompt increased funding. (1997, November). *Psychiatric Times* (mental health economic supplement).

Ax, R. K., & Morgan, R. (2002). Internship training opportunities in correctional psychology: A comparison of settings. *Criminal Justice and Behavior, 29,* 332-347.

Berkman, A. (1995). Prison health: The breaking point. *American Journal of Public Health, 85,* 1616-1618.

Briere, J. (1997). *Psychological assessment of adult posttraumatic states.* Washington, DC: American Psychological Association.

Bureau of Justice Statistics. (2000). *Prisoners in 1999.* Washington, DC: U.S. Department of Justice.

Butterfield, F. (1998, March 5). By default, jails become mental institutions. *New York Times,* p. A1.

Camp, C. G., & Camp, G. M. (1998). *The corrections yearbook, 1998.* Middletown, CT: Criminal Justice Institute.

Conklin, T. (1998). Look behind bars for key to control of STDs. *Journal of the American Medical Association, 279,* 1-4.

Conover, T. (2000). *New Jack: Guarding Sing Sing.* New York: Random House.

Donziger, S. (1998). Fear, crime, and punishment in the United States. *Tikkun, 12*(6), 24-27.

Harowski, K. (1999, Spring). HIV in the incarcerated population. *Division 18 Newsletter,* p. 12. (Public Service Psychology, American Psychological Association)

Harowski, K., Norton, S., Schlak, L., & Allen, J. (1993, May). *Psychology training in the correctional setting.* Paper presented at the meeting of the Minnesota Psychological Association, Minneapolis.

Hawk-Sawyer, K. (1997). Personal reflections of a career in correctional psychology. *Professional Psychology: Research and Practice, 28,* 335-337.

Janik, J. (1995). Correctional compassion fatigue: Overwhelmed corrections workers can seek therapy. *Corrections Today, 57*(7), 162-164.

Lamb, R., & Weinberger, L. (1998). Persons with severe mental illness in jails and prisons. *Psychiatric Services, 49,* 275-281.

Magaletta, P., Fagan, T., & Ax, R. (1998). Advancing psychology services through telehealth in the Federal Bureau of Prisons. *Professional Psychology: Research and Practice, 29,* 543-548.

Morgan, R. D., Winterowd, C. L., & Ferrell, S. W. (1999). A national survey of group psychotherapy services in correctional facilities. *Professional Psychology: Research and Practice, 30,* 600-606.

Norton, S. (1990). Supervision needs of correctional mental health counselors. *Journal of Addictions and Offender Counseling, 11,* 13-19.

Pietz, C. A., DeMier, R. L., Dienst, R. D., Green, J. B., & Scully, B. (1998). Psychology internship training in a correctional facility. *Criminal Justice and Behavior, 25,* 99-108.

Sewell, J. D. (1993). Traumatic stress of multiple murder investigations. *Journal of Traumatic Stress, 6*(1), 103-118.

Skolnick, A. A. (1998). Prison deaths spotlight how boards handle impaired, disciplined physicians. *Journal of the American Medical Association, 280,* 1387-1390.

Stamm, B. H. (2001, Fall). A tragic reminder of the importance of caring for the caregiver. *Division 18 Newsletter,* p. 14. (Public Service Psychology, American Psychological Association)

Strandberg, K. (2000, October). Dealing with the mentally ill. *Corrections Forum,* pp. 24-27.

Torrey, E. F. (1995). Jails and prisons: American's new mental hospitals [editorial]. *American Journal of Public Health, 85,* 1611-1613.

CHAPTER 13

Mental Health Professionals as Institutional Consultants and Problem Solvers

Joel Dvoskin, Erin M. Spiers, and Steven E. Pitt

The incarcerated population in the United States continues to grow at an exceptional rate. From the end of 1990 to mid-1999, federal, state, and local correctional institutions took in an additional 83,743 inmates each year, or 1,610 new inmates per week (U.S. Department of Justice, 2000a). By the end of 1999, state prisons were reported to be operating between 1% and 17% over capacity, while the federal prison system was estimated to be operating at 32% over capacity (U.S. Department of Justice, 2000b).

Commensurate with the increasing correctional population is the number of prisoners with mental illness (see Chapter 6). According to the American Psychiatric Association (2000), researchers estimate that 20% of prison and jail inmates are in need of mental health care. Unfortunately, as the incarcerated population continues to grow, the availability of resources to serve this population lags further and further behind. Fiscal constraints drain the minimal resources available, and to date, correctional systems have been largely unable to keep pace with

AUTHORS' NOTE: The authors thank Irwin Grossman, Sandra Williamson, Jason Dana, and Jason Lewis for their thoughtful comments and suggestions during the preparation of this chapter.

the dramatic increase in the populations they serve (Veysey, Steadman, Morrissey, & Johnsen, 1997). In fact, correctional personnel cite inmates with mental illness as one of their most significant concerns, second only to overcrowding (Lamb & Weinberger, 1998). Although the overall number of mental health professionals working in corrections is increasing (Ferrell, Morgan, & Winterowd, 2000), the estimated psychologist-to-inmate ratio is approximately half of what it was during the 1980s (Boothby & Clements, 2000). The incarceration of mentally ill offenders in facilities ill prepared to manage and treat them has negative ramifications not only for inmates with mental illness but also for correctional and security staff as well as the community at large (Morris, Steadman, & Veysey, 1997). Nevertheless, confronted with unprecedented growth and insufficient revenue, correctional systems are forced to make due, often with inadequate facilities, limited staff, and ineffective or less than adequate institutional programs. Environmental stressors lead to individual stress, which leads to interpersonal tension, which in turn creates a volatile atmosphere for both inmates and staff.

In addition to the abundant overt stressors, covert pressures further complicate matters. Correctional professionals are constantly faced with complex, and at times competing, objectives. Punishment has long been the fundamental purpose behind jails and prisons, and confinement itself remains the most common and (absent the death penalty) serious sanction imposed by our judicial system (Carlson, 1999c). Imprisonment incapacitates offenders, thereby precluding the commission of further free world crimes (at least for the duration of incarceration) and protecting society from further victimization (Gottfredson & Gottfredson, 1988).

Public perception dictates that the role of prisons and jails is primarily to provide secure housing to offenders, including those who are mentally ill (Dvoskin & Patterson, 1998). However, correctional institutions must do more than warehouse offenders. Law and social policy mandate ethical and humane treatment of inmates and require appropriate and adequate mental health care (Metzner, Cohen, Grossman, & Wettstein, 1998). Finally, it is anticipated that correctional institutions will "treat" inmates in such a way as to decrease the likelihood of future criminal acts. In essence, as organizations, correctional systems are expected to serve a punitive function, a protective function, and a rehabilitative function simultaneously (Carlson, 1999b).

Like correctional staff, there are several mechanisms by which mental health professionals can make important and cost-effective contributions. The bulk of consultation between security and mental health staff is related to the correctional management of inmates or detainees (Brodsky & Epstein, 1982). Several of the more complex inmate-management decisions (e.g., classification, work assignments, educational and vocational opportunities, disciplinary sanctions) can be managed successfully with a commitment to interdisciplinary communication and collaboration. It is incumbent on all prison employees, including mental health professionals, to take proactive steps toward the resolution of conflict and the development of an institutional climate conducive to safety, security, and the well-being of all inmates and staff. To be successful, mental health professionals need not, and in fact *cannot*, limit the scope of their activity to traditional treatment modalities and the provision of direct service. Rather, they must consider expanding the scope of their practice to include institutional consultation and problem solving if they are to be maximally effective correctional mental health practitioners. This chapter discusses several areas in which mental health professionals have served as effective institution consultants and problem solvers.

Assessing Institutional Climate

Correctional facilities are inherently stressful environments. Inmates and staff alike are subject to the constant pressures of overcrowding, extremes of cold or heat, noise, and filth. Information is often sparse, unreliable, and dependent on rumors. Inmates are typically forced to share their living spaces with strangers they might not like, respect, or trust. In addition, they fear for their personal safety on a daily basis. Generally speaking, jails tend to be even more stressful than prisons because most detainees have recently entered the system and are often uncertain as to the outcomes of their legal status. Furthermore, the high turnover in jails precludes the formation of predictable social groupings. Former inmates returning to prison after extended periods in the community are confronted by an ever-changing inmate subculture, with new rules and social demands that they might not understand (Hunt, Riegel, Morales, & Waldorf, 1998). For first-time offenders and new officers alike, expectations are likely to be colored by television or movie dramatizations stressing violence in corrections. For repeat offenders, particularly those who spent time under "old school" rules, modern prison life can be dramatically different from what they had come to expect.

Dvoskin (1994) has long favored conceptualizing the correctional setting as a community. Correctional facilities consist of groups of interdependent people, often divided along social and/or racial lines, living and working in close proximity and under the same conditions. In fact, it could be argued that inmates and staff in a correctional setting are significantly more dependent on one another than are civilians in most communities. Inmates are dependent on correctional staff to provide safety, security, and structure. Similarly, staff are dependent on inmates (who far outnumber them) to behave according to the rules and to provide a labor force necessary for daily facility functioning. Although interdependence does not imply equality, it is important to remember that all individuals in a jail or prison, staff and inmates alike, are subject to the same environmental stressors. Power differential notwithstanding, it is clearly in the best interest of the "community" if relations are good and morale is positive.

If one is to work effectively in a correctional setting regardless of professional capacity, then it is essential to have an adequate appreciation for the character or climate of the facility. As noted by McGee, Warner, and Harlow (1998), "There is an undeniable character associated with any prison that is hard to define . . . , yet it importantly affects what can be done within the institution" (p. 104). Understanding an institution's climate requires an appreciation of the nuances of inmate behavior and an understanding of the social and political structure that governs the correctional subculture. In fact, accurate assessment depends to a much greater extent on interpersonal skill and experience than on clinical acumen. To the seasoned professional, it is often readily apparent whether significant tension exists either between or within the staff and inmate populations. Some facilities are well known for tense relations, while others enjoy a sense of rapport among those living and working within their walls.

Although a given facility may maintain a reputation for its atmosphere, psychic tension within correctional institutions is dynamic in nature. On any given day, innumerable factors directly affect the state of relations. Broad variables such as legislative policy, departmental mandates, and unit-specific issues (e.g., changes in management or line staff) can have a direct impact on the quality of interpersonal relations. Widespread institutional unrest can also arise from a single incident with a single inmate, and tensions can build rapidly as a result of countless, seemingly random and unpredictable factors (e.g., gang activity, race relations, changes in operating policy). Nevertheless, disturbances that potentially place the safety and integrity of an institution in jeopardy often, but certainly not always, follow a clear course of escalation (Useem, Graham-Camp, & Camp, 1996). In other words, correctional catastrophes do not occur in a vacuum. Retrospectively, there are often clearly identifiable red flags signaling impending danger.

Cooksey (1999) accurately emphasized the importance of *listening* to inmates' complaints and concerns. Although it is true that some inmates will complain chronically, others conduct their daily activities in a respectful manner, working well with staff and peers. Trusted staff working directly with inmates will inevitably hear from the latter group when tensions are mounting or problems are developing in the facility. It is imperative that staff take inmate reports seriously and that administrators in turn take staff reports seriously. Understanding the nature of inmate complaints and the importance of attending to rumors is critical. It is also important to recognize each inmate as an individual *and* as a member of the broader social environment or correctional community.

Correctional staff have, by far, the most significant amount of contact with inmates on a daily basis. Consequently, they are the most likely observers of changes in institutional climate, escalating tension, and overall unrest. A well-trained, conscientious correctional officer is more likely to be responsible for defusing a potential problem than is any member of the mental health staff (Armstrong, 1999). Nevertheless, mental health professionals can contribute by taking a hands-on approach, maintaining a visible presence on the unit, walking the yard, and communicating openly with all levels of staff and inmates. Paying attention to details, observing interactions, and assessing nonverbal cues all are key to understanding the facility's atmosphere. Ultimately, mental health professionals could then offer assistance relevant to their primary area of expertise, that is, human behavior. For example, attending to what the inmates *do not* complain about may be even more telling and informative than attending to what they *do* complain about; if the inmates at a given facility complain primarily about their menu selection, then it is less likely that they are under extreme duress or fear of abuse by staff or peers. Conversely, if inmates in a facility offer no complaints at all, then it might signal content residents or, conversely, captives who have been brutally intimidated into silence.

Implications associated with an institution's climate extend beyond monitoring the ebb and flow of tension in the interest of elevating morale. Mental health professionals also have a vested interest in the accurate assessment of institutional climate as it relates to the placement of correctional programs (McGee et al., 1998). As programs continue to develop to meet the changing needs of the correctional population, administrators and policymakers are faced not only with identifying at-risk groups but also with determining where within the system to locate them. Designation of a program will be based on several factors, including physical plant, available staff, access to community resources, and institutional climate. Clearly, it would be detrimental for a program comprised of particularly vulnerable inmates (e.g., physically handicapped, geriatric) to be housed in a facility where the institutional climate would not support the program. By talking to one another and sharing observations and recommendations, mental health and correctional staff can work together toward selecting an institution that will optimize the potential for a program to succeed.

Consultation Within the Institution

Mutual distrust between mental health and correctional professionals has been cited as one of the largest barriers in caring for offenders (Roskes & Feldman, 1999). Apprehension and skepticism between disciplines are exacerbated by the challenges associated with complex and often competing demands of security and mental health systems (Kauffman, 1988; Ziegenfuss, 1985). Correctional administrators and line staff who have learned to trust their mental health personnel are more likely to value advice and attend to presented concerns. However, it is essential that consultation be viewed as interactive and mutually beneficial. In other words, trust is something that mental health professionals must earn. Mental health professionals would be well served to heed the advice of seasoned correctional staff who have a much greater appreciation of how to interact with inmates.

Classification

Classification is one of the most crucial steps in determining the course of a given inmate's incarceration. According to Cooksey (1999), "Classification can best be defined as the systematic grouping of inmates into categories based on shared characteristics and behavioral patterns" (p. 75). More specifically, the classification process is the mechanism by which the inmate's physical, medical, educational, vocational, spiritual, and mental health needs are weighed in the context of necessary security precautions to determine a "best fit" for offender and organization alike (Ziegenfuss, 1985). Accordingly, a thoughtful classification policy can be the key to heading off many potential institutional problems (Brennan, 1998). It is also one of the processes in which the involvement of mental health professionals is most important. Careful consideration of whether a given inmate will be capable of negotiating the demands of a given institution, as well as the treatment and/or growth opportunities available, will go a long way toward preventing unnecessary difficulties down the line.

Similar to most other areas of correctional management, the classification process is confronted with competing demands and divergent priorities. Maximizing bed space and guaranteeing security often take precedent over psychosocial needs and/or personal growth (Bartollas, 1985). When participating in classification procedures, mental health professionals must be mindful of the context in which they are working. Institutional safety and security must ultimately prevail; thus, the interest of the broad community will likely outweigh individual needs. Through participation in classification, mental health professionals have the opportunity, from the beginning, to offer opinions and/or suggestions that may defuse potential crises, thereby saving precious time, energy, and resources. Ideally, a representative from the mental health staff should participate in all classification decisions. However, given staffing constraints, psychological expertise may be in short supply and, if so, should be used strategically (e.g., for offenders with mental illness, with repetitive violent behavior, and/or with severe personality disorders). Formal written policies requiring trained mental health participation in classification decisions is not the norm (Morris et al., 1997). Nevertheless, within the context of a mutually respectful and esteemed relationship, informal consultation can be quite effective as well. In many cases, a simple decision, such as changing an inmate's work assignment, schedule, or housing status, can prevent significant problems, for example, impending assault or psychiatric decompensation (Dvoskin, Spiers, Metzner, & Pitt, in press). By heading off such potential disruptions, the institution will continue to function smoothly without unnecessary expense and escalating tension.

Case Management/Unit Teams

Traditional Case Management. Case managers (as well as correctional counselors) are responsible for a significant part of an institution's daily operation (Carlson, 1999a). An effective case management program is essential to the successful management of day-to-day institutional functioning. Case managers monitor and support the inmates on their caseloads, forestall potential crises, and reduce stress and pressure on correctional staff. The influence of case management extends both within and without the institution and spans the duration of incarceration. Within the institution, case managers link inmates with correctional services and programs, and they serve as a liaison between inmates and various institutional departments. The correctional setting is laden with detailed policies and stringent procedures that may be difficult for even the most mentally healthy inmate to negotiate. Often, a simple question (e.g., how to facilitate visitation, how to order reading material, how to enroll in educational programming) will result in an inmate being referred to several different staff members before an answer is provided. One of the most important yet often overlooked needs of the inmate population is simply to be heard. Getting the runaround is frustrating for anyone but can be particularly problematic for an already fragile inmate. Case managers serve as a single point of contact, allowing inmates the opportunity to address concerns, obtain information, and request services throughout their incarceration. Often, the simple provision of accurate information can dramatically decrease disruptive anxiety or frustration, and the refuting of rumors or offering of support can often significantly improve an inmate's response to an otherwise distressing situation (Dvoskin et al., in press).

In the absence of supportive services, the collective pressures of incarceration can intensify to the point of crisis. Crises of any kind are extremely disruptive to the institution, and after-the-fact intervention is often expensive. Fortunately, through active case management, such crises can usually be averted. In fact, for many inmates, case managers can supplement or even replace costly clinical contacts. Verbal counseling not only is the least intrusive intervention available but often also is the most effective, especially when the difficulty is in response to a specific event or the novelty of the incarceration itself. With general training in human relations, nonclinical staff can serve in a supportive capacity. Nevertheless, case managers must often rely on the expertise of mental health professionals to address concerns beyond the scope of their training. Depending on the size and staffing ratio of a given facility, case managers may be assigned to work with a designated mental health professional. Within this arrangement, informal consultation will also occur on a regular basis. Regularly (but infrequently) scheduled meetings/staffings are another useful mechanism to keep all parties apprised of inmates' status. The management of inmates who are repetitively violent or who have serious mental illness or severe personality disorders will require a collaborative effort. To this end, mental health professionals can contribute their knowledge of behavior toward the development of an effective treatment plan. Like security staff, mental health professionals should be readily available to *advise*, as well as to *listen to*, case management staff. Case managers should feel confident that if they seek consultation from mental health staff, their concerns will be met with attention and respect. Moreover, mental health staff should consistently provide feedback to case managers following receipt of referrals. Ultimately, it is the *mutual* sharing of impressions, ideas, and suggestions, with each discipline learning from the expertise of another, that is most beneficial for everyone.

Unit Management. Many correctional systems, including the Federal Bureau of Prisons, employ an integrated or team approach to institutional management. Inmates are generally designated to a unit team on the basis of their housing assignment. Team members include correctional counselors, case managers, and a team leader whose offices are usually located within the unit. Positive professional relationships are supported by the daily interaction between staff and team members facilitated by this modality. Moreover, by their nature, treatment teams create a sense of cooperation and unify effort. Allowing security staff to participate in treatment/programming decisions, as well as allowing treatment staff to participate in security decisions, generates continuity for inmates and staff alike. In institutions that have adopted the unit team modality, mental health professionals can function either as official team members or as consultants to the team. Mental health professionals can offer insight toward the management of special needs inmates and share knowledge regarding the behavioral sequelae of various mental illnesses.

Discharge Planning. Case management plays an integral role in guiding the daily lives of inmates and assisting with discharge planning. Although the great majority of mentally ill offenders need case management (Lamb & Weinberger, 1998), even mentally fit offenders can benefit from assistance and outreach services. Case managers are often the primary mechanism of communication between inmates and other staff as well as between inmates and the community (Carlson, 1999a). Continuity of care is critical to appropriate mental health service, and mental health professionals can—and should—work to assist case management staff toward the development of service plans. In the absence of appropriate post-release services, even the most impressive correctional mental health care program will be fruitless (Steadman, Morris, & Dennis, 1995).

Assertive case management programs, such as intensive case management and assertive community treatment teams, can serve to derail the unfortunate but common cycle of release and reincarceration experienced by many mentally ill offenders (Dvoskin & Steadman, 1994; Lamb & Weinberger, 1998). Case management after release may ultimately lower the likelihood of recidivism in the mentally ill offender population (Ventura, Cassel, Jacoby, & Huang, 1998).

Detail/Work Supervisors

Tension in the workplace can be problematic for individuals regardless of occupation or status. However, because of the uniqueness of the correctional setting, workplace stressors extend far beyond routine employment concerns. This applies to everyone who works in a prison, including staff, volunteers, and inmate workers alike. Although many jurisdictions do not compensate inmates for their work, most facilities are dependent on inmate labor. Regardless, correctional staff and inmates must work together to maintain day-to-day functioning of the facility. A line staff member within a correctional setting has a unique role as the direct or indirect supervisor of involuntary laborers, while at the same time responding to his or her own chain of command within the correctional hierarchy (Phillips & McConnell, 1996). The balance of cooperative effort necessary to maintain an inmate/staff labor force is delicate, and additional or unnecessary pressure at work is likely to have deleterious consequences for all.

Mental health professionals should be available for, and amenable to, regular collaboration with inmate work supervisors. Consultation with work supervisors, particularly with respect to mentally ill inmates, will go a long way toward defusing potential conflict. A work environment with minimal unnecessary pressure will inevitably improve rapport between inmates and staff. For example, everyone benefits if a detail supervisor has general information about mental illness and knows how to incorporate appropriate communication strategies into his or her interaction with inmates. When officers are trained, supported, and reinforced for therapeutic behavior, they are a tremendous asset to the inmates and the institution as a whole. For example, rather than refusing to take on an inmate worker with limited ability, a yard supervisor may create a position for a cognitively impaired inmate consistent with his or her functional capacity. This not only assists the institution but also can create an invaluable sense of self-worth and accomplishment for the inmate.

Disciplinary Proceedings

Every correctional system maintains formal policy dedicated to the secure and orderly management of inmates (Flanagan, 1998). Inmates who fail to abide by institutional rules and regulations will ultimately face some form of disciplinary action within the facility. However, the procedures by which inmates are served disciplinary reports (sometimes referred to as "write-ups" or "tickets"), appeal charges, and receive punishment vary significantly across correctional systems. In general, inmates who break rules are written up at the discretion of security staff. On receipt of a disciplinary report, the inmate will face some sort of in-house court or disciplinary panel. The disposition may include withdrawal of privileges (e.g., commissary, recreation), change in housing or custody status (e.g., movement to a higher custody status), or loss of "good time" toward early release.

Mental health involvement in disciplinary proceedings can be formal and mandated by institutional policy or informal and based on case-specific consultation. One example of a formal system involves the routine review of disciplinary reports received by inmates with documented mental illness. If a mentally ill inmate receives a ticket, a member of the mental health staff will first review the charges to determine whether or not the infraction was directly related to mental illness. For example, consider that an offender with a long history of schizophrenia is charged with talking out of place. The mental health professional would be faced with determining whether or not the inmate's rule breaking was volitional. If the mental health professional concludes that the ticket received was a direct result of the inmate's mental illness (analogous to an insanity defense), he or she would have the authority to dismiss the charge.

Another method of policy-driven, formal mental health participation allows inmates to compel mental health staff to testify during disciplinary proceedings (Hafemeister, Hall, & Dvoskin, 2000). Mental health professionals could then be called by inmates to provide testimony regarding the inmate's mental status. For example, if an inmate with documented mental illness is charged with refusing to obey an order, then the inmate can call mental health staff to testify about the possible influence of his or her mental status on the behavior in question.

Although either one of the aforementioned approaches may initially appear to serve the inmate's best interest, direct mental health involvement in disciplinary proceedings can create significant tension between security and mental health staff (Cohen, 1998). Moreover, the participation of in-house mental health staff may compromise their treatment role and divert resources from direct service provision (Hafemeister et al., 2000). In the interest of minimizing these problems, administrative policy in the state of New York bars mental health professionals employed by an institution from participating as "expert witnesses" in disciplinary processes (Dvoskin, Petrila, & Stark-Reimer, 1995), although they are encouraged to provide informal mental health consultation to the disciplinary officer. This policy was upheld by the Second Circuit of the U.S. Court of Appeals (*Powell v. Coughlin,* 1991). Mental health staff are also allowed to testify as "fact witnesses" (e.g., to report an eyewitness account of an assault) as necessary (Hafemeister et al., 2000). The goal is to provide meaningful psychological input into the decision-making process without compromising the role of the institution's mental health professionals.

Finally, Cripe (1999) emphasized the importance of identifying well-defined goals prior to the establishment of institutional disciplinary policy. In keeping with that sentiment, interdepartmental involvement in disciplinary policy and decision-making processes should be grounded in ethical, reasonable, and attainable goals. The most obvious goal of mental health participation in institutional disciplinary action would be to avoid the exploitation or unnecessary punishment of mentally ill offenders. A second, less overt goal would be to minimize unnecessary tension within the institution.

These authors contend that informal involvement of mental health professionals in disciplinary proceedings is most effective. Informal mental health involvement protects the rights of inmates by allowing mitigating information into the process without compromising mental health professionals' role with either inmates or staff. Open discourse and mutual respect between security and mental health staff remains the hallmark of effective intervention on virtually every level. In an atmosphere of cooperative collaboration, members of the disciplinary panel could consult informally with mental health staff and solicit opinions or advice on a case-by-case basis. When mental health professionals engage in the unilateral dismissal of charges brought by security staff, officers are (perhaps appropriately) likely to feel as though their authority and judgment have been called into question. Therefore, in some instances, even the best-intentioned mental health professionals and the most conscientious of security staff could conceivably present conflicting opinions. Given that the goal is to reduce, rather than elicit, interdepartmental tension, it seems prudent to refrain from developing policy that would inherently result in dissent. In the long run, the respectful submission of a *recommendation,* as opposed to an authoritative determination, is far more beneficial to everyone.

Conflict Resolution

Given the day-to-day tensions and competing demands inherent in the correctional setting, it is not uncommon for intra-institutional conflicts to arise. If the mental health department has established an atmosphere of trusting collaboration, then personnel from the department(s) in conflict are more likely to seek out the assistance of mental health staff. Alternatively, upper management or supervisory staff may enlist the support and/or advice of mental health personnel toward conflict resolution within an institution. In these cases, mental health professionals can function in the role of mediator. Drawing on their expertise in human behavior and conflict response, mental health professionals can assist in the development of an appropriate and constructive discussion of the issues. Ideally, each party would first have the opportunity to express its concerns and articulate its objectives on an individual basis. Subsequently, all parties in question would meet together in the interest of achieving an appropriate resolution. Mental health professionals can be beneficial to this process because they can assist in setting the tenor of the meeting and facilitating an atmosphere conducive to cooperative effort. Ideally, the outcome will be such that neither side feels shortchanged.

When in the role of mediator, it is important for mental health professionals to be mindful that some individuals may attach undue weight to their judgments because of their perceived professional stature. At the same time, mental health professionals are not immune from becoming blinded by personal biases. Although it may be tempting to lend opinions, particularly in the area of departmental conflict resolution, mental health professionals must strive to remain objective and limit their involvement to their area of expertise.

Conflict between staff and inmates can be even more problematic than interdepartmental discord. Every problem and/or conflict is embedded in both the physical and psychological aspects of the institution that creates the context in which inmates live (Ziegenfuss, 1985). As discussed previously, a hostile institutional climate can have a substantial and deleterious effect on everyone. On an institutional level, innovative strategies aimed at increasing communication can minimize the potential for conflict. Cooke (1998) cited a Scottish program developed, in part, by a mental health professional. The program included the implementation of staff-inmate committees. These committees met at regularly scheduled intervals to facilitate communication and provide an open forum to address concerns, grievances, and mutual goals. As a result, they noted a significant reduction in violence at that facility. The Scottish program is just one example of the impact that mental health professionals can have toward improving the quality of life behind bars.

Fundamental principles of human behavior and interpersonal relations can be applied in a variety of ways toward the prevention or resolution of conflict in the correctional setting. With a little creativity and a commitment to cooperative effort, seemingly insurmountable obstacles can be overcome.

Staff Screening and Selection

The selection and retention of qualified motivated personnel is critical to any professional enterprise. However, the high level of interdependence and structure necessary to operate a correctional facility successfully magnifies the importance of effective staffing procedures. In some jurisdictions, mental health professionals routinely participate in assessments, interviews, and staff selection decisions. Depending on the setting, mental health professionals may participate in selecting candidates for positions across all disciplines of correctional service.

Whenever mental health professionals play a role in human resource decision making, they must clarify the purpose and parameters of their involvement. To this end, staffing issues should be classified as one of two very distinct tasks: screening or selection. *Screening* refers to the process by which negative characteristics or problem behaviors are identified so as to remove an inappropriate candidate from further consideration. *Selection* involves selecting a candidate based on his or her likelihood of demonstrating positive performance over time. Screening is an evaluation of the candidate's immediate status, while selection focuses on future performance (Hibler & Kurke, 1995). Behavioral science is far more adept at determining an individual's current psychological state than it is at predicting an individual's future behavior. As a result, several authors have suggested that mental health professionals are more useful in terms of screening out problem candidates than of selecting effective employees (Chandler, 1990; Parker, Meier, & Monahan, 1989).

Notwithstanding the fact that there is a significant body of research dedicated to the reliability and validity of various personnel assessment measures, results thus far have been inconclusive. In any setting, psychological assessment of potential employees remains controversial, and researchers continue to work toward the development of accurate measures of performance (Hogan, Hogan, & Roberts, 1996; Landy & Shankster, 1994; Martin & Terris, 1991; Tenopyr, 1996). Regardless of the venue, when used for preemployment purposes, psychological instruments must be reliable and valid for the specific task for which the candidate is being evaluated (Chandler, 1990; Schofield, 1993). Although courts have routinely supported law enforcement agencies' ability to use psychological assessment instruments (Schofield, 1993), the selection of measures, identification of criteria, and interpretation of results must be carried out with caution (DeCicco, 2000) to withstand judicial scrutiny (Chandler, 1990). Candidates may pursue legal action if they believe that they were screened out inappropriately or subject to discrimination (Chandler, 1990; DeCicco, 2000), and members of the public can hold law enforcement agencies accountable for negligent hiring (Hibler & Kurke, 1995).

An overwhelming majority of the related personnel research to date has focused on police and community law enforcement populations (Blau, 1994; Kornfeld, 2000; Parker et al., 1989; Sarchione, Cuttler, Muchinksy, & Nelson-Gray, 1998; Varela, Scogin, & Vipperman, 1999). Inwald (e.g., 1985, 1990) has long been at the forefront of research related to law enforcement personnel, actively advocating and researching psychological screening programs (Chandler, 1990). Suggested guidelines for preemployment screening of law enforcement officers are readily available in the literature (Blau, 1994; Chandler, 1990; Inwald, 1990). Preemployment psychological assessment may include a clinical interview, intelligence testing, personality testing, or any combination thereof. In law enforcement arenas, the Minnesota Multiphasic Personality Inventory and the Inwald Personality Inventory are among the most commonly used (Blau, 1994; Chandler, 1990; DeCicco, 2000; Parker et al., 1989) and empirically investigated personality assessment instruments (Scogin, Schumacher, Gardner, & Chaplin, 1995). The California Psychological Inventory is another frequently used preemployment screening tool for law enforcement (Hargrave & Hiatt, 1989).

Despite the plethora of research addressing the screening and selection of law enforcement officers, relatively little attention has been paid to screening and selection issues specific to correctional officer selection. In one of the few studies available, Shusman and Inwald (1991) found preemployment Inwald Personality Inventory item responses to be a valid predictor of correctional officer absence, tardiness, and disciplinary problems over time.

Given the paucity of literature examining correctional staff selection, it may be tempting to apply broader law enforcement research in correctional decision making. However, as Blau (1994) appropriately cautioned, the duties and demands of police and correctional officers are very different, and these two populations are unlikely to be adequately served by using identical criteria for staff selection. Thus mental health professionals must be mindful of the inherent limitations to generalizing law enforcement research to the correctional setting. Any interpretation and application of such data should be undertaken with caution until such time as a more substantive research base is developed.

Whether psychological assessment instruments are used for screening or selection purposes, it is imperative that they never be used as the sole determinant of a hiring decision. As is the case with a clinical evaluation, data from a variety of sources must be integrated and considered cumulatively before any conclusions are drawn. It is incumbent on mental health professionals to be proactive in ensuring that psychological test data are used only in a capacity consistent with the limitations of the instruments used.

The value of mental health input in personnel selection is further clouded by policies that require the *presence* of mental health professionals in the *absence* of valid objective testing measures. Mental health staff may be perceived as having some unique or innate ability to determine the viability of a candidate solely as a result of his or her professional background. Of course, training in behavioral science does not, in and of itself, provide anyone with the ability to make such a decision. As such, there is no indication that mental health staff are any better (or worse) than anyone else at determining the ideal candidate for a given position.

Often, the most telling means of determining a given candidate's suitability for correctional work is through actual job performance. To that end, it is very helpful for institutional policy to include, and for institutional practice to make use of, a probationary period for all new hires. The use of a probationary period provides the new employee and supervisory staff with the opportunity to assess more accurately the appropriateness of a given personnel placement.

It is also worth noting that the use of in-house mental health staff to assist in personnel selection takes these professionals away from their clinical duties and may, at times, be an undesirable allocation of limited resources. As with any department in a correctional setting, mental health staff should be available to assist on an as-needed basis or when the interviewee in question is applying for a job in their department. If mental health professionals elect or are compelled to participate in correctional staff selection, it is important that they do so only with an appreciation of their limitations.

Program Development and Evaluation

Morris et al. (1997) postulated that insufficient mental health services in jail might result simply from a lack of knowledge related to the development and implementation of services. Mental health professionals have much to offer correctional administrators regarding the development, implementation, and evaluation of institutional programs. Regardless of nature or context, preliminary research and follow-up evaluation are integral to the development of quality programming. Data must be used in decision making around the creation and implementation of a program as well as in evaluating the program's effectiveness. Information gleaned from ongoing quality assessment and quality improvement efforts should be used to guide all decisions and to improve all phases of institutional programming (e.g., assessment, referral, treatment). Data collection is critical not only to ensuring quality and effectiveness of care but also to minimizing fiscal waste. Taxpayers expect that their dollars will be used to protect the public and reduce the likelihood of future crime (Elliott, 1997). The absence of effective institutional programs significantly limits the opportunity for inmates to learn new skills and strategies for improved decision making in the community (Dvoskin & Steadman, 1989). Research is a critical component in the evaluation of correctional programs.

Mental health professionals can contribute to institutional program development from both within and outside of the correctional system. In either case, correctional researchers will inevitably confront numerous practical and methodological difficulties associated with criminal justice settings (Megargee, 1995). Nevertheless, empirical investigation is a critical endeavor that provides information necessary to improve all areas of corrections. External consultants can assist with the implementation of sound research, and program developers should be prepared to provide consultation to interested institutions (Rice & Harris, 1997).

Crisis: Prevention and Response

Nowhere is the importance of consultation and collaboration more apparent than in a correctional emergency. Administration and staff must be vigilant in their preparation for potential crises. Staff must be adequately trained, and crisis plans must be tested and continually revised to meet the changing needs of the facility (Stepp, 1999). Historically, crisis response plans and training exercises were geared primarily toward the resolution of hostage situations. More recently, however, trained negotiators are increasingly equipped to address a variety of issues (e.g., suicidal individuals, barricades, standoffs). Although crisis negotiation teams are often primarily composed of law enforcement and/or security personnel (Burke, 1995; Hammer, Van Zandt, & Rogan, 1994), mental health professionals can play an instrumental role in preparing their institutions for the most serious of crises.

Training

The most commonly cited reason for including mental health consultants in crisis response plans is to support post-incident counseling activities (Hammer et al., 1994) (see Chapter 11). However, mental health professionals also frequently serve as on-scene advisers during crisis negotiations and in the selection and training of team members. Only a small percentage of teams use mental health professionals as primary negotiators.

Although mental health professionals do not typically serve as frontline negotiators, they have much to offer in the way of teaching therapeutic communication skills. The resolution of a crisis through negotiation is the "dominant philosophy of all modern crisis management training" (Burke, 1995, p. 50) and is the "principal tool of negotiators is the ability to communicate with subjects in a way that resolves the incident with a minimum of injury or loss of life" (Slatkin, 1996, p. 3). Therefore, strong interpersonal skills are a prerequisite for any effective negotiation team. In a crisis situation, verbal skills are negotiators' most powerful weapon; therefore, it is critical that negotiators are armed with a substantive repertoire of communication techniques.

Communication in a crisis differs from routine conversation in that, during a crisis, each exchange is calculated, deliberate, purposeful, and focused (Slatkin, 1996). Active listening skills, commonly used in therapy settings, can be beneficial for crisis negotiators. Mental health professionals can share their expertise on verbal communication; basic techniques, when applied appropriately, can go a long way toward safely resolving a critical incident. Paraphrasing, reflection, clarification, primary empathy, and summarization all are useful skills for negotiators that, if used correctly, will engage offenders and help the negotiation team to gain a better understanding of the meaning behind an offender's behavior. In addition to teaching communication skills, mental health professionals should provide negotiators with an overview of expected behavioral responses to stress and trauma as well as with an introduction to the signs and symptoms of mental illness.

Consultation

Mental health professionals can also be very useful to crisis negotiation teams via on-site consultation. The Federal Bureau of Investigation classifies all critical incidents into one of two categories: hostage situations or nonhostage situations (Noesner, 1999). As Noesner (1999) explained, hostage situations involve the holding of another person or persons to use as leverage against a third party in the interest of fulfilling demands. Offenders in hostage situations are typically goal directed in their behavior. Although they will often threaten to harm their victims if their demands are not met, these offenders are aware that harming hostages will lessen the likelihood of a positive outcome. Nonhostage situations may also involve the holding of another person against his or her will. However, in these incidents, the offender does not have well-defined goals and is more likely to behave in an erratic or self-destructive manner. Here, the offender is more likely to be acting out of anger, frustration, confusion, or depression. The offender's emotional reactivity may be directed toward a third party or toward the person he or she is holding. In such cases, the offender is more likely to have had a relationship with the person being held, and there is a greater risk of harm to that individual (Noesner, 1999).

When discussing strategy and negotiation tactics, the importance of the preceding distinction is critical. A hostage situation can be conceptualized primarily as a bargaining interaction, while a nonhostage situation is more in keeping with traditional crisis intervention (Noesner, 1999). Through active consultation, mental health professionals can help to assess the dynamics of a given incident, determine the category to which the event belongs, and assist in strategic planning.

Regardless of the type of critical incident, the presence of a mental health professional is crucial when confronting a suicidal or mentally ill individual. In these cases, knowledge of mental illness and its behavioral sequelae is of utmost importance in the development of an appropriate intervention. Mental health professionals can advise negotiators about the symptomatology associated with the offender's diagnosis. This is important not only in terms of strategic planning but also to avoid fear and confusion on behalf of negotiators unfamiliar with mental illness.

Negotiation is a labor-intensive and time-consuming proposition. Although the passage of time affords negotiators an opportunity to develop rapport and gain the trust of an offender (Noesner, 1999), it can also wear down even the most diligent member of a crisis negotiation team. In the interest of providing a step-by-step framework for negotiators, Fagan (2000) outlined the following six step model: (a) establishing contact and opening a line of communication; (b) restoring calmness to the situation; (c) exploring precursors, motives, and demands; (d) developing a plan or negotiation strategy; (e) selling the plan to the perpetrator; and (f) preparing for surrender. Fagan's model was intended to allow negotiators to focus on one step at a time, thereby decreasing frustration and emphasizing the *process* rather than solely anticipating the end, ultimately minimizing stress and enhancing performance.

Post-incident Response

The most traditional avenue for mental health involvement in correctional crises is during the aftermath of a critical incident. Hostage taking in any context is a terrifying and traumatic event. In the correctional setting, however, a hostage incident can be especially horrific for those involved. The unique reversal of roles and shift in power can have profound implications for victims (Campbell, 1992). Officers involved in hostage incidents have described their experiences as among the most traumatic events in their lives (Kauffman, 1988).

In addition to "crisis negotiation" teams, each facility should have designated and equally well-trained "crisis response" teams to address the needs of victims and their families during and after critical events. In this venue, mental health professionals can be instrumental in the training of staff and in the provision of services. Crisis response teams are usually comprised of mental health professionals, pastoral staff, and medical personnel. However, many systems include line staff who volunteer their services in the event of a crisis. All crisis response staff should be provided with training that includes acute stress management, crisis support, the signs and symptoms of trauma, and defusing and debriefing procedures (Fagan, 1994).

In correctional crisis or hostage situations, victims' families often become secondary victims, confronted first with their own fear for the safety of their loved ones and then coping with their subsequent responses to the trauma (Campbell, 1992). Planning should include the designation of a family command center that provides loved ones with a place to gather, receive information and intelligence, and gain access to emotional support (Fagan, 1994; Noesner, 1999). The long-term ramifications of a correctional crisis are difficult to measure. Some staff may return to work immediately, while others may take extended leaves or terminate their employment entirely. Individual responses to trauma vary tremendously, and correctional administrators and mental health staff must be mindful of the diverse needs of staff and their families. There is no right way in which to recover from a traumatic event.

Mental health personnel should take an active role in all facets of crisis response. However, their involvement is especially important immediately following a traumatic incident. Debriefing sessions that include all correctional personnel involved in the incident (regardless of capacity) provide an opportunity for frank discussion of the event. These sessions also provide mental health professionals with an opportunity to educate victims about post-traumatic symptoms and coping skill development (Fagan, 1994) (see Chapter 11 for a detailed discussion of debriefing procedures).

Mental Health Professionals as Correctional Administrators

The need for correctional mental health services is growing at an unprecedented rate and is unlikely to decline in the foreseeable future. Consequently, the demand for creative programming and innovative policy continues to rise (Dvoskin & Patterson, 1998). The responsibility for providing an environment capable of managing the demands of taxpayers, inmates and their families, and correctional staff ultimately rests with the uppermost management personnel (Elliott, 1997). Those in leadership positions must constantly negotiate conflicting demands in terms of punishment versus rehabilitation and in terms of safety versus liberty while simultaneously enduring constant scrutiny from the media, lay public, and politicians (DiIulio, 1999).

Correctional administrators must have a deep understanding of human behavior and interpersonal relations. To be effective in a correctional setting, administrators must have problem-solving, communication, motivation, and conflict resolution skills—skills that are part of the training, experience, and personal makeup of many mental health professionals. However, the position requires expertise beyond that which prepares mental health professionals for clinical work. Correctional administrators must also be competent in areas including, but not limited to, managerial ability, budgeting, strategic planning, and supervision. Although some mental health professionals may make excellent correctional administrators, mental health credentials alone do not imply that one will be competent or equipped for effective correctional management.

Conclusions

The demands of a correctional institution are complex. Unnecessary tension in an inherently stressful setting can create a dangerous and volatile milieu. By virtue of their training, mental health professionals are well versed in the nuances of human behavior and interpersonal relationships. Notwithstanding their expertise, to maintain institutional equilibrium, mental health professionals must work in concert with correctional staff skilled in the technical aspects of maintaining a secure environment. To this end, by modeling and fostering open communication across disciplines and between members of this unique and stressful community, mental health professionals can play a significant role in contributing to the improvement of a correctional institution's productivity, morale, and safety.

References

American Psychiatric Association. (2000). *Psychiatric services in jails and prisons* (2nd ed.). Washington, DC: Author.

Armstrong, J. J. (1999). Causes of institutional unrest. In P. M. Carlson & J. S. Garrett (Eds.), *Prison and jail administration: Practice and theory* (pp. 361-366). Gaithersburg, MD: Aspen.

Bartollas, C. (1985). *Correctional treatment: Theory and practice.* Englewood Cliffs, NJ: Prentice Hall.

Blau, T. (1994). *Psychological services for law enforcement.* New York: John Wiley.

Boothby, J. L., & Clements, C. (2000). A national survey of correctional psychologists. *Criminal Justice and Behavior, 27,* 716-732.

Brennan, T. (1998). Classification for control in jails and prisons. In T. J. Flanagan, J. W. Marquart, & K. G. Adams (Eds.), *Incarcerating criminals: Prisons and jails in social and organizational context* (pp. 168-173). New York: Oxford University Press.

Brodsky, C. M., & Epstein, L. J. (1982). Psychiatric consultation through continuing education in correctional institutions. *Comprehensive Psychiatry, 23,* 582-589.

Burke, F. V., Jr. (1995). Lying during crisis negotiations: A costly means to expedient resolution. *Criminal Justice Ethics, 14*(1), 49-62.

Campbell, J. F. (1992). *Hostage: Terror and triumph.* Westport, CT: Greenwood.

Carlson, P. M. (1999a). Case management/Unit management. In P. M. Carslon & J. S. Garrett (Eds.), *Prison and jail administration: Practice and theory* (pp. 82-93). Gaithersburg, MD: Aspen.

Carlson, P. M. (1999b). The legacy of punishment. In P. M. Carslon & J. S. Garrett (Eds.), *Prison and jail administration: Practice and theory* (pp. 3-7). Gaithersburg, MD: Aspen.

Carlson, P. M. (1999c). The organization of the institution. In P. M. Carslon & J. S. Garrett (Eds.), *Prison and jail administration: Practice and theory* (pp. 25-31). Gaithersburg, MD: Aspen.

Chandler, J. T. (1990). *Modern police psychology: For law enforcement and human behavior professionals.* Springfield, IL: Charles C Thomas.

Cohen, F. (1998). *The mentally disordered inmate and the law.* Kingston, NJ: Civic Research Institute.

Cooke, D. J. (1998). Prison violence: A Scottish perspective. In T. J. Flanagan, J. W. Marquart, & K. G. Adams (Eds.), *Incarcerating criminals: Prisons and jails in social and organizational context* (pp. 106-117). New York: Oxford University Press.

Cooksey, M. B. (1999). Custody and security. In P. M. Carlson & J. S. Garrett (Eds.), *Prison and jail administration: Practice and theory* (pp. 75-81). Gaithersburg, MD: Aspen.

Cripe, C. A. (1999). Inmate disciplinary procedures. In P. M. Carlson & J. S. Garrett (Eds.), *Prison and jail administration: Practice and theory* (pp. 208-218). Gaithersburg, MD: Aspen.

DeCicco, D. A. (2000, December). Police officer candidate assessment and selection. *FBI Law Enforcement Bulletin*, pp. 1-8.

DiIulio, J. J., Jr. (1999). Leadership and innovation in correctional institutions: New challenges for barbed-wire bureaucrats and entrepreneurs. In P. M. Carlson & J. S. Garrett (Eds.), *Prison and jail administration: Practice and theory* (pp. 32-40). Gaithersburg, MD: Aspen.

Dvoskin, J. A. (1994). The structure of prison mental health services. In R. Rosner (Ed.), *Principals and practice of forensic psychiatry*. New York: Chapman & Hall.

Dvoskin, J. A., & Patterson, R. F. (1998). Administration of treatment programs for offenders with mental disorders. In R. M. Wettstein (Ed.), *Treatment of offenders with mental disorders* (pp. 1-43). New York: Guilford.

Dvoskin, J. A., Petrila, J., & Stark-Reimer, S. (1995). *Powell v. Coughlin* and the application of the professional judgement rule to prison mental health [case note]. *Mental and Physical Disability Law Reporter, 19*(1), 108-114.

Dvoskin, J. A., Spiers, E. M., Metzner, J., & Pitt, S. E. (in press). The structure of correctional mental health services. In R. Rosner & R. B. Harmon (Eds.), *Principles and practice of forensic psychiatry* (2nd ed.). London: Arnold.

Dvoskin, J. A., & Steadman, H. J. (1989). Chronically mentally ill inmates: The wrong concept for the right services. *International Journal of Law and Psychiatry, 12*, 203-210.

Dvoskin, J. A., & Steadman, H. J. (1994). Using intensive case management to reduce violence by mentally ill persons in the community. *Hospital and Community Psychiatry, 45*, 679-684.

Elliott, R. L. (1997). Evaluating the quality of correctional mental health services: An approach to surveying a correctional mental health system. *Behavioral Sciences and the Law, 15*, 427-438.

Fagan, T. J. (1994). Helping hostages and their families through critical incident response. *Corrections Today, 56*(4), 78-84.

Fagan, T. J. (2000). Negotiating by the numbers. *Corrections Today, 62*(2), 132-136.

Ferrell, W., Morgan, R. D., & Winterowd, C. L. (2000). Job satisfaction of mental health professionals providing group therapy in state correctional facilities. *International Journal of Offender Therapy and Comparative Criminology, 44*, 232-241.

Flanagan, T. J. (1998). Discipline. In T. J. Flanagan, J. W. Marquart, & K. G. Adams (Eds.), *Incarcerating criminals: Prisons and jails in social and organizational context* (pp. 214-219). New York: Oxford University Press.

Gottfredson, M. R., & Gottfredson, D. M. (1988). *Decision-making in criminal justice: Toward the rational exercise of discretion* (2nd ed.). New York: Plenum.

Hafemeister, T. L., Hall, S. R., & Dvoskin, J. A. (2000). Administrative concerns associated with the care of adult offenders with mental illness within correctional settings. In J. B. Ashford, B. D. Sales, & W. Reid (Eds.), *Treating adult and juvenile offenders with special needs* (pp. 419-444). Washington, DC: American Psychological Association.

Hammer, M. R., Van Zandt, C. R., & Rogan, R. C. (1994, March). Crisis/Hostage negotiation team profile. *The FBI Law Enforcement Bulletin*, pp. 8-12.

Hargrave, G. E., & Hiatt, D. (1989). Use of the California Psychological Inventory in law enforcement officer selection. *Journal of Personality Assessment, 53*, 267-277.

Hibler, N. S., & Kurke, M. I. (1995). Ensuring personal reliability through selection and training. In M. I. Kurke & E. M. Scrivner (Eds.), *Police psychology into the 21st century* (pp. 57-91). Hillsdale, NJ: Lawrence Erlbaum.

Hogan, R., Hogan, J., & Roberts, B. W. (1996). Personality measurement and employment decisions. *American Psychologist, 51*, 469-477.

Hunt, G., Riegel, S., Morales, T., & Waldorf, D. (1998). Changes in prison culture: Prison gangs and the case of the "Pepsi generation." In T. J. Flanagan, J. W. Marquart, &

K. G. Adams (Eds.), *Incarcerating criminals: Prisons and jails in social and organizational context* (pp. 118-127). New York: Oxford University Press.

Inwald, R. (1985). Administrative, legal, and ethical practices in the psychological testing of law enforcement officers. *Journal of Criminal Justice, 13,* 367-372.

Inwald, R. (1990). The Hilson Research model for screening public safety applicants. In P. Keller & S. Heyman (Eds.), *Innovations and clinical practice: A sourcebook* (Vol. 9, pp. 361-388). Sarasota, FL: Professional Resource Exchange.

Kauffman, K. (1988). *Prison officers and their world.* Cambridge, MA: Harvard University Press.

Kornfeld, A. (2000). Harris-Lingoes MMPI-2 Pd subscales and the assessment of law enforcement candidates. *Psychological Reports, 86,* 339-343.

Lamb, H. R., & Weinberger, L. E. (1998). Persons with severe mental illness in jails and prisons: A review. *Psychiatric Services, 49,* 483-492.

Landy, F. J., & Shankster, L. J. (1994). Personnel selection and placement. *Annual Review of Psychology, 45,* 261-297.

Martin, S. L., & Terris, W. (1991). Predicting infrequent behavior: Clarifying the impact on false-positive rates. *Journal of Applied Psychology, 76,* 484 487.

McGee, R. A., Warner, G., & Harlow, N. (1998). In T. J. Flanagan, J. W. Marquart, & K. G. Adams (Eds.), *Incarcerating criminals: Prisons and jails in social and organizational context* (pp. 99-106). New York: Oxford University Press.

Megargee, E. I. (1995). Assessment research in correctional settings: Methodological issues and practical problems. *Psychological Assessment, 7,* 359-366.

Metzner, J. L., Cohen, F., Grossman, L. S., & Wettstein, R. M. (1998). Treatment in jails and prisons. In R. M. Wettstein (Ed.), *Treatment of offenders with mental disorders* (pp. 211-264). New York: Guilford.

Morris, S. M., Steadman, H. J., & Veysey, B. M. (1997). Mental health services in United States jails: A survey of innovative practices. *Criminal Justice and Behavior, 24,* 3-19.

Noesner, G. W. (1999, January). Negotiation concepts for commanders. *FBI Law Enforcement Bulletin,* pp. 6-15.

Parker, L. C., Meier, R. D., & Monahan, L. H. (1989). *Interpersonal psychology for criminal justice* (2nd ed.). St. Paul, MN: West.

Phillips, R. L., & McConnell, C. R. (1996). *The effective corrections manager: Maximizing staff performance in demanding times.* Gaithersburg, MD: Aspen.

Powell v. Coughlin, 953 F. 2nd 744 (2nd Cir. 1991).

Rice, M. E., & Harris, G. T. (1997). The treatment of mentally disordered offenders. *Psychology, Public Policy, and Law, 3*(1), 126-183.

Roskes, E., & Feldman, R. (1999). A collaborative community-based treatment program for offenders with mental illness. *Psychiatric Services, 50,* 1614-1619.

Sarchione, C. D., Cuttler, M. J., Muchinsky, P. M., & Nelson-Gray, R.O. (1998). Prediction of dysfunctional job behaviors among law enforcement officers. *Journal of Applied Psychology, 83,* 904-912.

Schofield, D. L. (1993, November). Hiring standards: Ensuring fitness for duty. *FBI Law Enforcement Bulletin,* pp. 27-33.

Scogin, F., Schumacher, J., Gardner, J., & Chaplin, W. (1995). Predictive validity of psychological testing in law enforcement settings. *Professional Psychology: Research and Practice, 26*(1), 68-78.

Shusman, E., & Inwald, R. E. (1991). Predictive validity of the Inwald Personality Inventory. *Criminal Justice and Behavior, 18,* 419-429.

Slatkin, A. (1996, May). Therapeutic communication. *FBI Law Enforcement Bulletin,* pp. 1-5.

Steadman, H., Morris, S. M., & Dennis, D. L. (1995). The diversion of mentally ill persons from jails to community-based services: A profile of programs. *American Journal of Public Health, 85,* 1630-1635.

Stepp, E. A. (1999). Preparing for chaos: Emergency management. In P. M. Carlson & J. S. Garrett (Eds.), *Prison and jail administration: Practice and theory* (pp. 367-378). Gaithersburg, MD: Aspen.

Tenopyr, M. L. (1996). The complex interaction between measurement and national employment policy. *Psychology, Public Policy, & Law, 2,* 348-362.

U.S. Department of Justice. (2000a). *Prison and jail inmates at midyear 1999* (NCJ-181643). Washington, DC: U.S. Department of Justice, Bureau of Justice Statistics.

U.S. Department of Justice. (2000b). *Prisoners in 1999* (NCJ-183476). Washington, DC: U.S. Department of Justice, Bureau of Justice Statistics.

Useem, B., Graham-Camp, C., & Camp, G. M. (1996). *Resolution of prison riots: Strategies and policies.* New York: Oxford University Press.

Varela, J. G., Scogin, F. R., & Vipperman, R. K. (1999). Development and preliminary validation of a semi-structured interview for the screening of law enforcement candidates. *Behavioral Sciences and the Law, 17,* 467-481.

Ventura, L. A., Cassel, C. A., Jacoby, J. E., & Huang, B. (1998). Case management and recidivism of mentally ill persons released from jail. *Psychiatric Services, 49,* 1330-1337.

Veysey, B. M., Steadman, H. J., Morrissey, J. P., & Johnsen, M. (1997). In search of the missing linkages: Continuity of care in U.S. jails. *Behavioral Sciences and the Law, 15,* 383-397.

Ziegenfuss, J. T., Jr. (1985). *Behavioral scientists in courts and corrections.* New York: Van Nostrand Reinhold.

CHAPTER 14

Research-Based Practice in Corrections: A Selective Review

Carl B. Clements and Alix M. McLearen

This chapter highlights examples of recent behavioral science research that could inform professional work in corrections. It also identifies barriers to effective practice and offers suggestions for surmounting them. Because the preceding chapters have documented developments in many of the major subfields of assessment and intervention, this chapter does not repeat those details. Its goal is rather to suggest how the research context and mission has been, and can be, the basis for advancement. Although it seems self-evident that practice *should* be informed by research, a number of observers have noted recurring barriers both to conducting research (Megargee, 1974) and to implementing programs and practices as they were designed and intended (Hollin, 1995; Quay, 1977).

This chapter reviews the underlying rationales for a variety of correctional research questions and inquiries. It summarizes the offender assessment and treatment intervention literature and makes special note of the value of theory-derived models and the importance of treatment integrity. The chapter also reviews current issues in assessment and intervention with individuals exhibiting psychopathic traits and those who may exaggerate psychological or medical symptoms. Finally, the chapter offers some suggestions about the constraints faced by clinical

AUTHORS' NOTE: The authors are grateful to Allyson Bennett for assistance in identifying research literature pertinent to the topics reviewed in this chapter.

professionals in carrying out research and in implementing those practices for which good evidence exists. It also notes areas that deserve additional attention, for example, female offenders.

Research Frameworks

It may be useful to categorize correctional research in terms of familiar psychological models of behavior as well as various points of focus, from individual to policy level. These differ in purpose, yet each requires an explicit commitment to objectively assessing or evaluating some aspect of offenders and the sanctions and interventions imposed on or offered to them. This chapter limits discussion to efforts that directly involve the goal of understanding and changing criminal behavior (classically, "rehabilitation") and does not review broad strategies such as prevention and the impact of policies based on other traditional justice goals (e.g., deterrence, retribution, incapacitation).

The Person-Centered Perspective: Offender Characteristics

Research addressing person-centered issues seeks to determine offender characteristics and traits, risk and need profiles, psychopathology, differential relapse rates, and the like. Such surveys and related approaches to understanding offenders emphasize "individual differences." Presumably, the more that is known about this target population, the more correctional professionals are able to proceed rationally. A substantial body of literature represents this offender-trait orientation, which asks questions such as the following. Who are these offenders? What are they like? What is their risk level? Are there distinct subgroups within the offender population? How do they respond differentially to the corrections experience? Which delinquents get transferred to adult courts and prisons? What is the recidivism rate for sex offenders?

This focus is a parallel search for both common elements and distinguishing characteristics. Within this tradition, it is becoming increasingly clear, for example, that many offenders have a cluster of attitudes, cognitions, and associates that put them at risk for reoffending (Andrews & Bonta, 1998). Another compelling example is the accumulating evidence that individuals exhibiting high levels of psychopathy present a continuing risk for recidivism, especially violent recidivism (Hare, 1996b). Another promising line of inquiry is how offenders cope with and respond to imprisonment (Zamble & Porporino, 1988). Within the person-centered perspective, research might also focus on the assessment of so-called malingering (e.g., Haskett, 1995; Walters, White, & Green, 1988).

All of these inquiries could inform practitioners as they establish intervention goals and treatment plans or arrange correctional environments that are responsive to recognizable, validly assessed offender profiles. Somewhat less obvious is periodic research aimed at understanding the characteristics and work of correctional employees. Who are these individuals, what do they do, and how satisfied are they with their work (Boothby & Clements, 2000; Finn, 1998; Schaufeli & Peeters, 2000)? Regardless of the target group being examined, such information can carry practitioners only so far in seating professional work in a research-derived knowledge base. It should be credited as progress, however, that researchers have moved well beyond some early assumptions that all offenders (or all correctional officers) are cut from the same cloth.

The Situation-Centered Perspective: Policies and Programs

In addition to addressing offender traits and deficits, it is also useful to consider situational factors that are associated with criminal behavior, prison misconduct, and recidivism—or, conversely, that encourage "mature coping" (Johnson, 1996; Soderstrom, Castellano, & Figaro, 2001). Although it is tempting to assign these outcomes exclusively to offender traits, perhaps repeating the well-known fundamental attribution error (Krull & Erickson, 1995), a closer analysis usually identifies situational influences as part of an overall behavior-in-context model (e.g., Zamble & Quinsey, 1997). Research has demonstrated, for example, that prison environments often can create their own kind of psychological maladjustment. Overcrowding, the presence of predatory aggressive offenders, and other prison stressors may lead some to seek protection, engage in self-injurious or suicidal behavior, or react aggressively. The correctional research mission includes examining these factors as well as evaluating practices such as isolating and confining offenders for long periods and the impact (e.g., potential stress reduction) of opportunities for meaningful work and training activities and access to mental health staff. This research tradition considers the entire spectrum of situational and environmental circumstances that shape offenders; it also underlies many policies with which society responds. Studies that evaluate or compare treatments (e.g., therapeutic communities, incarceration vs. alternative sanctions, cognitive-behavioral interventions vs. boot camp, intensive aftercare vs. none) are representative members of this focus. The situational focus asks the following questions. What works? Did the program succeed? How do policies compare? What are the nature and impact of the correctional experience? What external factors promote success?

The "what works" literature in corrections has a checkered legacy. Historically, public officials (and the public) have rarely called for objective examination of correctional strategies. Policies are more often announced than dispassionately derived. Punishment, as a public goal, seems to move under its own weight rather than being subjected to analysis. Even when evaluations are undertaken by interested staff or consulting researchers, other problems often emerge. For example, the "it" in "Does *it* work?" has often been so vaguely specified as to be nonreplicable. Furthermore, the treatment integrity or fidelity of many intervention schemes has been suspect because the actual implementation barely resembled the intended intervention (if, in fact, the intervention or policy was clearly articulated) (Hollin, 1995; Quay, 1977). Thus, no claims about success, one way or another, could be made. Interestingly, even when good evidence has been marshaled to discredit a particular practice (e.g., boot camps [MacKenzie, 1994]), political and "commonsense" arguments seem to hold sway over demonstrated lack of efficacy (Gendreau, Goggin, Cullen, & Paparozzi, in press).

Another potential weakness of the situation-centered research perspective is the seductive assumption that if "X" works (or does not work), then it succeeds (or fails) in some kind of universal fashion. This proposition—a "one-size-fits-all" model for correctional intervention—directly conflicts with the accumulating evidence that offenders represent multiple patterns of traits and needs. Nevertheless, careful attention needs to be paid to the developing literature, particularly meta-analyses that have begun to identify common ingredients of programs that are most consistently successful in changing offender behavior (e.g., Gendreau & Goggin, 1997; Lösel, 1995).

The Interactionist Perspective: Tailored Selected Interventions

Both trait- and situation-centered research foci provide invaluable sources of information and insight. These traditions must continue, but they do not answer all questions. A third model, the interactionist perspective, demands that consideration be given not just to the *who* (the offender) and *what* (some policy or intervention) questions but also to the *what works for which offenders* question. Offender assessment at any juncture, for example, is most meaningful when it is tied to a planning process that leads to differential intervention. Likewise, accumulating evidence suggests that treatment effectiveness is enhanced when targeted at "criminogenic" needs and when correctly matched to individuals at the appropriate risk and responsivity (readiness) levels (Andrews & Bonta, 1998).

The interactionist perspective also is consistent with contemporary theory about multiple causation of behavior. Most theorists assume that traits and vulnerabilities and coping skills interact with environmental risk factors to produce a range of adaptive and maladaptive responses. In the prison setting, it is tempting to focus purely on global trait-based risks (and to classify many of these as unchangeable) rather than to look at the complex pattern of traits, needs, thinking, and coping styles as well as the situational contexts that might promote adaptive learning and behavior change.

In the sections that follow, comments are presented on several research and practice trends that fit into these three broad frameworks: person focused, environment focused, and interactionist focused. Of note, the following sections do not focus primarily on mentally disordered offenders (see Chapter 6 for a more detailed discussion of this topic). Instead, these sections address a broader range of topics and questions faced by correctional systems. Psychologists and other mental health professionals have much to offer in the mental health context, but they also have made notable contributions to the general correctional enterprise.

Research in Offender
Assessment and Classification

Psychological assessment and offender classification represent a major component of correctional mental health practice (Boothby & Clements, 2000; Clements, 1996). The goals of assessment are multilayered, but the underlying theme should be to reliably document important individual differences that serve as a basis for differential interventions. Interestingly, this scope could include the identification of offenders for whom a given treatment might be of no benefit or even be counterproductive. Assessment occupies, on average, nearly 20% of correctional psychologists' time (Boothby & Clements, 2000). It is a concern, however, that some assessment practices do not go beyond the "routine" required for intake. Even in this context, assessments should be tied to clear objectives and developed from a stated conceptual framework or research base. Conversely, it also often seems that contemporary assessment tools and concepts are more sophisticated than the blunt instruments of current prison policy. The "race to incarcerate" (Mauer, 1999), particularly in the United States, reveals little patience for or interest in the nuances that distinguish offenders on a multitude of risks, needs, and related factors. Such negative systemic messages may defeat the goal of a dynamic assessment program. However, if for no other reason than to identify the increasing proportion of mentally ill offenders—now estimated to be approaching 20% (Ditton, 1999; Kupers, 1999)—support for such activity seems fully warranted.

A full-service assessment practice with offenders should include, but need not focus exclusively on, mental disorder. This clinical domain is an important niche; however, for the majority of offenders, many clinical instruments and concepts of pathology do not address the factors relevant to correctional decision making. Traditional tools have been notoriously ineffective, for example, in predicting risk (Monahan, 1984). Furthermore, for correctional purposes, it is not sufficient that an instrument has been found valid in some other context; rather, it must be validated for a particular set of clients, questions, and settings. Fortunately, some well-known instruments have been adapted for offender populations, resulting in specific norms and identifying important behavioral correlates (e.g., Minnesota Multiphasic Personality Inventory-2 [MMPI-2] [Megargee, 1994]). More promising still are instruments designed specifically for the correctional questions or decisions at hand. (The reader may recognize a parallel to forensic assessment in which the specific psycholegal questions [e.g., competency, mental state, malingering] are addressed with tailored validated instruments. Instead of the MMPI, the Rorschach, and drawings, for example, the forensic assessment lineup is more likely to consist of tools such as the MacArthur Competency Assessment Tool [Hoge et al., 1997], the Rogers Criminal Responsibility Assessment Scales [Rogers, 1984], and the Structured Interview of Reported Symptoms [SIRS (Rogers, Bagby, & Dickens, 1992)].)

During the past decade, psychological science has made strides in connecting assessments to outcomes within the context of offender risks and needs. In general, classification practices have become increasingly more objective and attentive to critical offender characteristics (Clements, 1996). New instruments have evolved with a sufficient research basis to credibly aid the correctional decision maker. Recent promising tools include the Levels of Service Inventory–Revised (LSI-R) (Andrews & Bonta, 1995) and the Psychopathy Checklist–Revised (PCL-R) (Hare, 1991), both of which have a decade or more of developmental research behind them—based largely in Canada. The development of these instruments as well as others noted subsequently has been no small undertaking. As Megargee (1995) pointed out, correctional assessment researchers can expect to encounter significant obstacles in areas such as data collection, funding, and institutional approval. Parenthetically, it would appear that the collaborations and partnerships forged by Canadian justice institutions and university-based researchers have been productive, in part, because they have successfully reduced such obstacles.

Risk Assessment

Debate continues about whether violence or a similar undesirable outcome (e.g., recidivism) is better predicted by personality traits or by evocative or coercive environments or circumstances. Current research argues for combining traits, criminal history, needs, and context factors. For example, in their meta-analytic review of prison misconduct prediction studies, Gendreau, Goggin, and Law (1997) found clusters reflecting antisocial attitudes and criminal history as well as institutional factors. Most studies (including Gendreau et al., 1997) also indicate that so-called "clinical judgment" approaches to prediction are usually inferior to more objective, mainly actuarial methods, including structured interview tools. The current authors' brief review of the psychopathy literature later in the chapter indicates the mounting efficacy for that construct and the predictive value of the assessment tools developed and researched by Hare and his colleagues. Likewise, the LSI-R (Andrews & Bonta, 1995) has enjoyed cumulative research support as a means of assessing the critical components of dynamic risk factors and criminogenic needs. Both of these instruments draw heavily on well-grounded theoretical and conceptual models. Currently, U.S. correctional psychologists report infrequent use of these promising instruments (Boothby & Clements, 2000).

Assessment for Treatment

In addition to risk, offenders' behavior patterns may be conceptualized as reflecting diverse "needs." These also have predictive value for the important concerns of institutional or community adjustment and recidivism. One of the authors pointed out elsewhere (Clements, 1986) that offender needs vary from minimal to severe, from acute to chronic, and from isolated to pervasive. Identifying such needs—objectively, systematically, and reliably—can become the basis for an informed intervention response or regime. To these distinctions, Andrews and Bonta (1998) made the compelling case for attending primarily to "criminogenic" needs—those most directly associated with criminal conduct.

To apply this model or comparable models effectively, one attends not simply to the aggregate correlations (offenders as a group) but also to individual assessments. Relying on the former, therapists might provide *all* offenders with interventions aimed at their cognitive distortions; relying on the latter, therapists might provide only those who reveal a pattern of such distortions with interventions. The normative database from assessment tools reveals frequently occurring offender characteristics and provides important theory and context, but individualized assessment remains critical.

Research on the importance of offender attitudes, values, beliefs, and thinking styles supports the utility of assessing these constructs. In addition to the LSI-R noted earlier, several focused instruments appear to be promising. These include the Criminal Sentiments Scale–Modified (CSS-M) (Simourd, 1997), a 41-item self-report inventory that assesses respect for law and justice, justifications for law violation, and identification with and beliefs about law violation. Studies have found significant relations between the CSS-M and disciplinary problems and recidivism (Simourd & van de Ven, 1999). Another example is Walters's (1990) continuing research on the "lifestyle" aspects of criminal behavior patterns. The Psychological Inventory of Criminal Thinking Styles (Walters, 1995) addresses cognitive components adopted by many offenders that appear to promote and justify law violation. Although both constructs—"criminal sentiments" and "lifestyle thinking"—are envisioned as risk factors, interventions designed to address these characteristics are the next logical step (e.g., Walters, 1999). Finally, another recently reported "thinking style" assessment tool is Simourd and Mamuza's (2000) Hostile Interpretations Questionnaire (HIQ). Their research draws on theory about how attributions influence one's response to interpersonal stimuli and from the well-demonstrated relations between hostile attribution bias and aggression in children (e.g., Dodge, 1980), delinquents (Dodge, Price, Bachorowski, & Newman, 1990), and adult offenders (Copello & Tata, 1990). The HIQ appears to identify learned attitudinal patterns that both predict negative hostile behaviors and can be targeted for behavioral change.

Offenders' ability to cope with imprisonment may also affect their adjustment both within institutions and on release. Zamble and Porporino (1988), in a pioneering longitudinal study, addressed the number and kinds of problems inmates experience and their coping strategies. They found that the Prison Problems Scale (Negy, 1995) was the strongest of several measures in predicting emotional maladjustment. Actual measures of coping styles have ranged from Zamble and Porporino's (1988) structured interview to inventories such as the eight-component Ways of Coping scale reported by Cooper and Livingston (1991), the Coping Strategy Indicator (Amirkhan, 1990, cited in Soderstrom et al., 2001), and the COPE, a 15-component measure of strategies used by Negy, Woods, and Carlson (1997). These studies represent advances in understanding how coping strategies influence offender adjustment and are further evidence of the importance of dynamic variables as targets for assessment and change.

Other interesting, highly focused assessment practices are also reported in the literature. For example, to assess sex offender behavior patterns, Happel and Auffrey (1995) developed a review panel interview to reduce the typically distorted and minimized information one expects from offenders. Like many local instruments, replication in other settings would be important. The widely used Abel Assessment for Sexual Interest (Abel, Huffman, Warberg, & Holland, 1998), in contrast, offers a large normative database. Abel et al.'s diagnostic profile is based on something other than (and often contradicts) offenders' verbal reports and instead directly assesses interest in sexual material presented via photo slides.

Finally, the recognized scarcity of treatment resources—reflected in shrinking staff ratios (Boothby & Clements, 2000)—makes careful allocation of intervention efforts particularly important. Focused tailored treatments, prescribed on the basis of high-quality assessment, hold promise. One feature of the current national trend in psychology toward empirically validated treatments (Chambless & Task Force on Psychological Interventions, 1996, 1998; Nathan & Gorman, 1998) is identifying the symptom pattern or diagnostic profile to inform treatment choice. Good treatment, when misdirected, fails as surely as does inadequate treatment. Aside from best use of scarce resources, a broader policy challenge faces interventionists. If support for a general "rehabilitation" stance is to reemerge and be sustained, then demonstrations of treatment impact must become common. Historically, opinions about the value of offender programs have vacillated widely, particularly during the past three decades—starting with an unbridled enthusiasm during the 1960s but followed by nearly two decades of the so-called *nothing works* mentality (Martinson, 1974). The current view is much more, if still guardedly, optimistic (Gendreau & Goggin, 1997). One lesson learned is that generic, all-purpose treatment efforts are likely to fail. The assessment function reveals the diverse traits and highly varied profiles exhibited by offenders; tailored treatment strategies should follow.

Treatment Outcomes Research

Fortunately, the catalog of promising intervention programs is growing, even as an era of increased punitiveness seems to have become entrenched (Haney, 1997; Mauer, 1999). This paradox is not new. Martinson's (1974) classic review launched, or at least gave credibility to, a reactive period of prison philosophy described as *nothing works*. The shortcomings of Martinson's analysis have been well documented, but the surrounding controversy stimulated a new generation of more sophisticated, better controlled studies, many with positive outcomes. Researchers now use the phrase *what works* to suggest a more targeted approach to treatment. In the *nothing works* dogma of the 1970s and 1980s, however, even Martinson's (1979) own recanting of his original negative analysis of outcome studies went unnoticed by most justice professionals and policymakers. Pessimism persisted despite reanalyses and data-based counterarguments put forth by a number of writers (Gendreau & Ross, 1979, 1987; Palmer, 1984, 1992). Similarly, McGuire and Priestly (1985) identified many programs that could not be dismissed as "bad research"—a frequent criticism—or as reflecting "poor outcomes," and Thornton (1987) found positive outcomes in nearly half of Martinson's original pool of studies (Lipton, Martinson, & Wilks, 1975). During the past two decades, the rigor of research methodology applied to correctional intervention has improved, thereby allowing firmer and more intervention-specific conclusions.

Meta-analysis and Correctional Outcomes

In the face of nearly intractable pessimism, a new age of increasingly harsh punishment (Haney & Zimbardo, 1998), and the seeming "industrialization" of the prison business (Schlosser, 1998), researchers have been able to accumulate aggregate evidence of success in reducing reoffending. The powerful statistical tool of meta-analysis allows comparison of a wide range of experimental studies and documents the general impact (average "effect size") of interventions. Perhaps more important, meta-analysis enables researchers to illuminate and extract common ingredients of those programs or interventions that seem most consistently successful (or unsuccessful). These reviews have made their way into the criminology, criminal justice, and psychology literature. In fact, by 1995, Lösel provided a major review and synthesis of 13 separate meta-analyses. Although far from definitive in answering the question of *what works,* reviews like Lösel's (1995) clearly signal that selected interventions hold promise, thus demanding the attention of correctional professionals.

Among the most consistent positive findings have been those from programs based on theoretically well-founded models and those employing cognitive-behavioral and multimodal types of treatment (Lösel, 1995). In other words, promising programs derive from models of human behavior that themselves have some recognized scientific validity and standing. In addition, the successful cognitive-behavioral approaches emphasize short-term positive consequences and are designed to alter both skills deficits and attitudinal correlates of offending (Gendreau & Goggin, 1997). Social skills training, prosocial modeling, and aggression replacement training are examples (Goldstein & Glick, 1997). Cognitive therapies aimed at a wide range of dysfunctional attitudes, beliefs, and problem-solving deficits have also shown promise (Lester & Van Voorhis, 1997), as have programs using well-validated behavioral therapies and contingency management techniques (Milan, 2001). Virtually every program model underscores the importance of transitional support into the community.

These writers, as well as others (e.g., Andrews & Bonta, 1998), also assert that programs should address multiple problems and that treatments should be intensive, be of some reasonable duration, provide transition to less secure and ultimately community settings, and provide follow-up support. As for differential effects, evidence continues to mount that interventions should be aimed at offenders who have relatively high-risk profiles, that is, those whose past criminal conduct and associated characteristics predict higher rates of recidivism (Bonta, Wallace-Capretta, & Rooney, 2000). Lower risk offenders may be unaffected or actually harmed by certain modes of treatment. As noted, offender traits and behavior patterns, as well as the correctional milieu, clearly present multiple challenges for intervention. But the growing evidence argues that even in the face of such barriers, meaningful change is possible.

A cautionary note is warranted. It is clear within the juvenile justice system that community-based, multisystemic approaches to treatment are among the most promising (e.g., Henggeler, 1998). And in general, meta-analyses regarding treatment of younger offenders reveal strong positive results for the kinds of programs just noted. It may be argued that adult offenders are more treatment resistant, although it can hardly be claimed that many actually received, as juveniles, any of the interventions now thought to be useful. Nevertheless, adult studies are somewhat less positive than their juvenile counterparts. In that context, Rice and Harris (1997) argued that innovative treatments—not just those found to be effective with youthful offenders—should be attempted. They also noted the presence, in adult prisons, of a higher proportion of offenders with psychopathic traits whose inclusion in treatment studies may distort both the process and outcomes. Nevertheless, Rice and Harris concluded that harsh punishment will continue to fail as effective social policy. In this sentiment, they join writers such as Andrews (1995), who stated, "Criminal sanctioning without the delivery of correctional treatment services does not work" (p. 42).

The Role of Theory

As the reader may recognize, importing programs and models with known efficacy outside corrections seems to have merit. This observation also reflects the growing capacity of broad psychological theories to encompass criminal behavior (e.g., Akers, 1998; Feldman, 1993; Pallone & Hennessy, 1992, 1996; Raine, 1993; Walters, 1990). The value of theory or conceptual models in building a productive applied research program has long been established (Elliott, 1980). Most writers embrace a multicausal model that, in turn, has potential for multiple points of intervention. One example in corrections is Andrews and Bonta's (1998) "personal, interpersonal, community–reinforcement" (PIC-R) perspective. Developed during the 1980s and elaborated on most recently in their 1998 book, the second edition of *The Psychology of Criminal Conduct*, this personality, cognitive, social learning model has led to a series of studies in which recidivism, prison misconduct, community adjustment, and other important outcomes are tied to specific measurable components of offender characteristics, attitudes, skills, relationships, and community support or barriers. Andrews and Bonta's (1995) 54-item LSI-R addresses these dynamic risk and need factors drawn specifically from their model. Not only does the LSI-R appear to be robust in predicting outcomes, it seems to be sensitive to changes within treatment programs. Furthermore, it can provide an intervention guide as to which deficits, attitudes, skills, and person-by-situation vulnerabilities could be targeted most productively. Obviously, no single instrument or theoretical model can account for or predict the complex phenomenon of criminal behavior. Correctional researchers gain ground, however, when a logical model or construct can be brought to life with measures that capture its components, predict adjustment, and reflect change.

Andrews and Bonta's approach is also squarely psychological and encouraging of targeted interventions. Underscoring the value of theory in organizing empirical evidence, Andrews (1995) described 16 principles of effective correctional treatment that flow from the PIC-R model. Although many writers have spotlighted the ills of the prison system, particularly in the United States (e.g., Haney & Zimbardo, 1998), and have continued to point out the social, economic, and racial disparities in the justice system, the PIC-R model addresses the crime reduction problem at a different juncture—at the individual's interaction with significant others and the community. "Treatment," then, *is* possible, even as one acknowledges the flawed system in which such efforts are embedded. The current authors would also argue that grounded intervention and assessment practices can do much to make the system more rational and, ultimately, provide more legitimate opportunities for offender change.

Other Evidence of Effective Programs

The evidence begins to converge. Not all is known about what is needed to implement effective programs, but researchers have begun to sort through the valid and promising, the partially valid and potentially promising, and those interventions (mostly of the case counseling and "get tough" varieties) that seem to have minimal or negative impact.

McGuire and Priestly (1995) provided one example of this sorting in a review that sets a treatment and research agenda for correctional practitioners. Among other points, they asserted that no one approach is guaranteed to reduce recidivism. If this seems obvious, then the need to restate it should be as well. As noted previously, high-risk offenders are the most promising targets for interventions—interventions aimed at their criminogenic needs that support or contribute to offending. Programs work best when staff and client learning styles match, when active participation is required across a breadth of offender skills and deficits, and when programs follow an established structure that can be observed and documented. Treatment or the construction of environments to increase offenders' "mature coping" may also have promise. Johnson (1996) suggested that prisons, as typically managed, are not supportive of offender reform. He argued for programs that encourage mature coping (i.e., environments that are safe and just), thus minimizing defensive vigilance, and programs that provide for and encourage personal efficacy, avoidance of deception, and learning of empathy. How to engineer such programs and measure the "maturing" of offenders remains a challenge, although a recent study by Soderstrom et al. (2001) identified several psychometric instruments that seem promising as intermediate in-program measures.

It has also been pointed out that treatment integrity is an important precondition of program success (Hollin, 1995; Lösel, 1995; Quay, 1987). There is a critical need to deliver a given program with a high level of fidelity, that is, for well-trained and well-supervised therapists to follow an established protocol or set of guidelines. This principle is too often ignored or not assessed. The correctional system's ability, or willingness, to rigorously implement such programs remains uncertain. Providing resources for staff training, appropriate treatment assignments, and the critical strategies of monitoring, program evaluation, and dissemination is both expensive and politically unpopular. The current authors would also argue that knowledge advancement would flourish if correctional research and evaluation branches were established within each jurisdiction. As evidence of effective interventions becomes more widely known, the necessary resources may follow. Given the United States' world-leading incarceration rates, the financial costs alone may encourage renewed attention to the promise of correctional treatment services.

Research on Special Populations and Issues

Good evidence exists on which to base many assessment and intervention practices in correctional settings. However, special attention has been directed to selected groups and topics that pose unique challenges to current models of practice. These are briefly reviewed in what follows.

Psychopathic Traits as a Special Risk/Need Factor

As noted by Rice and Harris (1997), some offenders may be unresponsive to psychological treatment. For example, within the group of offenders diagnosed as antisocial personality disordered, the criminal activity of an increasingly well-documented subgroup appears to be particularly persistent. Designated as psychopaths, these extremely challenging individuals are estimated to comprise between 15% and 25% of incarcerated law violators, and they present a continuing risk for recidivism, especially violent recidivism (Hare, 1996b). They not only have the impulsive lifestyle characteristic of the antisocial personality, but they also lack the capacity for remorse, empathy, or emotional depth. Their interpersonal style is described as manipulative, superficial, deceitful, and self-inflating. This combination of traits greatly increases the probability of violent reoffending and of institutional misconduct (Hare, 1996b; Hart & Hare, 1997). Such individuals appear to be less amenable to programs promoting positive behavior change, although superficially they may seem quite compliant and well motivated. Recent advances in assessment and treatment may provide a basis for designing specific programs for individuals exhibiting a high degree of these traits and, in turn, excluding them from certain other interventions. In any event, their presence in intervention studies must be documented to allow researchers to examine differential treatment effects.

Assessment of Psychopathy. Drawing on Cleckley's (1976) original conceptualization of psychopathy, and buttressed by more than 20 years of research that includes examination of collateral institutional behaviors and subsequent reoffending, Hare and his colleagues have developed the well-respected Psychopathy Checklist–Revised (Hare, 1991). The two-factor model that underlies the PCL-R has been consistently (but not always) found in offender populations, namely the impulsive antisocial lifestyle and the defining—and apparently uniquely predictive—affective and interpersonal personality features noted previously. Hare and others (e.g.,

Serin, 1996) have argued that this trait cluster—the exploitative, manipulative, low-empathy features (Factor 1)—make the so-called psychopath a greater risk than other antisocial offenders for continuing law violation and resistance to standard treatment (Hare, Hart, & Harpur, 1991). Thus, they argue, it is critical to assess this combination of traits. As noted recently by Lilienfeld (1998), the two-factor model of psychopathy (and the PCL-R) has sharpened the assessment of psychopathy and highlighted the differential correlates of the personality-based and behavior-based components of the construct. The 20-item PCL-R (Harpur, Hare, & Hakstian, 1989) has become the standard for such assessment, and scores on the PCL-R consistently predict treatment involvement and post-release adjustment (Hemphill, Hare, & Wong, 1998; Salekin, Rogers, & Sewell, 1996) over and above other demographics and risk scales. As a predictive instrument, the PCL-R also typically results in fewer decisional errors (Serin, 1996).

The PCL-R's robustness is due in part to its insistence on a thoroughgoing review of the offender's legal and social history as well as a comprehensive and focused clinical interview. Few shortcuts have been found, although a screening version (Hart, Cox, & Hare, 1995) is now available, as is a self-report version (Hare, 1996a). Clinical impressions, uncorroborated by systematic assessment, are likely to miss the mark. Other self-report assessment tools, such as the Pd subscale (Psychopathic Deviate–Scale 4) and the Antisocial Practices subscale of the MMPI-2, are relatively well suited to measuring a person's impulsive, law-violating features (Factor 2) but less accurate in assessing his or her affective interpersonal style (Factor 1).

In contrast, the recently developed Psychopathic Personality Inventory (PPI) (Lilienfeld & Andrews, 1996) was designed specifically to assess those features via self-report. This instrument, originally aimed at detecting subclinical levels of these traits, has identified eight factors, many of them similar to the personality hallmarks emphasized by Cleckley and Hare. Recent extensions to an offender population show some promise. For example, Poythress, Edens, and Lilienfeld (1998), in comparing PPI and PCL-R profiles of adult prison inmates, found significant correlations. Most notable, in contrast to other self-report measures of psychopathy, the PPI demonstrated a moderate and positive correlation with PCL-R Factor 1. In a follow-up study, these same researchers (Edens, Poythress, & Lilienfeld, 1999) found that both the PPI and the PCL-R were modestly, but significantly, correlated with indexes of aggressive institutional behavior. The two scales appeared to account for common variance in aggression, further suggesting their construct similarity. These results indicate that the PPI may well be worth additional evaluation as an index of offenders' psychopathic traits.

Psychopathic Traits and Treatment. These high-risk offenders present unique challenges for intervention. According to Rice and Harris (1997), psychopathic individuals are not just more deviant than other offenders. Rather, their criminal behavior is of a different, partly biological genesis, and treatment that is effective for "ordinary" offenders might have little relevance. The needs and deficits noted earlier might not be appropriate treatment targets. Instead, Rice and Harris recommended a focus on "increas[ing] the detection of and reducing the payoff for deception, exploitation, and antisocial conduct . . . [as well as] targeting irresponsibility and impulsivity" (p. 432).

Few well-controlled studies have actually been conducted on the response of psychopathic individuals to treatment. An initial challenge is to assess the presence or degree of psychopathy (depending on whether one views the construct as a diagnostic taxon or as a trait continuum) and to specify what treatments were provided. In some studies, these omissions, plus the lack of adequate follow-up and comparison groups, have been methodologically fatal (Hart & Hare, 1997). Informative studies are available, however. For example, in the context of a voluntary therapeutic community, Ogloff, Wong, and Greenwood (1990) found that higher levels of psychopathy, based on PCL-R scores, were associated with fewer days in treatment (104 days vs. 242 days for high- vs. low-psychopathy groups). Motivation and improvement ratings were also higher for the low-psychopathy group. Recidivism rates for the high-psychopathy group were nearly double those of their low-psychopathy counterparts (Hemphill & Wong, 1991). In another complex study involving several clinical groups in treatment, Rice, Harris, and Cormier (1992) found that high-psychopathy groups, while in treatment, had significantly more behavioral problems, disciplinary infractions, and seclusion penalties for disruptions. Recidivism data from this study provide classic support for the proposition that treatment may be effective for some groups and ineffective for others. Psychopaths, whether treated or untreated, had extremely high relapse rates. In addition, the rate of violent recidivism actually increased for those in treatment. For nonpsychopaths, treatment via the therapeutic community had a positive effect. Simply aggregating the data would have revealed "no effect."

The evidence from these studies supports Rice and Harris's (1997) general position that specially designed treatment approaches are needed for offenders who exhibit high levels of psychopathy. These results also are consistent with the interactionist perspective cited earlier, namely, the need to determine *what* treatment works for *which* offenders and how to encourage treatment engagement with appropriately designed and intensely administered services. Hart and Hare (1997) suggested that group- and insight-oriented methods are inappropriate or even counterproductive. They emphasized relapse prevention integrated with intense cognitive-behavioral programs in the context of tight supervision, an emphasis on responsibility and consequences, and the promotion of prosocial ways of satisfying personal needs and wants.

In contrast to the positions taken by Hart and Hare (1997) and Rice and Harris (1997), Simourd and Hoge (2000) demonstrated that psychopathy traits, as measured by the PCL-R, are highly correlated with other risk characteristics, history, and criminogenic needs, as assessed by the previously noted LSI-R, the CSS-M, and the Pride in Delinquency scale. They argued that although psychopathic offenders are clearly at high risk for reoffense, the assessment tools used in their study are better able to specify targets for intervention. The value of the psychopathy construct, they reasoned, may be to reveal how such offenders ought to be managed and how to maximize their response to treatment. Many of the attitudinal, interpersonal, and behavioral deficits exhibited by most offenders—not just those thought to have psychopathic traits—remain appropriate targets for intervention.

Malingering: Detection and Response

Another challenging group for correctional practice are those individuals who appear to produce false or exaggerated symptoms for external gain. These patterns of response have been studied extensively in correctional settings (American Psychiatric Association, 1994; Rogers, 1997). Inherent in the definition of "malingering" is the idea that dissimulation is likely to occur in medico-legal contexts such as jails and prisons. Incarcerated offenders, limited in their personal resources and residential accessories, may view the production of psychological difficulties as a method of gaining scarce benefits. A second component of the definition relevant to correctional settings is that malingering is to be strongly suspected when a comorbid diagnosis of antisocial personality disorder has been made. Investigations into the rates of mental illness among offenders (discussed elsewhere in this book) have demonstrated that the antisocial personality disorder taxon is warranted in nearly 50% of prisoners (Teplin, 1994), emphasizing the importance of studying malingering in correctional settings.

Research Background. Malingering has been typically investigated from one of three vantage points: assessing prevalence of the behavior, discovering characteristics of so-called malingerers, or designing or improving tools used to identify persons feigning mental illness. Results of prevalence studies suggest that, although malingering occurs at lower rates in correctional settings than in civil litigation cases, it is a common phenomenon because jails and prisons offer numerous external incentives, including psychotropic medication, special/segregated housing, reduced sentences, and insanity pleas (American Psychiatric Association, 1994; Norris & May, 1998; Walters et al., 1988). Of the few pure prevalence investigations, much variation between samples has been found. Walters et al. (1988) found that 46% of inmates reporting psychological distress were exaggerating their degree of impairment, while Haskett (1995) found a much lower rate of 16% of prison inmates to be malingering. Other studies using pretrial (jail) inmates as participants have found the prevalence of malingering to range from 8% (Cornell & Hawk, 1989) to a high of 37% (Wasyliw & Grossman, 1988). Rogers's (1997) review of malingering literature indicated that this pattern of behavior occurred in 15% to 17% of cases in forensic settings.

As noted, studies of malingering have gone beyond simple assessment of prevalence to examine the qualities of offenders engaging in deception and to distinguish dissimulators from honest respondents. Clearly, a large overlap between some characteristics of malingering and psychopathy exists. In addition, it has been suggested that substance abusers are more likely to engage in the false production of medical and psychiatric symptoms (Rogers, 1997; Sierles, 1984; Wilson, 2000). Race and age may affect malingering behavior, but few studies have investigated the interaction of such demographic factors (Haskett, 1995; Sierles, 1984).

Research on malingering conducted in correctional settings has also commonly focused on the development of objective measures of assessing the pattern of behavior associated with malingering. Although beyond the scope of this chapter, instruments such as the SIRS and MMPI-2 have been validated for use in jails and prisons. Typically, one of two designs is used in the development of such measures. The simulation design involves the assignment of participants to "honest" and "malingering" response style groups, which can then be compared with groups representing true pathology. Compromised by a lack of generalizability, the simulation design is often passed over in favor of the known groups method, a design that compares the responses of persons already identified as malingering with those of honest respondents (Rogers, 1997).

Malingering and the Correctional Environment. In addition to more common avenues for examining malingering behavior, current literature has attempted to explain how the correctional environment may contribute to the malingering behavior it is desirous of preventing. The adaptational model conceptualizes malingering as a tool of survival and posits that persons are likely to malinger when placed in negative or adversarial circumstances in which they believe that exaggerating or feigning mental illness—or other subclinical symptom patterns—is likely to lead to a beneficial outcome. According to Rogers (1997), under the adaptational model, "would-be malingerers engage in a cost-benefit analysis when confronted with an assessment they perceive as indifferent, if not inimical, to their needs" (p. 8). This explanatory framework was supported in Walters's (1988) study involving post-sentence federal inmates. Results demonstrated that dissimulation was not common under neutral circumstances but was more frequent when used to attain some important object or other advantage (e.g., a preferred bunk, special housing).

A recent addition to the literature is the development of methods of malingering detection that can be used for triage and treatment planning. Given staffing and funding concerns often present in correctional environments, individuals feigning or exaggerating illness can tax an already overburdened mental health system. Haskett (1995) stated that malingering must be addressed from a treatment standpoint to preclude the heightened development of a sense of entitlement to special services already present among malingerers and to reduce recidivism and the criminal lifestyle. In other words, malingering can be addressed in treatment as a counterproductive coping strategy rather than as an exclusion criterion for intervention. To date, no intervention studies have been reported. Other profitable future research in malingering may be in the direction of creating shorter and easier methods of detection that can be used in all correctional settings. Haskett's instrument, the Tehachapi Malingering Scale, is one such scale in which the cost-benefit scenario appears to be promising.

Ethical Issues in Correctional Research

Prior to the initiation of any data collection involving correctional detainees as participants, attention must be given to the protocol involved in undertaking such endeavors. Because inmates are not in positions of power, stringent guidelines governing research practices have been developed. Designed to prevent offenders from being taken advantage of, these standards stipulate the kinds of studies that can be conducted in jails and prisons. Furthermore, attention is given to the importance of confidentiality and ensuring that potential participants are not offered disproportionately large incentives to engage in risky or damaging investigations.

In 1977, the National Commission for the Protection of Human Subjects specified three types of research conducted in correctional settings. Treatment-oriented research consists of studies designed to improve or evaluate services offered to correctional detainees. A second desirable category of research involves prisoner-oriented projects. These endeavors examine the effects of variables tied to incarceration, including adaptation to the prison environment and the effects of various types of programs. A final section of this taxonomy, convenience research, is discouraged. Studies of this type use the inmates as participants simply because they are available while providing little in the way of direct benefit to the participants. Overholser (1987) suggested engaging in a cost-benefit analysis when considering research in such settings so that research with greater probable benefits to inmate participants is allowed greater leeway in the identification of possible discomforts to participants. In addition, adherence to general American Psychological Association (1992) ethical guidelines is emphasized.

A recent revision of standards put forth by the American Association for Correctional Psychology (AACP, 2000) encourages correctional psychologists to engage in both basic and applied research while still maintaining ethical standards. Although seemingly at odds with federal regulations, AACP does not encourage convenience research but rather notes that some studies may propose to increase knowledge while not directly evaluating programs that benefit inmates. Although AACP guidelines reiterate that research should be in compliance with both American Psychological Association and federal regulations, they provide little specific guidance outside that already stated. Another provision of the code emphasizes the importance of having on-site professionals evaluate the ethicality of any potential research projects prior to commencing data collection. This statement suggests that mental health workers have knowledge of those studies that are appropriate and those that may be harmful. AACP also encourages correctional psychologists to be involved in at least one relevant research project while employed in such settings.

In preparing correctional research for institutional review board (IRB) approval, several areas require attention. As in all projects, informed consent is particularly important. Although benefits to the participating inmates should be noted, risks must also be divulged and scripted in language comprehensible by persons with limited educational backgrounds. Inmates must be assured that they will not be denied privileges or face negative consequences from staff for refusing to participate (AACP, 2000; ACA, 1990). The rationale for the study and all methodologies must also be clearly stated. In general, research in correctional settings is subject to the same standards as is other psychological research. However, given the "captive audience" status of detainees, particular care must be used in designating incentives and examining the relevance of proposed studies. Dispassionate parties, including inmate representatives, usually serve on prison-based IRBs. Correctional systems differ as to the number of subsequent reviews and approvals required. In the experience of the current authors, faculty and graduate students proposing correctional research also have to address numerous queries from university review boards. All are quite understandable and designed to protect participants. Such review and approval can facilitate subsequent review by the correctional setting. Although some see IRB policies and procedures as barriers, the required steps often result in better projects. Finally, the authors would note that program evaluation studies that become part of a jurisdiction's routine—a highly desirable state—can provide for a series of follow-up studies that do not have to be individually re-reviewed. Ironically, it is because systematic research studies are so rare in many correctional agencies that review procedures may seem awkward and burdensome.

Constraints, Recommendations, and Future Issues to Consider

Extending Professional Capacity

Given the declining staff ratios in correctional institutions, methods of providing services to inmates in a less direct fashion should be evaluated for efficacy. The evidence for group and other indirect methods is promising. Although these are treatment oriented in nature, their justification can well be argued as promoting stability, productivity, and other goals of the correctional environment.

Group Therapy. Cost effectiveness has made group approaches one of the most attractive methods in the provision of psychological services to correctional inmates. In addition to efficiently using scarce resources, group therapy provides participants with the opportunity to realize that they share common traits and hardships with other detainees (Metzner, Cohen, Grossman, & Wettstein, 1998). Groups in prisons and jails focus on a variety of issues, ranging from social skills development to understanding symptoms of various illnesses and characterological traits (Biggam & Power, 1997; Scott, 1993; Sigafoos, 1994; Wilson, 1990). Assignments to groups may be based on type of offending, nature of illness, skill clusters, or cognitive capacity of the participants. In general, groups have been perceived as fairly successful and have received positive responses from participants. However, little systematic evaluation of this modality has occurred. Jemelka, Trupin, and Chiles (1989), who commented that "much more has been written about the legal issues in providing psychiatric treatment than has been written about the treatment itself," described the literature on group approaches to addressing inmate behavior. Treatment providers themselves have rated group approaches as effective in areas such as anger management and cognitive restructuring (Morgan, Winterowd, & Ferrell, 1999). Morgan et al. (1999) urged the development of treatment manuals and systematic follow-up studies.

Stein and Brown (1991) identified several obstacles to the use of group treatment in correctional settings, including distrust of staff, limited confidentiality, and the paradox of asking inmates to talk about their feelings in an environment where such behavior can lead to victimization. On the other hand, Demuth and Bruhn (1997) noted that the "no nonsense" correctional environment encourages insight and prevents group participants from saying what therapists want to hear by allowing other inmates to act as "bullshit detector[s]" (p. 30).

As noted, group approaches cover a wide range of topics, making meta-analytic studies difficult. Furthermore, as in other areas of correctional research, groups fall prey to many of the issues preventing solid empirical research, including limited time of staff to conduct studies and inability to conform to treatment protocols because of inmate behavior or institutional requirements. Isolated studies of groups based on psychodynamic, cognitive-behavioral, and atheoretical or other (e.g., art therapy) approaches have led to positive outcomes, including symptom improvement and reduction of behavioral infractions (Demuth & Bruhn, 1997; Marshall, Bryce, Hudson, Ward, & Moth, 1996; Sigafoos, 1994; Stallone, 1993; Teasdale, 1997). Group methods, focusing on the same patterns of offender risks and needs as were highlighted earlier, would appear to be readily translated from the individual work on which many research studies have been based. Anecdotal evidence also indicates that participants may derive enjoyment or other immeasurable benefits from the group process (Murphy, 1994).

Bibliotherapy. In addition to group therapy, correctional administrators have begun to examine other time- and staff-efficient methods of service delivery. Bibliotherapy, a minimal contact treatment approach that allows individuals to use self-help materials at their own pace, has demonstrated efficacy in treating depressive symptomatology in the general population, even when compared with traditional, therapist-intensive methods (Brown & Lewinsohn, 1984; Wollersheim & Wilson, 1991). Bibliotherapy in the treatment of depression has been found to be particularly effective with older adults (Scogin, Jamison, & Davis, 1990), a growing segment of the prison population.

Application of this approach to correctional settings has only recently been undertaken, but with promising results. Domino et al. (2000) randomly assigned jail inmates to cognitive bibliotherapy or delayed treatment conditions and found that both level of psychopathology and level of hostility were reduced for individuals participating in bibliotherapy. In addition to being a cost-effective form of treating detainees, this method has the benefit of being minimally invasive.

Mental Health Professionals as Managers

Correctional psychologists and other clinical professionals find themselves frequently involved in administrative or management responsibilities. One of the current authors found that, on average, some 30% of psychologists' professional time was spent carrying out administrative duties within correctional institutions (Boothby & Clements, 2000). Is this time simply a managerial "black hole"—impenetrable to the gaze of a research perspective? The current authors think not. In fact, it has been suggested that program directors have an ethical duty to learn management principles and skills (Goodstein, 1984). Among other valuable models, the tools and skills associated with industrial or organizational psychology have much to offer (Hesketh, Rawlings, & Allen, 1996). Managerial work should not be merely the "other" stuff—tackled by "seat of the pants" methods—but rather should be as rigorous and as theory or principle driven as is any other psychological task. Although most clinically trained professionals receive little instruction or supervised experience in management, there are resources and tools available, including many excellent management texts (see Clements, 1993, for a review).

Persons in leadership roles also confront the constraints and obligations of program implementation. Establishing programs that are carried out systematically is both an organizational and a personal challenge. Hollin (1995) provided one example of translating what is known to work in corrections into the managerial tasks and pitfalls faced by program managers and implementers. Clinical managers would also do well to focus on program evaluation; this role also fits into a community/organizational framework. Although most clinicians have not been systematically trained in outcome study models, many excellent examples exist, and continuing professional education ought to be devoted to such critical activities. In many cases, collaboration with other researchers may be productive.

Commitment to Correctional Research

Where will correctional professionals find the time to engage in research that informs their practice? One survey indicates that the interest is there for many (Boothby & Clements, 2000). The previously noted successful enterprise within the Canadian system suggests four needed conditions:

- A policy-level commitment to evaluating the outcomes of correctional interventions
- An openness to collaboration and funding that supports long-term studies needed for instrument development and validation and for assessment of well-matched intervention models (this condition is consistent with Megargee's [1974] early observation about the importance of collecting high-quality data over time)
- A commitment by university researchers to justice-based, psychologically relevant studies that build on current theory
- Training of scientist-practitioners who will bring an evidence-based agenda with them to correctional settings

These conditions, although perhaps facilitated because Canada's federal system is comparatively small, have led to an enviable and productive networking of researchers and practitioners who both design instruments and programs and have access to myriad outcome measures. The United Kingdom has made a parallel commitment to outcomes research and collaboration between academics and practicing clinicians. A number of studies reviewed in this chapter (e.g., Walters, 1990) also reflect examples of sustained and productive research activity within U.S. corrections.

Implementing Best Practices and Maintaining Therapeutic Integrity

If psychologists or other correctional professionals have neither the inclination nor the time to actually *conduct* research, correctional researchers should not lose heart. There is abundant support for many assessment and intervention approaches that have not yet been widely implemented. Practitioners, if nothing else, should negotiate personal and workplace goals to allow for the study and application of the current "best practices" in the literature. Gendreau and Andrews (1996) provided a very useful template for evaluating how closely correctional programs adhere to the known treatment literature and to principles derived from the past two decades of research. This kind of template can be useful both in selecting treatments and in monitoring program adherence.

The current authors have seen that maintaining such program integrity is critical to successful interventions. Evidence indicates a stubborn tendency for programs to "drift" toward weaker and nonspecific versions. In some cases, different sites or staff may implement altered forms of the programs such that actual negative effects may result (e.g., Bassett & Blanchard, 1977; Fagan, 1990). Practitioners need to adhere to standardized treatment protocols (Wilson, 1997), whether in the form of step-by-step treatment manuals or in the form of behavior analytic guidelines (Liberman, Kopelowicz, & Young, 1994), and need to monitor offenders' program involvement and staff compliance with milieu protocols. Otherwise, those who are treated might not be "treated as intended," and their subsequent success or failure would shed no light on the worth of the intended programs. Worse, negative outcomes (due to poor implementation) might push the pendulum back in the direction of *nothing works*—a moribund state to which corrections can ill afford to return.

Research With Female Offenders

Correctional researchers have made considerable progress in identifying what works for whom in correctional settings, but only when the *whom* criterion of being male has been satisfied. Growing numbers of females are being detained in correctional facilities, and it would be presumptuous to assume that assessment strategies and intervention programs designed for and validated on male inmates could be unilaterally applied. For example, Teplin, Abram, and McClelland (1996) found that women in jail show far higher rates of severe mental illness than do male offenders. In correctional settings, there is a need to provide services to female offenders whose mental health and health problems are likely to be more widespread and diverse than those of their male counterparts (Acoca, 1998; Ditton, 1999).

Clearly, a "gender gap" exists in terms of knowledge about and resources devoted to female offenders. Not only are important risk and need factors likely to be gender divergent, but the specification of targeted treatment is needed. During the past decade, several risk and need clusters have been highlighted as particularly germane to women. These include mental health needs, depression, physical and sexual victimization (Belknap, 1996; Walker, 1994), post-traumatic stress disorder, family-based problems, education-based problems, parental responsibilities, peer influence, distorted attributions and pro-crime attitudes, patterns of drug abuse, and dysfunctional relationships (Conley, 1998) (see Chapter 7 for a more detailed discussion of these and other female offender treatment needs). Integrating assessments of the extent and severity of these gender-specific risks and needs remains a challenge. To date, the development of female norms and the applicability of current conceptualizations of criminal behavior have been relatively few in number (Negy et al., 1997; Salekin, Rogers, & Sewell, 1997; Salekin, Rogers, Ustad, & Sewell, 1998; Walters, Elliott, & Miscoll, 1998). Such research must be accelerated.

Alternatively, the search for risk and need factors may be buttressed by the identification of potential protective factors—positive personal characteristics and/or environmental supports—that may serve to buffer other risks and reduce negative outcomes. Such factors might include attachment to prosocial adult figures, commitment to work and education, prosocial peers, and self-esteem. For girls and women, indirect familial controls (e.g., emotional bonds) appear to reduce violence. Other factors, broadly grouped into categories of personal strengths and relational and external support, include empathy, internal locus of control, self-efficacy, positive gender identification, prosocial values and skills, and nondelinquent peer activities. Virtually all such protective factors could be strengthened as part of a comprehensive intervention program (Morash, Bynum, & Koons, 1998; Peters, 1998). Many of these risk, need, and protective factors can be identified through several of the instruments noted earlier. Likewise, the same principles of—and urgent need for—innovative and tailored treatment selection and program evaluation are clearly applicable.

Research in Jail Settings

Jails have been fertile ground for research on the demographics, interpersonal styles, and psychopathology rates of offenders. However, assessment and treatment protocols are typically investigated in prison settings. Although many of the same inmates held in detention facilities eventually progress to prison, others charged with minor offenses do not. Furthermore, the chaos and high population and staff turnover of jails create environmental conditions that are vastly different from those experienced in prison. The current authors assert that, like females, jail populations are underresearched and that the *who* and *what works* methodologies must be applied to these settings. In a recent study providing the basis for this call to action, McLearen, Cannon, and Clements (2001) found that service providers in jail settings were trained in a number of disciplines but that the majority felt ill equipped to deal with the dilemmas and needs of inmates they were attempting to treat. Responding practitioners also noted a desire for greater access to treatment alternatives and to empirical research to guide in the selection of rehabilitative efforts.

The need for more extensive examination of treatment options and assessment in jail settings should not diminish the strides that have already been made in this area. Given the brief length of stay for most detainees, longitudinal data collection is often difficult, and inmates may be less likely to see the benefits of participating in research. In addition, funding for such projects may be scarce, and the problems of resources and time experienced in prison settings may be felt more profoundly in jails. Even with these limitations, an extensive body of literature has developed on certain facets of jail life. Beginning with the deinstitutionalization process several decades ago, the rate of mentally ill persons in jails nationwide began to rise (Abramson, 1972; Lamb & Weinberger, 1998). Reports from administrative staff led researchers to probe exactly who was serving time in jails. Studies have consistently demonstrated that between 6% and 15% of jail detainees meet criteria for severe mental illness and that more than half are diagnosable with substance abuse disorders or personality disorders (Abram & Teplin, 1991; Lamb & Weinberger, 1998; Teplin, 1994). Furthermore, 29% of jails surveyed reported holding mentally ill persons who were not suspected of crimes (Torrey et al., 1992). Advances have been made in screening and assessing these individuals. Teplin and Swartz's (1989) Referral Decision Scale, a screening instrument designed specifically for jail settings, has demonstrated the ability to quickly identify those detainees in need of further services (Hart, Roesch, Corrado, & Cox, 1993; McLearen & Companik, 2000; Veysey, Steadman, Morrissey, Johnsen, & Beckstead, 1998).

Lacking in the jail literature are empirical evaluations of treatment programs suitable for jails of moderate size or for replication outside the original study. Carr, Hinkle, and Ingram (1991) described a jail program for substance abusers, but many jails simply do not have the time or resources to evaluate existing programs. Furthermore, although a number of agencies, task forces, and administrators have called for the establishment and evaluation of diversion programs, little research on these alternatives exists. Continuity of care must also be explored given that only one quarter of responding jails in a nationwide survey provided discharge-planning services (Morris, Steadman, & Veysey, 1997). Although initial evaluation of jail programs may be costly and time-consuming, the long-term benefits of such research are likely to make those efforts worthwhile.

Conclusions

In this chapter, the authors have maintained that, even in the face of a correctional system that is stretched beyond its limits, psychologists and other clinicians and researchers can make substantial contributions to the goal of understanding, measuring, responding to, and facilitating change, both in offenders and in the correctional agencies and systems to which they are assigned. As Brodsky (1973) pointed out many years ago, corrections encourages employees to become "system professionals," a role in which one accepts many of the underlying assumptions and routines of the U.S. justice model. Can such professional staff perform effectively without being compromised? The current authors think so, particularly if staff maintain an outcomes orientation and if they harness what has been learned through research about valid assessment methods and treatment efficacy. But as Brodsky (2000) recently lamented, support for innovation or examination of the value of a particular policy is rare. Rarer still are "system challengers" who actually question those policies.

This chapter has implied that an outcomes, research-driven orientation is, in its own way, a challenge to the status quo in corrections. Indeed, a rational empirical approach may be especially critical given the continuing escalation of incarceration as a principal sanction. If common correctional goals are identified, irrespective of whether one is a clinician, a researcher, an administrator, or a custodial staff member, then how best to reach those goals—within a given milieu—becomes an empirical question. The research summarized here provides a launching point to initiate or continue programs and strategies of promise. The spectrum of potential professional roles is wide, as reflected in this handbook. All need not conduct their own research. All need not publish. But all need to inform their work with current evidence. Ideally, we would add to that evidence whenever possible.

References

Abel, G. G., Huffman, J., Warberg, B. W., & Holland, R. (1998). Visual reaction time and plethysmography as measures of sexual interest in child molesters. *Sexual Abuse: A Journal of Research and Treatment, 10,* 317-335.

Abram, K., & Teplin, L. (1991). Co-occurring disorders among mentally ill jail detainees: Implications for public policy. *American Psychologist, 46,* 1036-1045.

Abramson, M. F. (1972). The criminalization of mentally disordered behavior: Possible side effect of a new mental health law. *Hospital and Community Psychiatry, 23*(4), 101-105.

Acoca, L. (1998). Defusing the time bomb: Understanding and meeting the growing health care needs of incarcerated women in America. *Crime & Delinquency, 44,* 49-69.

Akers, R. L. (1998). *Social learning and social structure: A general theory of crime and deviance.* Boston: Northeastern University Press.

American Association for Correctional Psychology. (2000). Standards for psychology services in jails, prisons, correctional facilities, and agencies. *Criminal Justice and Behavior, 27,* 433-494.

American Correctional Association. (1990). *Adult correctional institutions* (3rd ed.). Lanham, MD: Author.

American Psychiatric Association. (1994). *Diagnostic and statistical manual of mental disorders* (4th ed.). Washington, DC: Author.

American Psychological Association. (1992). Ethical principles of psychologists and code of conduct. *American Psychologist, 47,* 1597-1611.

Amirkhan, J. H. (1990). A factor analytically derived measure of coping: The coping strategy indicator. *Journal of Personality and Social Psychology, 59,* 1066-1074.

Andrews, D. A. (1995). The psychology of criminal conduct and effective treatment. In J. McGuire (Ed.), *What works: Reducing reoffending—Guidelines from research and practice* (pp. 35-62). Chichester, UK: Wiley.

Andrews, D. A., & Bonta, J. L. (1995). *The Level of Service Inventory–Revised.* Toronto: Multi-Health Systems.

Andrews, D. A., & Bonta, J. (1998). *The psychology of criminal conduct* (2nd ed.). Cincinnati, OH: Anderson.

Bassett, J. E., & Blanchard, E. B. (1977). The effect of the absence of close supervision on the use of response cost in a prison token economy. *Journal of Applied Behavior Analysis, 10,* 375-379.

Belknap, J. (1996). *The invisible woman: Gender, crime, and justice.* Belmont, CA: Wadsworth.

Biggam, F. H., & Power, K. G. (1997). Social support and psychological distress in a group of incarcerated young offenders. *International Journal of Offender Therapy and Comparative Criminology, 41,* 213-230.

Bonta, J., Wallace-Capretta, S., & Rooney, J. (2000). A quasi-experimental evaluation of an intensive rehabilitation supervision program. *Criminal Justice and Behavior, 27,* 312-329.

Boothby, J. L., & Clements, C. B. (2000). A national survey of correctional psychologists. *Criminal Justice and Behavior, 27,* 716-732.

Brodsky, S. L. (1973). *Psychologists in the criminal justice system*. Urbana: University of Illinois Press.

Brodsky, S. L. (2000). Judging the progress of psychology in corrections: The verdict is not good. *International Journal of Offender Therapy and Comparative Criminology, 44,* 141-145.

Brown, R., & Lewinsohn, P. (1984). A psychoeducational approach to the treatment of depression: Comparison of group, individual, and minimal contact procedures. *Journal of Consulting and Clinical Psychology, 52,* 774-783.

Carr, K., Hinkle, B., & Ingram, B. (1991). Establishing mental health and substance abuse services in jails. *Journal of Prison and Jail Health, 10*(2), 77-89.

Chambless, D., & Task Force on Psychological Interventions. (1996). An update on empirically validated therapies. *The Clinical Psychologist, 49,* 5-18.

Chambless, D., & Task Force on Psychological Interventions. (1998). Update on empirically validated therapies, II. *The Clinical Psychologist, 51,* 3-16.

Cleckley, H. (1976). *The mask of sanity* (5th ed.). St. Louis, MO: C. V. Mosby.

Clements, C. B. (1986). *Offender needs assessment*. College Park, MD: American Correctional Association.

Clements, C. B. (1993). Principles of clinical management: A first course for future psychologist-managers. *The Clinical Psychologist, 46,* 19-24.

Clements, C. B. (1996). Offender classification: Two decades of progress. *Criminal Justice and Behavior, 23,* 121-143.

Conley, C. (1998). *The Women's Prison Association: Supporting women offenders and their families* (National Institute of Justice program focus, NJC 172858). Washington, DC: U.S. Department of Justice.

Cooper, C., & Livingston, M. (1991). Depression and coping mechanisms in prisoners. *Work and Stress, 5,* 149-154.

Copello, A. G., & Tata, P. R. (1990). Violent behavior and interpretive bias: An experimental study of the resolution of ambiguity in violent offenders. *British Journal of Clinical Psychology, 29,* 417-428.

Cornell, D. G., & Hawk, G. L. (1989). Clinical presentation of malingerers diagnosed by experienced forensic psychologists. *Law and Human Behavior, 13,* 374-383.

Demuth, P. W., & Bruhn, A. R. (1997). The use of the early memories procedure in a psychotherapy group of substance abusers. *International Journal of Offender Therapy and Comparative Criminology, 41,* 24-35.

Ditton, P. M. (1999). *Mental health and treatment of inmates and probationers* (Bureau of Justice Statistics special report, NCJ 174463). Washington, DC: National Criminal Justice Reference Service.

Dodge, K. A. (1980). Social cognition and children's aggressive behavior. *Child Development, 51,* 162-170.

Dodge, K. A., Price, J. M., Bachorowski, J., & Newman, J. P. (1990). Hostile attributional biases in severely aggressive adolescents. *Journal of Abnormal Psychology, 99,* 385-392.

Domino, M., Wilson, D., Boothby, J. L., Stump, J., Scogin, F., & Brodsky, S. L. (2000, March). *Cognitive bibliotherapy treatment of depression with jail detainees*. Poster presented at the biennial conference of the American Psychology-Law Society, New Orleans, LA.

Edens, J., Poythress, N. G., & Lilienfeld, S. O. (1999). Identifying inmates at risk for disciplinary infractions: A comparison of two measures of psychopathy. *Behavioral Sciences and the Law, 17,* 435-443.

Elliott, D. S. (1980). Recurring issues in the evaluation of delinquency prevention and treatment programs. In D. Schichor & D. H. Kelly (Eds.), *Critical issues in juvenile delinquency* (pp. 237-262). Lexington, MA: D. C. Heath.

Fagan, J. A. (1990). Treatment and reintegration of violent delinquents: Experimental results. *Justice Quarterly, 7,* 233-263.

Feldman, M. P. (1993). *The psychology of crime: A social science textbook*. New York: Cambridge University Press.

Finn, P. (1998). Correctional officer stress: A cause for concern and additional help. *Federal Probation, 62*(2), 65-74.

Gendreau, P., & Andrews, D. A. (1996). *Correctional Program Assessment Inventory (CAPI)* (6th ed.). Saint John, New Brunswick: University of New Brunswick.

Gendreau, P., & Goggin, C. (1997). Correctional treatment: Accomplishments and realities. In P. Van Voorhis, M. Braswell, & D. Lester (Eds.), *Correctional counseling and rehabilitation* (3rd ed., pp. 271-280). Cincinnati, OH: Anderson.

Gendreau, P., Goggin, C. E., Cullen, F. T., & Paparozzi, M. (in press). The common sense revolution and correctional policy. In J. McGuire (Ed.), *Offender rehabilitation and treatment: Effective programs and policies to reduce re-offending.* Chichester, UK: Wiley.

Gendreau, P., Goggin, C. E., & Law, M. A. (1997). Predicting prison misconducts. *Criminal Justice and Behavior, 24,* 414-431.

Gendreau, P., & Ross, R. R. (1979). Effective correctional treatment: Bibliotherapy for cynics. *Crime & Delinquency, 25,* 463-489.

Gendreau, P., & Ross, R. R. (1987). Revivification of rehabilitation: Evidence from the 1980s. *Justice Quarterly, 4,* 349-407.

Goldstein, A., & Glick, B. (1997). *Aggression replacement training.* Champaign, IL: Research Press.

Goodstein, L. D. (1984). Ethical pitfalls for managers. *Professional Psychology: Research and Practice, 15,* 749-757.

Haney, C. (1997). Psychology and the limits to prison pain: Confronting the coming crisis in Eighth Amendment law. *Psychology, Public Policy, and Law, 3,* 499-588.

Haney, C., & Zimbardo, P. (1998). The past and future of U.S. prison policy: Twenty-five years after the Stanford Prison Experiment. *American Psychologist, 53,* 709-727.

Happel, R. M., & Auffrey, J. J. (1995). Sex offender assessment: Interrupting the dance of denial. *American Journal of Forensic Psychology, 13*(2), 5-22.

Hare, R. C. (1991). *Manual for the Hare Psychopathy Checklist–Revised.* Toronto: Multi-Health Systems.

Hare, R. D. (1996a). *The Hare Self-Report Psychopathy Scale-II.* Toronto: Multi-Health Systems.

Hare, R. D. (1996b). Psychopathy: A clinical construct whose time has come. *Criminal Justice and Behavior, 23,* 25-54.

Hare, R. D., Hart, S. D., & Harpur, T. J. (1991). Psychopathy and the DSM-IV criteria for antisocial personality disorder. *Journal of Abnormal Psychology, 100,* 391-398.

Harpur, T. J., Hare, R. D., & Hakstian, R. A. (1989). A two-factor conceptualization of psychopathy: Construct validity and implications for assessment. *Psychological Assessment: A Journal of Consulting and Clinical Psychology, 1,* 6-17.

Hart, S. D., Cox, D. N., & Hare, R. D. (1995). *Manual for the Hare Psychopathy Checklist–Revised: Screening version* (PCL: SV). Toronto: Multi-Health Systems.

Hart, S. D., & Hare, R. D. (1997). Psychopathy: Assessment and association with criminal conduct. In D. M. Stoff, J. Breiling, & J. D. Maser (Eds.), *Handbook of antisocial behavior* (pp. 22-35). New York: John Wiley.

Hart, S. D., Roesch, R., Corrado, R. R., & Cox, D. N. (1993). The Referral Decision Scale: A validation study. *Law and Human Behavior, 17,* 611-623.

Haskett, J. (1995). *Tehachapi Malingering Scale: Research revision No. 5 manual.* Modesto, CA: Logocraft.

Hemphill, J. F., Hare, R. D., & Wong, S. (1998). Psychopathy and recidivism: A review. *Legal and Criminological Psychology, 3,* 139-170.

Hemphill, J. F., & Wong, S. (1991). Efficacy of the therapeutic community for treating criminal psychopaths [abstract]. *Canadian Psychology, 32,* 206.

Henggeler, S. W. (1998). *Multisystemic therapy* (Blueprints for Violence Prevention, Book 6). Boulder: University of Colorado Press.

Hesketh, B., Rawlings, R., & Allen, R. (1996). Organisational psychology applied to forensic issues [abstract]. *Australian Psychologist, 31*(1), 9-14.

Hoge, S. K., Bonnie, R. J., Poythress, N., Monahan, J., Eisenberg, M., & Feucht-Haviar, T. (1997). The MacArthur adjudicative competence study: Development and validation of a research instrument. *Law and Human Behavior, 21,* 141-179.

Hollin, C. (1995). The meaning and implications of "program integrity." In J. McGuire (Ed.), *What works: Reducing reoffending—Guidelines from research and practice* (pp. 195-208). Chichester, UK: Wiley.

Jemelka, R., Trupin, E., & Chiles, J. (1989). The mentally ill in prisons: A review. *Hospital and Community Psychiatry, 40,* 481-490.

Johnson, R. (1996). *Hard time: Understanding and reforming the prison* (2nd ed.). Belmont, CA: Wadsworth.

Krull, D. S., & Erickson, D. J. (1995). Inferential hopscotch: How people draw social inferences from behavior. *Current Directions in Psychological Science, 4,* 35-38.

Kupers, T. (1999). *Prison madness: The mental health crisis behind bars and what we must do about it.* San Francisco: Jossey-Bass.

Lamb, H. R., & Weinberger, L. E. (1998). Persons with severe mental illness in jails and prisons: A review. *Psychiatric Services, 49,* 483-492.

Lester, D., & Van Voorhis, P. (1997). Cognitive therapies. In P. Van Voorhis, M. Braswell, & D. Lester (Eds.), *Correctional counseling and rehabilitation* (3rd ed., pp. 163-185). Cincinnati, OH: Anderson.

Liberman, R. P., Kopelowicz, A., & Young, A. S. (1994). Biobehavioral treatment and rehabilitation of schizophrenia. *Behavior Therapy, 25,* 89-107.

Lilienfeld, S. O. (1998). Methodological advances and developments in the assessment of psychopathy. *Behavior Research and Therapy, 36,* 99-125.

Lilienfeld, S. O., & Andrews, B. P. (1996). Development and preliminary validation of a self-report measure of psychopathic personality traits in noncriminal populations. *Journal of Personality Assessment, 66,* 488-524.

Lipton, D., Martinson, R., & Wilks, J. (1975). *The effectiveness of correctional treatment.* New York: Praeger.

Lösel, F. (1995). The efficacy of correctional treatment: A review and synthesis of meta-evaluations. In J. McGuire (Ed.), *What works: Reducing reoffending—Guidelines from research and practice* (pp. 79-111). Chichester, UK: Wiley.

MacKenzie, D. L. (1994). Results of a multi-site study of boot camp prisons. *Federal Probation, 58*(2), 60-66.

Marshall, W. L., Bryce, P., Hudson, S. M., Ward, T., & Moth, B. (1996). The enhancement of intimacy and the reduction of loneliness among child molesters. *Journal of Family Violence, 11,* 219-235.

Martinson, R. (1974). What works? Questions and answers about prison reform. *Public Interest, 35,* 22-84.

Martinson, R. (1979). New findings, new views: A note of caution regarding sentencing reform. *Hofstra Law Review, 7,* 242-258.

Mauer, M. (1999). *Race to incarcerate.* New York: New Press.

McGuire, J., & Priestly, P. (1985). *Offending behavior: Skills and stratagems for going straight.* London: Batsford.

McGuire, J., & Priestly, P. (1995). Reviewing "what works": Past, present, and future. In J. McGuire, (Ed.), *What works: Reducing reoffending—Guidelines from research and practice* (pp. 3-34). Chichester, UK: Wiley.

McLearen, A. M., Cannon, D., & Clements, C. B. (2001, March). *The need for a unified code of ethics in jails.* Poster session presented at the annual meeting of the Southeastern Psychological Association, Atlanta, GA.

McLearen, A. M., & Companik, P. (2000, March). *Identification of severe mental illness: Analysis and variation of jail intake procedures.* Paper presented at the biennial meeting of the American Psychology-Law Society, New Orleans, LA.

Megargee, E. I. (1974). Applied psychological research in a correctional setting. *Criminal Justice and Behavior, 1,* 43-50.

Megargee, E. I. (1994). Using the MMPI-based classification system with the MMPI-2s of male prison inmates. *Psychological Assessment, 6,* 337-344.

Megargee, E. I. (1995). Assessment research in correctional settings: Methodological issues and practical problems. *Psychological Assessment, 7,* 359-366.

Metzner, J. L., Cohen, F., Grossman, L. S., & Wettstein, R. M. (1998). Treatment in jails and prisons. In R. M. Wettstein (Ed.), *Treatment of offenders with mental disorders* (pp. 211-264). New York: Guilford.

Milan, M. A. (2001). Behavioral approaches to correctional management and rehabilitation. In C. Hollin (Ed.), *Handbook of offender assessment and treatment* (pp. 139-154). New York: John Wiley.

Monahan, J. (1984). The prediction of violent behavior: Toward a second generation of theory and policy. *American Journal of Psychiatry, 141,* 10-15.

Morash, M., Bynum, T. S., & Koons, B. A. (1998). *Women offenders: Programming needs and promising approaches* (NIJ Research in Brief). Washington, DC: National Institute of Justice.

Morgan, R. C., Winterowd, C. L., & Ferrell, S. W. (1999). A national survey of group psychotherapy services in correctional facilities. *Professional Psychology: Research and Practice, 30,* 600-606.

Morris, S. M., Steadman, H. J., & Veysey, B. M. (1997). Mental health services in Unites States jails. *Criminal Justice and Behavior, 27,* 3-20.

Murphy, J. (1994). Mists in the darkness: Art therapy with long-term prisoners in a high security prison: A therapeutic paradox? In M. Liebman (Ed.), *Art therapy with offenders* (pp. 14-38). London: Jessica Kingsley.

Nathan, P. E., & Gorman, J. M. (1998). *A guide to treatments that work.* New York: Oxford University Press.

Negy, C. (1995). Coping styles, family dynamics, and prison adjustment. *Dissertation Abstracts International, 55,* 4610. (Doctoral dissertation, Texas A&M University)

Negy, C., Woods, D. J., & Carlson, R. (1997). The relationship between female inmates' coping and adjustment in a minimum-security prison. *Criminal Justice and Behavior, 24,* 224-233.

Norris, M. P., & May, M. C. (1998). Screening for malingering in a correctional setting. *Law and Human Behavior, 22,* 315-323.

Ogloff, J. R. P., Wong, S., & Greenwood, A. (1990). Treating criminal psychopaths in a therapeutic community program. *Behavioral Sciences & the Law, 8,* 81-90.

Overholser, J. C. (1987). Ethical issues in prison research: A risk/benefit analysis. *Behavioral Sciences & the Law, 5,* 187-202.

Pallone, N. J., & Hennessy, J. J. (1992). *Criminal behavior: A process psychology analysis.* New Brunswick, NJ: Transaction Publishers.

Pallone, N. J., & Hennessy, J. J. (1996). *Tinder-box criminal aggression: Neuropsychology, demography, phenomenology.* New Brunswick, NJ: Transaction Publishers.

Palmer, T. (1984). Treatment and the role of classification: A review of basics. *Crime & Delinquency, 30,* 245-267.

Palmer, T. (1992). *The reemergence of correctional intervention: Developments through the 1980s and prospects for the future.* Newbury Park, CA: Sage.

Peters, S. (1998). *Guiding principles for promising female programming: An inventory of best practices.* Washington, DC: Office of Juvenile Justice and Delinquency Prevention. Available: http://ojjdp.ncjrs.org/pubs/principles/contents.html

Poythress, N. G., Edens, J. F., & Lilienfeld, S. O. (1998). Criterion-related validity of the Psychopathic Personality Inventory in a prison sample. *Psychological Assessment, 10,* 426-443.

Quay, H. C. (1977). The three faces of evaluation: What can be expected to work. *Criminal Justice and Behavior, 4,* 341-354.

Quay, H. C. (1987). Institutional treatment. In H. C. Quay (Ed.), *Handbook of juvenile delinquency* (pp. 244-265). New York: John Wiley.

Raine, A. (1993). *The psychopathology of crime.* San Diego: Academic Press.

Rice, M. E., & Harris, G. T. (1997). The treatment of adult offenders. In D. M. Stoff, J. Breiling, & J. D. Maser (Eds.), *Handbook of antisocial behavior* (pp. 425-435). New York: John Wiley.

Rice, M. E., Harris, G. T., & Cormier, C. (1992). Evaluation of a maximum-security therapeutic community for psychopaths and other mentally disordered offenders. *Law and Human Behavior, 16,* 399-412.

Rogers, R. (1984). *Rogers Criminal Responsibility Assessment Scales.* Odessa, FL: Psychological Assessment Resources.

Rogers, R. (Ed.). (1997). *Clinical assessment of malingering and deception* (2nd ed.). New York: Guilford.

Rogers, R., Bagby, R. M., & Dickens, S. E. (1992). *Structured Interview of Reported Symptoms: Professional manual.* Odessa, FL: Psychological Assessment Resources.

Salekin, R. T., Rogers, R., & Sewell, K. W. (1996). A review and meta-analysis of the Psychopathy Checklist and Psychopathy Checklist–Revised: Predictive validity of dangerousness. *Clinical Psychology: Science and Practice, 3,* 203-215.

Salekin, R. T., Rogers, R., & Sewell, K. W. (1997). Construct validity of psychopathy in a female offender sample: A multitrait-multimethod evaluation. *Journal of Abnormal Psychology, 106,* 576-585.

Salekin, R. T., Rogers, R., Ustad, K. L., & Sewell, K. W. (1998). Psychopathy and recidivism among female inmates. *Law and Human Behavior, 22,* 109-128.

Schaufeli, W. B., & Peeters, M. C-W. (2000). Job stress and burnout among correctional officers: A literature review. *International Journal of Stress Management, 7*(1), 19-48.

Schlosser, E. (1998). The prison-industrial complex. *The Atlantic Monthly, 282*(6), 51-77.

Scogin, F., Jamison, C., & Davis, N. (1990). Two-year follow-up bibliotherapy for depression in older adults. *Journal of Consulting and Clinical Psychology, 58,* 665-667.

Scott, E. M. (1993). Prison group therapy with mentally and emotionally disturbed offenders. *International Journal of Offender Therapy and Comparative Criminology, 37,* 131-145.

Serin, R. C. (1996). Violent recidivism in criminal psychopaths. *Law and Human Behavior, 20,* 207-217.

Sierles, F. S. (1984). Correlates of malingering. *Behavioral Sciences & the Law, 2,* 113-118.

Sigafoos, C. E. (1994). A PTSD treatment program for combat (Vietnam) veterans in prison. *International Journal of Offender Therapy and Comparative Criminology, 38,* 117-130.

Simourd, D. J. (1997). The Criminal Sentiments Scale–Modified and Pride in Delinquency scale: Psychometric properties and construct validity of two measures of criminal attitudes. *Criminal Justice and Behavior, 24,* 52-70.

Simourd, D. J., & Hoge, R. D. (2000). Criminal psychopathy: A risk-and-need perspective. *Criminal Justice and Behavior, 27,* 256-272.

Simourd, D. J., & Mamuza, J. M. (2000). The Hostile Interpretations Questionnaire: Psychometric properties and construct validity. *Criminal Justice and Behavior, 27,* 645-663.

Simourd, D. J., & van de Ven, J. (1999). Assessment of criminal attitudes: Criterion-related validity of the Criminal Sentiments Scale–Modified and Pride in Delinquency scale. *Criminal Justice and Behavior, 26,* 90-106.

Soderstrom, I. R., Castellano, T. C., & Figaro, H. R. (2001). Measuring "mature coping" skills among adult and juvenile offenders. *Criminal Justice and Behavior, 28,* 300-328.

Stallone, T. M. (1993). The effects of psychodrama on inmates within a structured residential behavior modification program. *Journal of Group Psychotherapy, Psychodrama, and Sociometry, 46*(1), 24-31.

Stein, E., & Brown, J. D. (1991). Group therapy in a forensic setting. *Canadian Journal of Psychiatry, 36,* 718-722.

Teasdale, C. (1997). Art therapy as part of a group programme for personality disordered offenders. *Therapeutic Communities, 18*(3), 209-221.

Teplin, L. A. (1994). Psychiatric and substance abuse disorders among male urban jail detainees. *American Journal of Public Health, 84,* 290-293.

Teplin, L. A., Abram, K. M., & McClelland, G. M. (1996). Prevalence of psychiatric disorders among incarcerated women: Pretrial jail detainees. *Archives of General Psychiatry, 53,* 505-512.

Teplin, L. A., & Swartz, J. (1989). Screening for severe mental disorder in jails. *Law and Human Behavior, 13,* 1-18.

Thornton, D. M. (1987). Treatment effects on recidivism: A reappraisal of the "nothing works" doctrine. In B. J. McGurk, D. M. Thornton, & M. Williams (Eds.), *Applying psychology to imprisonment: Theory and practice* (pp. 181-189). London: Her Majesty's Stationery Office.

Torrey, E. F., Stieber, J., Ezekiel, J., Wolfe, S. M., Sharfstein, J., Noble, J. H., & Flynn, L. M. (1992). *Criminalizing the seriously mentally ill: The abuse of jails as mental hospitals.* Washington, DC: Public Citizens' Health Research Group and National Alliance for the Mentally Ill.

Veysey, B. M., Steadman, H. J., Morrissey, J. P., Johnsen, M., & Beckstead, J. W. (1998). Using the Referral Decision Scale to screen mentally ill jail detainees: Validity and implementation issues. *Law and Human Behavior, 22,* 205-215.

Walker, L. E. A. (1994). *Abused women and survivor therapy.* Washington, DC: American Psychological Association.

Walters, G. D. (1988). Assessing dissimulation and denial on the MMPI on a sample of maximum security, male inmates. *Journal of Personality Assessment, 52,* 465-474.

Walters, G. D. (1990). *The criminal lifestyle: Patterns of serious criminal conduct.* Newbury Park, CA: Sage.

Walters, G. D. (1995). The Psychological Inventory of Criminal Thinking Styles: I. Reliability and preliminary validity. *Criminal Justice and Behavior, 22,* 307-325.

Walters, G. D. (1999). Short-term outcome of inmates participating in the Lifestyle Change program. *Criminal Justice and Behavior, 26,* 322-337.

Walters, G. D., Elliott, W. N., & Miscoll, D. (1998). Use of the Psychological Inventory of Criminal Thinking Styles in a group of female offenders. *Criminal Justice and Behavior, 25,* 125-134.

Walters, G. D., White, T. W., & Green, R. L. (1988). Use of the MMPI to identify malingering and exaggeration of psychiatric symptomatology in male prison inmates. *Journal of Consulting and Clinical Psychology, 56,* 111-117.

Wasyliw, O. E., & Grossman, L. S. (1988). The detection of malingering in criminal forensic groups: MMPI validity scales. *Journal of Personality Assessment, 52,* 321-333.

Wilson, D. J. (2000). *Drug use, testing, and treatment in jails* (Bureau of Justice Statistics special report, NCJ Publication No. 179999). Washington, DC: National Criminal Justice Reference Service.

Wilson, G. L. (1990). Psychotherapy with depressed incarcerated felons: A comparative evaluation of treatments. *Psychological Reports, 67,* 1027-1041.

Wilson, G. T. (1997). Treatment manuals in clinical practice. *Behavior Research and Therapy, 35,* 205-210.

Wollersheim, J., & Wilson, G. (1991). Group treatment of unipolar depression: A comparison of coping, supportive, and delayed treatment groups. *Professional Psychology: Research and Practice, 22,* 496-502.

Zamble, E., & Porporino, F. J. (1988). *Coping, behavior, and adaptation in prison inmates.* New York: Springer-Verlag.

Zamble, E., & Quinsey, V. L. (1997). *The criminal recidivism process.* New York: Cambridge University Press.

CHAPTER 15

A Viable Future for Correctional Mental Health Care

Robert K. Ax

A disparate array of public and private health care systems currently leaves millions of Americans without regular access to medical, dental, and mental health care (Kovacs, 2000), with jails and prisons being the most dependable portals to treatment for many of these unfortunates. Other institutions—schools, families, and those of established religions—seem inadequate to socialize, educate, and acculturate, partly because, in an increasingly diverse and divided society, there is less agreement on what ought to constitute common and desirable values, knowledge, and conduct.

In contrast, the penal system continues to provide a reliable minimum return on investment and offers a sense, whether justified or not, of increased safety from crime and criminals, among them hundreds of thousands of seriously mentally ill individuals who other mental health systems could not or would not accommodate. Ironically, to the extent that jails and prisons are called on to rehabilitate, it is their task to educate, socialize, and (ideally) restore to health those individuals who have been refractory to the efforts, such as they are, of other societal institutions.

Along with this, American jail and prison systems have been characterized in the public consciousness as a "prison industrial complex" (Dyer, 2000; Hallinan, 2001; Mauer, 1999; Schlosser, 1998) that has generated business opportunities and large numbers of jobs, making the construction of new facilities much prized in economically depressed areas. Although it is not necessarily the economic juggernaut that its critics assert, the collective political influence of this special interest group at the state and national levels cannot be ignored in the shaping of prison policy.

As noted in Chapter 1, there is a long tradition, both in the United States and abroad, of imprisoning persons with serious mental illness. Ax, Fagan, and Holton (in press) framed the modern trend of incarcerating inmates far from their homes, further weakening family and community ties, in terms of the historical practice of exiling criminals and seriously mentally ill persons. Even now, many fear the mentally ill and want to keep their distance from them (Link, Phelan, Bresnahan, Stueve, & Pescosolido, 1999). Therein lies some of the appeal of the United States' policy of incarcerating greater numbers of its citizens during the past three decades as the impact of deinstitutionalization on the community has been increasingly felt. Consequently, any speculation as to the future of correctional mental health care must consider the ambivalence with which the public views the rehabilitative purpose of the criminal justice system, insofar as it implies the reintegration of devalued and feared individuals into the community, and the economic incentives for an entrenched industry to oppose large-scale programs, such as alternatives to incarceration, that might lower the prison population significantly.

For reasons of space, many of the ideas treated here can only be suggested rather than highly elaborated, such that any value the reader might derive from this chapter will be more heuristic than explanatory. In describing a necessarily hypothetical future, a broad-brush approach is likely to paint a clearer picture, and a paucity of detail may be more of an asset than a liability. Nor can this author consider, beyond a brief mention, those futures seen as undesirable, for example, a capitulation to a view that rehabilitation, broadly speaking, is a failed enterprise (Lykken, 2000). It is incumbent on mental health professionals to steward a vision of the future that affirms the potential for positive and perhaps permanent societal change, one that includes a meaningful reduction in the incidence of both crime and serious mental illness and in which helpful and humane treatment is provided to those who must be incarcerated. Finally, pragmatism also precludes consideration of objectives seen as unfeasible over the near term in the United States, such as the abolition of prisons and jails (Davis & Rodriguez, 2000; International Conference on Penal Abolition, 2001), as much as one might wish for a future in which they will be unnecessary.

Framing the Future

By way of introducing the future of correctional mental health care, three overarching and interrelated issues to be considered are the public health model, consumerism, and globalization, forces in terms of which more traditional health care issues are discussed subsequently. By attending to these first, the reader will better appreciate the changes taking place specifically in correctional health care.

Public Health

A public health model provides a framework that accommodates many of the components that would characterize a future in which correctional mental health practitioners could and should practice. It is prevention oriented and implies a view of prisoners, those otherwise under the purview of the criminal justice system (i.e., on probation or parole), and individuals identified as at risk for serious criminal offending (e.g., adolescents who have committed minor infractions) as members of the community rather than as separate from the larger society. A public health model applied to correctional mental health implies continuity among all components of the community, from mental and correctional institutions to the larger "free world" society. Hence, it is a systems model, and it readily incorporates a broad range of programs designed to prevent imprisonment and to help incarcerated citizens make smoother, more successful returns to the community.

Lorion (2001) described how one behavioral problem about which correctional mental health professionals are particularly concerned adapts to a public health model:

> Public health strategies for reducing environmental contamination range, for example, from killing mosquitoes that carry malaria, to draining the swamps in which they breed, to vaccinating and educating those exposed so that they neither acquire nor transmit the disease. By definition, pervasive community violence means that a substantial number of individuals in a community engage in violent behavior, and multilevel interventions are required to address this complex problem. To achieve the equivalent of "draining the swamp" in a neighborhood or community where violence is pervasive would require identifying and altering setting characteristics that encourage and sustain violent behavior, including the public's general acceptance of violence. (p. 108)

Gun control programs, including enforcement of existing laws, could be part of such an intervention, which, when successful, reduces crime and is conducive to a more generally benign environment. Thus, fewer citizens are emotionally and physically traumatized and desensitized to violence, in turn reducing the incidence of serious mental illness. Family planning and parenting, well baby care, and similar interventions can also be seen as part of a public health effort whose broad range of intended long-range effects would include reducing the incidence of crime and mental illness, thereby lowering the incarceration rate in general and that for the seriously mentally ill in particular.

This model implies a global perspective, a vital component because neither crime nor pathogens respect national boundaries and because migration patterns are increasingly a factor in American society and in prisons. Also, it more readily enables those whose focus is American correctional mental health to see the potential relevance to local concerns of assessment techniques and programs developed and implemented by practitioners in other countries. As noted in Chapter 14, for example, a great deal of innovative work has been done in Canada during the past several years.

A desirable framework must be one that, at least theoretically, provides the maximum possible options for interventions and that in turn increases the roles that mental health professionals can play and the contributions they can make in correctional mental health care. Public health models can incorporate traditional rehabilitation and correctional mental health care programs and would be considered secondary or tertiary prevention interventions in community mental health models, while those that seek to reduce the initial occurrence of crime and mental illness would be considered primary prevention approaches (Rappaport, 1977).

Citizens as Consumers

Populist Health Care. Unfortunately, public health approaches can and often do fail for a variety of reasons. These include harmful interventions (e.g., vaccination programs with iatrogenic effects) and, related to this, mistrust and resistance on the part of the community. Support for prevention programs tends to flag in the absence of a health threat such as an infectious disease epidemic seen as likely to affect a broad segment of the population (Garrett, 2000). Their introduction may be resisted in societies where individual rights are seen as paramount, trumping those of the larger society under most circumstances, as is common in democracies.

Although economic considerations are often the enemy of best health practices, they do create situations in which the potential for innovation becomes greater. The term *populist health care* is used here to denote a multidimensional phenomenon that occurs when segments of the population see their health care needs, broadly construed, as not met and take action to correct the situation:

> Liberals are accustomed to thinking it is conservatives who employ moral crusades, particularly on issues involving drugs or sex, the classic examples being Prohibition in the 1920s and the venereal disease control laws in the late 19th century. But getting AIDS research and treatment funded in the United States was also a moral crusade, driven by gay activism and powered by the idea that stigmatization should not prevail. It was because it was a moral crusade that the movement to make AIDS a fundable disease on a par with cancer or heart disease was successful. The lesson that moral crusades work, and subsidiary lessons learned in the AIDS campaign such as the importance of activism, the necessity of mobilizing patients, and the overwhelming power of the media, have been passed on to other disease constituencies, and these lessons have formed the public health universe that we all live in now. (Moss, 2000, p. 1386)

The first step is frequently to organize, whether formally or informally, around a specific concern. Groups may remain small and local or may become larger and highly structured, perhaps by affiliating in coalitions with other organizations such as those that Falk and Strauss (2001) included under the rubric of *civil society*. Populist health care may complement the services provided by existing health care systems, although it is often seen as a force in opposition to those systems. Group interests may be more general or more specific and are manifest in a variety of ways, through public demonstrations (e.g., ACT-UP, the AIDS activist group that successfully pushed a variety of health care initiatives [Moss, 2000]; the Million Mom March on behalf of gun control) or the dissemination of health care information (e.g., the publication of *Our Bodies, Ourselves* by the Boston Women's Health Collective [1973]). They are frequently politicized and increasingly international in their reach. Although such conflicts between the public and the health care establishment (Starr, 1982) have existed in the United States for more than a century, the invigoration of civil society groups, or nongovernmental organizations, whose focus is fundamentally health related has been fueled during recent years by the availability of the Internet, which has enabled these groups to form, communicate, strategize, and recruit more easily.[1]

These groups' interests are often served, or so their members may believe, by other technological advances and the marketplace, which place more health care within the reach of the lay public. Examples include home test kits for diabetes, pregnancy, or illegal drugs and automated external defibrillators (AEDs), now widely available and successfully used by, among others, flight attendants (Page et al., 2000) and casino security personnel (Valenzuela et al., 2000) to prevent death in victims of sudden cardiac arrest. (These are also examples of the *portability* of health care, an issue discussed in more detail later.)

As consumers, their collective power constitutes a challenge to the authority of the health care establishment.[2] From the standpoint of the health care provider, the choices people make from among their alternatives may be good or bad. Their goal, however, is to create health care options for themselves. Sometimes they do this by using newly achieved political influence to force providers, insurance companies, and prisons or other government agencies to provide improved services. They may bypass the health care establishment entirely, as in choosing nontraditional (e.g., homeopathic) health treatments. A relevant example is the formation of health-related support and information groups formed for *and by* prison inmates in the perceived absence of sufficient services from prison health officials. Notable among these is the AIDS Counseling and Education (ACE) program founded by the female inmates at Bedford Hills Correctional Facility in New York (described in Braithwaite, Hammett, & Mayberry, 1996). The initiation of litigation ("health care by tort") by inmates aggrieved about some aspect of their health care, especially when organized or supported by a larger civil society group (e.g., the American Civil Liberties Union), would be another example. Needle exchange programs, which exist illegally in many American cities and are sometimes initiated or staffed by laypersons (including drug addicts themselves), fit this paradigm; the focus is on the prevention of disease, particularly (for current purposes) among a group at high risk for coming to prison.

Many of these groups have an explicit interest in correctional health and mental health issues, for example, Amnesty International, Human Rights Watch, and the

National Alliance for the Mentally Ill (NAMI). It is important to remember that an increasing prison population may also increase the constituency for changing the criminal justice system, creating new groups, such as Families Against Mandatory Minimums (FAMM), and swelling the ranks of existing organizations. The impact of these organizations, many of which have international support bases, is likely to grow as globalism becomes more of an economic and political force affecting U.S. social policy. Ultimately, this aggregation of forces can provide fresh viewpoints and valuable support for the enactment of prison reform where appropriate, including health care initiatives, especially to the extent that they attract a more mainstream following.

Purchasing Prisons. Writing on the 25th anniversary of the landmark Stanford Prison Experiment, Haney and Zimbardo (1998) decried the lack of impact that psychologists have had in the shaping of recent correctional policy: "Historically, psychologists once contributed significantly to the intellectual framework on which modern corrections was built. . . . In the course of the past 25 years, they have relinquished voice and authority in the debates that surround prison policy" (p. 721).

Mental health professionals in the United States seem not so much absent as ignored, even as the influence of researchers and practitioners within the correctional systems of Canada and the United Kingdom appears to be growing (see Chapter 14). They continue to be a presence in prisons and jails and have provided data concerning the effectiveness of treatment programs for correctional populations. Yet American citizens have chosen to buy prisons in huge numbers, beginning in the 1970s and continuing through the 1990s.

It may be argued that purchasing prisons has been a poor choice, a reflexive response to media influence and political demagoguery. However, the American public accepted the deal—more prisons and more of its citizens incarcerated in return for the promise of safety from crime and drugs—and might only now be rethinking, however tentatively, the terms of that arrangement. This is the political and economic reality to be confronted by correctional mental health workers who seek to implement effective diversion and rehabilitation programs. Punishment, retribution, and incapacitation, much more than rehabilitation, constitute the contemporary solution to the problem of crime and, de facto, to that of serious mental illness.

If this situation is to change and correctional mental health professionals are to have a role in the reascendance of rehabilitation as a correctional mission, then they will have to become more politically sophisticated, particularly with respect to the ways in which program outcome research, on which they base assertions for the effectiveness of their work, may be viewed by the public and their elected representatives. Citizens as consumers may choose to discount or disregard data and may, under any circumstances, interpret them idiosyncratically.[3] Psychologists, who have the most rigorous research training among mental health care professionals, should well understand how subjectively data may be viewed, distorted, or discounted.

Spelman's (2000) work serves as a useful illustration in this regard. He analyzed data on crime rates and other factors related to the increase in the prison population and concluded, "In short, the prison buildup was responsible for about one-fourth of the crime drop. Other factors were responsible for the vast majority of the crime drop. Some will find this estimate disturbingly low; others, astonishingly high" (pp. 122-123). Spelman's results raise two questions: Are they credible, and (given their credibility) how will the data be interpreted outside the professional community? Some citizens as consumers would view a one-fourth drop in the crime rate as *excellent* value received in return for costs paid in financial and human terms. Others would be aghast, decrying the allocation of funds that could have been used for schools or hospitals and what they might see as the foreclosure on the legal rights of many of those incarcerated—predominantly poor and non-white, unable to hire their own lawyers, forced to depend on "public pretenders" (as some of their clients call court-appointed attorneys), and given short shrift by the legal system. There is a great deal of evidence that selected corrections-based rehabilitation interventions are effective (see Chapters 5 and 14). Yet Lykken (2000) stated, in his reply to Haney and Zimbardo's (1998) article, "The fact is, however, that Haney and Zimbardo cannot point to a single convincing study indicating that prison reforms designed to augment rehabilitation have ever been successful" (p. 14). The credibility and interpretability of research data, particularly with respect to an issue as politically sensitive as prison programming, are crucial to their ultimate utility.[4]

Purchasing prisons has entered the popular consciousness as a military metaphor, as "the war on crime/drugs," but when seen as a health care issue, it contains elements of both populist health care (marginalizing health care experts and an ad hoc alliance with industry and the legislature) and a public health intervention (a large-scale response to a perceived crisis, a moral tone, and the incapacitation of a minority [albeit an increasingly large one] for the benefit of the majority, much as victims of infectious diseases might be quarantined to prevent the spread of an epidemic). As the reader will see later, this decision process relates to the more conventional issues of assessment and programming. Historical trends and abiding fears of the seriously mentally ill constitute a formidable force opposing real and lasting reform of correctional mental health practices. It falls to mental health professionals, among others, to serve as a counterforce, as Haney and Zimbardo (1998) stated:

So, perhaps it is this one last thing that the Stanford Prison Experiment stood for that will serve the discipline best over the next 25 years. That is, the interrelated notions that psychology can be made relevant to the broad and pressing national problems of crime and justice, that the discipline can assist in stimulating badly needed social and legal change, and that scholars and practitioners can improve these policies with sound data and creative ideas. (p. 722)

Creating the space to implement programs (i.e., reasserting psychology's place in the policy arena) and advocating for diversion, treatment, and rehabilitation—as well as, perhaps most important, community-based prevention—programs will demand more than simply data documenting their effectiveness. Good data will not guarantee the acceptance of good programs or assessment procedures. However, they can serve as the foundation of discussions and debates that must ultimately take place in local, state, and national political arenas; corporate boardrooms; government agencies; and the popular media. Some mental health professionals will be directly involved, helping to transform the way in which we see imprisonment, particularly of the seriously mentally ill, and its ramifications from a military and adversarial concern to a social and health care issue.

Globalization: American Correctional Mental Health in a Connected World

Civil society, made up of nonprofit organizations and voluntary associations dedicated to civic, cultural, humanitarian, and social causes, has begun to act as an independent international force. The largest and most prominent of these organizations include Amnesty International, Greenpeace, Oxfam, and the International Committee of the Red Cross; in addition, the U.N. [United Nations] now lists more than 3,000 civil society groups. During the 1990s, these transnational forces effectively promoted treaties to limit global warming, *establish an international criminal court,* and outlaw antipersonnel land mines. (Falk & Strauss, 2001, p. 214, emphasis added)

Crime, punishment, and the treatment of incarcerated citizens have become irreversibly global concerns. The U.S. economy is increasingly dependent on international commerce. Social policy may soon be more amenable to influence from abroad as well. Falk and Strauss (2001), noting that "globalization is dispersing political authority throughout the international order" (p. 213), suggested the formation of a "global parliament" to empower public opinion as currently expressed separately from states and within civil society forums. Understandably, among the issues Falk and Strauss saw as central is that of human rights. The weight of global public opinion, particularly if articulated through an organized and respected body, might be highly influential in some areas of American social policy, possibly including corrections and the treatment of the mentally ill within this country's jails and prisons. Many international organizations are already active in promoting human rights issues in American prisons, including Human Rights Watch, Amnesty International, and the Sentencing Project. The UN Committee Against Torture, using reports from groups such as Amnesty International, recently determined that the use of electric stun belts and restraint chairs, as used in many U.S. jurisdictions to control persons in custody, constituted torture (Olson, 2000).

More generally, globalization and the increased interdependence of American and foreign economies may compel increased sensitivity to foreign public opinion, including some of the more controversial aspects of U.S. correctional policy. In particular, capital punishment is strongly opposed in Europe. It has engendered considerable criticism in the press and from politicians there, and on several occasions, it has induced formal protests of specific executions by the European Union (Reid, 2000).

However, globalization is also important in ways as closely related to prison health as to prison health policy. It is likely to be of concern to correctional mental health professionals and central to their role in patient treatment as it evolves and perhaps expands. Public health is typically thought of in terms of issues such as prevention of infectious disease. Prisons in other countries often spread these diseases, including tuberculosis, a particularly serious problem throughout Russia and one indivisible from its prisons (Garrett, 2000). From 1993 to 1998, the percentage of U.S. tuberculosis cases that were foreign born grew from 29.8% to 41.6% (Talbot, Moore, McCray, & Binkin, 2000). American correctional facilities could become staging areas for the spread of new diseases, such as drug-resistant tuberculosis, as employees are infected and bring the diseases home or as inmates, especially those from jails where turnover rates are often high, are released to the community. Hence, infectious disease is one way in which prisons are unavoidably contextualized within the larger community. The future may well witness a greater involvement of mental health professionals in primary health care provision, compelled by the economic necessity that supports innovative practices, particularly with regard to health promotion and the prevention of infectious diseases such as HIV, hepatitis, and drug-resistant tuberculosis.

Finally, it will be helpful for American correctional health care providers to consider an international perspective and learn from their colleagues in other countries. As Gendreau (1996) noted, "More blatant examples of ethnocentrism are the fact that American reviews on treatment effectiveness almost never reference the literature from foreign countries where different approaches to the 'crime problem' exist (e.g., less incarceration)" (p. 152). Concerns specific to American society notwithstanding, as the United States becomes more multicultural, it will be vital to consider viewpoints and interventions that our colleagues from other countries have developed and implemented.[5]

Building a Viable Future: Changes in Health Care Delivery

Within the broader parameters discussed previously, it becomes possible to see the relevance of specific health care trends to correctional mental health. This section provides some speculative extrapolations to the future of correctional mental health care based on current practices.

Technology

A defining feature of technology as it affects health care is portability, a fact of particular importance in prison mental health care. New services and service delivery media can simultaneously cut costs and expand the catchment area by reducing or eliminating the impact of geographic and temporal factors in health care delivery as well as the "distance" between the prison environment and the outside community. They can empower those with less formal training to provide highly sophisticated health care services (recall the use of AEDs by flight attendants and casino operators discussed earlier) and leverage specialty skills. Implicit in this is the notion that technology makes *knowledge* portable. For example, physicians are now using handheld computers to improve the quality of care and safety with respect to medication delivery. They can carry with them patients' medical records as well as information on medication side effects and have all of this available during appointments (Freudenheim, 2001). Furthermore, combining or bundling technologies with specialty skills can synergistically increase benefits to patients and lower costs to payers.

Finally, ownership of technology will influence the way in which it is used. Will interactive television (IATV) equipment be networked throughout a prison setting or be centralized, making some entity (e.g., the hospital, the dispensary) the gatekeeper and perhaps narrowing access and the range of services provided? Broad or narrow availability will frame and entrench perceptions. If system access is owned by medical services, then staff will see it as *telemedicine.* If all health care providers have access, then it will be *telehealth,* leading to broader acceptance and more innovative, cost-effective use.

It is clear that telehealth (see Chapter 2) has an important place in the provision of correctional health services given its cost-effectiveness and acceptance by patients (Magaletta, Fagan, & Ax, 1998; Magaletta, Fagan, & Peyrot, 2000; McCue et al., 1997). IATV will enable systems to make more efficient use of the specialized skills that their own staff or outside consultants possess. For example, a neuropsychologist can currently conduct parts of the assessment process via this modality (Schopp, Johnstone, & Merrell, 2000). Bundling technologies (e.g., adapting conventional neuropsychological assessment instruments for online administration) will add further value. Inmate-patients will benefit from specialty services for which they might otherwise need to wait months or never get.

Government or private agencies could hire a minimum number of specialists to provide services throughout the system (local, state, or federal) or else conveniently outsource the service, perhaps to bidders from around the country, thereby reducing redundancy of expensive and unneeded services. One might have a bank of consultants to dial up on a fee-for-service basis such that, for example, neuropsychologists could be employed only on an as-needed, case-by-case basis for systemwide consultation. This approach might make it unnecessary to employ such highly specialized and costly providers on a full-time basis. At the same time, agencies could employ less credentialed mental health technicians to provide the bulk of day-to-day care, knowing that specialists were available as needed.

Those with technological skills who also bring appropriate sensitivity to patient concerns may become a more central part of technology-based treatment. For example, Hodges et al. (1999) described a "virtual environment" (VE) consisting of a series of video combat vignettes created to assist veterans in coping with posttraumatic stress disorder. Hodges et al. noted, "The implication seems to be that enough virtual stimuli must be provided to support at least some aspects of the patient's recounting of his experiences. These details can be approximations to the real events, but they must not be clearly incorrect" (p. 13). If this particular use of virtual reality proves to be therapeutically effective, then more skillfully realized video simulations might further enhance therapy outcomes. Hence, one might imagine a specialty in therapeutic video environment design, perhaps requiring some training in applied mental health care, as many now have careers designing video games or Web pages. VE might prove useful in dealing with other traumas faced by incarcerated individuals, such as sexual abuse, which many female inmates report having experienced (see Chapter 7).

Technology and cost-cutting pressure could lead to more assessment, counseling, and psychoeducational services being offered online. Inmate-patients, particularly those in restricted housing or in rural facilities, who cannot secure in-person services might use computers with security procedures in place that allow access only to selected Web sites or chat rooms. Self-help group formats with appropriate monitoring, such as Narcotics Anonymous and Alcoholics Anonymous, might lend themselves particularly well to such an arrangement. Online therapists might facilitate virtual groups with patients from several different correctional facilities.

The combination of electronic monitoring with global positioning system technologies now enables authorities to track offenders outside of prison. For example, 20 states now use this technology to monitor sex offenders in the community (Raffaele, 2001). Similarly, stalkers (some of whom suffer from diagnosable mental illness) could be effectively prevented from violating the terms of restraining orders, and their victims could be made aware of their proximity. It may soon be possible to implant monitoring and tracking devices in the body, making them much more difficult to defeat ("Microchip Implants," 1999, cited in Fabelo, 2000). Obviously, the use of such an invasive technology raises ethical concerns, a complete discussion of which would include not only the intrusiveness of this kind of monitoring but also the measure of freedom the offender may gain (with the alternative being incarceration) by agreeing to this as a condition of probation or parole. It may also be anticipated that mental health professionals from other countries and civil society groups will engage in the debate about the ethics of this and other proposed treatment innovations.

Psychotropic Medication

Psychotropic medications have become safer, and in many cases more effective, during the past several years. The newer antidepressants, including the selective serotonin reuptake inhibitors, carry a lower degree of health risks than do the monoamine oxidase inhibitor and tricyclic antidepressant classes. The advent of the atypical antipsychotic medications, which treat both the positive and negative symptoms of schizophrenia and characteristically do not cause extrapyramidal side effects at therapeutic doses, should lead to greater compliance and benefit from treatment of individuals with schizophrenia. Similarly, anticonvulsant medications (e.g., valproic acid) have been found to be effective in treating bipolar disorder. The decoding of the human genome offers the promise of medications customized to the neurochemistry of the individual patient. In addition to assisting seriously mentally ill persons already incarcerated, effective use of new psychotropic medications could lead to stabilization within the community of a greater number of impaired individuals and, accordingly, to fewer being sent to prison. These medications could also improve relapse prevention programs.

New medications such as naltrexone have been approved for treating substance abuse. Because this is often the root cause or specific criminal offense for which seriously mentally ill citizens are incarcerated, combination pharmacological and psychotherapeutic treatments may soon comprise an effective means for reducing the incarceration of dually diagnosed offenders through drug abuse diversion programs and lowering reincarceration rates through prison-based interventions.

Another example of bundling would be that of psychotherapy with pharmacotherapy, as appropriate to the needs of different patients. Providers competent in both could offer the optimal treatment, whether a combination or only one type of intervention, as dictated by each patient's presenting issues, presumably increasing the cost-effectiveness of providers' services and thereby adding value (see Sammons & Levant, 1999, for an overview of the issues related to combining these therapies). Those providing mental health services to incarcerated patients with serious mental illness will be particularly challenged by the need to help them adjust to these difficult and demanding environments and will benefit, toward this end, from good working relationships with custody and other correctional personnel (as noted in Chapters 6 and 13).

Who will prescribe psychotropic medications? The American Psychological Association has committed itself to changing scope of practice laws for psychologists with additional training to allow them to prescribe psychotropic medications (Martin, 1995). However, specialty training and the support of computer technology (e.g., handheld computers) might enable many others to prescribe them effectively and safely. One can imagine clinical social workers, who also have training in psychodiagnosis, providing this service at considerable cost savings.

Programming, Assessment, and Provider Issues

In a desirable—if not likely—future, correctional mental health treatment would involve a coordinated continuum of services between the "free world" community and total institutions (i.e., prisons and mental hospitals), with an emphasis on prevention and diverting individuals from the criminal justice system. This would include community mental health services as they were originally envisioned: targeting the most impaired individuals for accessible and affordable treatment and integrating them with correctional mental health services at both the provider and agency levels. If this approach is to be implemented reliably and on a broad basis, then consumers—citizens and their legislators, public and private correctional systems, the courts—must be convinced of their worth, meaning at a minimum that good data must be available to support claims of clinical effectiveness, assertions that can survive the scrutiny of the popular media and the political process. The support of civil society groups, such as FAMM and NAMI, may be valuable in that regard.

This approach would likely mean reevaluating deinstitutionalization as well. For some chronically mentally ill individuals, longer periods—weeks or perhaps months, but not years—of inpatient care in safe, well-staffed facilities must continue to be an option if they are to avoid the criminal justice system. Others with serious mental illness who are at risk for incarceration could live in the community with greater support than they currently receive. A notable example would be the long-term group living and work arrangements that characterize the "Fairweather Lodges" (Fairweather, Sanders, Maynard, Cressler, & Bleck, 1969). Still others might live more autonomously but still require some of the structure and stability that inpatient care provides, including assistance with obtaining and taking antipsychotic medication, adequate transportation to community health care centers, and in-home visits by health care professionals. Such supportive care effectively lowers the response cost of treatment compliance. The Program of Assertive Community Treatment (PACT), as designed, appears to offer a comprehensive range of services, including round-the-clock availability of services and providers, that could enable patients to make successful community adjustments (NAMI, 2001). Having a continuum of services available, including inpatient care, can lower overall monetary costs as seriously mentally ill citizens are given appropriate levels of care, neither more nor less than they require. The benefits might include a reduction in the bias that the general population has toward persons with serious mental illness as more stable individuals who can rely on care that is truly adequate to meet the needs of the mentally ill represent this group in the community.

Prison-based programs, in terms of Fagan's model (see Chapter 1), are also part of the treatment continuum and focus on helping some individuals to adjust to incarceration and others to prepare for release. As basic (Level 1) programs prove their worth, it becomes more likely that the funding will be available, and that practitioners will have the credibility, to implement Level 2 and Level 3 services of the kind described elsewhere in this handbook. However, over the near term, competition for resources and other pressures to reduce costs will raise the standard for acceptability of programs. Providers should bear in mind that in correctional settings where inmates are expected to work, particularly in for-profit enterprises, prisoners' labor is considered a valuable resource, and time spent in programming is considered a fiscal cost to these institutions.

Reducing the response cost for appropriate behavior is crucial to relapse prevention. Making health care, employment, and social support and acceptance more accessible will contribute meaningfully to reducing recidivism. Consequently, academic and vocational education and the teaching of job-finding skills (Azrin & Philip, 1979; McCollum, 2000) join traditional mental health and substance abuse treatment as components of effective rehabilitation programs. Beyond this, lowering barriers to full citizenship, at least for some ex-offenders, can help to strengthen their endorsement of prosocial attitudes and behavior. These could include restoration of suffrage, providing removal (via laser procedure) of gang tattoos on request, sealing criminal records subsequent to a set period of crime-free behavior for those individuals without histories of violence, and (similarly) permitting those with drug convictions to apply for financial aid for college. Interestingly, an advocacy group, Students for Sensible Drug Policy, has already formed around the latter issue (Groppe, 2001), consistent with the civil society dynamics that gave rise to FAMM.

As noted earlier, merely having good data will not guarantee the acceptance of rehabilitation programs, particularly in corrections. Those designing and administering the programs must also confront the troublesome issue of treatment failures, that is, individuals who complete programs, perhaps gaining early release or avoiding incarceration in so doing, and then recidivate. In such instances, considerable publicity may be generated and treatment successes ignored. After all, it is the spectacular failures, rather than the quiet successes, that are featured in the popular media.[6] Perhaps it is partly the frustration over past treatment failures that has led to the practice of labeling sex offenders as mentally ill and then institutionalizing them indefinitely on completion of their prison sentences. Efforts to validate the clinical effectiveness of psychological procedures in general are under way at this time (Borkovec, Ragusea, & Echemendia, 1999), and the onus will be even greater on correctional mental health professionals to create, validate, and market cost-effective treatments if they are to expect payers (e.g., public and private correctional systems, the courts) to purchase these programs or win the public's acceptance. For this and other reasons, assessment and treatment are inextricably interlinked.

For some individuals, prison may be the most appropriate "treatment." The tone of this handbook has been positive, informed by a belief that progress will continue to be made in the treatment of mental illness in correctional settings. However, this should not blind us to the existence of a core of psychopathic individuals among the prison population who currently appear intractable to treatment. It should be a high priority to identify these individuals. Because of their characteristic predisposition toward interpersonal manipulation, including an ability to mask their true intentions from others (including, sadly, correctional mental health professionals), they are likely to constitute a high percentage of those who recidivate after being certified as treatment successes (see Chapters 6 and 14). Hare (1996) wrote,

> The uninformed views of the judge and the protestations and anecdotes of those who run prison programs notwithstanding, there is no known treatment for psychopathy. This does not necessarily mean that the egocentric and callous attitudes and behavior of psychopaths are immutable, only that there are no methodologically sound treatments or "resocialization" programs that have been shown to work with psychopaths. Unfortunately, both the criminal justice system and the public routinely are fooled into believing otherwise. As a result, many psychopaths take part in all sorts of prison treatment programs, put on a good show, make "remarkable progress," convince the therapists and parole board of their reformed character, are released, and pick up where they left off when they entered prison. (p. 41)

Although it is vital to continue attempting to find ways in which to treat (or socialize) these individuals, mental health professionals should make every attempt not to underwrite the early release of individuals at high risk for victimizing the community through unwarranted assertions that these people have been rehabilitated when, in fact, they are at high risk for committing further serious offenses once released. In fact, it is reasonable to assume that prison will still be the treatment of choice for some individuals who, by dint of varying degrees of interplay between heritability and environmental factors, cannot currently be socialized. Hare (1996) noted that among a group generally resistant to treatment, psychopathic sexual offenders are particularly refractory. Although it is undoubtedly true that some—perhaps a great many—sex offenders are helped by treatment programs, the consequences wrought by the recidivistic behavior of even a small number of these individuals have undoubtedly helped to create the movement toward civilly committing many of them after they have served their prison sentences. The credibility of mental health treatment programs and of the specialty of correctional mental health is highly related to the validity of the assessments that psychologists and other mental health professionals provide. Reducing the "false positive" and "false negative" rates of the tests and techniques they use must be an especially high priority for those working in corrections.

Documenting the quality of treatment programs alone will not ensure the preservation of service provider positions. Related to the issue of program effectiveness is that of provider effectiveness. Clinical psychologists have not yet proven that the rigorous programs they undertake, involving years of academic training, practica, and internships, reliably produce practitioners with superior treatment skills (Bickman, 1999). (This is not to say that the proof is not out there to be gotten, of course.) Corrections as a health care system must deal with its own version of managed care, and the future may well show that selected behavioral and psychoeducational programs in correctional settings can be implemented cost-effectively using paraprofessionals and nonprofessionals (e.g., correctional counselors, inmates, volunteers) as facilitators or that faith-based rehabilitation programs run by religiously oriented and trained providers have merit.

One way in which providers will be able to make themselves more valuable to correctional systems will be to provide services to a wider range of inmates. Increased cultural heterogeneity will place greater demands on the correctional health care system to accommodate the needs of foreign inmates. Speaking a foreign language, particularly Spanish, may be the most useful single skill that correctional mental health care professionals can acquire. Those who have this capacity, or who can otherwise appropriately enhance their scope of practice (e.g., using telehealth technology, obtaining prescription privileges), can serve as direct providers of services and/or program designers for a broader range of patients. Documenting the quality and effectiveness of services will help to preserve both new and traditional practice niches.

Staff Issues

The lives and careers of prison guards are not coveted ones. The guards produce nothing and this gnaws at them. A good day, they say, is a day when they and their colleagues have not been hurt and when they have not been pelted with feces or doused with urine. (LeDuff, 2001, p. A25)

The realization of a more desirable future must involve greatly increased attention to staff issues, particularly staff professionalism and morale, which are largely a function of selection, training, and institutional culture. They are central to the maintenance of a more benign, or at least less pathogenic, prison environment, a fact less easily appreciated by those who have little or no experience working in prison settings. Prison systems often fail to recognize the skills and qualities that the better correctional officers possess, including the ability to tolerate hours of boring routine, interrupted by occasional crises that may involve life-and-death decisions on their part; a capacity for self-restraint balanced with the ability to act decisively but appropriately in a confrontation that may involve direct physical threat; and integrity, that is, the ability to resist the temptation to accept bribes and other forms of compromise despite low pay and often stressful work conditions. Good correctional workers, particularly uniformed correctional officers, are much less valued than they are valuable. Helping prison system administrators, legislators, and the public to understand, value, and reward the skills that correctional line staff bring to their jobs, thereby improving the correctional environment for all inmates, is one of the most important things that mental health providers in prisons and jails can do to ensure a better future for correctional mental health programs for offenders.

Chapter 14 discussed the interaction of individual characteristics and situations as related to offender programs such as rehabilitation. This is certainly a concern for staff as well. Person-environment fit (Caplan, 1983) has direct implications for their emotional and physical well-being. Stress management programs work best when both the correctional environment and the individual employees are targeted for intervention. In the absence of the former approach, the latter (and more common) approach often amounts simply to blaming the victims.

Stress management can be integrated into existing job designs and training programs. Karasek and Theorell (1990) argued persuasively that features such as low levels of control over one's duties and insufficient levels of challenge are conducive to cardiovascular disease. Appropriate job redesign at the organizational level would also ensure that adequate staffing patterns, training, and tools (for correctional employees, tools could be anything from hammers and saws to computers and body alarms) are available.

The steeply hierarchical structure of prison bureaucracies does not provide appreciable advancement opportunities for most line staff. Rotating shift work taxes health (Monk & Tepas, 1985), puts further strains on outside support systems (e.g., family, friends, social activities commonly organized to accommodate diurnal work schedules), and constrains options in terms of training (e.g., taking college courses for advancement within or outside the correctional system). Many of the skills in which correctional officers are trained do not generalize readily from this largely pre-industrialized and labor-intensive environment to the requirements of a post-industrial economy. If specific prison populations decrease, then staff may be laid off. This recently occurred in the New York State prison system (LeDuff, 2001). The introduction of new technology-based correctional management techniques (see Chapter 12), driven by security concerns and cost savings mandates, may further reduce staffing requirements. The prospect of downsizing is a particular problem for recruitment and retention of well-qualified employees because job security is one of the most highly valued aspects of prison work.

Prevention and community mental health models have direct implications for staff well-being. Those working in policy and administrative positions can promote staff wellness by taking a more prevention-oriented, systems approach to employee assistance programs. For example, one might seek to design and/or advocate policies allowing officers to promote "up and out" of corrections to other law enforcement agencies or government positions under traditional civil service, taking benefits with them. Agency support for online education and training classes would remove a significant impediment to promotion and advancement. Officers could be offered training (e.g., in computer skills) as part of a benefits package that would allow them to be more generally marketable if they choose to move out of law enforcement or would increase their promotion potential within corrections. Those choosing to remain as uniformed correctional officers would generally be a better fit with the prison environment. Correctional officers more motivated to stay would find more promotion opportunities within the system. As their job satisfaction increases, it is reasonable to expect a generally improved prison environment.

Role Transformations: Toward a Biopsychosocial Scope of Practice and Self-Concept

> In addition, the Stanford Prison Experiment and the perspective it advanced also suggest that prison change will come about only when those who are outside of this powerful situation are empowered to act on it. (Haney & Zimbardo, 1998, p. 721)

> The rich complexity of each individual is produced by a cognitive architecture, embodied in a physiological system, which interacts with the social and nonsocial world that surrounds it. (Tooby & Cosmides, 1992, p. 21)

It is hoped that the reader will find in this section a satisfactory theoretical confluence of the ideas and issues discussed previously and the basis for extrapolating reasonable forecasts and plans for the future of mental health practice in corrections. If it seems that this chapter has been insufficiently focused on corrections per se, the emphasis reflects this author's belief that a desirable future will be one in which correctional mental health will involve the community to a greater extent, altering the relationship between society and its correctional institutions and transforming the nature of mental health care in corrections. Academics, policymakers, and others would become nearly as much a part of correctional mental health care as are those providing direct services. The latter, in turn, would begin to focus more of their time and energy on effectiveness and outcome research, prevention and post-release issues, and policy matters, thereby promoting better communication and improved research-based treatment.

A range of forces imposes mandates and constraints but will also provide opportunities for innovation and improved service. Starr (1982) documented the rise of the American medical profession and its subsequent subordination to business interests during the last century. The experience of organized medicine is highly relevant to allied health care professionals, who have never enjoyed the power, credibility, and influence that physicians once possessed and who must now struggle even harder to earn and maintain a place in an increasingly competitive health care marketplace (see Chapter 2).

When practitioners talk about a biopsychosocial model of practice (see Chapters 5 and 6), they give themselves the freedom to conceptualize problems using a broad range of variables and thereby the potential for much more effective solutions, using the talents of many others, including practitioners from outside the current boundaries of the correctional system. In turn, they find themselves reinventing their professional self-concepts by choosing to grow and evolve proactively so as to provide better patient care rather than simply reacting to technological and market forces. Such a model acknowledges that conceptualizations of the biological, psychological, and social realms as discrete entities constitute arbitrary and outdated distinctions, more suited to turf battles among the various health care professions than to the care and treatment of the whole patient. Regarding corrections, this seems especially true in terms of prevention, where changes in law and social policy could meaningfully reduce the numbers of citizens with serious mental illness sent to prison in the first place. Those whose professional titles currently define them as mental health care professionals can use this state of affairs to redefine their roles, attain new knowledge and skills, and expand their scope of practice to make greater contributions to patient care and earn their marketplace niches by continuing to "add value."

Most likely, these role transformations will include a move for some, paralleling that already under way within organized psychology, toward primary care and prevention-oriented roles for practitioners (as reflected in the recent adoption of CPT codes enabling psychologists to bill for assessment and treatment of selected conditions outside the mental health domain [Foxhall, 2000]). Chapter 7 provides an overview of the medical and mental health needs of female inmates that underscore the interrelationship between the psychological and somatic realms. The desirability of changing high-risk behavior to reduce rates of new cases of infectious diseases such as HIV is obvious in prison environments. The high rates of depression among HIV-infected individuals (Breitbart, Rosenfeld, & Passik, 1996; Kaplan & Sadock, 1996) further illustrate the interrelationship of medical and mental health issues. In one prison, a physician, a physician's assistant specializing in infectious diseases, and a psychologist have worked together in a clinic providing an array of services for HIV-infected inmates. Marcus Forbes, cofounder of the clinic, noted that, as a psychologist, he had to learn a great deal about the disease process, the medications used to treat HIV, and related health issues. Given the increasing comorbidity of other diseases with HIV, for example, hepatitis and tuberculosis are now routinely discussed with patients at the clinic. Also important to his role are the social work aspects of preparing patients for release and providing for continuity of care in the community. "As a psychologist," he said, "I have to be willing to wear a lot of different hats" (M. Forbes, personal communication, June 4, 2001). He added that among the ways in which he was able to contribute distinctively as a psychologist was by helping physicians to communicate with patients more effectively. In a viable and desirable future, best practices will often mean interdisciplinary collaboration to respond to emerging health issues, including, but not limited to, mental health concerns.

For other professionals, it will mean different, and perhaps even more radical, transformations of their traditional practice boundaries and role definitions, involving in some cases a direct engagement with the political process. The U.S. Senate recently passed a bill, S. 1865, creating mental health diversion courts. This bill was cosponsored by Ted Strickland (D-Ohio), a psychologist who once worked in a maximum-security prison and is now a congressman (Strickland, 2001; U.S. Congress, 2000). David Kaczynski, a social worker and the brother of convicted "Unabomber" Theodore Kaczynski, recently became executive director of a civil society group, New Yorkers Against the Death Penalty (Purdy, 2001).

Even as those with advanced training in mental health care assessment and treatment pursue new skills, others may increasingly offer the services now being performed by these "high-end" practitioners. As has been discussed, the portability of health care made possible largely through technology has enabled less credentialed professionals and laypersons to provide more sophisticated health care services. Paraprofessionals—even inmates—are also providing more counseling and psychoeducational services in corrections (but see Chapter 2 regarding concerns about inmates as service providers). As treatments become safer and easier to administer, and as their effectiveness is documented, demand for the treatments will increase. This is likely to result in both pressure to reduce costs (so as to increase the supply) and an attendant societal tolerance of innovative means of delivering these services. Accordingly, for example, it might be expected that regulatory barriers (e.g., licensure and reimbursement regulations) to the delivery of health care, including counseling and psychotherapy via IATV and online, will be suitably modified. At the same time, the use of other health care professionals, technicians, and paraprofessionals to deliver those services that were once the exclusive purview of a few will continue and become even more common. The safer the antidepressant, the more likely it is that psychologists, social workers, and others will be allowed to prescribe it or that it will eventually become available as an over-the-counter agent, such that the inmate-patient could simply self-diagnose and purchase the medication at the prison commissary.

Perhaps this appears nothing like a desirable future. It may seem like the need for adaptation is overwhelming, that professional autonomy will continue to erode, and that practitioners' professional identities will be transformed beyond recognition. After all, isn't it difficult enough to provide effective mental health services in settings where health care is at best a subordinate mission and where the inmate-patients and the executive staff may be hostile to the best efforts of mental health professionals?

However, this state of affairs is really what is meant when progress is discussed. Mental health's scope of practice can evolve just as its knowledge of mental illness and how best to treat it increases. Even as services that mental health practitioners have provided devolve to other, less credentialed providers, new interventions become available to these practitioners. Practitioners who resist change will eventually find their skills unmarketable, but those who are willing to learn and grow professionally will find a much broader range of opportunities available to them. Learning a foreign language, attending to correctional issues and practices in other countries, and/or becoming more comfortable in delivering care via interactive television will enable correctional mental health care providers to survive and thrive during the coming decades. Having the competence to provide both psycho-therapeutic and pharmacological interventions in accordance with the particular needs of patients will help to ensure practitioners' marketplace niches. Regularly collecting outcome data, particularly regarding an understudied population such as prison inmates, and basing new treatments on this information will enhance both the knowledge base and the professional credibility of mental health practitioners.

Just as important as direct service provision is the policy that dictates mental health treatment of those in prison, including the laws that send them there. The policy arena will be one in which health care providers can have a considerable impact over the next several years (as exemplified by the work of Strickland noted previously) alongside, and in partnership with, health care activists from a range of civil society advocacy groups. More than two decades ago, Rappaport (1977) wrote, "To create social change, community psychology will need to engage in political battles at the local level. Politics as well as science must be accepted as a legitimate domain" (p. 262). He asserted that the role of the "system challenger" (a concept adapted from Brodsky, 1973) in the criminal justice system was as an outside critic challenging the status quo. We now live in a society in which challenging the system has become institutionalized within civil society organizations. A viable and desir-able future for correctional mental health practice will include a reinvigoration of its roles in policy, and appropriate system challenge and change, without (it is hoped) taking an adversarial stance but with a viewpoint informed by science and a commitment to patient care and social well-being by those practicing both inside and outside "the fence."

Conclusions

Is it possible to create communities so benign that few are motivated to commit crimes and in which the development of serious mental illness is minimized? How can mental illness be destigmatized, and how can a more secure place for the seriously mentally ill be created in the community? Can a greater acceptance and understanding of these individuals be enculturated, or must each new generation be taught? How long will it be before scientific advances bring "cures" for mental illness and drug addiction? These questions illuminate the gaps between what may be practically achievable during the next decade and what is more consistent with a long-term, perhaps utopian future. It is hoped that this chapter has provided a glimpse into a viable future, one that will bring mental health practi-tioners and other invested parties a step closer to answering these fundamental questions.

Viable does not mean probable. Positive change will be realized only through the combined efforts of those whose intentions are to create a more inclusive society, one in which its members understand that preventing crime and reducing the incidence of mental illness are in the best interests of all and that best practices in caring for those with serious mental illness in the criminal justice system have positive consequences in the free world as well as in prison.

Perhaps such a future is closer than most think. As this chapter was being written, the nation's prisons had actually shown a recent leveling in population (Beck & Karberg, 2001). There is growing support in many states for a moratorium on the death penalty. Civil society groups, such as NAMI, FAMM, and Amnesty International, have an increasingly powerful voice that they are bringing to bear on behalf of more progressive correctional policies. Some alternatives to incarceration are being tried, particularly with regard to drug offenses. Strickland's bill creating federal mental health courts is a high-profile manifestation of this initiative. Conservative prison experts such as John DiIulio are calling for changes in sentencing policy with respect to some offenses (DiIulio, 1999). Taken together, these may signal the advent of a watershed moment in American correctional policy, one that promises greater consideration of correctional rehabilitation and prevention programs and more involvement of mental health professionals in policymaking (Haney & Zimbardo, 1998).

One wonders, however, how likely it is that these data reflect a legitimate societal homeostasis, moving law and policy back toward a theoretical center in which innovation in the treatment of mentally ill offenders and the prevention of crime can play a part. Perhaps they are only an artifactual aberration, a blip in a long-term trend line pointing to ever increasing numbers of incarcerated citizens, a disproportionate number of whom are seriously mentally ill and otherwise devalued (e.g., members of racial and ethnic minority groups). A prolonged economic downturn might erase whatever gains have been made during the past few years. Certainly, the Internet has created the opportunity for more crime, more punishment, and more prisons. An even bleaker scenario might suggest that as the demographics of this nation change and immigrants constitute an ever larger percentage of the population, society will react with a renewed xenophobia, especially in the wake of the events of September 11, 2001, using prisons and mental institutions to incapacitate these individuals to an even greater extent than has been done heretofore. However, the existence of countervailing forces—such as civil society groups, international opinion and pressure, and (especially) the willingness to resist extremes of intolerance that has characterized the United States at its best—argues in favor of a brighter outlook. The aim of this chapter has been to limn a desirable and feasible future so that mental health professionals and others with an interest in corrections can begin to prepare for it and help to realize it.

Notes

1. A similar phenomenon exists in poor countries, where indigenous peoples have organized and learned to use the Internet and World Wide Web to promote their concerns, for example, preservation of their habitats (Kunitz, 2000).

2. Two examples illustrate different aspects of the notion of patients as consumers, another facet of the populist health care phenomenon. First, Eisenberg (2000) suggested that AEDs might eventually be sold over-the-counter, driving down costs to as low as $250

and allowing consumers greater control over their own health care. Second, the increasingly common marketing of medications, including psychotropics, directly to consumers through print and electronic media tacitly encourages them to self-diagnose and to use physicians more as middlemen than as traditional providers.

3. From the laboratories of cognitive psychologists (Tversky & Kahneman, 1981, 1983) and social psychologists (Latané & Darley, 1970; Lerner, 1970) comes evidence of the logical fallacies to which decision makers are prone, even when in possession of the facts and of people's predispositions to think about and act uncharitably toward others, including the "innocent victims."

4. The review of prison rehabilitation programs by Robert Martinson, published during the mid-1970s, is considered one of the most highly influential studies ever done on the subject (Martinson, 1974). However, the context, as recounted by Hallinan (2001), exemplifies the ways in which data can be mischaracterized and misinterpreted. Hallinan noted, for example, that its publication helped to galvanize anti-rehabilitation sentiment: "The people against rehabilitation, [Andrew] Sullivan [former curator of Martinson's papers] said, could hold this up and say, 'Here's a scholarly study saying it doesn't work. So let's take the money out of it and let's go in a different direction'" (p. 35). Yet Martinson refuted his own findings in a later article. Furthermore, he apparently meant the results of the original study as an argument *against* prisons rather than for them (Hallinan, 2001).

5. The Hispanic (all races) population of the United States rose by 57.9%, and the Asian population rose by 48.3%, between 1990 and 2000. In several states (including California, Oregon, Washington, and Maine), these minorities now constitute larger segments of the population than do African Americans. In contrast, the white (non-Hispanic) population grew at the slowest rate of all population subgroups, 5.9%, during this period (U.S. Bureau of the Census, 2001). Note that all figures are approximate due to differences in reporting between the 1990 and 2000 censuses.

6. A recent *New York Times* article, "Class Time and Not Jail Time for Anger, but Does It Work?" (Lewin, 2001), notably on the newspaper's front page, made the point. Anger management classes are readily available, inexpensive, and seen as desirable alternatives to incarceration, particularly for first-time offenders. However, the article raised questions about effectiveness, cited cases of treatment failures, and asserted that many programs, rather than being based on sound research, are attempts at quick fixes.

References

Ax, R. K., Fagan, T. J., & Holton, S. M. B. (in press). Individuals with serious mental illness: Rural perspectives and issues. In B. H. Stamm (Ed.), *Rural behavioral healthcare: An interdisciplinary guide.* Washington, DC: American Psychological Association.

Azrin, N. H., & Philip, R. A. (1979). The Job Club method for the job handicapped: A comparative outcome study. *Rehabilitation Bulletin, 23,* 144-155.

Beck, A. J., & Karberg, J. C. (2001, March). Prison and jail inmates at midyear 2000. *Bureau of Justice Statistics Bulletin,* pp. 1-12.

Bickman, L. (1999). Practice makes perfect and other myths about mental health services. *American Psychologist, 54,* 965-978.

Borkovec, T. D., Ragusea, S. A., & Echemendia, R. J. (1999, July). *Report to the American Psychological Association and the Pennsylvania Psychological Association on the Pennsylvania Practice Research Network.* Task force report, Pennsylvania Psychological Association.

Boston Women's Health Collective. (1973). *Our bodies, ourselves.* New York: Simon & Schuster.

Braithwaite, R. L., Hammett, T. M., & Mayberry, R. M. (1996). *Prisons and AIDS: A public health challenge.* San Francisco: Jossey-Bass.

Breitbart, W., Rosenfeld, B. D., & Passik, S. D. (1996). Interest in physician-assisted suicide among ambulatory HIV-infected patients. *American Journal of Psychiatry, 153,* 238-242.

Brodsky, S. L. (1973). *Psychologists in the criminal justice system.* Urbana: University of Illinois Press.

Caplan, R. D. (1983). Person-environment fit: Past, present, and future. In C. L. Cooper (Ed.), *Stress research: Where do we go from here?* (pp. 35-78). Chichester, UK: Wiley.

Davis, A., & Rodriguez, D. (2000). The challenge of prison abolition. *Social Justice, 27,* 212-218.

DiIulio, J. J. (1999, May 17). Against mandatory minimums. *National Review,* pp. 46-51.

Dyer, J. (2000). *The perpetual prisoner machine: How America profits from crime.* Boulder, CO: Westview.

Eisenberg, M. S. (2000). Is it time for over-the-counter defibrillators? *Journal of the American Medical Association, 284,* 1435-1438.

Fabelo, T. (2000, May). Technocorrections: The promises, the uncertain threats. *Sentencing & Corrections,* pp. 1-6.

Fairweather, G. W., Sanders, D. H., Maynard, H., Cressler, D. L., & Bleck, D. S. (1969). *Community life for the mentally ill: An alternative to institutional care.* Chicago: Aldine.

Falk, R., & Strauss, A. (2001). Toward global parliament. *Foreign Affairs, 80,* 212-220.

Foxhall, K. (2000, November). New CPT codes will recognize psychologists' work with physical health problems. *APA Monitor,* pp. 46-47.

Freudenheim, M. (2001, January 8). Digital doctoring. *New York Times,* pp. C1, C4.

Garrett, L. (2000). *Betrayal of trust: The collapse of global public health.* New York: Hyperion.

Gendreau, P. (1996). Offender rehabilitation: What we know and what needs to be done. *Criminal Justice and Behavior, 23,* 144-161.

Groppe, M. (2001, August 27). Drugs trigger withdrawal of student financial aid. *USA Today,* p. 4A.

Hallinan, J. T. (2001). *Going up the river: Travels in a prison nation.* New York: Random House.

Haney, C., & Zimbardo, P. (1998). The past and future of U.S. prison policy: Twenty-five years after the Stanford Prison Experiment. *American Psychologist, 53,* 709-727.

Hare, R. D. (1996). Psychopathy: A clinical construct whose time has come. *Criminal Justice and Behavior, 23,* 25-54.

Hodges, L. F., Rothbaum, B. O., Alarcon, R., Ready, D., Shahar, F., Graap, K., Pair, P., Hebert, P., Gotz, D., Wills, B., & Baltzell, D. (1999). A virtual environment for the treatment of chronic combat-related post-traumatic stress disorder. *CyberPsychology & Behavior, 2,* 7-14.

International Conference on Penal Abolition. (2001). [Online]. Accessed April 11, 2001, from www.justice action.org.au/ icopa/icopa.html

Kaplan, H. I., & Sadock, B. J. (1996). *Pocket handbook of psychiatry* (2nd ed.). Baltimore: Williams & Wilkins.

Karasek, R., & Theorell, T. (1990). *Healthy work: Stress, productivity, and the reconstruction of working life.* New York: Basic Books.

Kovacs, A. (2000, November). *America's broken health care systems: How we got here and what can be done.* Invited address given at the fall meeting of the Virginia Psychological Association, Williamsburg.

Kunitz, S. J. (2000). Globalization, states, and the health of indigenous peoples. *American Journal of Public Health, 90,* 1531-1539.

Latané, B., & Darley, J. M. (1970). Social determinants of bystander intervention in emergencies. In J. Macauley & L. Berkowitz (Eds.), *Altruism and helping behavior: Social psychological studies of some antecedents and consequences* (pp. 13-27). New York: Academic Press.

LeDuff, C. (2001, February 22). They call it tobacco road. *New York Times,* p. A25.

Lerner, M. J. (1970). Desire for justice and reactions to victims. In J. Macauley & L. Berkowitz (Eds.), *Altruism and helping behavior: Social psychological studies of some antecedents and consequences* (pp. 205-229). New York: Academic Press.

Lewin, T. (2001, July 1). Class time and not jail time for anger, but does it work? *New York Times,* pp. A1, A16.

Link, B. G., Phelan, J. C., Bresnahan, M., Stueve, A., & Pescosolido, B. A. (1999). Public conceptions of mental illness: Labels, causes, dangerousness, and social distance. *American Journal of Public Health, 89,* 1328-1333.

Lorion, R. P. (2001). Exposure to urban violence: Shifting from an individual to an ecological perspective. In N. Schneiderman, M. A. Speers, J. M. Silva, H. Tomes, & J. H. Gentry (Eds.), *Integrating behavioral and social sciences with public health* (pp. 97-113). Washington, DC: American Psychological Association.

Lykken, D. T. (2000). Psychology and the criminal justice system: A reply to Haney and Zimbardo. *The General Psychologist, 35*(1), 11-15.

Magaletta, P. R., Fagan, T. J., & Ax, R. K. (1998). Advancing psychology services through telehealth in the Federal Bureau of Prisons. *Professional Psychology: Research and Practice, 29,* 543-548.

Magaletta, P. R., Fagan, T. J., & Peyrot, M. F. (2000). Telehealth in the Federal Bureau of Prisons: Inmates' perceptions. *Professional Psychology: Research and Practice, 31,* 497-502.

Martin, S. (1995, September). APA to pursue prescription privileges. *APA Monitor,* p. 6.

Martinson, R. (1974). What works? Questions and answers about prison reform. *The Public Interest, 35,* 22-54.

Mauer, M. (1999). *Race to incarcerate.* New York: New Press.

McCollum, S. (2000, June). Mock job fairs in prison: Tracking participants. *Federal Probation, 64,* 13-18.

McCue, M. J., Mazmanian, P. E., Hampton, C., Marks, T. K., Fisher, E., Parpart, F., & Krick, R. S. (1997). The case of Powhatan Correctional Center/Virginia Department of Corrections and Virginia Commonwealth University/Medical College of Virginia. *Telemedicine Journal, 3*(1), 11-17.

Microchip implants closer to reality. (1999, October). *The Futurist,* p. 9.

Monk, T. H., & Tepas, D. I. (1985). Shift work. In C. L. Cooper & M. J. Smith (Eds.), *Job stress and blue collar work* (pp. 65-84). Chichester, UK: Wiley.

Moss, A. R. (2000). Epidemiology and the politics of needle exchange. *American Journal of Public Health, 90,* 1385-1387.

National Alliance for the Mentally Ill. (2001). *PACT* [Program of Assertive Community Treatment] [Online]. Accessed March 4, 2001, from www. nami.org/about/pactfact. html

Olson, E. (2000, May 18). Geneva panel says U.S. prisoner restraints amount to torture. *New York Times,* p. A11.

Page, M. D., Joglar, J. A., Kowal, R. C., Zagrodzky, J. D., Nelson, L. L., Ramaswamy, K., Barbera, S. J., Hamdan, M. H., & McKenas, D. K. (2000). Use of automated external defibrillators by a U.S. airline. *New England Journal of Medicine, 343,* 1210-1216.

Purdy, M. (2001, August 5). Crime, punishment, and the brothers K. *New York Times,* p. A21.

Raffaele, M. (2001, October 1). Satellites track sex offenders. *Richmond Times-Dispatch,* p. A2.

Rappaport, J. (1977). *Community psychology: Values, research, and action.* New York: Holt, Rinehart & Winston.

Reid, T. R. (2000, December 17). Many Europeans see Bush as executioner extraordinaire. *Washington Post,* pp. A36, A41.

Sammons, M., & Levant, R. F. (1999). Combined psychosocial and pharmacological treatments: Introduction. *Journal of Clinical Psychology in Medical Settings, 6,* 1-10.

Schlosser, E. (1998, December). The prison-industrial complex. *Atlantic Monthly, 282,* 51-77.

Schopp, L., Johnstone, B., & Merrell, D. (2000). Telehealth and neuropsychological assessment: New opportunities for psychologists. *Professional Psychology: Research and Practice, 31,* 179-183.

Spelman, W. (2000). The limited importance of prison expansion. In A. Blumstein & J. Wallman (Eds.), *The crime drop in America* (pp. 97-129). New York: Cambridge University Press.

Starr, P. (1982). *The social transformation of American medicine.* New York: Basic Books.

Strickland, T. (2001, Winter). Mental health courts bill becomes law. *AAP Advance,* pp. 1, 8.

Talbot, E. A., Moore, M., McCray, E., & Binkin, N. J. (2000, December 13). Tuberculosis among foreign-born persons in the United States, 1993-1998. *Journal of the American Medical Association, 284,* 2894-2900.

Tooby, J., & Cosmides, L. (1992). The psychological foundations of culture. In H. Barkow, L. Cosmides, & J. Tooby (Eds.), *The adapted mind: Evolutionary psychology and the generation of culture* (pp. 19-136). New York: Oxford University Press.

Tversky, A., & Kahneman, D. (1981). The framing of decisions and the psychology of choice. *Science, 211,* 453-458.

Tversky, A., & Kahneman, D. (1983). Extensional versus intuitive reasoning: The conjunction fallacy in probability judgment. *Psychological Review, 90,* 293-315.

U.S. Bureau of the Census. (2001). U.S. census tables of changes in ethnic population groups by state, 1990-2000. [Online]. Accessed April 14, 2001, from www.census.gov/population/ cen2000/phc-t1/tab.04.pdf and from http://factfinder.census.gov/home/cen/pldata/ html

U.S. Congress (2000). *Public Law 106-515.* [Online]. Accessed June 9, 2001, from http:// frwebgate.access.gov/cgi-bib/getdoc.cgi?dbnamexxx106_cong_public_1:publ515.10

Valenzuela, T. D., Roe, D. J., Nichol, G., Clark, L. L., Spaite, D. W., & Hardman, R. G. (2000). Outcomes of rapid defibrillation by security officers after cardiac arrest in casinos. *New England Journal of Medicine, 343,* 1206-1209.

Index

Abel, G., 154, 280
Abikoff, H. A., 173
Abram, K. M., 63, 88, 293, 295
Abramson, M. F., 294-295
Acoca, L., 89, 293
Adams, K., 59, 103, 104
Administration on Aging, 207
AIDS/HIV-infected offenders, 208,
    210-212, 240, 307, 320
Akers, R. L., 282
Alaska Department of Corrections, 158
Alcoholics Anonymous, 13, 31, 43, 76, 77,
    84, 86, 313
Alexander, T., 15
Alison, L., 229
Allegations of Poor Psychiatric Care, 241
Allen, D., 105, 200
Allen, J., 246
Allen, R., 291
Alterman, A. I., 88
Alzheimer's disease, 207
Amaro, H., 131-132, 133
American Association for Correctional
    Psychology (AACP), 289
American Bar Association, 93
American Correctional Association, 11,
    78-79, 117, 200, 205, 206, 209, 213
American Psychiatric Association, 45, 108,
    111, 112, 113, 115, 155, 167, 170, 173,
    212, 230, 251, 287
American Psychological Association, 29,
    47, 49, 50, 51, 67, 289, 314
American Red Cross, 231
Amirkhan, J. H., 279
Andrews, B. P., 285
Andrews, D. A., 274, 276, 278, 281, 282,
    283, 293
Anglin, M. D., 79, 90
Anthenelli, R. M., 132
Anti-Drug Abuse Acts, 22, 74, 79
Antisocial personality disorder, 6,
    113, 114, 284
Araji, S., 154

Arbiter, N., 91
Armstrong, J. J., 254
Arrigo, B. A., 65
Assessment. *See* Mental health services
    in correctional institutions,
    assessment
Atkinson, L., 131
Auffrey, J. J., 279-280
Austin, J., 15, 79
Ax, R. K., 23, 62, 119, 246, 247, 304, 312
Azrin, N. H., 315

Bachorowski, J., 279
Bagby, R. M., 277
Baird, C., 15
Balch, D. C., 119
Ball, J. C., 74-75
Balla, D. A., 183, 194
Barbaree, H. E., 159
Barg, J., 131
Barnes, H. E., 22, 32
Barnum, R., 170
Bartizal, D. E., 23
Bartoi, M. G., 193
Bartol, C. R., 26
Bartollas, C., 256
Bassett, J. E., 293
Bean, G. J., 176
Beauford, J., 87
Beck, A. J., 5. 9, 10, 323
Becker, J., 154, 157, 158
Beckman, L. J., 132, 133
Beckstead, J. W., 295
Beecher, H. K., 131
Beeler, A., 201, 202, 203, 207, 209
Begun, A. M., 6
Behavioral science
    and crime, 4
    and employee evaluation, 15-16
    and employee training, 16
    and institutional climate, 15-16
    and treatment services, 15
Belenko, S., 74-75, 76, 89, 90

Stieber, J., 5
Strandberg, 241
Strauss, A., 307, 310
Strickland, T., 321, 322, 323
Stringer, T. L., 176
Strozier, A. L., 89
Strupp, H., 35
Stuart, P., 226, 229
Students for Sensible Drug Policy, 315
Stueve, A., 103, 304
Substance abuse, 114, 115
Substance Abuse and Mental Health
    Services Administration, 76, 89
Substance abuse treatment programs
    and drug courts, 92-93
    and peer support, 13
    as alternatives to incarceration, 74,
        93-94
    biopsychosocial, 13-14, 79
    drug abuse education, 81, 86
    dual diagnosis, 85
    economic benefits of, 87
    elements of, 13, 76-86
    "essential" services of, 78
    Federal Bureau of Prisons, 79-82
    federal initiatives for, 75
    Florida Department of Corrections,
        82-84
    for females, 89-91
    funding for, 75-76, 83
    future of, 81-82, 84, 86, 91-94
    history of, 75-76
    "important" services of, 78
    jail versus prison, 87
    legal standards for, 77
    need for, 74-76
    nonresidential, 80-81
    Oregon Department of Corrections,
        84-86
    outcomes, 86-88
    outpatient, 83-84
    post-release, 87
    pre-release, 83-84, 85-86, 93
    professional standards for, 77-79
    research on, 94
    residential, 80, 83, 85
    state initiatives for, 74, 82-83
    statistics on, 75-76
    success of, 13, 14, 86-88, 92
    therapeutic communities, 82-83, 85,
        86-87, 94
    transitional services, 81, 91-93
Suicide
    and "deliberate indifference," 117
    and depression, 112
    ethical issues concerning, 118
    liability and, 117
    prevention programs, 9, 46, 62,
        117-118
    risk assessment, 53, 62

    staff training in, 106
    statistics, 62, 111, 112
    watch, 118
    See also Juvenile offenders, and suicide
"Supermax" facilities, 103
Swartz, J. A., 87, 295
Sykes, G. M., 126, 128

Talbot, E. A., 311
Tan, S. Y., 131
Task Force on Psychological
    Interventions, 280
Tata, P. R., 279
Tauber, J., 92
Taxman, F. S., 87
Teague, G. B., 88
Teasdale, C., 291
Technology, in correctional
        health care
    and portability of health services,
        311-313, 321
    use in providing services, 23, 242,
        311-313, 321
Teir, R., 146, 148
Temin, C. E., 125, 126, 134-135, 136
Tenopyr, M. L., 262
Teoh, S. K., 132
Tepas, D. I., 318
Teplin, L. A., 63, 88, 102, 287,
        293, 295
Terminally ill offenders, 208-210
Terris, W., 262
Testa, M., 133
Tewksbury, R., 34
Theorell, T., 318
Thomas, C. R., 22
Thomas, G., 87
Thornton, D. M., 280
"Three strikes" legislation, 5
Timmermans, G., 131
Tims, F. M., 79, 81-82
Tittle, C. R., 128
Toch, H., 60, 103, 104, 106
Tomkins, A. J., 29
Tooby, J., 319
Torrey, E. F., 5, 60, 295
Transinstitutionalization, 240
Triad Drug Evaluation Project, 14
Trupin, E., 103, 290
Tucker, T. C., 87
Tunis, S., 79, 87
Turk, D. C., 131

University of Alabama, Ph.D. program, 29
Urbano-Marquez, A., 132
U.S. Department of Justice, 74, 75, 83, 92,
        94, 241, 251
U.S. General Accounting Office, 104
Useem, B., 254
Ustad, K. L., 294

About the Editors

Thomas J. Fagan, Ph.D., is a licensed clinical psychologist and American Psychological Association Fellow. He currently consults with correctional and law enforcement agencies on a variety of mental health and crisis management issues and is an adjunct psychology professor at two Virginia colleges. For many years, he was a psychology practitioner and administrator in the Federal Bureau of Prisons, where he actively participated in the development of correctional programs and mental health policies and procedures and where he trained professional, paraprofessional, and correctional staff. He was also the bureau's chief hostage negotiator and coordinator of its crisis negotiation training program for a number of years, was on-site for several of its most serious hostage incidents, and has served as a consultant to numerous state, local, and other law enforcement agencies in the areas of crisis negotiation, critical incident stress debriefing procedures, and management of mental health services and programs. He has published regularly in correctional and psychological journals, has authored several book chapters, and is a nationally recognized trainer of law enforcement personnel. He currently serves on the editorial board of the *Journal of Correctional Health Care* and represents the American Psychological Association on the National Commission on Correctional Health Care's board of directors. He received his bachelor's degree from Rutgers University and his master's and doctoral degrees from Virginia Polytechnic Institute and State University.

Robert K. Ax, Ph.D., received his doctorate in clinical psychology from Virginia Polytechnic Institute and State University. He has worked in corrections fo nearly 20 years, providing direct services and administering an American Psychological Association (APA)-accredited internship program. He served as president (2001-2002) of Division 18 (Psychologists in Public Service) of the APA and is also an APA Fellow.

About the Authors

Andrea Fox Boardman, Ph.D., is Chief Psychologist at the Federal Detention Center in Philadelphia. A Bureau of Prisons psychologist for more than 5 years, she has previously served in the capacities of staff psychologist and drug abuse program coordinator at the Federal Correctional Institution in Fort Dix, New Jersey. Her current responsibilities include the administrative and clinical oversight of psychology services as well as the assessment and treatment of incarcerated offenders. She is actively involved in the Bureau of Prisons' annual crisis management training, particularly with respect to the use of critical incident stress management techniques following crisis situations in correctional settings. The Federal Bureau of Prisons recently recognized her as its Psychology Services Staff Member of the Year. In addition to her work in the federal prison system, she serves as an adjunct assistant professor in the Department of Clinical and Health Psychology at the Medical College of Pennsylvania–Hahnemann University, where she teaches graduate courses in personality assessment and correctional psychology. She has participated in research projects on sexual aggression, conducted pre-parole evaluations of sexual offenders, and facilitated treatment groups for inmates convicted of sexual crimes. She has published on topics such as sexual aggression and the insanity defense.

Lisa Melanie Boesky, Ph.D., is a clinical psychologist. She specializes in the identification, management, and treatment of juvenile offenders with mental health disorders, including youth who are suicidal and/or who self-injure. She has designed several mental health training programs for correctional staff and trains justice personnel across the country. She has consulted on mental health policy and programming to a variety of juvenile correctional facilities and helped to develop a mental health screening instrument for juvenile justice agencies to use with youth in their care. She received her bachelor's degree from the University of California, Santa Barbara, and her master's and doctorate degrees from Wayne State University. Adolescents have always been the focus of her research and clinical interests, and her initial clinical work was in inpatient psychiatric settings. However, her interest in youth involved with the juvenile justice system grew and eventually became her primary focus. She has worked directly with juvenile offenders within a correctional setting providing crisis intervention, psychological screening/assessment, and management services, and she has served as the primary member of a mental health mobile team that traveled to a variety of correctional facilities providing consultation related to the mentally ill youth in their care. She is the author of a book as well as a number of chapters, articles, and training curricula on the topic of juvenile offenders with mental health disorders.

Jennifer Boothby, Ph.D., is Assistant Professor of Psychology at Indiana State University. She is a recent graduate of the University of Alabama, where she earned her doctorate in clinical psychology. She received specialized training in the area of psychology and law and completed a predoctoral internship at the Federal Medical Center in Butner, North Carolina, and at the University of North Carolina at Chapel Hill. She has published several articles on offender adjustment to incarceration, the professional roles of correctional psychologists, and the development of attorney-client trust.

Carl B. Clements, Ph.D., is a clinical psychologist and Professor of Psychology at the University of Alabama, Tuscaloosa, where he has helped to train psychologists and others for correctional and justice system work for some 30 years. He has consulted with a number of state and federal agencies and has served as a court-recognized expert in litigation involving prison conditions, offender classification systems, and professional standards. At the University of Alabama, he has also served as director of clinical training and as department chairman, and he is a fellow of the American Psychological Association. His recent publications and research activity have addressed issues of offender classification, prison overcrowding, attitudes about crime, delinquency intervention, program evaluation, professional roles in corrections, and risk and needs assessment. He also serves on the editorial board of *Criminal Justice and Behavior.*

David DeMatteo, M.A., J.D., is completing his Ph.D. in clinical psychology at the Medical College of Pennsylvania–Hahnemann University, where he has been focusing on forensic psychology. He is currently completing his predoctoral clinical psychology internship at the Medical College of Virginia in Richmond. He earned his B.A. (psychology), magna cum laude, from Rutgers University in 1995. He earned his M.A. (clinical psychology) from the Medical College of Pennsylvania–Hahnemann University in 1999 and his J.D., magna cum laude, from Villanova University School of Law in 2001. He has worked with several forensic and correctional populations over the past six years in Pennsylvania, New Jersey, and Virginia.

John T. Dignam, Ph.D., is Psychology Services Administrator for the Federal Bureau of Prisons' Mid-Atlantic Region. He is a clinical psychologist who has worked for the bureau since 1987. He has served as the bureau's employee assistance program administrator (1994-1998); psychology services administrator in its northeast region (1991-1994); chief of psychology services at the Federal Correctional Institution in Fairton, New Jersey (1989-1991); and staff psychologist and drug abuse program coordinator at the Metropolitan Correctional Center in New York City (1987-1989). He received his M.A. and Ph.D. in clinical psychology from Arizona State University and served his clinical internship at the Beth Israel Medical Center in New York City. Among his previous publications in the area of correctional mental health are book chapters and journal articles on the topics of substance abuse, suicide prevention, job stress and burnout, workplace violence, and critical incident stress management.

Joel Dvoskin, Ph.D., A.B.P.P., teaches at the University of Arizona College of Medicine and maintains a private forensic and consulting psychology practice in Tucson, Arizona. He has worked as a clinician, an administrator, a consultant, an expert witness, a researcher, a trainer, and a scholar in the provision of mental health services in criminal justice settings for more than 25 years. He has worked on many of the nation's most important prison and jail mental health lawsuits, and he has authored a number of important scholarly articles on correctional mental health care. In addition to serving as New York State's acting commissioner of mental health, he also ran that state's forensic and correctional mental health system for more than a decade.

Richard Ellis, Ph.D., has been a psychologist with the Federal Bureau of Prisons for 12 years. He has held the positions of staff psychologist, forensic study center coordinator, drug and alcohol program coordinator, and chief psychologist in federal prisons; senior examiner and chief of the program analysis section in the bureau's central office; and western regional psychology administrator in the bureau's western regional office. He also supervised the development and accreditation of an American Psychological Association psychology internship program. He has taught courses for the bureau on critical incident stress debriefing and federal forensic evaluations, and he has been an instructor for U.S. attorneys on the cross-examination of expert witnesses. Prior to his employment with the bureau, he developed community residential treatment programs for the chronically mentally ill in the Boston metropolitan area. He received a bachelor's degree in psychology from the University of California, Davis; a master's degree in psychology from California State University, Sacramento; and a Ph.D. from the California School of Professional Psychology, San Diego.

Kathy J. Harowski, Ph.D., is a clinical psychologist who has worked as a supervisor and manager for the Federal Bureau of Prisons as well as for a state and county correctional system in Minnesota. With the bureau, she worked with staff and offenders in a medical referral center, serving mentally ill and medical cases; trained staff; and served as administrator for a residential drug and alcohol abuse treatment program. With the Minnesota Department of Corrections, she served as director of psychology services at a maximum-security prison. Currently, she works at a county juvenile detention center. Throughout her decade of correctional work, she has both formally and informally trained and mentored psychologists, other mental health providers, and correctional staff on effective functioning in a high-stress environment.

Shelia M. B. Holton, Psy.D., is a licensed clinical psychologist who is currently Drug Abuse Program Coordinator at the Federal Correctional Institution in Waseca, Minnesota. Prior to holding this position, she served as a staff psychologist with the Wisconsin Resource Center, where her duties consisted of providing psychological services to inmates who had been removed from the general population of the Wisconsin Department of Corrections due to clinical or management issues related to their psychopathology. She also worked for the Virginia Department of Corrections first as a staff psychologist in a correctional facility and later as the director of a mental health unit. The latter was a 60-bed unit located within a medium-security prison. The primary diagnoses of inmates housed in this unit included schizophrenia, bipolar disorder, delusional disorder, and major depressive disorder. She received her clinical training from the Minnesota School of Professional Psychology. During her training, she worked with mentally ill offenders at the Federal Medical Center in Rochester, Minnesota, where she conducted psychological and forensic evaluations for federal inmates requiring inpatient or structured services within the correctional environment. She also completed a practicum placement at the Minnesota Security Hospital, where she provided psychotherapy, conducted psychoeducational groups, and completed psychological evaluations with inmates who were committed under the Mentally Ill and Dangerous statute in the state of Minnesota. She completed her predoctoral internship at the Federal Correctional Institution in Petersburg, Virginia. During this experience, she provided psychological services and conducted forensic evaluations with inmates experiencing a wide range of psychopathology.

Phil Magaletta, Ph.D., provides psychology services in the Federal Bureau of Prisons as the clinical training coordinator in Washington, DC. In this role, he has administrative responsibilities for the recruitment of and continuing education for more than 300 doctoral-level psychologists. He also provides national administration for the bureau's predoctoral psychology internship programs. He is a licensed clinical psychologist who earned his doctorate from St. Louis University. He has been practicing correctional psychology for 5 years and has published and presented papers on the practice of telehealth in the correctional environment, psychological treatment in segregation, and parenting from prison. He has been a bureau employee at the U.S. penitentiary in Allenwood, Pennsylvania, where he worked as a staff psychologist and drug abuse program coordinator. He was also responsible for the implementation and treatment coordination for a 120-bed residential program for violent offenders. In 1998, the director of the bureau recognized him for his innovative work in developing and implementing Allenwood's telehealth program for treating the mentally ill.

Charles O. Matthews, Ph.D., serves as National Institute on Drug Abuse Public-Academic Fellow in Substance Abuse Services Research in the Department of Mental Health Law and Policy at the Louis de la Parte Florida Mental Health Institute (FMHI), University of South Florida, and at the Substance Abuse Program Office of the Florida Department of Children and Families. Prior to coming to FMHI, he served as a research consultant on a joint project examining the impact of managed care on human resources in public behavioral health care systems. He also previously served as a research consultant to the American Psychological Association's Office on AIDS. He received his Ph.D. in clinical and community psychology from the University of Maryland at College Park, following completion of a predoctoral internship at the Perry Point and Baltimore VA Medical Centers in Maryland. He has developed a number of co-occurring disorders (substance abuse/mental health) group treatment manuals for the Suncoast Practice and

Research Collaborative and has provided training on the topic of co-occurring disorders treatment in a number of settings. He has also developed relapse prevention group treatment manuals for the Florida Department of Corrections dual diagnosis prison programs. He is currently involved in a Center for Mental Health Services community action grant focused on implementing evidence-based practices and improving integration of treatment for co-occurring disorders. He has also recently co-authored book chapters on substance abuse treatment in jails and prisons.

Alix M. McLearen, M.A., received her master's degree from Southwest Missouri State University and is currently a doctoral candidate in the University of Alabama's clinical psychology-law program. In addition to a wide range of therapy, testing, and teaching activities, she has worked in several correctional facilities, including prisons and jails at the county, state, and federal levels. She currently works at a state forensic hospital. Her research and professional interests include assessment of malingering, identification and treatment of mentally disordered offenders, forensic assessment, correctional ethics, and jail policy and staff training.

Robert Morgan, Ph.D., is Assistant Professor in the Department of Psychology at Texas Tech University. He completed his doctoral studies in counseling psychology at Oklahoma State University; predoctoral internship at the Federal Correctional Institute in Petersburg, Virginia; and postdoctoral fellowship in forensic psychology in the Department of Psychiatry at the University of Missouri–Kansas City and the Missouri Department of Mental Health. His research interests include group psychotherapy for incarcerated adults, correctional mental health treatment, issues in forensic psychology, and professional development/training issues.

Roger H. Peters, Ph.D., is Professor in the Department of Mental Health Law and Policy at the Florida Mental Health Institute (FMHI), University of South Florida, where he has been a faculty member since 1986. He serves as coordinator of the FMHI Collaborative on Substance Abuse Treatment and Policy Research and is an adjunct professor with the Department of Rehabilitation and Mental Health Counseling. He is the principal investigator and director for several grant projects, including the Suncoast Practice and Research Collaborative (SPARC) project. He has served since 1995 as the lead consultant to the National GAINS Center for People With Co-occurring Disorders in the Justice System. He received his Ph.D. in clinical psychology from Florida State University, following completion of a predoctoral internship at the University of North Carolina School of Medicine in association with the Federal Bureau of Prisons. He has pursued research, consultation, and training initiatives involving substance abuse treatment within the criminal justice system. He has published frequently in major journals and served on federal expert panels, grant and document reviews, and national advisory boards and committees. His research, consultation, and training efforts have focused on six interrelated areas within the justice system: treatment of dually diagnosed offenders, relapse prevention strategies, screening and assessment approaches, evaluation of treatment program effectiveness, alternative case processing approaches such as drug courts, and knowledge adoption and application strategies.

Steven E. Pitt, D.O., is Clinical Associate Professor of Psychiatry at the University of Arizona Health Sciences Center. He is a board-certified psychiatrist with specialty training and board certification in forensic psychiatry. A graduate of Michigan State University's College of Osteopathic Medicine, he completed his residency training in psychiatry at the University of Michigan Medical Center and a fellowship in forensic psychiatry at the University of Maryland School of Medicine. He is the former director of forensic psychiatric services at the Arizona State Hospital. In addition to maintaining a private practice in forensic and general psychiatry, he is an associate at Park Dietz and Associates, serves as a physician adviser to Magellan Behavioral Health, and is on the advisory panel of Legalvote.com.

Linda Richardson, M.S.N., Ph.D., is currently with the Los Angeles County Department of Mental Health as head of the Community Reintegration of Mentally Ill Offenders (CROMIO) program, a state funded clinical and research grant project with the goal of reducing recidivism among dually diagnosed offenders at high risk for incarceration in state prisons. She is also an adjunct professor at Alliant International University. She received her bachelor's degree in nursing and French from Simmons College, a master's degree in psychiatric nursing from Yale University, and a Ph.D. in clinical psychology from the University of Houston. She served her internship in clinical psychology at the University of Rochester Medical School. A registered nurse and licensed psychologist, she has been on the faculties of the University of Michigan, Texas Christian University, Louisiana Tech University, and the University of Louisiana, Monroe. In addition, she has served as a program manager for mental health services in prison units with the Texas Department of Corrections, the North Carolina Department of Corrections, the Louisiana Department of Corrections, and the Harris County Jail (Houston). She has published book chapters and journal articles and has made numerous presentations at local, state, and national organization meetings, and she has consulted with many groups and organizations on mental health issues.

Erin M. Spiers, M.A., completed her master's degree at Sam Houston State University and is currently a doctoral student of clinical psychology at the Arizona School of Professional Psychology. She has extensive correctional mental health experience at the state and federal levels. She has practiced in a wide range of correctional settings, including intake and diagnostic units, medical centers, and special and general population facilities. She has worked with mentally ill offenders across multiple security levels. In addition to her clinical work, she has been actively involved in correctional program development and outreach service planning.

G. Lane Wagaman, Ed.D., is a licensed psychologist who currently maintains a private practice dedicated to the provision of clinical, forensic, and consultative services. Prior to establishing this practice, he served for many years as the chief psychologist at the federal prison for female offenders in Alderson, West Virginia, where he offered a variety of assessment and treatment services and programs to female offenders. He also served as a resource on many regional and national workgroups tasked with developing programs for female offenders, substance abusers, and mentally ill individuals as well as on many quality assurance teams formed to assess the overall functioning of psychology programs. He developed both pre- and postdoctoral training programs in correctional psychology and served as an expert consultant for U.S. attorneys and the federal courts. Throughout his professional career, he has been an active member of numerous professional organizations and has demonstrated a long-standing commitment to professional education and training. He has held a number of adjunct faculty appointments and has taught a variety of courses at the undergraduate, graduate, and professional school levels. He has also conducted numerous workshops, seminars, and training sessions at the local, state, and national levels.